New Testament Backgrounds

The Biblical Seminar
43

NEW TESTAMENT BACKGROUNDS
A Sheffield Reader

edited by
Craig A. Evans &
Stanley E. Porter

Sheffield
Academic Press

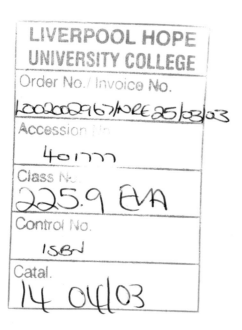
Published by
Sheffield Academic Press Ltd
Mansion House
19 Kingfield Road
Sheffield S11 9AS
England

Printed on acid-free paper in Great Britain
by The Cromwell Press
Melksham, Wiltshire

British Library Cataloguing in Publication Data

A catalogue record for this book is available
from the British Library

ISBN 1-85075-796-8

CONTENTS

This Series, of which *New Testament Backgrounds* is one, collects what the Series editors believe to be the best articles on the topic published in the first 50 issues (1978–1993) of *Journal for the Study of the New Testament*. Founded in 1978, with one issue in its inaugural year, *JSNT* was produced from 1979 to 1990 in three issues a year, and then, from 1991 to the present, in four issues a year. The continuing success of the journal can be seen in several ways: by its increasing circulation, by its increased publication schedule, by its fostering of a significant supplement series, which has now reached its 130th volume (*JSNT* Supplement Series), by its public exposure and influence within the scholarly community, and, most of all, by the quality of the essays it publishes. This volume contains a representative group of such articles on a specific area of New Testament studies.

Once it was decided that such a Series of volumes should be issued, the question became that of how the numerous important articles were going to be selected and presented. The problem was not filling the volumes but making the many difficult choices that would inevitably exclude worthy articles. In the end, the editors have used various criteria for determining which articles should be reprinted here. They have gathered together articles that, they believe, make significant contributions in several different ways. Some of the articles are truly groundbreaking, pushing their respective enquiry into new paths and introducing new critical questions into the debate. Others are assessments of the critical terrain of a particular topic, providing useful and insightful analyses that others can and have built upon. Others still are included because they are major contributions to an on-going discussion.

Even though back issues of *JSNT* are still in print and these essays are available in individual issues of the journal, it is thought that this kind of compilation could serve several purposes. One is to assist scholars who wish to keep up on developments outside their areas of specialist research or who have been away from a topic for a period of time and wish to re-enter the discussion. These volumes are designed to be representatively selective, so that scholars can gain if not a thorough grasp of all of the developments in an area at least significant insights into major topics of debate in a field of interest. Another use of these volumes is as textbooks for undergraduates, seminarians and even graduate students. For undergraduates, these volumes could serve as useful readers, possibly as supplementary texts to a critical introduction, to provide a first exposure to and a sample of critical debate. For seminary students, the same purpose as for undergraduates could apply, especially when the seminarian is beginning critical study of the New Testament. There is the added use, however, that such material could provide guidance through the argumentation and footnotes for significant research into a New Testament author or topic. For graduate students, these volumes could not only provide necessary background to a topic, allowing a student to achieve a basic level of knowledge before exploration of a particular area of interest, but also serve as good guides to the detailed critical work being done in an area. There is the further advantage that many of the articles in these volumes are models of how to make and defend a critical argument, thereby providing useful examples for those entering the lists of critical scholarly debate. While some of the contributors may have altered their positions, or at least have moved further along in their opinions—it is often dangerous to accept any scholarly opinion as definitive—we believe that there is still much of merit in the variety of positions represented in this volume.

Many more articles could and probably should be re printed in further volumes, but this one and those published along with it must for now serve as an introduction to these topics, at least as they were discussed in *JSNT*.

The editors would like to thank Ted Goshulak, Reference Librarian for Trinity Western University's Marion Alloway Library, and Wendy Porter, for assistance in tracking down many obscure bibliographical references.

Craig A. Evans   Stanley E. Porter
Trinity Western University   Roehampton Institute London
Langley, B.C.   England
Canada

ABBREVIATIONS

AB	Anchor Bible
ABD	D.N. Freedman (ed.), *Anchor Bible Dictionary*
AGJU	Arbeiten zur Geschichte des antiken Judentums und des Urchristentums
AJA	*American Journal of Archaeology*
AnBib	Analecta biblica
ANRW	*Aufstieg und Niedergang der römischen Welt*
ATR	*Anglican Theological Review*
BAGD	W. Bauer, W.F. Arndt, F.W. Gingrich and F.W. Danker, *Greek–English Lexicon of the New Testament*
BBB	Bonner Biblische Beiträge
BARev	*Biblical Archaeology Review*
BDF	F. Blass, A. Debrunner and R.W. Funk, *A Greek Grammar of the New Testament*
BETL	Bibliotheca ephemeridum theologicarum lovaniensium
Bib	*Biblica*
BJRL	*Bulletin of the John Rylands University Library of Manchester*
BNTC	Black's New Testament Commentaries
BR	*Biblical Research*
BTB	*Biblical Theology Bulletin*
BZ	*Biblische Zeitschrift*
BZNW	Beihefte zur *ZNW*
CBQ	*Catholic Biblical Quarterly*
CJT	*Canadian Journal of Theology*
ConBNT	Coniectanea biblica, New Testament
CSEL	Corpus scriptorum ecclesiasticorum latinorum
DJD	Discoveries in the Judaean Desert
DTT	*Dansk teologisk tidsskrift*
EncJud	*Encyclopaedia Judaica*
ETL	*Ephemerides theologicae lovanienses*
EvQ	*Evangelical Quarterly*
ExpTim	*Expository Times*
FFNT	Foundations and Facets: New Testament
FRLANT	Forschungen zur Religion und Literatur des Alten und Neuen Testaments
GNB	Good News Bible

HibJ	*Hibbert Journal*
HNT	Handbuch zum Neuen Testament
HNTC	Harper's New Testament Commentaries
HTKNT	Herders theologischer Kommentar zum Neuen Testament
HTR	*Harvard Theological Review*
HTS	Harvard Theological Studies
HUCA	*Hebrew Union College Annual*
IB	*Interpreter's Bible*
IBS	*Irish Biblical Studies*
ICC	International Critical Commentary
IEJ	*Israel Exploration Journal*
Int	*Interpretation*
JAC	*Jahrbuch für Antike und Christentum*
JAOS	*Journal of the American Oriental Society*
JBL	*Journal of Biblical Literature*
JBLMS	Journal of Biblical Literature Monograph Series
JEH	*Journal of Ecclesiastical History*
JewEnc	*The Jewish Encyclopedia*
JJS	*Journal of Jewish Studies*
JQR	*Jewish Quarterly Review*
JR	*Journal of Religion*
JRH	*Journal of Religious History*
JRS	*Journal of Roman Studies*
JSHRZ	Jüdische Schriften aus hellenistisch-römischer Zeit
JSJ	*Journal for the Study of Judaism in the Persian, Hellenistic and Roman Period*
JSNT	*Journal for the Study of the New Testament*
JSNTSup	*Journal for the Study of the New Testament*, Supplement Series
JSOT	*Journal for the Study of the Old Testament*
JSOTSup	*Journal for the Study of the Old Testament*, Supplement Series
JSP	*Journal for the Study of the Pseudepigrapha*
JSPSup	*Journal for the Study of the Pseudepigrapha*, Supplement Series
JSS	*Journal of Semitic Studies*
JTS	*Journal of Theological Studies*
KD	*Kerygma und Dogma*
LCL	Loeb Classical Library
LSJ	Liddell–Scott–Jones, *Greek–English Lexicon*
LThJ	*Lutheran Theological Journal*
MNTC	Moffatt New Testament Commentary
NCB	New Century Bible
NEB	New English Bible
Neot	*Neotestamentica*
NHS	Nag Hammadi Studies
NICNT	New International Commentary on the New Testament

NIDNTT	C. Brown (ed.), *The New International Dictionary of New Testament Theology*
NIGTC	New International Greek Textual Commentary
NIV	New International Version
NovT	*Novum Testamentum*
NovTSup	*Novum Testamentum*, Supplements
NRT	*La nouvelle revue théologique*
NTS	*New Testament Studies*
NumenSup	*Numen* Supplements
PEQ	*Palestine Exploration Quarterly*
PG	J. Migne (ed.), *Patrologia graeca*
PL	J. Migne (ed.), *Patrologia latina*
PVTG	Pseudepigrapha Veteris Testamenti graece
RAC	*Reallexikon für Antike und Christentum*
RB	*Revue biblique*
REJ	*Revue des études juives*
Rel	*Religion*
RevQ	*Revue de Qumran*
RGG	*Religion in Geschichte und Gegenwart*
RivB	*Rivista biblica*
RSR	*Recherches de science religieuse*
RSV	Revised Standard Version
RV	Revised Version
SBEC	Studies in the Bible and Early Christianity
SBLDS	SBL Dissertation Series
SBLMS	SBL Monograph Series
SBLSCS	SBL Septuagint and Cognate Studies
SBLSP	SBL Seminar Papers
SBLTT	SBL Texts and Translations
SBT	Studies in Biblical Theology
Sem	*Semitica*
SJ	Studia judaica
SJLA	Studies in Judaism in Late Antiquity
SJT	*Scottish Journal of Theology*
SNTSMS	Society of New Testament Studies Monograph Series
SPB	Studia postbiblica
Str–B	H. Strack and P. Billerbeck, *Kommentar zum Neuen Testament aus Talmud und Midrasch*
TAPA	*Transactions of the American Philological Association*
TBl	*Theologische Blätter*
TDNT	G. Kittel and G. Friedrich (eds.), *Theological Dictionary of the New Testament*
TDOT	G.J. Botterweck and H. Ringgren (eds.), *Theological Dictionary of the Old Testament*
TEV	Today's English Version

ThWAT	G.J. Botterweck and H. Ringgren (eds.), *Theologisches Wörterbuch zum Alten Testament*
TLZ	*Theologischer Literaturzeitung*
TRu	*Theologische Rundschau*
TS	*Theological Studies*
TSAJ	Texte und Studien zum antiken Judentum
TU	Texte und Untersuchungen
TynBul	*Tyndale Bulletin*
TZ	*Theologische Zeitschrift*
USQR	*Union Seminary Quarterly Review*
VC	*Vigiliae christianae*
VT	*Vetus Testamentum*
VTSup	*Vetus Testamentum*, Supplements
WBC	Word Biblical Commentary
WTJ	*Westminster Theological Journal*
WUNT	Wissenschaftliche Untersuchungen zum Neuen Testament
ZNW	*Zeitschrift für die neutestamentliche Wissenschaft*
ZPE	*Zeitschrift für Papyrologie und Epigraphik*
ZRGG	*Zeitschrift für Religions- und Geistesgeschichte*
ZTK	*Zeitschrift für Theologie und Kirche*

LIST OF CONTRIBUTORS

Richard Bauckham, University of St Andrews, Scotland

Deborah Bleicher Carmichael, Ithaca, New York

D.R. de Lacey, University of Cambridge, England

T.L. Donaldson, College of Emmanuel and St Chad, Saskatoon, Saskatchewan, Canada

Ruth B. Edwards, Ripon College, Cuddesdon, Oxford, England

R. Joseph Hoffman, Keble College, Oxford, England

Richard A. Horsely, University of Massachusetts, Boston, Massachusetts

Pieter W. van der Horst, Utrecht University, The Netherlands

A.H. Mead, St Paul's School, London, England

David Mealand, University of Edinburgh, Scotland

John G. Nordling, Valparaiso University, Valparaiso, Indiana

J.C. O'Neill, University of Edinburgh, Scotland

J. Andrew Overman, University of Rochester, Rochester, New York

Christopher Rowland, University of Oxford, England

T. Ewald Schmidt, Santa Barbara, California

Klyne R. Snodgrass, North Park Theological Seminary, Chicago, Illinois

Herold Weiss, St Mary's College, Notre Dame, Indiana

Andrew Wilson, Lancaster University, England

JSNT 19 (1983), pp. 85-97

HOSTILITY TO WEALTH IN PHILO OF ALEXANDRIA

T. Ewald Schmidt

David Mealand's article, 'Philo of Alexandria's Attitude to Riches',[1] focuses on the influence of Greek philosophical schools in Philo's writings about poverty and wealth. Mealand documents Stoic, Cynic, Aristotelian, and Platonic ideas; and he likens Philo's aristocratic praise of poverty to that of Seneca, but concludes that the best explanation of his disparagement of wealth is 'Philo's adherence to a religion some of whose texts reflect the outlook of less privileged groups'.[2] It is the primary purpose of the present article to call into question this conclusion. Mealand's argument is clearly *non sequitur*; but it also falls prey on the one hand to a misinformed conception of the 'outlook' of Jewish texts, and on the other hand to a misreading of Philo's use of the Jewish tradition.

Mealand documents Philo's personal wealth, remarking that 'the basic puzzle is the discrepancy between his recorded statements and his personal affluence'.[3] But a survey of Near Eastern ethical tradition reveals this as a familiar situation: almost every source that exhibits a degree of hostility to wealth, from ancient Babylonian works to contemporary Jewish pseudepigraphical literature, shows evidence of aristocratic production.[4] Philo is in fact the example *par excellence* of this pheno-

1. *ZNW* 69 (1978), pp. 258-64.
2. 'Philo of Alexandria's Attitude to Riches', p. 264, a claim for which he cites no texts, but two sociologists (Max Weber and J.M. Yinger) and his own dissertation.
3. 'Philo of Alexandria's Attitude to Riches', p. 258. For further discussion of Philo's wealth, see S. Sandmel, *Philo of Alexandria* (Oxford: Oxford University Press, 1979), pp. 10-12; V. Burr, *Tiberius Iulius Alexander* (Bonn: Rudolf Habelt, 1955), *passim*.
4. In addition to external and internal biographical data that suggest production by members of the upper classes, there are general implications in the material itself: the rich and not the poor are often addressed in the second person, commands to do

menon. As a member of an established and wealthy family, possessed of means sufficient to allow for substantial study and voluminous writing, and influential enough to represent his community to the Emperor, Philo was hardly ripe for millenarist resentment. Yet from his pen came no less than 38 passages reflecting radical disparagement of wealth. Clearly there are possibilities for the production of such texts other than the author's socio-economic circumstances. In Philo's case, it seems likely that philosophical ideas working in conjunction with religious-ethical traditions produced what seems to be a theoretical position inconsistent with a socio-economic position. The religious-ethical traditions in the Philonic synthesis are of primary interest here: as we narrow our focus to the texts that reflect hostility to wealth, we must consider Philo's use of features common to other Jewish texts.

Passages that make reference to wealth are common in Philo's writings. We will consider over 200 of these, concentrating on those using πλοῦτος, which constitute about two thirds of the total.[5] Other words commonly used for wealth are ἄργυρος and/or χρυσός,[6] and χρῆμα.[7]

---

justice assume an economic capability, and a high degree of literacy is required for authorship. Many examples could be listed, but the following are representative of 'radical' views expressed by members of privileged groups: The *Maxims of Ptahhotep* 30; *The Poem of the Righteous Sufferer*, tab. 2, l. 46; *The Instruction of Amenemope* 16.10; 18.8; 26.12; *The Babylonian Theodicy* ll. 63-64; 70-71; 237; 253; *The Words of Ahiqar* l. 136; Job 21.7; 22.23-30; Ps. 73.12; Prov. 8.10; 23.4; Eccl. 10.20; Isa. 2.7; Mic. 6.10-12; LXX Ps. 33.11; Sir. 13.2-19; *T. Benj.* 6.2-3; *T. Job* 18.8; 48.2; *LAB* 35.5; *Jos. Asen.* 10–12.

5.   See G. Mayer, *Index Philoneus* (Berlin: de Gruyter, 1974), p. 235, for a list of the 149 passages cited below.

6.   Roughly half the references (Mayer, *Index Philoneus*, pp. 42, 307) use ἄργυρος and χρυσός to denote wealth (parentheses indicate that the passage also contains πλοῦτος): *Leg. All.* 2.107; *Cher.* 34; 48; 80; *Sacr.* 21; 26; 55; *Det. Pot. Ins.* 20; 157; *Poster. C.* 150; *Deus Imm.* 169; *Ebr.* 85-86; 95; *Sobr.* 41; *Conf. Ling.* 93; *Migr. Abr.* 97; 103; *Rer. Div. Her.* 44; 216–17; *Congr.* 112; 113–14; *Fug.* 15; (26); 35; *Mut. Nom.* 89–90; 93; *Somn.* 2.44; 57–62; *Abr.* (209); (220); *Jos.* 120; 125; 150; (258); *Vit. Mos.* 1 (152); (317); *Dec.* 4 (71); 133; *Spec. Leg.* 1 (21–25); *Spec. Leg.* 2 (20); *Spec. Leg.* 4 (74); (158); 223; *Omn. Prob. Lib.* (9) 31; (65); (76); *Vit. Cont.* 49; *Flacc.* (131); 142; *Leg. Gai.* (9, context includes χρήματα); (108); 343.

7.   *Op. Mund.* 79; *Leg. All.* 1.75; *Leg. All.* 2.17; *Det. Pot. Ins.* 135; *Poster. C.* 114; 117; *Gig.* (15); 36–37; *Deus Imm.* 163; *Plant.* 66; 171; *Ebr.* 22; *Sobr.* 67; *Migr. Abr.* 217; *Rer. Div. Her.* (48); 92; *Fug.* (28); 39; *Somn.* 1.124; 2.128; *Abr.* 228; *Jos.* 76; 135; *Vit. Mos.* 1.141; 267–93; *Dec.* 151; (153); *Spec. Leg.* 178; 104; 143; 151; *Spec. Leg.* 1.93; *Spec. Leg.* 2.170; 82; 139; 168; 181; *Spec. Leg.* 4.10; 33;

The word πλοῦτος is used in a figurative sense 51 times in Philo,[8] occasionally as a foil to negatively regarded material wealth, as in *Somn.* 1.179: 'Of what riches can we any longer stand in need, when we have Thee who art alone the true riches…?'[9] πλοῦτος is used nine times without critical evaluation,[10] and in eight other passages which address the justice imperative to the wealthy without giving a contextual indication of valuation or hostility.[11]

The imperative to do justice, a command fundamental to Old Testament and postcanonical piety,[12] is not a burning issue to Philo. Although he praises the just laws of the Pentateuch (e.g. *Spec. Leg.* 2.107; *Virt.* 97), he does not mention ἐλεημοσύνη, and only rarely does he mention the formulaic 'widow, orphan, and poor' as the recipients of aid (*Dec.* 40–43; *Spec. Leg.* 4.176–78). Instead, he offers a vague ideal of general welfare or commonality (*Spec. Leg.* 4.159; *Virt.* 169; *Praem. Poen.* 168) epitomized by the practice of the Essenes (*Apol. Iud.* 11.4, 11). When he does approach the familiar form of the justice imperative, Philo's aristocratic perspective and penchant for mere token response become clear: 'You have abundance of wealth, give a share to others, for the excellence

82; 87; (159); *Virt.* (82); 182; *Praem. Poen.* (104) 142; *Omn. Prob. Lib.* 55; 65; 145; *Vit. Cont.* 14; 16; *Flacc.* 60; *Leg. Gai.* 9; 17; 156; 172; 232; 315.

8.   *Op. Mund.* 23; *Leg. All.* 1.34; 45; *Leg. All.* 2.12; *Leg. All.* 3.24; 39; 163; 211; *Sacr.* 124; *Det. Pot. Ins.* 131; *Poster. C.* 139; 144; 151; 174; *Agr.* 54; *Plant.* 66; *Migr. Abr.* 71; *Rer. Div. Her.* 27; 48; 76; *Congr.* 76; *Fug.* 17; 102; *Somn.* 1.179; *Abr.* 25; *Vit. Mos.* 1.153; 155; *Vit. Mos.* 2.38; *Dec.* 178; *Spec. Leg.* 2. 23; 107; *Spec. Leg.* 4.75; 194; *Virt.* 5; 6; 7; 8; 10; 81; 85; 94–148; *Praem. Poen.* 36; *Omn. Prob. Lib.* 8; 77; *Vit. Cont.* 17; 35; *Flacc.* 63; *Leg. Gai.* 51; 141; 203.

9.   See also *Rer. Div. Her.* 148; *Vit. Mos.* 1.153; 155; *Spec. Leg.* 2.23; *Virt.* 85.

10.   *Poster. C.* 109; *Rer. Div. Her.* 212; *Congr.* 5; *Somn.* 1.155; *Somn.* 2.35; *Jos.* 72; *Spec. Leg.* 1.139; 277; *Spec. Leg.* 4.172. See also *Poster. C.* 114; *Deus Imm.* 163; *Plant.* 66; *Abr.* 228; *Jos.* 135; *Spec. Leg.* 1.104; 143; *Spec. Leg.* 3.70; 82; 168; 181; *Spec. Leg.* 4.10; 33; 159; *Leg. Gai.* 156; 315; where χρήματα is used in a noncritical sense; and *Op. Mund.* 49; *Poster. C.* 35; *Plant.* 126; *Ebr.* 141; *Rer. Div. Her.* 246; *Spec. Leg.* 1.342; *Leg. Gai.* 4; 215; 295; where χρῆμα is used for tribute money.

11.   *Jos.* 144; *Spec. Leg.* 2.71; 87; 107; *Virt.* 97; 169; *Leg. Gai.* 13; 199.

12.   There are over 200 passages in Jewish literature that reflect this 'justice imperative'. Almsgiving (ἐλεημοσύνη) becomes a primary focus of these in postcanonical literature. See e.g. Exod. 22.21-22; Lev. 19.9-10; Deut. 15.1-14; Job 22.6-9; Ps. 10.12-18; Prov. 14.31; 19.17; Isa. 1.17; Jer. 5.26-29; Ezek. 18.10-17; Amos 2.6-7; Mic. 2.2; Zech. 7.10; Tob. 1.7-8; Sir. 4.1-10; *T. Zeb.* 7.1–8.3; Wis. 2.10; *Ass. Mos.* 7.6; *T. Job* 9.2–15.5; *2 En.* 9.1; 63.1-2; 1QS 10.26; CD 6.16-17; 14.12-16.

of wealth consists not in a full purse but in succouring the needy' (*Jos.* 144).

Although about 80 per cent of the passages in question exhibit a degree of hostility to wealth, the remainder needs to be accounted for. Does Philo simply contradict himself, does his socio-economic position at times overcome his philosophical understanding, or is there an observable pattern that accounts for the discrepancies? There is indeed a pattern, and one which deals a blow to the argument that Philo's hostility to wealth reflects sympathy toward underprivileged co-religionists. For in 31 of 43 passages exhibiting a positive critical estimation of wealth, Philo writes of wealth belonging to Jews.[13] Perhaps his thinking was influenced by the scriptural narratives on which he was commenting; in any case, it is clear that he distinguishes between wealth as given by God to the Jews (*Leg. All.* 3.197) and wealth as an ethical subject. When he demonstrates even a remote awareness of deprivation among the Jews, it is to promise them wealth (*Praem. Poen.* 168). Clearly, Philo's praise of poverty and disregard for wealth are not determined by borrowed feelings of disenfranchisement.

The other twelve passages that exhibit valuation of wealth are instructive with respect to nuances in Philo's position, but they do not contradict his ethical teaching. When he allows for the possibility of 'good' wealth, he includes in the context a negative statement (*Plant.* 171; *Sobr.* 40) or a goal more worthy of striving (*Rer. Div. Her.* 286–87). In *Praem. Poen.* 104 he makes a statement very similar to Mt. 6.33:

> For those who possess stored up in Heaven the true wealth whose adornment is wisdom and godliness have also the wealth of earthly riches in abundance (cf. 118).

A careful reading of the context reveals that Philo defines this abundance in terms of an ongoing provision of food and shelter (98–100), and not the superfluity of luxury which he condemns elsewhere. Six of the seven remaining references value wealth in a particular context, exemplified by *Leg. Gai.* 123:

---

13. *Leg. All.* 3.24; 86; 197; *Sacr.* 19; 43; *Sobr.* 21; 41; 61; *Migr. Abr.* 94; 103; 172; 217; *Rer. Div. Her.* 216–17; *Fug.* 15; *Mut. Nom.* 88–89; 173; *Somn.* 2.44; *Jos.* 120; 150; 198; *Vit. Mos.* 1.141; 293; 312–17; *Spec. Leg.* 1.78; 151; *Spec. Leg.* 2.87; 208; *Spec. Leg.* 4.223; *Praem. Poen.* 142; 168; *Leg. Gai.* 232. Another indication of the distinction is that the passages reflecting valuation of wealth are almost all narrative, whereas the passages reflecting hostility to wealth are usually didactic.

> These things are horrible... when the rich become poor, the well-to-do destitute, suddenly through no fault of their own rendered hearthless and homeless (cf. *Flacc.* 58; 60; 77; *Leg. Gai.* 108; 343).

The remaining reference, *Leg. Gai.* 9 (cf. 18–21; 343) speaks sympathetically of inherited wealth, completing the picture of valuation of involuntarily acquired or deprived wealth. The will is the key. Where Philo is positive toward wealth, he regards its acquisition as involuntary: it is a gift of God to the Jews, an inheritance, or a plundered fortune. Where he is negative, wealth represents for Philo the acquisitiveness that cannot exist side by side with virtue, and renunciation represents the choice for virtue. The involuntary poverty of his fellow Jews scarcely attracts Philo's notice, and hardly relates to this scheme. Apparently, then, Philo does not regard his co-religionists as disinherited or plundered. It is to the extent that Jewish ethics support, or Jewish examples illustrate, his scheme of virtue in relation to wealth that Philo reveals his Jewishness.

In order to distinguish between degrees of hostility to wealth in Philo's writings, we will employ a scheme of categorization in which five logically successive stages[14] lead from the justice imperative to the most radical hostility to wealth (i.e., the recommendation that virtue be served by disparagement of, and separation from, wealth).

The first of these stages moves just beyond the justice imperative to an equation of greed and injustice; or more generally, greed and evil. The specific equation is found in *Vit. Cont.* 17, where Philo states that 'injustice is bred by anxious thought for the means of life and for money-making'.[15] Vices other than injustice are also linked with greed,[16] and among these equations is a reference to desire/covetousness as 'that insidious foe and source of all evils' (*Virt.* 100). Thirteen occurrences of the Greek-borrowed term φιλαργυρία/φιλοχρηματία[17] mark 'love of money' as a standard phrase used by Philo in condemning greed.

The second stage in the movement toward hostility to wealth is the

14. It should be emphasized that these stages are not chronological, nor does one stage necessarily produce the next; rather, the 'higher' stages tend to assume the 'lower' stages.

15. See also *Spec. Leg.* 4.65; 87; 212; 215; *Virt.* 82; *Flacc.* 130–31; 142.

16. See *Cher.* 34; *Det. Pot. Ins.* 157; *Poster. C.* 150; *Conf. Ling.* 93; *Rer. Div. Her.* 44; *Mut. Nom.* 226; *Somn.* 2.40; *Jos.* 125; 140; *Omn. Prob. Lib.* 31; 65.

17. *Mut. Nom.* 226; *Abr.* 221; *Vit. Mos.* 1.141; *Spec. Leg.* 1.23; 24; 281; *Spec. Leg.* 2.78; *Spec. Leg.* 4.65; 212; 215; *Omn. Prob. Lib.* 21; *Flacc.* 60. See examples in LSJ which demonstrate the commonness of these words in Greek literature.

equation of wealth and injustice. Again, the idea of injustice broadens to include other vices, making this stage a transition from the relation of wealth to behaviour to the consideration of wealth as an object. In Philo we encounter a number of examples of the equation 'wealth = injustice',[18] but certainly more characteristic of his writings are disparaging remarks about wealth itself. Typical of these is *Spec. Leg.* 1.25–28, in which riches are described as 'blind', 'unstable', and 'idols and unsubstantial shadows'.[19] Wealth is also commonly linked with pride[20] and excessive luxury or pleasure.[21] It is the fool's desire (*Conf. Ling.* 112; *Jos.* 254) and the antithesis of virtue (*Somn.* 2.12; *Vit. Mos.* 2.53); it is 'no true blessing, but actually a grievous evil' (*Gig.* 37).[22]

Comparative devaluation is the third stage. Here wealth is portrayed as lower on a scale of values than something else. In Philo's writings, this usually takes the form of valuation of virtue over wealth. *Abr.* 24–25 is typical: 'What wealth is equal in worth to these [virtues]...for in very truth the wealth which is not blind but keen in sight is abundance of virtue'.[23] Related to this form are valuations of prudence[24] or right relation to God[25] over material wealth. But requiring distinction are a few passages that express comparative devaluation without truly disparaging wealth itself. *Det. Pot. Ins.* 122 lauds justice because of 'its complete indifference to objects on the borderline between vice and virtue, such as wealth...' *Gig.* 38 advocates that one neither seek nor refuse wealth, but rather cultivate detachment from it. *Det. Pot. Ins.* 164 recommends 'economy', and *Omn. Prob. Lib.* 145 'moderate livelihood', as the proper middle road. One passage defies categorization, but may be included here as a way of demonstrating detachment without hostility. In *Fug.* 25–29 Philo suggests that one 'expose the worthless mode of life'; rather, says Philo, 'do not refuse abundance of wealth', but practice

18. See *Spec. Leg.* 3.139; *Spec. Leg.* 4.158; *Virt.* 85–86; 161–62; 166; *Omn. Prob. Lib.* 72.

19. Cf. *Cher.* 48; 80; *Det. Pot. Ins.* 135; *Gig.* 15; *Ebr.* 95; *Sobr.* 67; *Rer. Div. Her.* 48; 92; *Congr.* 112; *Fug.* 39; *Somn.* 1.248; *Abr.* 220; *Jos.* 131–33; *Dec.* 133; *Spec. Leg.* 4.82; *Praem. Poen.* 24; *Vit. Cont.* 14; *Flacc.* 148; *Leg. Gai.* 17.

20. *Poster. C.* 115; *Mut. Nom.* 214; *Somn.* 2.57–62; *Dec.* 4; *Virt.* 174.

21. *Abr.* 209; *Dec.* 71; 151; *Omn. Prob. Lib.* 9; *Vit. Cont.* 49.

22. See also *Det. Pot. Ins.* 20–21; *Ebr.* 22; *Fug.* 28; *Somn.* 1.124; 126; *Somn.* 2.128; *Vit. Mos.* 1.267; *Spec. Leg.* 1.93; *Vit. Cont.* 16; *Leg. Gai.* 172.

23. See also *Sacr.* 26; *Abr.* 219–21; *Jos.* 76; *Virt.* 188; cf. *Omn. Prob. Lib.* 55.

24. *Ebr.* 85–86; *Sobr.* 3; *Congr.* 113–14.

25. *Sacr.* 55; *Ebr.* 52; *Migr. Abr.* 101; *Virt.* 182.

generosity to such an extent that 'you will all but throw your private property into the common purse'. The exaggeration of the last line should not disguise Philo's implicit defence of (his own?) wealth. Virtue may be above it, but virtue can also redeem it (*Sobr.* 40). Whatever this passage may hint about Philo's underlying belief or practice, it represents only an exception to his written rule. It may be seen in terms of Jewish prerogative, and it should be noted that Philo here advocates 'not refusing' rather than 'acquiring'.

Alternative devaluation, the fourth stage, goes beyond the third stage by avowing value X *instead of* wealth rather than avowing value X *more than* wealth. With this stage we encounter truly radical hostility to wealth. Up to this point most of Philo's statements find parallels in earlier Semitic literature, despite the Greek cast which he gives to them.[26] But at this stage he seems to see less of a tension and more of an opposition between the delights of wealth and the demands of virtue. Eighteen passages reflect this thinking;[27] we will consider three of these as representational, giving the bulk of attention to stage five. In *Gig.* 15 Philo disparages

> glory, wealth, and offices, and honours, and all other illusions which like images or pictures are created through the deceit of false opinion by those who have never gazed upon the true beauty.

Ebr. 75 extols the one who has

> learnt that nothing else, neither wealth, nor glory, nor honour...nor the whole world, but only the true cause, the Cause Supreme among causes, deserves our service and highest honour.

This mutual exclusivity of values takes its most typically Philonic form in *Congr.* 27, which states that

> (virtue) trains us to despise (καταφρονητικῶς ἔχειν) all that should be held of little account, reputation and wealth and pleasure...

This opposition between the pursuit of virtue and the pursuit of wealth is taken a step further in 20 passages that evince the fifth and final stage,

26. This cast is most noticeable in the use of words like φιλαργυρία and χρηματία, the substitution of virtue for justice and wisdom, and the comparatively large number of references to wealth as an object rather than to the wealthy as a group.

27. *Det. Pot. Ins.* 33–34; *Poster. C.* 112; *Gig.* 15; 35; *Deus Imm.* 169; *Agr.* 31–39; 54; *Plant.* 69; *Ebr.* 75; *Migr. Abr.* 97; *Rer. Div. Her.* 48; *Congr.* 27; *Fug.* 17–19; 151; *Somn.* 1.179; *Abr.* 262–65; *Spec. Leg.* 1.311; *Spec. Leg.* 3.1.

teleological devaluation. Here, in passages containing some interesting parallels to Synoptic material, Philo makes voluntary dispossession of wealth a means or way of achieving virtue. *Leg. All.* 142–45 is notable for the verb used to indicate the act of renunciation. Philo says of Moses that

> not only does he renounce (ἀποτάττεται) the whole belly, but with it he scours away the feet, that is, the supports of pleasure... We must not fail to notice that Moses, when he refuses the entire belly, that is the filling of the stomach, he practically renounces (ἀποτάττεται) the other passions too.

The same verb is used in Lk. 14.33. Philo usually employs ἀποτάσσω/ ἀποτάττω to indicate purely mental activity,[28] and that sense may be implicit here, but it is interesting to encounter the word in such a context. A stronger statement is found in *Deus Imm.* 147–51:

> Have you won the Olympic crown of victory over all wealth, and so risen superior to all that wealth involves, that you accept nothing of what it brings for your use and enjoyment?... Will you see all the treasuries of wealth, one after the other, full to the brim, yet turn aside from them and avert your eyes?... For (a celestial and heavenly soul) taking its fill of the vision of incorruptible and genuine goods (ἀγαθῶν), bids farewell (ἀποτάττεται) to the transient and spurious.[29]

Here it is clear that hostility goes beyond attitude to active separation from wealth. *Plant.* 66 makes explicit the junction of attitude and action:

> This is the mind which, as the lawgiver insists, should be that of those who provide themselves with no property that has its place among things created, but renounce (ἀπογινώσκοντας) all these on the ground of that intimate association with the Uncreate, to possess Whom, they are convinced, is the only wealth, the only gauge of consummate happiness.

In *Vit. Mos.* 1.152–55 Philo praises the lawgiver because 'he did not treasure up (ἐθησαυρίσατο) gold and silver'; and states that 'God rewarded him by giving him instead the greatest and most perfect wealth' (cf. Lk. 12.21). Similarly, Philo advises in *Spec. Leg.* 4.74:

---

28. *Leg. All.* 2.25; *Leg. All.* 3.41; 238; *Sobr.* 5; but see *Migr. Abr.* 92; *Vit. Mos.* 1.38; *Leg. Gai.* 325; where physical action is implied.

29. The last sentence is my own translation. Colson and Whitaker (LCL) translate ἀγαθῶν as 'good': θέας γὰρ ἐμπιπλαμένη τῶν γνωσίων καὶ ἀφθάρτων ἀγαθῶν εἰκότως τοῖς ἐφημέροις καὶ νόφοις ἀποτάττεται. See *Mut. Nom.* 32 for a similar use of ἀγαθῶν.

So then let not the rich man collect great store of gold and silver and hoard it at his house, but bring it out for general use that he may soften the hard lot of the needy with the unction of his cheerfully given liberality... (cf. *Praem. Poen.* 104).

Philo's descriptions of the Essenes and Therapeutae provide additional examples of teleological devaluation. He lauds the former because

they have become moneyless and landless by deliberate action rather than by lack of good fortune, [but] they are esteemed exceedingly rich, because they judge frugality with contentment to be, as indeed it is, an abundance of wealth (*Omn. Prob. Lib.* 77; cf. 76).

He praises the latter, likewise, because they

preferred magnanimity to negligence and gave away (χαρισάμενοι) their possessions (τὰς οὐσίας) instead of wasting them, benefiting both others and themselves... (*Vit. Cont.* 16).

The Therapeutae garner further praise from Philo in that

when they have divested themselves of their possessions and have no longer aught to ensnare them they flee without a backward glance and leave their brothers, their children, their wives, their parents, the wide circle of their kinfolk, the groups of friends around them, the fatherlands in which they were born and reared, since strong is the attraction of familiarity and very great its power to ensnare (*Vit. Cont.* 18; cf. Mk 10.29-30).

Clearly, Philo presents these groups as contemporary examples of the biblical figures he describes elsewhere as embodiments of his ideal. Other examples of teleological devaluation could be given,[30] but these suffice to complete the picture of Philo's ideal as that of a man who voluntarily scorns and leaves his wealth by practising charity and frugality. Although he praises such action, he does not make it an absolute (*Fug.* 25–29) or universal (*Mut. Nom.* 32, 39) requirement, nor does he laud poverty. Instead, his focus is upon virtue as an exercise of the will, of which hostility to wealth is one important form.

In order to assess more carefully Philo's severity and its relation to previous Jewish and subsequent Christian traditions, it is useful at this point to consider Greek attitudes toward wealth. Summaries and

---

30. *Ebr.* 57; *Fug.* 26; 35; *Mut. Nom.* 32 (cf. 39); *Jos.* 258; *Spec. Leg.* 2.18–23; *Spec. Leg.* 4.159; *Praem. Poen.* 54; 100; *Omn. Prob. Lib.* 86; *Vit. Cont.* 13; *Apol. Iud.* 11.4–5, 11.

numerous references are provided by Hauck and Kasch on the subject
of wealth in general,[31] and by Bolkestein and Hands on the subject of
charity.[32] If we compare these works with our knowledge of Philo, we
discover that Philo's eclectic approach mirrors many elements of Greek
thought, from pre-Socratic to Stoic.[33] His expressions of teleological
devaluation, however, most closely resemble Cynic ideals, not only in
their radical extent of renunciation, as opposed to the mere detachment
of Stoics,[34] but also in their individual point of reference, as opposed to
the *polis* in Plato and Aristotle.[35] Diogenes, Crates, and Demetrius
appear as *personae classicae* for various authors,[36] prompting doubt as
to the prevalent practice of Cynic ideals. Seneca, who in social status and
teaching can be compared to Philo,[37] exemplifies this inconsistency. In
Epist. 62.3, praising Demetrius for renouncing his wealth, he pens the
concise maxim, 'The shortest cut to [true] riches is to despise riches'. In
a later epistle he makes the fuller statement that

> we must spurn wealth; wealth is the diploma of slavery. Abandon gold
> and silver, and whatever else is a burden on our richly furnished homes;
> liberty cannot be gained for nothing. If you set a high value on liberty, you
> must set a low value on everything else (*Epist.* 104.34).

Yet in *Vita Beata* 18.1–3 Seneca freely admits to neglecting the practice
of his ideals, arguing that the praise of virtue is necessary despite his
own lapses. It may be that Philo's scriptural and sectarian Jewish heroes

---

31. F. Hauck and W. Kasch, 'πλοῦτος', *TDNT*, VI, pp. 319-23. The authors
demonstrate a general valuation of wealth tempered by attention to the polis and
virtue (Plato and Aristotle) or by mental detachment (Stoics).

32. H. Bolkestein, *Wohltätigkeit und Armenpflege im vorchristlichen Altertum*
(Utrecht: A. Oosthoek, 1939); A.R. Hands, *Charities and Social Aid in Greece and
Rome* (Ithaca, NY: Cornell University Press, 1968).

33. Mealand, 'Philo of Alexandria's Attitude to Riches', pp. 259-63.

34. See e.g. Horace, *Satires* 2.3.82-157, 225-80; Seneca, *Epist.* 20.9-13.

35. Hauck and Kasch, 'πλοῦτος', p. 322 n. 30.

36. Diogenes: *Dio* 6.61–62; 9.12; Crates: *Diog. L.* 6.87; Demetrius: Seneca, *Vita
Beat.* 18.3; *Epist.* 62.3.

37. This is not the case, as Mealand suggests ('Philo of Alexandria's Attitude to
Riches', p. 259), in Philo's 'praise of poverty'. Philo values only voluntary renunciation, and he does not praise poverty. Seneca values poverty however it comes,
even involuntarily (see *Epist.* 4.9–11; 17.5; 20.7; 62.3; 87.41; 98.13). Another
important difference is Seneca's bent toward Stoic detachment (*Epist.* 20.9–13;
14.17–18).

correspond to these Cynic heroes, and that his practice was equally far removed from his ideals.

Another similarity between Philo and Greek authors is his lack of concern for almsgiving.[38] Despite occasional attention to the cause of the needy,[39] Philo tends to share the Greek characteristic that 'the giver's action is self-regarding'.[40] That is, he concentrates on the dangers of wealth to the individual, and not on the need of it by others less fortunate. Praise or compassion for the poor are rare both for Philo and for Graeco-Roman writers.[41] Generosity to society in the forms of grain doles, feasts, buildings, and other public benefits only incidentally benefited the poor as part of the general population.[42]

But if we look closer at the motivation for giving, we observe a crucial distinction that sets Philo apart from the Greeks who influenced so many aspects of his expression. The self-regarding action of the giver in the Greek world is such 'in the sense that he anticipates from the

38. See n. 12 above. Bolkestein (*Wohltätigkeit*, p. 114) states that in Greece 'Mahnungen an die Reichen, den Armen Almosen zu geben, fehlen...'

39. *Fug.* 29 (needy *friends*); *Spec. Leg.* 4.74; 159; 172.

40. Hands, *Charities*, p. 26.

41. Hands, *Charities*, pp. 77-88. A notable instance in Philo, to which my attention has been drawn by Dr William Horbury, is *Spec. Leg.* 4.176–81. Although 'widow', 'orphan', and 'incomer' are the words used, and there is no explicit mention of economic condition, Philo goes as far as to liken the Jewish race to an orphan, who gets help from God rather than from natural helpers. But any meritorious economic austerity implicitly referred to here is voluntary (179) and even then not necessarily contemporary (181). The passage cannot be adduced as evidence that Philo saw Jews as poor and therefore saw wealth as bad. *Dec.* 40–43 suggests that one become 'affable and easy of access to the poorest...the lonely...orphans [and] wives on whom widowhood has fallen' not out of sympathy or social consciousness, but 'because the lot...may change to the reverse,...but also because...a man should not forget what he is'. *Fragments* II Mang. 678 states that 'Poverty by itself claims compassion, in order to correct its deficiencies, but when it comes to judgement...the judgement of God is just'. Sympathy appears stronger here; but significantly, it does not extend beyond charity to identification of God—much less the writer—with the plight of the needy.

42. Hands, *Charities*, pp. 62, 115. Interestingly, when Philo mentions Caligula's grain doles, in which Jews were included as Roman citizens, he makes no mention of need. See *Leg. Gai.* 158; R.M. Grant, *Early Christianity and Society* (New York: Harper & Row, 1977), p. 142. I am indebted to Dr Christopher C. Rowland for this reference.

recipient some sort of return'.[43] This principle of reciprocity, which Bolkestein calls one of the *Grundlagen* of Greek society,[44] operated primarily among the upper classes[45] and brought either equivalent gifts or honor to the giver.[46] Philo's economic ethic is not informed by this dominant pagan ideal. Rather, his expression of Greek ideas is combined with a Jewish cast of characters, suggesting that he perceived a strong link between hostility to wealth and Jewish tradition. If he was primarily a Cynic in orientation, he was so only to the extent that he saw a warrant or a precedent for Cynic ideas in the Hebrew Scriptures and in contemporary Jewish sectarian practice.

With respect to subsequent Synoptic tradition, we must grant the possibility of familiarity with Cynic and even Philonic writings among the Christians of the middle decades of the first century. But given the warrant/precedent in Jewish sources for the same ideas, the similarities in expression are perhaps best regarded in terms of coincidence and not dependence.

Our consideration of Philo's writings can be summarized by four statements:
1. Philo writes from an aristocratic point of view.
2. Philo consistently expresses hostility to wealth, including a significant number of passages exhibiting alternative and teleological devaluation of wealth.
3. Philo's hostility to wealth is not determined by sympathy for oppressed Jews.
4. Philo's affinities to Greek thought, especially to that of the Cynics, are limited in scope to those that he perceives to be consistent with Jewish tradition.

These conclusions should give pause to contemporary scholars who too hastily wed modern sociological data and ancient texts. The 'puzzle' of Philo's simultaneous affluence and hostility to wealth is such only for

---

43. Hands, *Charities*, p. 26. See also Sir. 12.1-7; Pseudo-Phocylides 80.
44. Bolkestein, *Wohltätigkeit*, p. 158.
45. S.C. Mott, 'The Power of Giving and Receiving: Reciprocity in Hellenistic Benevolence', in G.F. Hawthorne (ed.), *Current Issues in Biblical and Patristic Interpretation* (Grand Rapids: Eerdmans, 1975), p. 72.
46. Hands, *Charities*, pp. 48-61.

those who follow Mealand's assumption that there exists a causative relation between socio-economic circumstances and critical evaluation of wealth. Philo is in fact a compelling argument that this assumption is false.[47]

47. Translations are from F.H. Colson and G.H. Whitaker, *Philo*, I–X (LCL; London: William Heinemann, 1949). I follow F.C. Conybeare (*Philo and the Contemplative Life* [Oxford: Clarendon Press, 1895], pp. 325-58) against P.E. Lucius (*Die Therapeuten und ihre Stellung in der Geschichte der Askese* [Strassburg, 1879]) with respect to the authenticity of *De Vita Contemplativa*: Conybeare argues persuasively for authenticity on linguistic grounds. See now also T.E. Schmidt, *Hostility to Wealth in the Synoptic Gospels* (JSNTSup, 15; Sheffield: JSOT Press, 1987), esp. pp. 76-84.

JSNT 24 (1985), pp. 111-15

THE PARADOX OF PHILO'S VIEWS ON WEALTH

David Mealand

The article 'Hostility to Wealth in Philo of Alexandria' by T. Ewald Schmidt contains some useful analysis of Philo's views, but does not do justice to the full range of Philo's views and misconstrues my article on the subject.[1] I wish to reply by setting out some of the facts as I see them.

Schmidt regards Philo as the supreme example of an aristocratic attitude to wealth, and he writes as though my article focused chiefly or exclusively on socio-economic factors. In fact the bulk of my article was directed to the debt Philo's ideas owe to various philosophical traditions. Towards the end I mentioned that Philo's debt to Judaism is, of course, more important. I then added three brief sentences pointing out that Philo's loyalty to Judaism rendered his social position in Alexandria ambiguous, despite his obvious wealth. It is the combination of all these factors which is in my view relevant to a study of Philo's conflicting attitudes to wealth.

Thus even though I give far more emphasis than Schmidt concedes to the importance of philosophical and religious traditions for Philo, there is also a genuine disagreement which needs to be explored. Schmidt gives the impression that he believes that there only 'seems' to be an inconsistency[2] between Philo's personal wealth and his praise of frugality, renunciation and avoidance of wealth. He speaks of it only as an apparent 'puzzle'.[3] While noting that others, especially Seneca, also exhibit such an inconsistency it is too simple to attribute so flagrant a contra-

---

1. T.E. Schmidt, 'Hostility to Wealth in Philo of Alexandria', *JSNT* 19 (1983), pp. 85-97 [reprinted in this volume]; D.L. Mealand, 'Philo of Alexandria's Attitude to Riches', *ZNW* 69 (1978), pp. 258-64.

2. Schmidt, 'Hostility', p. 36.

3. Schmidt, 'Hostility', p. 93.

diction solely to a gap between inherited wealth and inherited ideals. It is only a palliative to argue that Philo does not make his ideal absolute or universal.[4] He constantly commends renunciation, and yet he was a man of great wealth. Of course Philo drew on ethical traditions highly critical of wealth. That was one of my own main points. But Philo's wealth and Philo's views on wealth are in conflict. The puzzle is a real one. It is not puzzling that Philo retained his wealth. It is puzzling that being so rich he so emphasizes a set of traditions which reflect hostility to wealth. Even if most people inherit rather than choose their religious and ethical traditions they are able to choose which elements in those traditions they wish to emphasize. Philo could have emphasized Stoic indifference rather than Cynic frugality, he could have focused on the wealth of the patriarchs or the unsought wealth of Solomon or the prudential morality of Proverbs rather than the laws concerned with the plight of the poor. But Philo says of Moses that he has 'filled almost all his legislation with commandments to show mercy and kindness (ἔλεον καὶ φιλανθρωπίαν) and that he 'offers great rewards to those who hold it a duty to rectify the misfortunes of their neighbours and who regard abundant wealth not as their own property but common to those in need'.[5] Naturally Philo as a good Jew focuses more on the laws, but he chooses to emphasize this element in the laws.

Schmidt argues that Philo is 'the example *par excellence*' of aristocratic writers who exhibit 'a degree of hostility to wealth'. Now I readily grant that one does find texts written by members of a privileged and wealthy minority which exhibit 'a degree of hostility to wealth'. This is a well-known phenomenon, and it is not surprising that those with inherited wealth should criticize wealth acquired by wickedness or wealth obtained by great exertion. Job 21.7 and Prov. 23.4 may well be examples of such a tradition, as Schmidt argues. But the Jewish texts Schmidt cites either only exhibit a degree of hostility to wealth or are not obviously produced by the wealthy. Schmidt rightly says that Philo's ideal is that of one who voluntarily scorns and leaves his wealth by practising charity and frugality. But here surely Philo is using non-aristocratic Cynic and Jewish traditions.

There is also another radical element in Philo which appears only rarely. This echoes Jewish reversal theology. We find a radical protest by the victims of violence in a whole series of other Jewish texts. In the canonical psalms, in the *Admonitions of Enoch*, in the Qumran texts,

4.   Schmidt, 'Hostility', p. 91.
5.   *Spec. Leg.* 4.72.

and in the *Psalms of Solomon*,[6] to name but a few, we find a protest by those who describe themselves as poor and/or as the victims of oppression by others. Even if we hold that the psalms are court productions, and that the leaders of the Qumran sect were once priestly aristocrats, these texts themselves make it very clear that they are produced by people now in a situation of relative disprivilege due to the hostility and/ or oppression of the enemies. The role of relative disprivilege is here important and has been much emphasized in the classics of historical sociology.[7] Max Weber specifically notes this motif in his study of Judaism to which I made reference.

I do not claim that Philo was himself in so reduced a state, or that he makes any great use of this motif. But Philo cannot simply be described as an aristocrat writing from an aristocratic point of view. He was a very wealthy Jewish citizen of a *Greek*-ruled *Egyptian* city. He was a man of influence in his community, but not an aristocrat pure and simple. His social situation was not one of disprivilege but one of ambiguity. Those who are allergic to sociological theory could consider the historical circumstances of the Jews in Alexandria in Philo's lifetime. Under Flaccus the Jews of Alexandria were attacked and plundered. It was Philo who wrote a whole work against Flaccus describing the outrages. Yet Schmidt can write, 'Apparently, then, Philo does not regard his co-religionists as disinherited or plundered'. He also writes, 'When he [Philo] demonstrates even a remote awareness of deprivation among the Jews it is to promise them wealth'.[8] Now I do not claim that the extreme circumstances of the reign of Gaius obtained earlier (though there had been earlier troubles). But Philo certainly saw it as his duty to represent his

6.   Pss. 12, esp. v. 6; 14.46; 86.1-2 (cf. v. 14); 140; *1 En.* 94–104 (for the future judgment on wealthy oppressors see 103); *Pss. Sol.* 5.2, 11; 15.1; 18.2; 1QH 2.32; 1QpHab 12.2-10; 4QpPs 37.21-22. Cf. D.L. Mealand, *Poverty and Expectation in the Gospels* (London: SPCK, 1980), pp. 101-102.

7.   M. Weber, *The Sociology of Religion* (London: Methuen, 1965), pp. 107-17, a work written before 1920. (Of course his views on Old Testament scholarship need updating.) Refinement of the sociological theory is to be found in C.Y. Glock, 'The Role of Deprivation in the Origin and Exolution of Religious Groups', in R. Lee and M.E. Marty (eds.), *Religion and Social Conflict* (New York: Oxford University Press, 1964), pp. 24-36. Further qualifications in B. Wilson, *Religion in Sociological Perspective* (Oxford, 1982), pp. 116-18. (On the role of petty nobles and intellectuals, see N. Cohn, *The Pursuit of the Millennium* [London: Temple Smith, 3rd edn, 1970], Conclusion, esp. p. 284.)

8.   Schmidt, 'Hostility', p. 87 (both references).

people when the Jewish population of Alexandria was under attack. Surely Philo even earlier in his life *was identified* with his people? He cannot simply be portrayed as a representative of an aristocratic viewpoint. Also, if Philo in 38 CE identified himself with his people (a slightly different issue) as their representative, how can Schmidt be so confident that Philo did not so identify himself earlier?

That Philo is neither unaware of the eschatological hopes of his people nor untouched by feeling for his people's sufferings emerges in *Praem. Poen.* 168–72. This contains more than 'a remote awareness of deprivation among the Jews'. Philo describes a future return from the diaspora, echoes texts about the rebuilding of ruins and talks about reversal: 'There will suddenly be a change (μεταβολή, reversal) of everything. God will turn the curses against the enemies...who rejoiced in the misfortunes (κακοπραγίαις) of the nation and mocked and railed at them.' Philo goes on to say the enemies thought to see the Jews in unswerving misfortune (ἀκλινεῖ δυστυχίᾳ), and they laughed while the Jews lamented, and rejoiced at their ill fortune (171) (τὴν ἑτέρων κακοδαιμονίαν εὐδαιμονήσαντας). Their enemies treat them as obscure and neglected, but will find them of 'high lineage' and 'noble birth'. This passage is unusual but very revealing. It shows the wealthy well-placed Philo speaking clearly of the sufferings of his people and of the scorn and ignominy heaped on them. These enemies did not see him or his people as aristocrats. Philo only speaks of such indignities in passages like this and in his two political writings, but we can hardly maintain that his wealth made him immune to the insults offered to his people, nor for that matter did it leave him unconcerned about the fate of his co-religionists. Philo does indeed 'promise them wealth' (*Praem. Poen.* 168) but he promises 'wealth to each individually and to all in common' (πλοῦτον ἰδίᾳ τε ἑκάστῳ καὶ πᾶσι κοινῇ). Schmidt only finds here and elsewhere 'a vague ideal of general welfare or commonality'.[9] Is it vague?

I conclude from the arguments given here or previously that:

1. Philo praised voluntary poverty but possessed great wealth.
2. Philo's views on wealth are indebted to Cynic and radical Platonist ideals, though his indebtedness to Judaism is more important.
3. Philo did express concern for the sufferings of his people and also used his written and personal influence on their behalf.

---

9. Schmidt, 'Hostility', p. 86.

4. Philo did not write solely from an aristocratic point of view.

5. Philo is not unaware of the relative disprivilege of his people or of the theology of reversal.

6. Philo's own position is neither that of the secure aristocrat nor one of marked relative disprivilege. His social position is ambiguous[10] despite his wealth and influence.

7. Philo was a complex character who wrote complex and voluminous works. It is unlikely that one simple explanation will do justice to the data.[11]

10. Philo is clearly *not* an example of severe disprivilege; he was wealthy and influential and that fact has never been in dispute. But his situation was ambiguous: his wealth gave him a good position, his loyalty to Judaism rendered him less acceptable than his apostate nephew. This element of ambiguity, along with his philosophical ethical traditions and his religious ethical traditions, may help to explain why he is more radical than the aristocratic tradition of Proverbs, though only rarely displaying even a hint of the apocalyptic extremism of those subjected to more marked or unexpected relative disprivilege. That the Jewish population in Alexandria normally had sound businesses and tolerable relations with their neighbours is not in dispute.

11. Translations of Philo given above are indebted to, though not always wholly identical with, the translation by F.H. Colson, *Philo*, VIII (LCL; London: Heinemann, 1939).

On attitudes to Judaism in first-century Egypt, see J.G. Gager, *The Origins of Anti-Semitism* (Oxford: Oxford University Press, 1983), pp. 42-54, who carefully notes the anti-Roman component. The existence of communal tensions in the ancient world should neither be minimized nor exaggerated. On status inconsistency, see the comments of W.A. Meeks, *The First Urban Christians* (New Haven: Yale University Press, 1983), pp 22, 54, 191. On relative deprivation, see the important refinements of method in V.H. Hine, 'The Deprivation and Disorganization Theories of Social Movements', in I.I. Zaretsky and M.P. Leone (eds.), *Religious Movements in Contemporary America* (Princeton: Princeton University Press, 1974), pp. 646-61.

JSNT 24 (1985), pp. 99-110

A MAN CLOTHED IN LINEN:
DANIEL 10.5-9 AND JEWISH ANGELOLOGY

Christopher Rowland

There has been a growing interest in Jewish angelology in recent years, particularly with regard to the contribution it might have made to early Christology.[1] Several Old Testament passages have attracted attention, especially those concerning the מלאך יהוה, but of greater importance, not least because of the way it has contributed to the christophany in Rev. 1.13-16, is the angelophany in Dan. 10.5-9.[2] It is the assessment of the influence of this passage on several later Jewish texts, particularly *Joseph and Asenath* 14, which is the aim of this study.

That early Christologies owed much to angelomorphic categories is

---

1. Particular mention should be made of J. Barbel's important study *Christos Angelos* (Bonn: Hanstein, 2nd edn, 1964), and more recently R. Lorenz, *Arius judaizans* (Göttingen: Vandenhoeck & Ruprecht, 1980); A.F. Segal, *Two Powers in Heaven* (SJLA, 25; Leiden: Brill, 1978); K. Berger, *Die Auferstehung des Propheten und die Erhöhung des Menschensohnes* (Göttingen: Vandenhoeck & Ruprecht, 1976); J.-A. Bühner, *Der Gesandte und sein Weg im vierten Evangelium* (WUNT, 2.2; Tübingen: Mohr–Siebeck, 1977); cf. J.D.G. Dunn, *Christology in the Making* (London: SCM Press, 1980), pp. 149-59; R. Bauckham, 'The Worship of Jesus in Apocalyptic Christianity', *NTS* 27 (1980–81), pp. 322ff.; L. Hurtado, *One God, One Lord: Early Christian Devotion and Ancient Jewish Monotheism* (London: SCM Press, 1988); and C. Fletcher-Louis, *Luke–Acts: Angelology, Christology and Soteriology* WUNT; Tübingen: Mohr–Siebeck, forthcoming).

2. On this see my article, 'The Vision of the Risen Christ in Rev. 1.13ff.', *JTS* 31 (1980), pp. 1-11; T. Holtz, *Die Christologie der Apokalypse des Johannes* (Berlin: Akademie–Verlag, 1962), p. 116; L. Stuckenbruck, *Angel Veneration and Christology: A Study in Early Judaism and in the Christology of the Apocalypse of John* (WUNT; Tübingen: Mohr–Siebeck, 1955); and P.R. Carrell, 'Jesus and the Angels: The Influence of Angelology on the Christology of the Apocalypse of John' (doctoral thesis, University of Durham, 1993).

not now disputed, at least as far as the post-New Testament period is concerned. Nevertheless the fact that the New Testament writings do not contain any passage which speaks of Christ as an angel has persuaded many that, if there was an angel Christology, it was merely a peripheral phenomenon, rapidly rejected by mainstream Christianity (e.g. Heb. 1–3; cf. Col. 2.18).[3] It is the implicit threat to both the uniqueness and divinity of Christ involved in the attribution of the title 'angel' that has led to suspicion of this particular development. Such a negative assessment of the theological implications on angelomorphic Christology should not be too precipitate, however. There is clear evidence that at least one New Testament writer identified the divine figure on the throne of glory, seen by the prophet Isaiah, with the pre-existent Christ (Jn 12.41).[4] The rich theological tradition prompted by the throne-theophany tradition has been recognized in recent scholarship.[5] The angelomorphic categories linked with this interpretative stream provide evidence of subtle variations within the parameters of monotheism, by the delegation of divine authority and attributes to other beings in the divine hierarchy. It has become possible to glimpse something of the raw material for christological reflection available in Second Temple Judaism; but this has made

3.   See C. Rowland, 'Apocalyptic Visions and the Exaltation of Christ in the Letter to the Colossians', *JSNT* 19 (1983), pp. 73-83.

4.   On the importance of this passage and its relationship to Jewish apocalyptic tradition, see N.A. Dahl, 'The Johannine Church and History', in W. Klassen and W. Snyder (eds.), *Current Issues in New Testament Interpretation* (New York: Harper & Row, 1962), pp. 124ff.; Segal, *Two Powers in Heaven*; Berger, *Die Auferstehung des Propheten*; Bühner, *Der Gesandte und sein Weg*; C. Rowland, 'John 1.51, Jewish Apocalyptic and the Targumic Tradition', *NTS* 30 (1984), pp. 498-507; J. Ashton, *Understanding the Fourth Gospel* (Oxford: Clarendon Press, 1991); and J.J. Kanagaraj, '"Mysticism" in the Gospel of John: An Inquiry into the Background of John in Jewish Mysticism' (doctoral thesis, University of Durham, 1995)..

5.   See further M. Black, 'The Throne-Theophany Prophetic Commission and the "Son of Man": A Study in Tradition-History', in B. Hamerton-Kelly and R. Scroggs (eds.), *Jews, Greeks and Christians* (Leiden: Brill, 1976), pp. 56-73; C. Rowland, *The Open Heaven: A Study of Apocalyptic in Judaism and Early Christianity* (London: SPCK, 1982), pp. 94-112; and S. Kim, *The Origin of Paul's Gospel* (WUNT, 30; Tübingen: Mohr–Siebeck, 1981), pp. 239-52. There is a comprehensive survey of Jewish angelology in J.E. Fossum, *The Name of God and the Angel of the Lord* (Utrecht: Drukkerij Elinkwijk, 1982). See also J.E. Fossum, *The Image of the Invisible God: Essays on the Influence of Jewish Mysticism on Early Christology* (forthcoming).

clarification of what is meant by monotheism at this period very necessary.

Those of us who have sought to explain this rich seam of Jewish theology have in the past been a little too imprecise in our identification of what exactly may have been going on in the appropriation of Jewish angelology in primitive Christianity. It is probably a mistake simply to talk of angel Christology, at least in the primitive period, without further qualification. It is, in my view, more appropriate to speak of angelomorphic Christology in the earliest period. This kind of description in no way implies that Christ was identified entirely with the created order. There is an implicit recognition, that, while there may indeed be a *prima facie* case for the transference of angelomorphic categories in passages like Mk 9.2-8 and Rev. 1.13-16, this need not necessarily mean that Christ was identified as an angel, if by that is meant a being ontologically distinct from God.

Commentators have for a long time been perplexed by the identity of this figure, but, unlike the equally mysterious figure of the כבר אנש in Dan. 7.13, it has not attracted anything like as much attention. Several commentators recognize that we are dealing here with an angel who in his person manifests the divine *kabod* and not just a known messenger like Gabriel. Not least important is the fact that there is evidence in this passage of dependence on the vision of the divine glory in Ezekiel 1.[6] I have examined the links with Ezekiel 1 in more detail elsewhere.[7] Suffice it to say here that they indicate that the writer of this passage gives the impression that the angelophany has some of the ingredients of a theophany.

That there was a continuing interest in the angelophany in Dan. 10.5-9 is indicated by the evidence of dependence on it in descriptions of heavenly beings: Christ in Rev. 1.13-16, Jaoel in the *Apocalypse of Abraham* 11 and Michael in *Joseph and Asenath* 14.[8] Indeed, so close are the links that the parallel passages may be set out in synoptic form. The synopsis on the two pages above includes the MT of Dan. 10.6 together with the Greek versions of Theodotion and the Septuagint,

6. *ThWAT*, I, col. 688, 'בן אדם' (*TDOT*, II, p. 165).

7. Rowland, 'Vision', pp. 3-4.

8. The translation of the *Apocalypse of Abraham* is that by G.H. Box, *The Apocalypse of Abraham* (London: SPCK, 1918) and the edition of *Joseph and Asenath* is that by M. Philonenko, *Joseph et Aséneth* (SPB, 13; Leiden: Brill, 1968). There are only minor variations between the shorter and longer Greek recensions in this passage.

parallel passages from Dan. 7.9 and the descriptions of the heavenly beings in *Apocalypse of Abraham*, and *Joseph and Asenath*, Revelation and, by way of comparison, passages from Rev. 10.1; 14.14 and *Apoc. Zeph.* 6.11-12.

When the material is placed in a synopsis, it is possible to see at a glance the extent of the relationship between Daniel and the later passages. As the link between Daniel 10, Revelation 1 and *Apocalypse of Abraham* has been examined elsewhere, I should like to pay particular attention to the angelophany in *Joseph and Asenath* 14. The links between Daniel and *Joseph and Asenath* are, if anything, more obvious than between Daniel and *Apocalypse of Abraham*. Certainly *Apocalypse of Abraham* mentions the clothing,[9] body and face of the angel (lines 13, 15 and 28), but its comparisons differ from Daniel.[10] Despite mentioning the clothing only in passing[11] and omitting reference to the body of the angel,[12] *Joseph and Asenath* starts in a similar fashion to Daniel 10 and

---

9. The description of the robe shows some differences. Θ has βαδδιν, a transliteration of MT בדים. One variant in Θ has δόξαν, an indication of the celestial appearance of the angel, as also is ἐξαίρετα in LXX v.5 (cf. sy[h]) (see further J. Montgomery, *Daniel* [ICC; Edinburgh: T. & T. Clark, 1927], p. 409).

10. The Hebrew בכתם אזופ is variously interpreted by the versions. Θ has ἐν χρυσίῳ Ὠφάζ, whereas LXX has ἐκ μέσου αὐτοῦ φῶς. The latter surely reflects Hebrew מתכו פ.

11. The Peshitta has an interesting variant here: 'And behold, a man who was clothed with clothes of honour, and his loins girt with honour of glory. And his look was changed and he had no form.' A.G. Kallarakal ('The Peshitta Version of Daniel' [doctoral dissertation, University of Hamburg, 1973], p. 119) fails to note the significance of this variant.

12. Some MSS of the LXX compare the body of the angel to the sea (θαλάσσης is read for תרשיש). The most notable example of this reading is to be found in P. 967. See A. Giessen, *Der Septuaginta-Text des Buches Daniel, Kap. 5-12, nach dem Kölner Teil des Papyrus 967* (3 vols.; Bonn: Habelt, 1968), and Montgomery, *Daniel*, p. 409. Attempts to explain this variant have usually resorted to theories of textual corruption. The possibility of a deliberate theologically motivated change deserves consideration, however. In pursuit of this possibility I would like to mention three other passages which may point in this direction: (a) the replacement in Symmachus *Ezek.* 1.16 of θαρσις by ὑακίνθου; (b) the description of the body of the angel in *Apocalypse of Abraham*: 'the appearance of his body was like sapphire' (though this may derive from Ezek. 9.2 ζωνὴ σαπφίρου); and (c) a saying of R. Meir in *b. Men.* 43b which compares the colour of the throne of glory with the colour of the thread of blue (הכנף פתיל תכלת ונתנו על ציצת): 'It is not said here "that you may look upon them", but "that you may look upon Him". Thus Scripture teaches that whoever observes the commandment of the fringes is deemed as though

goes on to speak of the face, eyes and limbs of the angel in very similar, though not identical, terms (lines 15-21).

A superficial glance at *Joseph and Asenath* may seem to suggest that the similarities with Daniel, far from being the result of direct dependence on the latter, indicate borrowing from Rev. 1.13-16. Of course, the relationship between *Joseph and Asenath* and Christian ideas is a matter about which there has been considerable divergence of opinion, though most recent commentators consider it to be a product of pre-Christian Egyptian Judaism.[13] The connections between *Joseph and Asenath* and Revelation are certainly close. Reference to the face (line 15), eyes (line 17) and feet (line 31), for example, can all be paralleled in Revelation as well as Daniel. But when one comes to a detailed examination of these common elements, we note that in no case do we have exact verbal parallels between Revelation and *Joseph and Asenath*. Thus, whereas in Revelation the eyes of Christ are compared to φλὸξ πυρός (line 24), this phrase in *Joseph and Asenath* describes the hair of the angel. Also, whereas in *Joseph and Asenath* φέγγος ἡλίου describes the eyes of the angel (line 18), in Revelation ἥλιος describes the face of Christ (line 46). In Revelation the feet are likened to χαλκολίβανος (cf. Daniel ὡς ὅρασις χαλκοῦ στίλβοντος [Θ]; ὡσεὶ χαλκὸς ἐξαστράπτων [LXX], lines 32-33), whereas *Joseph and Asenath* has σίδηρος ἐκ πυρός (line 33). These differences indicate that there is no compelling evidence to suggest that *Joseph and Asenath* is dependent on Revelation 1; it most probably depends on the source common to both it and Revelation, namely Dan. 10.5-9.

he had received the Divine Presence, for תכלת resembles the colour of the sea, and the sea resembles the colour of the sky, and the colour of the sky resembles the colour of the throne of glory' (on this see further B.Z. Bokser, 'Thread of Blue', *PAAJR* 31 [1961], pp. 1ff.). What is more, it may be pointed out that the word used to translate תכלת in the LXX of Num. 15.38 is ὑάκινθος. Three points may be made about these passages: (a) there is a link between the colour of the sea and the throne of glory in *b. Men.* 43b; (b) as we have seen, the angelophany in Daniel 10 has many affinities with the vision of the throne-chariot in Ezekiel 1; and (c) there is a link between תרשיש and ὑάκινθος in Symmachus *Ezek.* 1.16. The possibility must be put forward, therefore, that the reading θαλάσσης could reflect some of the discussions concerned with the colour of the divine throne in these texts.

13. On this subject particular mention should be made of P. Battifol, *Le Livre de la Prière d'Asénath* (Paris: Leroux, 1889–90) and C. Burchard, *Untersuchungen zu Joseph und Aseneth* (Tübingen: Mohr–Siebeck, 1965), and *idem, Der dreizehnte Zeuge* (Göttingen: Vandenhoeck & Ruprecht, 1970).

Let us now turn to examine some of the details in these passages. *Joseph and Asenath*, like Daniel, describes the angel as a man (lines 3-4), though adding that he was in all respects like Joseph. The angel is probably to be identified with Michael as he is called ἀρχιστράτηγος in 14.7, a title given to Michael in *Testament of Abraham* 7 and *2 En.* 33.10. The link between a patriarch and an exalted angel is to be found also in the Jewish apocryphal work *The Prayer of Joseph*, quoted by Origen in his commentary on Jn 2.6 (*Comm.* 2.31).[14] In the fragment quoted by Origen we learn that Jacob is said to be the incarnation of an angel: 'When I, Jacob, was coming from Mesopotamia of Syria, Uriel, the angel of God, came forth and said that I had come down to earth and tabernacled among men and that my name was Jacob' (κατέβην ἐπὶ τὴν γῆν καὶ κατεσκήνωσα ἐν ἀνθρώποις...).

Unlike the Septuagint, *Joseph and Asenath*, and *Apocalypse of Abraham*, Revelation does not use either ἀνήρ (*Joseph and Asenath*) or ἄνθρωπος (Daniel, LXX). Rather, the author describes Christ as ὅμοιον υἱὸν ἀνθρώπου. Most commentators have argued, rightly in my opinion, that we havean allusion to Dan. 7.13 אנש כבר/ὡς υἱὸς ἀνθρώπου. Recently, however, Maurice Casey,[15] referring to Dalman,[16] has challenged this assumption. He points out that in Dan. 10.16 (Θ) we find ὁμοίωσις υἱοῦ ἀνθρώπου (cf. LXX ὁμοίωσις χειρὸς ἀνθρώπου and MT כדמות בני אדם). The fact that Rev. 1.13-17 is a vision which utilizes elements mainly from Daniel 10 rather than Daniel 7, he argues, makes it more likely that the phrase ὅμοιον υἱὸν ἀνθρώπου is borrowed from Dan. 10.16, 18 rather than 7.13. There are, however, good reasons why we should prefer the explanation which finds an allusion here to 7.13.

Although Rev. 1.13 is not exactly the same form as the Greek of Dan. 7.13, R.H. Charles has pointed out that the author of Revelation uses ὅμοιος as synonymous in meaning with ὡς.[17] What is more, he demonstrates that Rev. 1.13 and 14.14, where the phrase ὅμοιον υἱὸν ἀνθρώπου occurs, exhibit not only an identification of ὅμοιος and ὡς in respect of meaning but also in respect of construction. Thus the differ-

14. See further J.Z. Smith, 'The Prayer of Joseph', in J. Neusner (ed.), *Religions in Antiquity* (NumenSup, 14; Leiden: Brill, 1968), pp. 253ff.

15. *The Son of Man* (London: SPCK, 1979), p. 144.

16. *The Words of Jesus* (ET Edinburgh: T. & T. Clark, 1902), pp. 251-52; cf. G.K. Beale, 'The Use of Daniel in Jewish Apocalyptic Literature and in the Revelation of St John' (doctoral thesis, University of Cambridge, 1980), p. 142.

17. *Revelation* (ICC; Edinburgh: T. & T. Clark, 1920), I, p. 35.

ence between Revelation and the Greek versions of Dan. 7.13 should not be taken as indicative of an origin in Daniel 10 for the phrase.

We have an explicit allusion to Dan. 7.13 in 14.14. Whatever problems this passage may present for the interpretation of the Christology of Revelation, both the presence of the phrase ὅμοιον υἱὸν ἀνθρώπου and the reference to ἐπὶ τὴν νεφέλην make a link with Dan. 7.13 virtually certain. Thus the fact that one of the two instances of the use of υἱὸς ἀνθρώπου in Revelation is to be found in a context where Dan. 7.13 is alluded to makes it likely, in view of the identical form in which the expressions appear in 2.13 and 14.14, that both refer to Dan. 7.13 rather than that Rev. 1.13 is dependent on Dan. 10.16.

Joseph and Asenath and *Apocalypse of Abraham* refer to the garment of the angel only in passing (lines 5-6), with only *Apocalypse of Abraham* pausing to describe its colour ('like purple', line 29). Revelation is much closer to Daniel, though the priestly garb of the figure is given even more prominence (lines 9ff.).[18] Various explanations of this development have been offered, though we ought not to lose sight of the possibility that what we have in Revelation may be a reformulation of Daniel 10 due in part to the apocalyptist's visionary imagination.

Both *Joseph and Asenath* and Revelation agree in omitting all reference to the body of the angel (line 13), though in *Apocalypse of Abraham* Jaoel's body is compared to sapphire (line 14). The reason for the omission of this particular element is not entirely clear. Holtz explains its absence in Revelation as John's attempt to explain a difficulty in the Danielic vision.[19] He points out that the body of the angel is described as well as the garment which covered the angel's body. John, he suggests, avoids the confusion by replacing the reference to the body by the references to the head and hair (lines 19-20). Reference to the body of the angel is also absent in the Peshitta of Daniel 10, which departs quite significantly from the Hebrew ('and his appearance was changed, and he had no form').[20] The reluctance we find here to describe the body of the angel is similar to the reluctance found in some apocalyptic texts to describe the details of a theophany (e.g. *2 En.* 22.2, 'And who am I to tell of the Lord's unspeakable being and of his very wonderful face?').[21] This deviation in the Peshitta may indicate that *Joseph and Asenath* and

18. See further on this Holtz, *Christologie*, p. 118.
19. *Christologie*, p. 117.
20. On this reading see Kallarakal, 'Peshitta Version of Daniel', p. 118.
21. See also *Targ. Ezek.* 1.27 (also 8.2).

Revelation may have omitted reference to the body of the angel for reverential reasons.

The closest similarities between Daniel, *Joseph and Asenath* and Revelation are to be found in the descriptions of the face and eyes of the heavenly being (lines 15ff.). *Joseph and Asenath* only, however, follows the order in Daniel, whereas Revelation has the references to the face tacked on at the end of the description of the vision, and the reference to the eyes follows immediately after the description of the head and hair (line 23); *Apocalypse of Abraham* has a reference to the face only (line 15). Similar to these passages is the description of the angel who guides Enoch in *2 Enoch* 1 ('And there appeared to me two men, exceeding big,[22] so that I never saw such on earth; their faces were shining like the sun; their eyes were like burning candles, out of their mouths was fire coming forth, and their arms like golden wings...').

The major difference between Daniel 10 and the other three texts we have been examining is the fact that *Joseph and Asenath*, *Apocalypse of Abraham* and Revelation all make mention of the hair of the heavenly being (lines 19-21) (cf. *1 En.* 106.2). Although the wording of *Joseph and Asenath* differs from *Apocalypse of Abraham* and Revelation (*Joseph and Asenath*: ὡς φλὸξ πυρός; Revelation: ὡς ἔριον λευκὸν κτλ.; lines 21 and 24), this difference is not so marked as to set *Joseph and Asenath* apart from the other two passages. Commentators on Rev. 1.14 all assume that there is an allusion to Dan. 7.9 here. Holtz, for example,[23] asserts that the bestowal of this divine attribute on Christ is the conscious endowment of divinity from the theophanies of Daniel 7 and *1 Enoch* 46, so that the angelophany of Daniel 10 is given a new dimension with the attribution of this element to Christ.[24]

Considerations of this feature in Rev. 1.14 have usually ignored the parallel developments in Jewish literature. The fact that we have a feature of the theophany of Dan. 7.9 given to an angelic being in two texts in addition to Rev. 1.14 demands some explanation. There seem to me to be two possibilities: either in *Joseph and Asenath*, *Apocalypse of Abraham* and Revelation we have three texts which have independently used Daniel 10 as the basis of a description of a heavenly being and then added to that

22. On this feature of Jewish-Christian angelology see J. Danielou, *The Theology of Jewish Christianity* (ET London: Darton, Longman & Todd, 1964), p. 121.

23. *Christologie*, p. 121.

24. Holtz (*Christologie*, p. 122 n. 1) wrongly asserts that such an attribution is unique.

description a feature of the theophany in Dan. 7.9; or, there was already an established exegetical tradition in Judaism which linked the angelophany in Daniel 10 with the passage about the Ancient of Days in 7.9.

In the light of the fact that the combination of Dan. 10.6 and 7.9 can be found in no less than three texts, and may be hinted at in other passages,[25] the first alternative seems to be ruled out. But if we assume that the second alternative is correct, the question arises how it came about that Dan. 10.6 was combined with this particular aspect of the description of the Ancient of Days in Dan. 7.9. Two possible explanations suggest themselves.

(1) From a very early stage the connections between Dan. 10.5-9 and descriptions of theophanies were recognized, and as a result items from these theophanies contributed to the later use of Dan. 10.5-9. In the light of the close connections which exist between Dan. 10.3-5 and Ezekiel 1 it should not surprise us to find that Daniel 10 was linked with theophanic passages, and that it attracted material from them.[26]

(2) A rather more complicated process seems possible, which deserves consideration.

If in the tradition there had been identification of the angel in Dan. 10.6 with כבר אנש of Dan. 7.13,[27] then it becomes possible to see why

---

25. There may well be evidence of it elsewhere also. Reference should be made in particular to *y. Yom.* 42c, a story of Simeon the Just:

כל שנה ושנה שהייתי נכנס לבית קודש הקדשים
היח זקן אחד לבוש לבנים ועטוף לבנים נכנס עמי

There are two features here which seem to point to some connection with the angelic tradition manifested in *Joseph and Asenath*, *Apocalypse of Abraham* and Revelation: (a) the fact that the being is described as an old man, like the עתיק יקמיא in Dan. 7.9; and (b) his white raiment as in Daniel 10 (בדים) and Revelation (ποδήρη). That we are dealing with a theophany here is stressed by A. Marmorstein, *The Old Rabbinic Doctrine of God* (London: Oxford University Press, 1927), II, p. 49: 'In the circle of R. Abbahu this report roused some surprise, for it is written that no one shall be in the tent of appointment during the time when the High Priest is atoning in the sanctuary (Lev. 16.17). Not even one of the angels was permitted to stay there at that moment. R. Abbahu says that surely the venerable old man was not a human being but God himself.'

26. See my article, 'Vision', pp. 1-11, and the literature cited there; and also Beale, 'Use of Daniel', especially pp. 138ff.

27. On the angelic character of the Son of Man, see J.J. Collins, *The Apocalyptic Vision of the Book of Daniel* (HSM, 16; Missoula, MT: Scholars Press, 1977); but cf. Casey, *Son of Man*, pp. 31ff.

the angel should have white hair, an attribute of the Ancient of Days. It can be explained by the Septuagint reading of Dan. 7.13, ὡς παλαιὸς ἡμερῶν (cf. Θ ἕως παλαιοῦ ἡμερῶν), a reading of some antiquity.[28] The significance of this variant, whatever the reason for its origin, is that an identification is made between the man-like figure and the Ancient of Days.

It is suggested that *Apocalypse of Abraham, Joseph and Asenath* and Revelation all reflect an exegetical tradition which (a) knew of the identification of the man-like figure with the Ancient of Days implied by the Septuagint variant, (b) identified the human figure of 7.13 as an angelic being, and (c) as a result linked this verse with the parallel angelophany in Dan. 10.5-9.

Evidence for such a process is not entirely lacking in the passages we have been considering. After all Rev. 1.13-16 shows that Dan. 7.13 has been linked with the angelophany in Daniel 10, as has already been suggested. Such a link between angelic beings may well have been prompted by the similarity between כבר אנש and איש אחד, not to mention the links with Ezekiel 1 which are to be found in both passages. In the later development of theophanic passages in apocalyptic texts there is evidence of a tendency to combine features from several related passages.[29] It is suggested that Dan. 10.5-9 also attracted material from related passages. Certainly Rev. 1.13-16 offers evidence of this process, for, in addition to Daniel 10, Ezek. 9.2 may have contributed to 1.13 (line 9) (ἐνδεδυκὼς ποδήρη καὶ ζώνη σαπφείρου ἐπὶ τῆς ὀσφύος αὐτοῦ; cf. Rev. 1.13 ἐνδεδυμένον ποδήρη καὶ περιεζωσμένον πρὸς τοῖς μαστοῖς ζώνην χρυσᾶν), and in Rev. 1.16 Ezek. 1.24 is used (line 37) (ὡς φωνὴν ὑδάτων πολλῶν). Evidence of the expansion of Daniel 10 in *Joseph and Asenath* and *Apocalypse of Abraham* is not so easy to find, with the exception of the reference to the hair of the angel, though it is possible that the words 'the appearance of his body was like sapphire' (lines 13-14) and 'countenance of chrysolite' (line 16) may reflect Ezek. 9.2 and 28.13 respectively.

Thus the second explanation deserves consideration, namely, that

---

28. So J. Lust, 'Dan. 7.13 and the Septuagint', *ETL* 54 (1978), pp. 62ff.

29. See further I. Gruenwald, *Apocalyptic and Merkavah Mysticism* (AGJU, 14; Leiden: Brill, 1978), pp. 32ff., and my article, 'The Visions of God in Apocalyptic Literature', *JSJ* 10 (1979), pp. 138-52; C. Newsom, 'Merkabah Exegesis in the Qumran Community', *JJS* 38 (1987), pp. 1ff.; I. Chernus, 'Visions of God in Merkabah Judaism', *JSJ* 13 (1982), pp. 123ff.

Joseph and Asenath, Apocalypse of Abraham and Revelation all depend on an interpretation of Dan. 10.5-9 which had linked the latter with Dan. 7.13 in the form known to us in the Septuagint. Whatever may be thought of this explanation of the development of Daniel 10, there is evidence to suggest that we have in *Apocalypse of Abraham, Joseph and Asenath* and Revelation an interpretative tradition of significance not only for Jewish angelology but also for early Christology. That the latter is true is confirmed by evidence of the persistence of this tradition in the christophanies in works like the *Passio Perpetuae et Felicitatis* (chs. 4, 11). But this is just a small part of the developing angelology which is of considerable importance for the study of Judaism and early Christianity alike.[30]

30. The importance of angelomorphic Christology in the ongoing apocalyptic tradition of Jewish Christianity is brought out in J.M. Knight, *Disciples of the Beloved One: The Christology, Social Setting and Theological Context of the Ascension of Isaiah* (JSOTSup, 18; Sheffield: Sheffield Academic Press, 1996).

	Dan. 10 (Θ)	Dan. 10 (LXX)	*Joseph and Aseneth*	Dan. 10 (MT)	Rev. 1	*Apocalypse of Abraham*
1.					καὶ ἐν μέσῳ	And the angel came
2.					τῶν λυχνιῶν	whom he had sent to
3.	ἰδοὺ ἀνὴρ εἷς	ἰδοὺ ἄνθρωπος εἷς	ἰδοὺ ἀνὴρ ὅμοιος	הנה איש אחד	ὅμοιον υἱὸν ἀνθρώπου	me, in the likeness of
4.			κατὰ πάντα τῷ			a man...
5.			Ἰωσὴφ τῇ στολῇ		[14.14 ὅμοιον υἱὸν	
6.			καὶ τῷ στεφάνῳ		ἀνθρώπου ἔχον ἐπὶ τῆς	
7.			καὶ τῇ ῥάβδῳ τῇ		κεφαλῆς αὐτοῦ	
8.			βασιλικῇ		στέφανον χρυσοῦν καὶ	[and a golden sceptre
9.	ἐνδεδυμένος βαδδιν	ἐνδεδυμένος βύσσινα	[*Apoc. Zeph.*	לבוש בדים	ἐν τῇ χειρὶ αὐτοῦ δρέπανον ὀξύ]	in his right hand]
10.	καὶ ἡ ὀσφὺς αὐτοῦ	καὶ τὴν ὀσφὺν	6.11-12...he was	ומתניו	ἐνδεδυμένον ποδήρη	[and the clothing of
11.	περιεζωσμένη ἐν	περιεζωσμένος βυσσίνῳ καὶ	encircled by a	חגרים	καὶ περιεζωσμένον	his garments like
12.	χρυσίῳ Ωφάζ	ἐκ μέσου αὐτοῦ φῶς	golden girdle]	בכתם אופז	πρὸς τοῖς μαστοῖς	purple]
13.	καὶ τὸ σῶμα αὐτοῦ	καὶ τὸ σῶμα αὐτοῦ		וגויתו	ζώνην χρυσᾶν	...and the appearance
14.	ὡσεὶ θαρσεις	ὡσεὶ θαρσις		כתרשיש		of his body was like
15.	καὶ τὸ πρόσωπον αὐτοῦ	καὶ τὸ πρόσωπον αὐτοῦ	πλὴν τὸ πρόσωπον	ופניו	[v.16 ὄψις αὐτοῦ	sapphire
16.	ὡσεὶ ὅρασις ἀστραπῆς	ὡσεὶ ὅρασις ἀστραπῆς	αὐτοῦ ἦν ὡς ἀστραπή	כמראה ברק	ὡς ὁ ἥλιος φαίνει ἐν τῇ δυνάμει αὐτοῦ]	and the look of his
17.	καὶ οἱ ὀφθαλμοὶ αὐτοῦ	καὶ οἱ ὀφθαλμοὶ αὐτοῦ	καὶ οἱ ὀφθαλμοὶ αὐτοῦ	ועיניו	[1.14b καὶ οἱ ὀφθαλμοὶ	countenance like
18.	ὡσεὶ λαμπάδες πυρός [7.9	ὡσεὶ λαμπάδες πυρός [7.9	ὡς φέγγος ἡλίου	כלפידי אש [7.9]	αὐτοῦ ὡς φλὸξ πυρός]	chrysolite
19.	ἡ θρὶξ τῆς κεφαλῆς	τὸ τρίχωμα τῆς κεφαλῆς	καὶ αἱ τρίχες τῆς		ἡ δὲ κεφαλὴ αὐτοῦ	and the hair of
20.	αὐτοῦ	αὐτοῦ	κεφαλῆς αὐτοῦ	ושער רישה	καὶ αἱ τρίχες λευκαὶ	his head
21.	ὡσεὶ ἔριον καθαρόν	ὡσεὶ ἔριον λευκὸν καθαρόν		כעמר נקא	ὡς ἔριον λευκὸν	like snow
22.					ὡς χιὼν	
23.	ὁ θρόνος αὐτοῦ	ὁ θρόνος		כרסיה	καὶ οἱ ὀφθαλμοὶ αὐτοῦ	
24.	ὡσεὶ φλὸξ πυρός]	ὡσεὶ φλὸξ πυρὸς		די נור	ὡς φλὸξ πυρός	
25.		βαδίζουσα]			[10.1 καὶ ἡ ἶρις ἐπὶ	and the turban upon
26.					τῆς κεφαλῆς αὐτοῦ]	his head like the ap-
27.						pearance of a rainbow
28.						and the clothing of his
29.						garments like purple
30.	καὶ οἱ βραχίονες αὐτοῦ	καὶ οἱ βραχίονες αὐτοῦ	καὶ αἱ χεῖρες	וזרעתיו		[Rev. 10.1

	Dan 10 (Θ)	Dan 10 (LXX)	Dan 10 (MT)	Joseph and Aseneth	Rev. 1	Apocalypse of Abraham
31.	καὶ τὰ σκέλη	καὶ οἱ πόδες	ומרגלתיו	καὶ οἱ πόδες αὐτοῦ	καὶ οἱ πόδες αὐτοῦ	καὶ οἱ πόδες αὐτοῦ
32.	ὡς ὅρασις	ὡσεὶ	כעין	ὥσπερ	ὅμοιοι	ὡς
33.	χαλκοῦ στίλβοντος	χαλκὸς ἐξαστράπτων	נחשת קלל	σίδηρος	χαλκολιβάνῳ ὡς ἐν	στῦλοι πυρός.]
34.				ἐκ πυρός.	καμίνῳ πεπυρωμένης	
35.	καὶ ἡ φωνὴ	καὶ φωνὴ λαλιᾶς	וקול		καὶ ἡ φωνὴ	
36.	τῶν λόγων αὐτοῦ	αὐτοῦ	· דבריו		αὐτοῦ	
37.	ὡς φωνὴ ὄχλου	ὡσεὶ φωνὴ θορύβου	כקול המון		ὡς φωνὴ ὑδάτων	
38.					πολλῶν	
39.				[καὶ τῇ ῥάβδῳ	καὶ ἔχων	[and a golden sceptre
40.				τῇ βασιλικῇ]	ἐν τῇ δεξιᾷ χειρὶ αὐτοῦ	was in his right hand]
41.				[Apoc. Zeph.	ἀστέρας ἑπτὰ	
42.				9.12ff.]	καὶ ἐκ τοῦ στόματος	
43.				I raised myself up then	αὐτοῦ ῥομφαία	
44.				and stood there and	δίστομος ὀξεῖα	
45.				saw a tall angel who	ἐκπορευομένη	
46.				took his stand in front	καὶ ἡ ὄψις αὐτοῦ	[Rev. 10.1 καὶ τὸ
47.				of me; whose counten-	ὡς ὁ ἥλιος φαίνει	πρόσωπον αὐτοῦ ὡς
				ance shone like the	ἐν τῇ δυνάμει αὐτοῦ	ὁ ἥλιος…]
48.				rays of sun in his		
49.				magnificence;		
				and he was encircled		
				by a golden girdle,		
				likewise, upon his		
50.				breast;	[v. 15 καὶ οἱ πόδες	
51.				his feet were like brass	αὐτοῦ ὅμοιοι	
52.				which glows in a fire.]	Χαλκολιβάνῳ ὡς ἐν	
53.					καμίνῳ πεπυρωμένης]	

JSNT 2 (1979), pp. 2-30

THE LAMB OF GOD
IN THE *TESTAMENTS OF THE TWELVE PATRIARCHS*

J.C. O'Neill

How could we possibly find out whether the term 'Lamb of God' in the *Testaments of the Twelve Patriarchs* was Jewish before it was applied to Jesus? Everything seems to count against us. Although it is still debated at what point a Christian editor came on the scene in the history of the growth of our *Testaments of the Twelve Patriarchs*, everyone agrees that, by the end, the text was being copied and added to by Christian scribes. It is, therefore, always possible that the two passages referring to the Lamb were added by Christians, however strongly one might argue that the basic work was Jewish.

We seem to be in a fix. We certainly cannot prove that a passage like *Testament of Joseph* 19 is Christian, as Jeremias tries to do, by listing the New Testament echoes (Mt. 1.23; Heb. 7.14; Rev. 12.1; 1 Pet. 1.19; Rev. 17.3-6, 12-13, 14; Lk. 1.78; Jn 1.29, 36; Mt. 1.21); for the fact that these words and ideas appear in the New Testament may be due to the fact that they had already appeared in this sort of Jewish literature before Christ.[1] But we seem unable to prove that they did appear in this sort of Jewish literature before Christ because at least in the case of the 'Lamb of God', we have few undoubtedly Jewish parallels, and our main source has been copied and added to by Christians.

In theory, our quest seems hopeless. Turn to the two passages themselves, however, and the difficulties lift like mist in the morning. The closer we look, the less likely that the future figure of the Lamb is a Christian interpolation, after the event.

---

1. J. Jeremias, 'Das Lamm, das aus der Jungfran hervorging (Test Jos 19, 8)', *ZNW* 57 (1966), pp. 216-19. See further J.C. O'Neill, 'What is *Joseph and Aseneth* about?', *Henoch* 16 (1994), pp. 189-98; *Who Did Jesus Think he Was?* (Leiden: Brill, 1995).

I

Testament of Joseph 19 in a translation of the Greek says,

> Hear, my children, even what I saw as a dream. (2) Twelve harts were grazing and nine were divided and scattered in all the earth. Likewise also the three... (8) And I saw that from Judah was begotten a virgin having a robe of fine linen. And from her was begotten [or 'went out'] a spotless lamb, and on his left hand [there was one] like a lion. And all the beasts began to attack him but the lamb conquered them and destroyed them underfoot. (9) And because of him angels and men and all the earth rejoiced. (10) These things will happen in their season, in the last days. (11) You therefore, my children, keep the commandments of the Lord and honour Judah and Levi, for from them [or 'from their seed'] will arise to you the Lamb of God by grace saving all the Gentiles and Israel [or 'the Lamb of God who takes away the sin of the world, so saving all the Gentiles and Israel']. (12) For his kingdom is an eternal kingdom which will not be shaken. But my kingdom among you will end like a hut of a watcher in the garden: after summer it will appear no more [a reference to the 'cottage in a vineyard', the 'lodge in a garden of cucumbers' of Isa. 1.8; 24.20].

As the text stands, the reference to the lamb is unlikely to be Christian. We should have to imagine a Christian's wanting to insert a reference to Jesus the Lamb of God in a context where another great figure shares in his work. The passage seems to assume a doctrine of the two anointed figures, the anointed priest and the anointed king. No early Christian writer, so far as I know, has ever even toyed with the idea that another man, also anointed, would stand beside Jesus and share in his work. The idea that a Christian interpolator would rename one of two such figures 'the Lamb of God' seems highly unlikely.

This point is not new, but I think it is made unassailable by a further observation, which perhaps is new.

The two figures are, pretty clearly, an intrusion; they have been foisted on to an original text which knew of only one figure, the figure of the Lamb. In other words, the lamb imagery has been locked into the tradition by a scribe who held a theory of two Messiahs. Such an editor could not have been a Christian; therefore the tradition he was using is doubly unlikely to have been Christian.

Notice first the confusion. Of the lion and the lamb, surely the lion would represent Judah, yet it is the lamb who is born of the virgin, and she is of Judah.[2] Can the lion represent Levi? In any case, what is the lion doing in the story? He does not fight, nor does he take part in the victory.

The solution to all these questions seems to lie in the clause in v. 8, καὶ ἐξ ἀριστερῶν αὐτοῦ ὡς λέων. The word αὐτοῦ is a false reading for αὐτός, either a natural mistake after ἐξ ἀριστερῶν or an unconscious change made by a scribe who believed there had to be two figures.[3] We should accordingly translate, 'And there came forth from her a spotless lamb and he was at (her) left hand like a lion'. Because the lamb was like a lion he was able to destroy the wild animals when they attacked him.

But what are we to make of the reference to Judah and Levi in v. 11? It is important to notice that, even if I had not been able to remove the supposed separate figure of the lion from v. 8, there would still not be two figures in v. 11. As the text stands, the lamb is descended both from Judah and from Levi. This is, of course, perfectly possible, and some commentators, beginning with Charles, have argued that the common phrase 'Messiah from Aaron and from Israel' in the Damascus Document referred to one Messiah and not two.[4] However, the Greek MSS vary in the order of precedence, MS C reading 'Levi and Judah' against all the rest. This suggests that 'Levi' was originally a gloss which was incorporated in varying order into the text and that ἐξ αὐτῶν was originally ἐκ τοῦ σπέρματος (cf. C) or ἐξ αὐτοῦ. The original text here too referred to the Lamb of God from the seed of Judah, whose kingdom, as promised to David for his son, would be an eternal kingdom.

It seems that v. 8 has been misread by scribes who were accustomed to thinking of two great figures as taking part in the final victory, and v. 11 has been added by a glossator who believed that the Lamb of God would be descended from both Judah and Levi. Neither the scribe (unless it was a sheer mistake) nor the glossator can have been Christians, for no Christian would have wanted either to associate another figure with the Lamb in the work of salvation or to suggest that the Lamb of

---

2.   Gen. 49.9; *4 Ezra* (2 Esd.) 12.31-32.

3.   There is no direct manuscript evidence for αὐτος, but the last letter υ in MS B is an erasure, and the only possible under-letter, if not a sheer mistake, is σ.

4.   CD 12.23-24; 14.19; 19.10-11; 20.1. In 1QSa 2 the Messiah of Israel is the King Messiah, and the Priest, although not called Messiah explicitly, appears beside him to play an important part in the feast. CD 7.18-20 seems to speak of two figures, the Star who is the searcher of the Law, and the Sceptre who is the prince of all the congregation. Finally, 1QS 9.11 uses the plural, Messiahs of Aaron and Israel.

God was descended from Levi as well as from Judah.

The scribe who changed αὐτός to αὐτοῦ, if he was not simply making a mistake, cannot have been a Christian. The scribe who added a reference to Levi to a text that referred only to Judah cannot have been a Christian. But the scribe who put 'the Lamb of God *who bears the sin of the world* saving the Gentiles and Israel' in v. 11 where all the other manuscripts have 'the Lamb of God by grace saving the Gentiles and Israel' was almost certainly a Christian (MS C; cf. Jn 1.29).

We have these small but precious pieces of evidence that the *Testaments of the Twelve Patriarchs* were transmitted by scribes who were not Christians, as well as, later, by scribes who were Christians.

Before we see whether this tentative conclusion, based on two verses of one Testament, can be extended any further, let us turn to the other occurrence of the term 'Lamb of God'.

II

The other reference to the Lamb in the *Testaments of the Twelve Patriarchs* is in the *Testament of Benjamin* 3. Here is a translation of v. 1 and of vv. 6-8:

> Now therefore my children love the Lord the God of heaven and keep his commandments, imitating the good and holy man Joseph... (6) For he[5] even besought our father to pray for our brothers that the Lord would not account against them whatever evil they had harboured against him. (7) And so Jacob cried out, O child, O good child, you have overcome the bowels [of compassion] of Jacob your father. And embracing him he kissed him for two hours saying, (8) Heaven's prophecy of the Lamb of God and saviour of the world will be fulfilled through you, for as spotless for the lawless will he be given up, and as sinless for the godless will he die in the blood of covenant, for the salvation of the Gentiles and of Israel; and he will destroy Beliar and those who minister to Beliar.

The language is so familiar that we can hardly entertain the possibility that it is not Christian. Christian, however, it can scarcely be. Although early Christian writers like Melito of Sardis and Justin Martyr recognize in the patriarch Joseph a prototype of Jesus Christ, no Christian writer

---

5.   Reading ἐδεήθη with A C D E F G against B, which have the first person. The third person is right; the first person arose because a scribe thought Benjamin would speak about himself, and this scribal blunder led to many strange attempts to put the matter straight in the subsequent lines.

would ever have called a Messiah ben Joseph 'Lamb of God', for Jesus was of the tribe of Judah.[6]

In the previous case I was able to leave aside the Armenian version of the *Testament of Joseph*, because it contained almost all the key features of the Greek, even if it had much else besides. But we cannot ignore the Armenian version of *Testament of Benjamin* 3. It reads, in Charles's translation:

> Do ye also, therefore my children follow the good and holy man... [Then comes a much shorter version of vv. 2-5; v. 6 continues:] For Joseph also besought our father that he would not impute to them this evil. And thus Jacob cried out: My good child, thou hast prevailed over the bowels of thy father Jacob. And he embraced him, and kissed him for two hours, saying, In thee shall be fulfilled the prophecy of heaven, which says that the blameless one shall be defiled for lawless men, the sinless one shall die for ungodly men.

All the decisive elements are lacking. It is possible that the Armenian represents a text pre-dating the work of a Christian interpolator, but that is not the only possible solution to a puzzling problem.[7]

Notice that all that is contained in v. 8 is the Old Testament reference to Isaiah 53. The 'prophecy of heaven' in the Armenian version is a strict Old Testament prophecy. It is possible that a Christian editor removed a specific reference to the Messiah ben Joseph, but not very likely. There is no copy of the *Testaments of the Twelve Patriarchs* that explicitly claims to be a Christian book, and the name of Jesus never occurs. A Christian scribe would therefore not feel bound to answer for everything in the book he copied; he could well accept the prefiguring of the Messiah in the virtues of Joseph without bothering with the fact that, strictly speaking, the prophecy looked forward to a son from the tribe of Joseph. Perhaps a messianic prophecy about the son of Joseph would be held not to be inappropriate concerning him who was known as Joseph's son (Lk. 3.23-24; 4.22; Jn 1.45; 6.42). If the shorter text is not the result of a Christian excision, it is likely that the shorter Armenian text represents a tradition before the last of the Jewish additions was made.

My point is that it is scarcely possible to argue that a Christian inter-

---

6.   Melito, *Paschal Homily* 69; Justin, *Dialogue* 91.1-2; 126.1.

7.   See C. Burchard, 'Zur armenischen Überlieferung der Testaments der zwölf Patriarchen', in *idem*, J. Jervell and J. Thomas, *Studien zu den Testamenten der zwölf Patriarchen* (BZNW, 36; Berlin: de Gruyter, 1969), pp. 1-29.

polator would make the text say that the Lamb of God was to be son of Joseph, even though it is very likely that he would transmit the text without demur.

There is other Jewish evidence that such a Messiah was expected in some circles. In *Joseph and Asenath* Joseph is called Son of God; he prays for the conversion of Asenath, the type of the proselyte; the Spirit of God is upon him and the grace of the Lord is with him; and he appears clothed in heavenly glory.

In *b. Suk.* 52a there is a Messiah ben Joseph who will fall in battle, with references to Deut. 33.17 and Zech. 12.10. In the Jerusalem Targum to Ezek. 40.11 the Messiah ben Joseph will fight against Gog, and there are some late traditions that he would fall in that battle. Finally, there is the well-attested rabbinic tradition about the Lamb who in Pharaoh's dream outweighed the whole of Egypt in the balance.[8]

If my previous arguments hold, we may conclude that the Greek *Testament of Benjamin* was an expanded version of a shorter Testament, represented in the Armenian, which did not yet identify the martyr of Isaiah 53 with the Messiah ben Joseph; but that the addition of the reference to the Messiah ben Joseph was not the work of a Christian.

We may go further. The Greek *Testament of Benjamin* incorporates a tradition that Joseph was the model for the suffering Messiah and that the Messiah would be of Joseph's tribe, whereas the *Testament of Joseph* thinks of the Lamb of God as born of a virgin from the tribe of Judah. Perhaps we should explore the possibility that the virgin from Judah was an intrusion into an original *Testament of Joseph* which taught that the Lamb from the tribe of Joseph would conquer, for such a hypothesis would bring the two references to the Lamb of God much closer together. But we do not need, in this discussion, to pursue that train of thought, for we have already established an important point, sufficient for our purpose. It is perfectly clear that the *Testaments of the Twelve Patriarchs* are the repository for diverse Jewish traditions, traditions diverse in teaching as well as diverse in literary form; and it is also perfectly clear that diverse traditions may be both put alongside one another (as the Lamb of God son of Judah has been put alongside the Lamb of God son of Joseph) and slid over one another (as the Lamb of

---

8.   K. Koch, 'Das Lamm, das Ägypten vernichtet: Ein Fragment aus Jannes und Jambres und sein geschichtlicher Hintergrund', *ZNW* 57 (1966), pp. 79-93; C. Burchard, 'Das Lamm in der Waagschale: Herkunft und Hintergrund eines haggadischen Midraschs zu Ex. 1.15-22', *ZNW* 57 (1966), pp. 219-28.

God has been slid over a reference to Isa. 53).

These conclusions are scarcely controversial, and they are just the conclusions that make a certain answer to our original question so hard to obtain. If the Testaments are compilations, it is very difficult to distinguish between a Christian-Jewish addition and a Jewish-Jewish addition, if I may put it like that. In terms of the present case, the harder I argue that a Christian editor could have let pass a Jewish tradition that Joseph was a type of Christ, the more likely I make it that this could have been a Christian addition. Is there any evidence that the Testaments as a whole existed as a Jewish entity before they were copied and circulated by Christians? And if so, what were the boundaries of that entity?

III

Let us turn to discuss this, the hardest question of all, the question of whether or not there was a Jewish book, *Testaments of the Twelve Patriarchs*, and the question of whether or not we can establish its likely boundaries.

A good place to start is with the *Testament of Benjamin* again, but this time in connection with the problems I raised in Part I. There I argued that the *Testament of Joseph* showed clear signs of having been altered and glossed by scribes who were interested in the messianic status of a priest of the house of Levi. There were two rather different results of this interest: in 19.8 a scribe was betrayed into making two out of one—a lion and a lamb out of a lamb like a lion—and in 19.11 a glossator could not resist adding that the Lamb of God would descend from Levi as well as from Judah. Notice that neither of these processes is quite like the processes I argued were at work in the *Testament of Benjamin*: in that case a massive tradition was both set alongside another massive tradition—the Messiah ben Joseph alongside the Messiah ben David— and used to enrich another massive tradition—the Messiah ben Joseph to enrich the Suffering Servant. Both these latter instances may be called the work of compilers, whereas the former instances are the work of scribes transmitting a given document.

The distinction between compilers on the one hand and scribes on the other hand cannot, however, be pressed home until I have shown, if I can, that the scribal work lightly pervades the whole document. Compilers work massively and in blocks, but scribes betray themselves by the smallest of signs found pervasively.

My case is that the *Testaments of the Twelve Patriarchs* existed as a complete document in Greek, and that we possess good evidence that it was transmitted by non-Christian scribes. It follows that it was once a complete Jewish document. If so, it also follows that the scribal contamination inevitably introduced by the later Christian scribes was likely to have been exceedingly slight.

The passage in the *Testament of Benjamin* I want to discuss now, which betrays clear signs of having been glossed by a scribe not a Christian, is *T. Benj.* 11.2. It is another example of a scribal gloss akin to the gloss in *T. Jos.* 19.11.

The text is not well transmitted, which suits our purpose admirably, for it neatly displays the fact that our Greek manuscripts go back to at least two recensions. Sometimes one of these recensions, sometimes the other, shows signs of having been transmitted by non-Christian scribes; if this can be proven, then the common text to which they bear witness cannot have been Christian.

Here, in *T. Benj.* 11.2, a scribe with the set of interests betrayed by the scribe in *T. Jos.* 19.11 contaminated the original text as he copied it, and this scribe could not have been a Christian. The original copy of the *Testaments of the Twelve Patriarchs* probably read: 'And there shall arise from my seed in the latter times the beloved of the Lord, hearing his voice and doing good pleasure at his mouth, enlightening all the Gentiles with the light of knowledge...' It is likely that a Christian scribe has added a reference to St Paul in the latter part of the verse, but it was no Christian scribe who changed the messianic reference at the beginning of the passage to 'And there shall arise in the latter times the beloved of the Lord from the seed of Judah and Levi doing good pleasure at his mouth'.[9]

The two examples from *T. Jos.* 19.11 and *T. Benj.* 11.2 do not stand alone. From beginning to end the *Testaments of the Twelve Patriarchs* show signs of having been transmitted by scribes who expected to find that the Messiah would be of the tribe of Levi. Some of them thought that the one Messiah would be descended from both Levi and Judah, others that the Messiah of Judah would be subordinate to the Messiah of Levi, and others again that the Messiah of Levi would stand alone. Their glosses and alterations always had some basis in the text, for there are

9.   I have listed the passages at the end of this article, giving there the more important variants to B: first, the minimum necessary to recover a better text; and secondly, those I attribute to scribal corruption.

clear passages that look forward to the coming of the Priest as well as the King, but the glosses and alterations are of a quite different character from the basic text; they are always small-scale remarks which disturb the flow of the passages where they are found.

I shall discuss every passage in the Testaments that either mentions a great future son of Levi or could be held to refer to him.

Testament of Reuben 6 foretells the coming of Levi and Judah. Levi is to make known the Law, to pronounce judgment, and to sacrifice for Israel. He will bless Israel and Judah, for the Lord has chosen Judah to rule, to fight, and perhaps to die in visible and invisible battles, before ruling for ever. A scribe could have taken the 'him' in v. 11, which says 'The Lord has chosen him to rule', as referring to Levi rather than to Judah. That possible reading would have provided a foothold for the small changes noted in the appendix. I conjecture that v. 8 originally simply put a limit to the work of Levi, 'until the completion of the time [or times] of which the Lord spoke'. A glossator added either words to say that these times were 'of the anointed high priest' or simply a note that the figure was 'high priest of the Messiah [or of the Lord]'.

T. Sim. 5.4-6 is a very obscure passage. In the Blessing of Jacob in Genesis 49 Simeon and his brother Levi are men whose weapons of violence are their swords, and who will be divided in Jacob. Our present text of the Testament makes Levi Simeon's opponent who will fight the battle of the Lord and conquer Simeon. There will be few of Simeon, and they will be divided among Levi and Judah. I strongly suspect that the reference to Levi and Judah is another gloss, but cannot adduce positive evidence, except to draw attention to the fact that MS D adds 'concerning Levi and Judah' at the end of v. 6, which is certainly a gloss.

T. Sim. 7.2 gives a clear statement of the respective roles of Levi and Judah: 'For the Lord will raise up from Levi one as High Priest and from Judah one as King both God and man: he will save all the Gentiles and the people of Israel'. In v. 1, however, scribes have been at work who believed that the Messiah would be one person descended from two tribes. An original that said 'And now my children, obey Levi and you will be redeemed by Judah, and do not revolt against these two tribes for from them shall arise for you God's salvation' has suffered two small alterations: 'obey Levi and Judah' (C) and 'from him shall arise' (E).

In *T. Levi* 2.10 and 12 Levi is told that he will have the high office of standing by the Lord and proclaiming to Israel the coming redemption. As a result, his life will be to share the Lord's portion: the Lord 'will be your field, vineyard, fruits, gold, silver'. Verse 11 originally said, I con-jecture, 'And through Judah the Lord shall appear to men, saving by him every tribe of man'. A glossator who thought the Messiah would be of Levi as well as of Judah added 'through you and Judah' and subsequent scribes, mistaking his intention, changed 'by him' to 'by them'. My con-jecture at least explains the present anomaly that Levi is given a special blessing in v. 12 as though he had not been already mentioned in v. 11.

In *Testament of Levi* 4 the easiest way of taking the text has appeared to be to regard the original as describing a Messiah son of Levi which Christian scribes have altered to refer to Jesus Christ. What else could the last sentence of v. 4 imply: 'But your sons will lay hands upon him to crucify him'? However, the verb 'crucify' is probably a Christian alteration, and MS B gives us a text, not necessarily Christian, that any Christian scribe would be only too ready to alter: 'But your sons will lay hands upon him to remove him as a stumbling block'.

But if the christianizing of the passage looks like the work of a scribe, so do the features of the passage that refer to the Messiah son of Levi look like the work of scribes. The scope of the passage is a warning by Levi to his sons that, although his prayer to the Most High for salvation will be answered, they are all too likely to reject the one who is given them in answer to that prayer. Levi himself is given counsel and knowl-edge to make known to his sons concerning the one who is to come (v. 5). Now this is just the role of the great son of Levi at the end in relation to the great son of David (*T. Sim.* 7.1, 2; *T. Levi* 2.9-12; 5.2; 8.11-19; 10.2; *T. Iss.* 5.7-8). Taken as a whole, the passage fits perfectly into the picture of the Priest who announces the coming of the King.

Some manuscripts put forward a different picture. They assume that the one sent by the Lord in answer to Levi's prayer will be Levi's son: 'For the Most High has heard your prayer to separate you from unrighteousness and you will be to him Son and Servant and Minister of his face. As a shining light of knowledge will you enlighten in Jacob, and you will be as the sun.' Yet the textual support for reading the passage as referring to a Messiah the son of Levi is most uncertain. There is plenty of textual evidence to suggest an original that fits in with the scope of the context and reads: 'For the Most High has heard your prayer to separate you from unrighteousness, and to be to you Son and Servant and Minister of his presence. As a shining light of knowledge he shines to Jacob, and as the sun to all the seed of Israel.' In that case v. 4 then follows on completely naturally: 'And he will be given to you as a blessing and to all your seed...', as do vv. 5 and 6: 'And therefore counsel and wisdom are given to you to inform your sons about him, for he who blesses him will be blessed and those who destroy him will be destroyed'. None of these latter verses needs to be emended, and their text is quite solid. They refer to a Messiah not son of Levi.

Again, the likeliest hypothesis is that an original text which gave Levi a high office as proclaimer or the Messiah has been slightly altered by scribes in order to suggest that the Messiah himself was to be son of Levi. No Christian scribe would have made these alterations, although almost all the later Christian scribes could not resist making one alteration, of a single letter, to provide a reference to the crucifixion (v. 4).

In *T. Levi* 5.2 all manuscripts bear witness to Levi's role as announcing the incarnation of the Son of God: 'Levi, to you I have given the blessings of priesthood until I come and dwell in the midst of Israel'. This passage neither invites nor forbids a theory that the Messiah would be son of Levi, but in fact it belongs firmly among those that see Levi as announcing the advent of the King who will be God incarnate (*T. Sim.* 6.5, 7; 7.1-2; *T. Jud.* 22.2; *T. Iss.* 7.7; *T. Zeb.* 9.8; *T. Dan.* 5.1, 13; *T. Naph.* 4.5?; 8.3; *T. Ash.* 7.3; *T. Jos.* 10.2?; *T. Benj.* 6.4?; 10.7-8).

In *T. Levi* 8.11-19 the text as it stands says that the third part of the seed of Levi will be called by a new name (v. 14). This new name will patently be given to the descendant of Levi by the king who will arise out of Judah and who will create a new priesthood. Schnapp explicitly, and Charles implicitly, take this to mean that the third part of the seed of Levi will arise as a king out of Judah, and that no doubt is how the scribes who believed that the Messiah would be of both Levi and Judah read the verse too.[10] But this reading is forced, and unlikely to be the original sense. The only reason for adopting this translation lies in ch. 18, and to that we must now turn.

The key passage for the theory that the Testaments originally contained clear teaching about the Messiah of Levi who was identified with the King Messiah is ch. 18. On close examination, however, vv. 2 and 3 should be taken rather to refer to the King Messiah, again subtly glossed

---

10. F. Schnapp in E. Kautzsch (ed.), *Die Apocryphen und Pseudepigraphen des Alten Testaments* (Tübingen: Mohr–Siebeck, 1900), II, pp. 458-506; R.H. Charles, *The Apocrypha and Pseudepigrapha of the Old Testament in English* (Oxford: Clarendon Press, 1913), II, pp. 282-367; cf. J. Becker, *Die Testamente der zwölf Patriarchen, Jüdische Schriften aus hell.-röm. Zeit* (JSHRZ, 3.1; Gütersloh: Mohn, 1974), III.

in another sense, and only v. 9 remains as weighty evidence for the
theory that the Testaments originally taught about a Priest Messiah who
did all that was expected of the King Messiah.

Verses 2 and 3 are normally translated

> Then the Lord will raise up a new priest to whom all the words of the
> Lord will be revealed. And he [the new priest] will make a judgment of
> truth on the earth in the fulness of days. (3) And his star will arise in
> heaven as a King, giving light of knowledge as by the sun of day.

This can hardly be right, however; not only because *T. Levi* 8.14 says
that the King from Judah will create the new priesthood, but because all
the rest of ch. 18 (apart from v. 9) ascribes to the coming one attributes
of the King Messiah, attributes which are never elsewhere ascribed to
the coming great Priest.

The solution appears to be that an original text has been subtly
misread and miscopied by scribes who held that the King Messiah would
also be of Levi's tribe. The MSS H and I, with support from D, give
evidence that the original Testament read, 'And there shall arise for him
a star in heaven as King'. The star is the King Messiah, the son of David
(cf. *T. Jud.* 24.1).[11]

Only v. 9 stands decisively in the way. The shorter text of MS B reads,
'And in his priesthood all sin shall fail and the lawless will fall [E] into
evil but the righteous will rest in him' (cf. 1QpHab 8.2-3). There seems
no way of avoiding the conclusion that the Priest Messiah is meant—and
yet the massive difficulty remains that nowhere else is the Priest Messiah
said to be the one who opens up paradise again;[12] and it is always the
son of David whose kingdom will have no end (*T. Levi* 18.8; cf. Gen.
49.10; 2 Sam. 7.13, 16; 1 Chron. 17.14; Ps. 89.4, 29, 36, 37).

The solution seems to be that a glossator, while not wishing to deny
the Davidic descent of the Messiah, also wished to claim that he was a
son of Levi. There is one small piece of evidence that such a glossator
was at work. The MS I at the end of the long section of 18.9 that does
not appear in B reads, 'on the earth by his priesthood (sin has ceased)'.

---

11. The only passage that comes near to helping the hypothesis that the Star could
be identified with Levi is CD 7.18-19, where the Star is said to be the Interpreter of
the Law and the Sceptre the Prince of the whole congregation. Otherwise the Star is
always the King Messiah (especially Rev. 22.16).

12. The theme of the restoration of paradise is common: *4 Ezra* (2 Esd.) 7.36;
8.52; *Sib. Or.* 3.769-95; *2 En.* (Slavonic Enoch) 8; *2 Bar.* (Syriac) 51.11; 1QS 4.25;
1QH 11.13-14; 13.11-13.

No other manuscript reads 'on the earth', but this would fit the context beautifully, and I conjecture that a marginal gloss 'by his priesthood' has forced out the original 'on the earth', becoming 'during his priesthood'.[13] If this conjecture be accepted, ch. 18 of the *Testament of Levi* ceases to appear to be a strange freak in late Jewish literature, and rejoins the passages that speak of the Messiah son of David.

Before we leave the *Testament of Levi*, we should notice one more passage. In *T. Levi* 13.9 the innocent remark that, if anyone teaches and practises the fear of the Lord, 'he will be enthroned with kings as was our brother Joseph' is perhaps turned in the direction of teaching that the ideal son of Levi 'will be enthroned with a king' by the scribe whose alteration of 'kings' to 'king' is preserved in the MSS A and B.

T. Jud. 17.6 states the standard view, 'And I know that from me shall the kingdom be established', but 21.1-5 seems to subordinate the kingdom to the priesthood. The usual text reads,

> And now children, love Levi in order that you may abide. And do not rise up against him in order that you may not be destroyed. (2) For to me the Lord gave the kingdom and to him the priesthood, and he subordinated the kingdom to the priesthood. (3) To me he gave the things upon earth and to him the things in heaven. (4) As heaven is higher than the earth, so is the priesthood of God higher than the kingdom upon earth, unless it fall away from the Lord through sin and be ruled by the earthly kingdom. (5) For the Lord has chosen him above you, to be near him and to eat at his table and to offer to him the first fruits, the choicest gifts of the sons of Israel.

The first three sentences, except for the words 'and he subordinated the kingdom to the priesthood', convey ideas that are well attested elsewhere: the Priest and the King have each their part to play in the last days, and all honour and attention must be given to the Priest. The idea that the King should be subordinated to the Priest is more doubtful. One manuscript, the MS G, omits the difficult words both here and in v. 5, but no account is normally taken of this omission, since the longer reading seems harder and therefore more likely to be original. However, the shorter reading of G should not be so lightly dismissed. The same teaching as G omits is found in v. 4, and there it is clearly secondary.

Notice, first, that the second half of v. 4 is omitted by B and D, 'unless it fall away from the Lord through sin and be ruled by the earthly kingdom'. This looks very like a remark inserted to rebuke priests who

---

13. See further evidence in the textual note.

were thought by the author to have been unfaithful to the Lord, and it should probably be omitted as a gloss. In any case, it is a strange remark, for it teaches that the (heavenly) high priesthood retains supremacy over the (earthly) kingdom only if the heavenly high priesthood be not ruled by the earthly kingdom. Verse 3, however, meant nothing derogatory about things heavenly and things earthly: Levi and Judah had each their important sphere, and Judah's 'things on earth' were of great honour and importance. Verse 5, in speaking of Levi's special sacrificial role, did not imply any denigration of Judah (even if, which I doubt, the words 'above you' be original).

The second half of v. 4 implies that the priesthood is superior to the earthly kingdom so long as it retains its moral and spiritual authority over the earthly kingdom, which is the teaching of the words omitted in vv. 3 and 5 by G. The glossator in v. 4 has in mind a specific historical priesthood and a specific historical royal house, and the same would seem to be true of the author of the words omitted in vv. 3 and 5 by G. But if we regard the second half of v. 4 and the omitted words in vv. 3 and 5 as glosses, we are left with a very different picture. This writer regards the priesthood and the kingdom as two different spheres of activity and the priesthood as high above the kingdom as heaven is above the earth simply because the priest is chosen to eat at the Lord's table and to offer Israel's choicest gifts. This writer, who must be the writer of the original Testament, was not talking of historical figures but of the great Priest and King who would come at the end. He does nothing to diminish the role on earth of the Messiah son of David, however much he wishes Levi to be honoured.

T. Iss. 5.7, 8 contains the standard teaching about honouring Levi and Judah, 'for to one [the Lord] gave the priesthood and to the other the kingdom'. Yet even here a glossator has been at work; the MS B says 'Levi and Judah *has* been glorified by the Lord among the sons of Jacob' where all the other manuscripts give the plural. The plural has been changed to a singular by a scribe who held that the Messiah would come from both tribes and would therefore be priest as well as king.

Judah's honour is fully and clearly affirmed in *Testament of Judah* 24: the descendant of Judah is compared to the sun of righteousness; he is sinless; he is the Branch and the Fountain of life; he wields the rod of his kingdom; and from his root arises a stem which will become a rod of righteousness for the Gentiles. The text is in no doubt, unlike the passages which press the claims of a Priest Messiah. The fact that Levi is put first over Judah in the lists of honour in ch. 25 by no means disturbs the picture, for Levi as priest is charged with the highest role in the heavenly court; but Levi does not displace the Messiah of Judah from his regal position on earth.

In *T. Dan* 5.4 a prophecy of the last days predicts that the children of Dan will be offended at Levi and rebel against Judah. This is standard teaching about Levi, who will proclaim the word of the Lord, and Judah, who will come as king. But all the Greek manuscripts go on to make both Levi and Judah into warriors: 'but you will not be able (to fight) against them for an angel of the Lord will guide both of them, for in them shall Israel stand'. Verse 10 later says, 'And the salvation of the Lord shall arise to you from the tribe of Judah and Levi. And he will make war against Beliar and the vengeance of victory will he give to our borders.'

However, this text has been retouched by scribes. The opening reference to both Levi and Judah, in the standard order, has given the scribes the opportunity to import their favourite theories about the Messiah or the Messiahs. In v. 4 some manuscripts of the Armenian read the singular, thus taking the figure against whom the rebellious sons of Dan try to fight as Judah alone. This singular reading is likely to be right, since the warlike Priest always occurs in passages that are textually doubtful.

In v. 10 only one tribe is mentioned, and either Judah or Levi is likely to be an interpolation. Charles thought the interpolation was Judah, but this is unlikely, for had Levi stood alone in the text a glossator would probably have added Judah in the second position, which is the customary order (only reversed in *T. Jos.* 19.11—except MS C—and in *T. Gad* 8.1). The 'he' who will make war against Beliar, in the next sentence, will then be Judah, not the Lord. Judah will restore paradise (*T. Dan* 5.12; cf. *T. Levi* 18.10-12 as taken above).

Again we have evidence of two scribal alterations, in the first of which a scribe raised Levi to equality with Judah as a warrior Messiah, and in the second of which a scribe added the gloss that the one Messiah would be of both Judah and Levi. Neither glossator could have been a Christian, so the text they were glossing was definitely not Christian.

There is another strange reference to Levi in some manuscripts of v. 6 which can hardly be original. The MS B supported by D G L* gives the curious information that 'I have read in the book of Enoch the Righteous that your commander is Satan and that all the spirits of fornication and of pride *will obey Levi* to attend the sons of Levi to make them sin before the Lord.' The text of C E F H omits *Levi* in the phrase italicized, and L as corrected and Athos Laura K 116 say the spirits *will rise in insurrection*. The text of B can hardly be right, since the evil spirits are obedient to Satan not to Levi, even though v. 7 says that the sons of Dan will draw near to Levi, for the writer there means they will attach themselves to the sinful sons of Levi. Nevertheless, v. 7 has given a scribe sufficient reason to transmit an obviously corrupt text of v. 6 that says the evil spirits will obey Levi.

The question is, how did the corruption arise, and what was the original text? The reading that best explains all the other readings is the one that says all the spirits *will rise in insurrection*. The author meant the evil spirits would *rise against* the Lord. One glossator suggested they would not rise against Satan but would *obey* Satan, pedantically regarding Satan as their lord. Another glossator suggested they would rise against *Levi*. All our manuscripts, except L as corrected and Athos Laura K 116, take one or both of the glosses into the text to produce either sense (they will obey Satan) or close to nonsense (they will obey Levi).

One of the glosses, the gloss that suggested the evil spirits would rise in insurrection against Levi, was made by a scribe who thought the Messiah would be the true Levi who would stand against the false sons of Levi. This scribe could scarcely have been a Christian.

In *Testament of Naphtali* 5 and 6 Levi is identified with the sun and Judah with the moon, Levi and Judah are together on the one plank in the shipwreck, and when Levi prays the storm is calmed. All these ideas are fully in line with the idea that a son of Levi will be the Priest and a son of Judah the King.

In ch. 8, however, we find an interesting manuscript variant that gives us for the only time a phrase approaching the standard phrase found in the Damascus Document and the Qumran scrolls, 'the Messiah of Aaron and Israel'. The MS A reads, '(2) And as for you, command therefore your children to be united to Levi and to Israel and in him will Jacob be blessed' instead of the longer form, '(2) And as for you, command therefore your children to be united to Levi and Judah, for through Judah shall arise salvation to Israel and in him will Jacob be blessed'. The scribe whose work is preserved in MS A allowed his belief that the Messiah would be descended from both Levi and Judah to let him produce a more familiar phrase than in fact his text offered him. He has not, of course, omitted that the Messiah would be from Judah, for that is what 'Israel' means in the context of the Qumran and Damascus Document phrase, but he has made the two figures, each with a distinct function, into one. Judah must be the figure through whom salvation would arise to Israel, for only Judah wields the rod: 'for through his rod God will appear dwelling among men on earth to save the people of Israel and to gather the righteous from the Gentiles' (v. 3).

T. Gad 8.1, 2 contains the second of three passages in which the order is Judah and Levi (with *T. Dan* 5.10 and *T. Jos.* 19.11 bar MS C). The words 'and Levi' are almost certainly added by a scribe who thought that the next clause 'for from them the Lord will shine to us as salvation in Israel' could refer to two tribes.[14] The glossator would not have thought he was doing more than adding correct information, that the Messiah would be from the tribe of Levi as well as from the tribe of Judah. However, the scribe who changed v. 2 from 'at the end your children will fall away from him' into 'will fall away from them' possibly thought there were two Messiahs, or was just making a pedantic and incorrect consequential emendation to bring v. 2 into line with v. 1.

I have been covering some well-trodden ground. The theories that have been put forward at various times to explain the rather different roles given to Levi and Judah in the Testaments raise almost every possibility: that the Messiah from Judah was original and the Messiah from Levi added;[15] that the Messiah from Levi was original, the Messiah from Judah added;[16] that the Two Messiahs belonged to the earliest strata;[17]

---

14. I am following mainly the text of C; see appendix. The verb ἀνατέλλω always takes an indirect object in the Testaments, so that texts with accusatives are out.

15. K. Kohler, 'Testaments of the Twelve Patriarchs', *JewEnc*, XII, pp. 113-18.

16. W. Bousset, 'Die Testamente der zwölf Patriarchen', *ZNW* 1 (1900), pp. 141-75, 187-209 at 201-202; R.H. Charles, *The Testaments of the Twelve Patriarchs* (London: A. & C. Black, 1908); the argument is reproduced in *The Apocrypha and Pseudepigrapha*, p. 294; M. de Jonge, 'Christian Influence in the *Testaments of the Twelve Patriarchs*', *NovT* 4 (1960), pp. 182-235; reproduced in *Studies on the Testaments of the Twelve Patriarchs: Text and Interpretation* (SVTP, 3; Leiden: Brill, 1975), pp. 193-246 at pp. 228-29, although he takes Levi and Judah to refer to tribes rather than to individuals.

17. G.R. Beasley-Murray, 'The Two Messiahs in the *Testaments of the Twelve Patriarchs*', *JTS* 48 (1947), pp. 1-12; K.G. Kuhn, 'Die beiden Messias Aarons und Israels', *NTS* 1 (1954–55), pp. 168-79; trans. in K. Stendahl (ed.), *The Scrolls and the New Testament* (New York: Harper & Row, 1957), pp. 54-64; A.S. van der Woude, *Die messianischen Vorstellungen der Gemeinde von Qumran* (SSN, 3; Assen: Van Gorcum, 1957), ch. 2: 'Die messianischen Vorstellungen der Testamente der Zwölf Patriarchen'.

that the Two Messiahs belonged to the later strata;[18] that the Two Messiahs belonged to the earliest strata but that later the Messiah was to be from both Levi and Judah or from Levi alone;[19] or that originally the Testaments said God himself would come to earth, and this tradition was combined with another tradition of the future priesthood and the Davidic kingdom in which the Messiah would be Davidic, but that this initial editing of the Testaments was modified in the first century BCE by the addition of the Priest-Saviour, a messianic figure of a new and independent type.[20] We can learn from all these theories, but only Charles makes the crucial distinction between layers of tradition and textual corruption, and he thought the corruption was in the adding of Judah to Levi rather than the other way round.

I have been arguing that the Testaments originally held that only one Messiah would come, usually the son of Judah, but sometimes the son of Joseph or of Benjamin. However, the Testaments also contain passages in which Levi is highly exalted as the Priest at the end of the days who would prepare Israel for salvation and who would minister in heaven. The Testaments often called on their readers to honour Levi and Judah. This basic teaching has been subjected to alterations and glosses by scribes who held either that the one Messiah would be descended from Levi as well as from Judah, or that there would be two Messiahs, one from Levi and one from Judah, or even that there would be one Messiah, from Levi alone. All our Greek manuscripts at one time or another espouse each of the three theories, but in just over half the verses there is textual evidence that scribes have been responsible for adding these

18. J. Becker, *Untersuchungen zur Entstehungsgeschichte der Testamente der Zwölf Patriarchen* (AGJH, 8; Leiden: Brill, 1970).

19. A. Dupont-Sommer, 'Le Testament de Lévi (XVII-XVIII) et la secte juive de l'Alliance', *Sem* 4 (1952), pp. 33-53, summarized in a book *Nouveau aperçus sur les manuscrits de la mer morte* (Paris: Adrien-Maisonneuve, 1953) which was translated as *The Jewish Sect of Qumran and the Essenes: New Studies on the Dead Sea Scrolls* (London: Valentine, Mitchell; New York: Macmillan, 1954), pp. 38-57 at pp. 53-54; M. Philonenko, *Les interpolations chrétiennes des Testaments des Douze Patriarches et les Manuscrits de Qoumrân* (RHPR, 35; Paris: Presses Universitaires de France, 1960).

20. A. Hultgård, *L'eschatologie des Testaments des Douze Patriarches. I. Inter-prétation des textes* (Uppsala: Almqvist & Wiksell, 1977); *idem*, 'L'universalisme des Test. XII. Patr.', in C.J. Blecker, S.G.F. Brandon and M. Simon (eds.), *Ex orbe religionum: Studia Geo Widengren...oblata* (Studies in the History of Religions, 21; Leiden: Brill, 1972), I, pp. 192-207.

theories to the text. In all instances, arguments from context and from parallels in other texts have indicated the presence of scribal corruption.

The evidence is cumulative. The clear examples of textual corruption, such as in *T. Benj.* 11.2, raise the probability that we should look to textual corruption to explain examples that have usually been regarded as anomalous traditions, such as in *Testament of Levi* 18. And when we do look closely, we often find variant readings that point in the direction of just the sort of corruption that was present in the more obvious examples.

My case is that no scribe who added this sort of gloss or made this sort of alteration would have been a Christian. If so, the text that was subjected to glossing and alteration cannot possibly have been a Christian text. Since the glosses and alterations affect almost every possible instance of a messianic reference in the Testaments, and these references appear in ten of the twelve Testaments, it seems reasonable to conclude that the Testaments as a whole were put together into one connected document by compilers who were not Christians, for the document as a whole was transmitted by various scribes who were not Christians before it was transmitted as a whole by scribes who were Christians.

It is almost certain, then, that Jews before Jesus Christ looked for the Messiah who would be called the Lamb of God. A wider investigation of all the messianic passages in the *Testaments of the Twelve Patriarchs* has confirmed the argument in Parts I and II of this article. Indeed, we may go further, and conclude that no statement of doctrine in the Testaments should be taken as purely a Christian idea unless there is clear evidence that it arose from a scribal corruption; and even then we must allow for the possibility that the corruption occurred in the text while it was still being transmitted by scribes who were not Christians.

Text-Critical Notes

The passages are in the order of the Testaments, not in the order of discussion in the article. The basic text is that of MS B (Cambridge University Library MS Ff 1.24). No attempt has been made to give a complete set of variants; only enough to restore a reasonable text and to explain which readings I take to be scribal corruptions.

M. de Jonge, *Testamenta XII Patriarcharum Edited according to Cambridge University Library MS Ff 1.24 fol. 203a-261b with Short Notes* (Leiden: Brill, 2nd edn, 1970); R.H. Charles, *The Greek Versions of the Testaments of the Twelve Patriarchs Edited from Nine MSS together with the Variants of the Armenian and Slavonic Versions and Some Hebrew Fragments* (Oxford: Clarendon Press, 1908;

repr. Darmstadt: Wissenschaftliche, 1960); M.R. James, 'The Venice Extracts from the *Testaments of the Twelve Patriarchs*', *JTS* 28 (1927), pp. 337-48 (= K).

T. Reub. 6.7-12
7 την αρχην] a scribal alteration; better text χαριν D (cf. later reference to Reuben, Dan, and Joseph as rulers)
μετ αυτων] better text μετ αυτω D (cf. μετ αυτου C E F H I); scribal alteration μετ αυτον A G
8 χρονων αρχιερεως χριστου ον] better text either χρονον ον (cf. D) or χρονων ων (cf. E F); a gloss αρχιερευς χριστου H or αρχιερευς κυριου (cf. D), later incorporated into the text.
T. Sim. 5.6
ευλογιαις] glossator added περι Λευι και Ιουδα D
T. Sim. 7.1
υπακουετε Λευι και εν Ιουδα λυτρωθησεσθε] scribal alteration επακουσατε του Λευι και του Ιουδα C
εξ αυτων] scribal alteration εξ αυτου E
T. Levi 2.11
και δια σου και Ιουδα] conjectured original και δια του Ιουδα (cf. C H I)
εν αυτοις] a scribal alteration; original εν αυτω A F G; Christian alteration (?) εν εαυτω C (E?) H I
T. Levi 4.2-6
2 και γενεσθαι αυτω υιον] conjectured original σοι; scribes took previous σε as subject of infinitive; then either a glossator suggested αυτω for σοι (= σοι αυτω H), or changed σοι to σεαυτω (C) or to αυτου (D), or omitted the word (G)
3 φωτιεις] a scribal alteration, like φωτισεις D, for the original φωτιει A C F H I
εση] a scribal alteration for the original εν C H I, επι K
4 υιοι first occurence] a mistake for υιου A C E F H I, cf. του υιου D G
αποσκολοπισαι] the original, changed by Christian scribes to ανα- in all MSS except B (K)
6 αυτον...αυτον] note that Schnapp, Charles, and Becker have to conjecture σε, without any textual evidence
T. Levi 18
3 και ανατελει αστρον αυτου] scribal alteration; original και ανατελει αστρον αυτω H I cf. και ανατελει αυτω αστρον αυτου D
9 επι της ιερωσυνης αυτου] originally επι της γης to which a marginal note (τω) ιερωσυνη αυτου was added; the gloss was incorporated into the text as above, or as in C: επι τη ιερωσυνη αυτου, or as in I (second time): επι της νης ιερωσυνη αυτου
T. Jud. 21.1-5
2 και υπεταξε την βασιλειαν τη ιερωσυνη] scribal gloss; omitted by G
4 υπερεχει θεου ιερατεια της επι γης βασιλειας] υπερεχει η ιερατεια του θεου της επιγειου βαειλειας C (cf. H I): υπερεχει θεου ιερατειας της επι γης βασιλειας D. All MSS except B D add εαν μη δι αμαρτιας εκπεση απο κυριου και κυριευθη απο της επιγειου βασιλειας, with variants. The shorter text is right,

and I conjecture the original read υπερεχει η ιερατεια της επι γης βασιλειας; the words (του) θεου are a gloss

5 αυτον υπερ σε εξελεξατο] υπερσε is a scribal gloss; omitted by G

T. Iss. 5.7

και ο Λευι και ο Ιουδας εδοξασθη] the singular verb a scribal alteration; original εδοξασθησαν A C D E F G H

T. Dan 5.4, 6, 10

4 προς αυτους...εκατερους...εν αυτοις] plurals are scribal alterations; Armenian B* D E F G have singular in all three cases, A has singular in first and third case

6 τω Λευι υπακουσονται] original text επαναστησονται L corr. Athos Laura K 116: one gloss υπακουσονται put in place of this true reading C E F H: another gloss τω Λευι added with the first gloss to produce the text of B D G L*

10 εκ της φυλης Ιουδα και Λευι] conjecture και Λευι a scribal addition

T. Gad 8.1, 2

1 οπως τιμησωσιν Ιουδαν και τον Λευι] conjecture και τον Λευι a scribal gloss

οτι εξ αυτων ανατελει κυριος σωτηρα τω Ισραηλ] a Christian scribal alteration; original οτι εξ αυτων ανατελει ημιν κυριος σωτηρια εν τω Ισραηλ = (C) (cf. A D E F σωτηρ; G K σωτηριαν) (G rightly has εν τω)

2 απ αυτων] scribal alteration; original απ αυτου A C E F G H or, more likely, (αναστησονται) επ αυτον D

T. Benj. 11.2

φωνην αυτου] to obtain better text add και ποιων ευδοκιαν εν στοματι αυτου cf. A D E F with C

εκ του σπερματος μου] scribal alteration εκ σπερματος Ιουδα και Λευι C

Supplementary Note

In October 1978, more than two months after this article had been accepted for publication, Harm Hollander kindly sent me a copy of the magnificent new critical edition of the Testaments: *The Testaments of the Twelve Patriarchs: A Critical Edition of the Greek Text* by M. de Jonge in cooperation with H.W. Hollander, H.J. de Jonge, T. Korteweg (PVTG, 1; Leiden: Brill, 1978). I have checked all the references in my article, but have not added the additional evidence now available from the manuscripts I, J, L, M and C. As far as I can see the evidence I have given is reliable, except perhaps sometimes in citing MS G. The small discrepancies do not affect my case. I append notes on two verses where de Jonge differs from Charles.

T. Reub. 6.8

The gloss may well have been αρχιερεα χριστου I J or αρχιερεα κυριου M. (De Jonge prints αρχιερεα χριστου as the text of H too; he notes in the Preface, p. viii, that H and J have been newly collated for his edition from microfilms obtained from the Monastery of St Catharine, Mount Sinai.)

T. Levi 2.11

De Jonge gives εν εαυτω C H I J; εαυτω A E F G. My point remains, that the plural was a scribal alteration.

JSNT 26 (1986), pp. 97-117

THE APOCALYPSES IN THE NEW PSEUDEPIGRAPHA

Richard Bauckham

The publication of *The Old Testament Pseudepigrapha* (*OTP*), edited by
J.H. Charlesworth,[1] is a major event for the current renaissance of
pseudepigrapha studies and for biblical studies generally. The purpose of
this article is to offer some assessment of the treatment of apocalyptic
literature in volume I of *OTP*,[2] with the interests of New Testament
students and scholars especially in mind.

OTP is the first collected edition of the pseudepigrapha in English
translation since 1913, when *The Apocrypha and Pseudepigrapha of the
Old Testament* (*APOT*), edited by R.H. Charles, was published. Its most
obvious difference from *APOT* is the very much larger number of works
which are included. *APOT* contained only six apocalyptic works (*4 Ezra,
2 Baruch, 3 Baruch, 1 Enoch, 2 Enoch,* and *Sib. Or.* 3–5). *OTP* includes
these six, three of them in longer forms (*4 Ezra* with the additional
chs. 1–2, 15–16; *2 Enoch* with the final chs. 69–73; and the complete
collection of *Sib. Or.* 1–14), and in addition thirteen other works in its
section 'Apocalyptic Literature and Related Works'. None of these
thirteen appear in *APOT*. In fact there are also two more works which
really belong in this section of *OTP*, since they are unambiguously
apocalypses (*Ladder of Jacob* and *Ascension of Isaiah*), but which have
been assigned to volume II.[3] *OTP*'s selection of apocalypses is also larger

1. *Vol. I: Apocalyptic Literature and Testaments* (Garden City, NY: Doubleday;
London: Darton, Longman & Todd, 1983).

2. In order to keep this article within reasonable bounds, I shall not discuss the
testaments, which are also in vol. I, even though some of them include apocalyptic
material.

3. Since this article was written before the publication of vol. II, it does not discuss these two works. Presumably they are included in vol. II because they are

than that projected for the series Jüdische Schriften aus hellenistisch-römischer Zeit (JSHRZ) or included in *The Apocryphal Old Testament*, edited by H.F.D. Sparks.[4]

Of course, biblical scholars have never depended solely on *APOT* for their knowledge of the pseudepigrapha, but it has tended to influence their sense of the range of pseudepigraphical works which are really relevant as 'background' to the New Testament. Certainly, the common views of the character of ancient Jewish apocalyptic have been largely based on *APOT*'s selection of apocalypses, and illuminating parallels to the New Testament have usually been sought in these. The standard studies of apocalyptic are based on these apocalypses, usually with the addition of the *Apocalypse of Abraham*. As *OTP* becomes the standard work of reference, this may or may not change. Much depends on whether *OTP*'s additional apocalypses can really be treated as in any way reliable evidence for the Judaism of the New Testament period, a question which requires careful assessment in each case. In what follows I shall offer comments on *OTP*'s treatment of each apocalyptic work, with the exception of the two calendrical works (*Treatise of Shem* and *Revelation of Ezra*), which belong in a distinct category of their own. These comments will, I hope, be of use to those who will be using *OTP* as a work of reference. I shall then offer some more general comments on the range of apocalypses which have been selected for inclusion in *OTP*.

1. *1 Enoch* (E. Isaac) is probably the most important non-canonical apocalypse for students of the New Testament, though its *direct* influence on the New Testament has often been vastly exaggerated (as here: p. 10). It has also been the object of a great deal of important recent research, rather little of which is reflected in Isaac's introduction and notes.

Essentially Isaac gives us an introduction to and translation of the Ethiopic version of *1 Enoch*. Controversy is likely to surround his use of the Ethiopic manuscripts, in particular his judgment that one manuscript (Lake Ṭana 9) is not only the oldest but very much the best, so that its

---

regarded as legendary expansions of the Old Testament, but they are no more so than *1 Enoch* or the *Apocalypse of Abraham*, both of which include narrative material as well as apocalyptic visions.

4. This volume (Oxford: Clarendon Press, 1984) was not yet published when this article was written. I owe the information about its contents and those of JSHRZ to J.H. Charlesworth, *The Pseudepigrapha and Modern Research with a Supplement* (SBLSCS, 75; Chico, CA: Scholars Press, 1981), pp. 29-30.

readings are usually to be preferred.[5] His translation is of this manuscript, correcting only its obvious errors, though many variants in other manuscripts are given in the apparatus. As far as a reader who is not an Ethiopic scholar can judge, a fair number of this manuscript's unique or unusual readings are preferable, sometimes because they agree with the Greek version against other Ethiopic manuscripts (e.g. at 1.9; 24.5), but its readings cannot be preferable in every instance. This translation may supplement, but cannot replace, that of Knibb (whose edition of Ethiopic Enoch[6] appeared after Isaac's work was completed).

The Greek versions of *1 Enoch* are cited quite often in the apparatus, the Qumran Aramaic fragments only rarely. But the latter, though very fragmentary, are evidence of *1 Enoch* in its (probably) original language, while the Greek versions cover about 40 chapters of the book. In view of the special importance of *1 Enoch* among the pseudepigrapha, should we not have been given translations of all versions, Greek, Ethiopic, and Aramaic, in parallel columns?

2. *2 Enoch* (F.I. Andersen). Of all the apocalypses in *APOT*, *2 Enoch* has always been the most puzzling and controversial. Some have insisted that it is Christian and of relatively late date, and the problems of provenance and date have scarcely been helped by disagreements over the relative priority of the two recensions, longer and shorter. Andersen's principal achievement is to provide us with a translation (of the two recensions in parallel) based on more and better manuscripts than previous translations, though he is the first to insist on its provisionality. More work on the text still needs to be done before we have an entirely secure basis for answering other questions. Andersen rightly argues that the question of priority between the two recensions should not be hastily answered: the evidence is too complicated to allow the assumption that either the shortest or the longest text is always the original.

Andersen inclines to regard *2 Enoch* as an ancient work from some group (perhaps of God-fearers) on the fringes of Judaism, but he is more frankly cautious about his conclusions than many contributors to this volume: 'In every respect *2 Enoch* remains an enigma. So long as the date and location remain unknown, no use can be made of it for histori-

5.   This judgment is maintained in greater detail in E. Isaac, 'New Light Upon the Book of Enoch from Newly-Found Ethiopic MSS', *JAOS* 103 (1983), pp. 399-411.

6.   M.A. Knibb, *The Ethiopic Book of Enoch* (2 vols.; Oxford: Clarendon Press, 1978).

cal purposes' (p. 97). Rereading *2 Enoch* in Andersen's translation, I found myself constantly deciding that the material must be ancient. But a great deal of patient study of all the available parallels to *2 Enoch*'s contents will be necessary before New Testament scholars are able to base anything on quotations from *2 Enoch*.

3. *3 Enoch* (P. Alexander) is the one Merkabah text already quite well known to New Testament scholars, through Odeberg's edition and translation. Alexander's improved translation is based on a corrected text, and is accompanied by abundant, very informative notes. The introduction is in fact a masterly brief introduction to Merkabah mysticism in general, including its relationship to ancient Jewish apocalyptic and specifically to some of the texts in *OTP*. The links between aspects of apocalyptic texts of the first and second centuries CE and the Merkabah texts are becoming increasingly apparent, and make an acquaintance with the latter essential for scholars interested in the former. Perhaps this justifies the inclusion of at least one Merkabah text in *OTP*, but not necessarily the inclusion of this text, which, despite its dependence on some very old traditions, is in Alexander's view to be dated in the fifth or sixth century CE; that is, it is probably not, as Odeberg thought, one of the earliest, but one of the later Merkabah texts. Reliable translations of the other major texts are an urgent need.

4. *Sibylline Oracles* (J.J. Collins). Although the *Sibylline Oracles* are part Jewish, part Christian, and were written over a long period (book 14 is probably seventh century), they form a continuous tradition of writing, and it is extremely useful to have for the first time an accessible translation of the whole collection, with excellent introductions and notes.

Particularly neglected but important are the Jewish parts of books 1–2, which were left out of *APOT*, and also out of Hennecke's *New Testament Apocrypha*, in which translations of only the Christian parts of books 1–2 were given.[7] However, Collins overestimates the possible extent of Jewish material in book 2 (p. 330), because he has taken no account of M.R. James's demonstration that 2.196–338 is dependent on the *Apocalypse of Peter*[8] (in fact, it is largely a poetic paraphrase of

---

7. E. Hennecke, *New Testament Apocrypha* (ed. W. Schneemelcher and R.McL. Wilson; London: Lutterworth, 1963, 1965), II, pp. 709-19; and in the new edition (Cambridge: James Clarke; Louisville: Westminster/John Knox, 1992), II, pp. 656-63.

8. M.R. James, 'A New Text of the Apocalypse of Peter', *JTS* 12 (1911), pp. 39-44, 51-52. The material is all ultimately Jewish in origin, but reached the

Apoc. Pet. 4–14). Since the passages in book 2 which are paralleled in book 8 (p. 332) are precisely the parts of this section which are not borrowed from the *Apocalypse of Peter*, the priority of book 8 to book 2 can also be demonstrated, with implications for the date of both books.

5. *Apocryphon of Ezekiel* (J.R. Mueller and S.E. Robinson). The *Apocryphon of Ezekiel* survives only in a few fragments: the five which can be fairly securely identified are translated here (though the two longest are not, despite the claim in the section heading, *new* translations). Clement of Alexandria in fact gives a little more of fragment 5 than is translated here (while the Chester Beatty papyrus gives a good deal more, but in a highly fragmentary, untranslatable state). It would have been useful to have some reference to other possible fragments (such as the quotation in Tertullian, *De res.* 22).

That the work dates from the late first century BCE or early first century CE is well established. Its parable of the resurrection (the longest fragment) is well known, but has probably not been given the attention it deserves as evidence of Jewish ideas about resurrection in New Testament times. It also has some relevance to the study of Gospel parables (cf. Mt. 22.2; Mk 12.9), as may the expansion of Ezekiel's image of the shepherd in fragment 5.

6. *Apocalypse of Zephaniah* (O.S. Wintermute). Of the apocalypses which *OTP* adds to *APOT*'s selection, this is the only one which has a real chance of being a pre-Christian Jewish work (apart from the fragmentary *Apocryphon of Ezekiel*). It has also been extraordinarily neglected by scholars.[9] Its inclusion in *OTP* is therefore fully justified, and any discussion which served to bring it to general scholarly attention would be welcome. While Wintermute's treatment is not wholly satisfactory, it is a significant start. His notes to the text are gratifyingly extensive. It is unfortunate that he apparently wrote before Martha Himmelfarb's dissertation and book became available:[10] her discussion of the *Apocalypse of Zephaniah* (which she continues to call 'the

Sibylline Oracles via the *Apocalypse of Peter*.

9. Surprisingly it is not mentioned in G.W.E. Nickelsburg, *Jewish Literature between the Bible and the Mishnah* (London: SCM Press, 1981) or in C. Rowland, *The Open Heaven: A Study of Apocalyptic in Judaism and Early Christianity* (London: SPCK, 1982).

10. M. Himmelfarb, *Tours of Hell: The Development and Transmission of an Apocalyptic Form in Jewish and Christian Literature* (Philadelphia: University of Pennsylvania Press, 1983).

Anonymous Apocalypse') within the broad context of tours of hell in Jewish and Christian apocalyptic is one of the most important contributions so far to the study of this apocalypse. It has the general effect of vindicating a fairly early date. Wintermute has also missed Scholem's discussion of the passage quoted by Clement of Alexandria:[11] both Scholem and Himmelfarb would have alerted him to the contacts between these texts and the Merkabah literature.

The texts in question are three: a short quotation in Clement of Alexandria, a brief manuscript fragment in Sahidic, and a long manuscript fragment in Akhmimic. The two Coptic fragments are from manuscripts which also contained the Coptic *Apocalypse of Elijah*. Clement's quotation is explicitly said to be from the *Apocalypse of Zephaniah*; the Sahidic fragment contains the words, 'I, Zephaniah, saw these things in my vision'; but the Akhmimic fragment contains no indication of the identity of the seer (and has therefore sometimes been called the Anonymous Apocalypse). Two problems arise: (a) Are Clement's quotation and the Sahidic fragment from the same *Apocalypse of Zephaniah*? (b) Are the Sahidic and Akhmimic fragments from the same work? Wintermute answers both questions affirmatively, but probably with too much assurance. It is true that the two Coptic fragments are closely related in style and content, but we could be dealing with two distinct apocalypses, either by the same author or one based on the other. My hesitation about identifying the Akhmimic text as the *Apocalypse of Zephaniah* arises from 6.10, in which the seer refers to events of the Babylonian exile as past historical events. This could be a slip on the author's part, but ancient pseudepigraphal writers, including apocalyptists, were usually careful to avoid such blatant anachronisms. (In the apocalypses in this volume, I think the only other examples are *Greek Apocalypse of Ezra* 1.19; 2.1; 4.11; 5.22; *Vision of Ezra* 38; *Apocalypse of Sedrach* 15.2-5—an indication that the authors or redactors of these late Christian apocalypses had lost any real sense of the historical identity of the pseudonym.) If the seer is therefore a post-exilic Old Testament figure,[12] not many candidates are available. I wonder whether the text might be

---

11. G.G. Scholem, *Jewish Gnosticism, Merkabah Mysticism, and Talmudic Tradition* (New York: Jewish Theological Seminary of America, 2nd edn, 1965), pp. 18-19.

12. A New Testament pseudonym seems ruled out by the purely Old Testament context of the account: cf. 3.4; 6.10; 7.7; 9.4; 11.4.

the *Apocalypse of Zechariah*,[13] which in the Stichometry of Nicephorus is listed after the *Apocalypses of Elijah and Zephaniah*.[14] Some support for this suggestion, which can only be conjecture, may come from the fact that the visions are partly modelled on those of Zechariah 16 (though this is also true of the Sahidic fragment).[15] At any rate, the relationship between the Sahidic and Akhmimic texts cannot be regarded as settled. Just as problematic is the relationship between these texts and the quotation in Clement: the difficulties in supposing that the latter is from the same work as even the Sahidic fragment alone seem to me greater than Wintermute allows (p. 500).

I agree with Wintermute that there is no reason to regard the Coptic texts as (a) Christian work(s), though I am more inclined than he is to see 10.9 as a minor Christian embellishment. On the other hand, 8.9 ('my sons...') does not have to be a 'homiletical aside', indicating that the text was meant to be read in a religious assembly. It could be that the seer is represented as recounting his visions to his sons (cf. Isaiah's apostrophes to 'Hezekiah and Jasub my son', which punctuate his account of his vision in *Asc. Isa.* 4.1; 8.24; 9.22; 11.16), perhaps in a testamentary context (cf. Enoch's account of his visions, mixed with homiletical comments to his sons, in *2 En.* 40–47).

The extraordinary incoherence of the Akhmimic text (which not even the *Greek Apocalypse of Ezra* equals) must, it seems to me, result from abbreviation. We know from other cases where more than one recension survives that scribes not infrequently tried to abbreviate apocalypses (cf. *2 Enoch*, *3 Baruch*, *Ascension of Isaiah*, *Apocalypse of Peter*), sometimes resulting in the kind of *non sequiturs* and abrupt transitions which the Akhmimic text here shows. But in that case we cannot rely on the length given for the *Apocalypse of Zephaniah* (or for the *Apocalypse of Zechariah*) in the Stichometry of Nicephorus for calculations related to

13. The quotation which Origen (comment on Eph. 4.27, in J.A.F. Gregg [ed.], 'The Commentary of Origen upon the Epistle to the Ephesians: Part III', *JTS* 3 [1902], p. 554) ascribes to Zechariah the father of John (cf. next note) would not be out of place in the work of which the Akhmimic text is part.

14. It is there called 'Of Zechariah the father of John', but this may be a mistaken Christian identification of the seer. The ancient lists of apocryphal books nevertheless include this work among the Old Testament apocrypha in the chronological position of Zechariah the prophet.

15. This dependence on Zech. 1–6 needs to be studied in connection with Himmelfarb's study of the 'demonstrative explanations' in tours of hell: 'Tours of Hell', ch. 3.

our fragment (cf. *OTP*, pp. 497-98). The manuscript which contained our Akhmimic fragment could have included abbreviated versions of two apocalypses (*Apocalypse of Zephaniah* and *Apocalypse of Zechariah?*) as well as the *Apocalypse of Elijah*.

Probably the most important aspect of the Coptic texts is that they may well be, along with a fragment of the *Apocalypse of Elijah*,[16] the earliest examples, in the apocalyptic tradition, of detailed visions of the punishments of the damned in hell. The tradition of such visions is very old (cf. *1 En.* 22, 27), and from brief references to such visions in apocalypses which do not actually describe them (*2 Apoc. Bar.* 59.10-11; *Apoc. Abr.* 21.3; *Asc. Isa.* 1.3;[17] *4 Ezra* 7.84; *3 Apoc. Bar.* 16.4 S; *2 En.* 40–41; cf. *LAB* 23.6), we can be sure that they were to be found in apocalypses of the New Testament period. Scholars have tended to think of the genre of the apocalyptic tour of the punishments of hell as belonging to a later period, from the second century CE onwards,[18] but in fact the evidence is good that it flourished already in the first century CE.[19] These Coptic '*Apocalypse of Zephaniah*' texts may well be among the early sources of the whole tradition. At least in the present abbreviated texts, they refer only in a perfunctory way (9.4) to the parallel tradition of visions of the bliss of the righteous in paradise.

These rather extended comments may serve to welcome one of the more important 'newcomers' to the pseudepigrapha, and also to indicate that much work needs to be done on it.

7. *4 Ezra* (B.M. Metzger). Here the words 'a new translation' included in the title of this, as of other sections of the volume, are quite misleading:

---

16. This is the fragment quoted in the apocryphal Epistle of Titus. It is published, with related material, in M.E. Stone and J. Strugnell, *The Books of Elijah: Parts 1–2* (SBLTT, 18; Missoula, MT: Scholars Press, 1979), pp. 14-26.

17. In my opinion this is not meant to be a reference to any of the contents of the present *Ascension of Isaiah*, but refers to a lost *Testament of Hezekiah*, which must have been a work of the first century CE or earlier, in which Hezekiah described his descent to Hades (the idea no doubt developed from Isa. 38).

18. The classic treatments are the Christian apocalypses of Peter, Paul and the Virgin; cf. also, in *OTP*, the *Greek Apocalypse of Ezra* and the *Vision of Ezra*. In both Jewish and early Christian apocalyptic the genre flourished right through the medieval period.

19. The account of the punishments in hell in the early second-century *Apocalypse of Peter* must be based on a Jewish apocalypse, perhaps that of Elijah: cf. my discussion in 'The Apocalypse of Peter: An Account of Research', in *ANRW* 2.25.6 (1988), pp. 4712-4750; and Himmelfarb, *Tours of Hell* ch. 5.

the translation is that of the RSV Apocrypha (prepared by Metzger), first published in 1957, and only slightly amended here.[20] Notes to the text are purely textual, and the marginal references do not even include the important parallels in *2 Baruch*. The study of *4 Ezra* is not advanced by this contribution, but probably we should not expect it to be, since *4 Ezra* is one of the few non-canonical apocalypses on which much of the basic scholarly work has already been done.

Much more disappointing is the treatment of the additions to the original apocalypse: chs. 1–2 (*5 Ezra*) and 15–16 (*6 Ezra*), which were not included in *APOT*, though they have always been well known from their inclusion in the Protestant Apocrypha, as well as the appendix to the Vulgate. *OTP* includes them as part of the translation of *4 Ezra*, but readers are given practically no guidance on what to make of them. Metzger's introduction to *4 Ezra* scarcely mentions them, except to inform us (with unjustified dogmatism) that 'Near the middle or in the second half of the third century four chapters were added...by one or more Christian writers' (p. 520). In fact, *5 Ezra* has been most commonly and most plausibly dated in the second century, as most recently by Daniélou[21] and by Stanton.[22] It is scarcely conceivable that both *5* and *6 Ezra* come from the same author.

5 Ezra is a patently Jewish-Christian work. In the case of *6 Ezra*, which lacks any overtly Christian characteristics, the Jewish or Christian origin of the text is certainly open to debate. Against the usual, but not very well-founded, belief in its Christian origin, Schrage[23] and Harnisch[24] have argued that it is a purely Jewish apocalyptic work, to be dated perhaps earlier than *4 Ezra*. Such arguments should have been discussed and assessed in *OTP*, which may thus have missed an important opportunity of rehabilitating a neglected Jewish apocalypse. Even if *5* and *6 Ezra* are both Christian, they bear the same kind of relationship to underlying Jewish apocalyptic traditions as do several other Christian

20. Metzger points this out: *OTP*, p. 518.

21. J. Daniélou, *The Origins of Latin Christianity* (ET; ed. J.A. Baker; London: Darton, Longman & Todd; Philadelphia: Westminster Press, 1977), p. 18.

22. G.N. Stanton, '5 Ezra and Matthean Christianity in the Second Century', *JTS* 28 (1977), pp. 67-83.

23. W. Schrage, 'Die Stellung zur Welt bei Paulus, Epiktet und in der Apokalyptik: Ein Beitrag zu 1 Kor. 7.29-31', *ZTK* 61 (1964), pp. 139-54.

24. W. Harnisch, *Eschatologische Existenz* (FRLANT, 110; Göttingen: Vandenhoeck & Ruprecht, 1973), pp. 72-74.

works included in *OTP*, and are also probably earlier in date than the other Ezra apocalypses (apart from *4 Ezra*) which *OTP* includes. They therefore merit the same kind of extended treatment as pseudepigraphal works in their own right.

Furthermore, the same principles which have led to the inclusion of *5* and *6 Ezra* and the later Ezra apocrypha in *OTP* should also have led to the inclusion of a translation of the Armenian version of *4 Ezra*.[25] This is, in effect, a rather thoroughly revised version of *4 Ezra*, including substantial additions to the text. Stone argues that these did not originate in Armenian, but derive from the Greek text behind the Armenian version and date from the fourth century at the latest. Though they constitute a Christian version of *4 Ezra*, they may depend on early Jewish sources.[26] The inclusion of these additions to *4 Ezra* in *OTP* would have been particularly useful because they belong to the same category of material inspired by *4 Ezra* as do the *Greek Apocalypse of Ezra*, the *Vision of Ezra* and the *Apocalypse of Sedrach*. With their inclusion, *OTP* could have given us a fairly complete collection of apocalyptic works inspired by *4 Ezra*.[27] Another missed opportunity!

8. *Greek Apocalypse of Ezra* (M.E. Stone). The translation of this work was made from one manuscript (that used by Tischendorf) and was completed before the publication of Wahl's edition of the text,[28] which is based on two manuscripts, but in fact the latter would have made practically no difference to the translation. The introduction and notes are thorough and learned, and constitute the fullest study of this work so far produced (fuller than Müller's in JSHRZ).[29]

It is important to realize that this work's Old Testament pseudonym, which is one of the criteria for its inclusion in *OTP*, probably results simply from the fact that its author took *4 Ezra* as a model for the kind

---

25. M.E. Stone, *The Armenian Version of 4 Ezra* (University of Pennsylvania Armenian Texts and Studies, 1; Missoula, MT: Scholars Press, 1979).

26. Stone, *Armenian Version*, p. ix; cf. also M.E. Stone, 'Jewish Apocryphal Literature in the Armenian Church', *Le Muséon* 95 (1982), p. 292. Stone gives detailed evidence in *A Textual Commentary on the Armenian Version of IV Ezra* (Septuagint and Cognate Studies Series, 34; Atlanta: Scholars Press, 1990).

27. The Syriac *Apocalypse of Ezra* and the Falasha *Apocalypse of Ezra* are also inspired by *4 Ezra*.

28. O. Wahl (ed.), *Apocalypsis Esdrae, Apocalypsis Sedrach, Visio Beati Esdrae* (PVTG, 4; Leiden: Brill, 1977).

29. Once again, it is a pity that it was written too soon to take account of Himmelfarb, 'Tours of Hell'.

of work he wished to write (a debate with God about his righteousness and mercy in judging sinners). It is no necessary indication of the Jewish (as opposed to Christian) character of its contents, and there is no real reason to regard this work (which is unquestionably Christian in its present form) as a Christian edition of an earlier Jewish apocalypse. (The same comments apply to other Ezra apocrypha: *Vision of Ezra* and *Questions of Ezra*.) As Stone recognizes, the work itself is Christian, but, as both the jumbled nature of its contents and the parallels with other works indicate, it is closely reliant on several sources, probably Jewish as well as Christian. That there is ancient Jewish apocalyptic material here is very probable. Its reliable identification must await further study especially in conjunction with parallel material in other Jewish and Christian apocalypses.

In view of the nature of the work and the state of scholarship on it, Stone wisely draws almost no conclusions about date or provenance: 'a date sometime between AD 150 and 850 is probable. Its provenance cannot be discerned' (p. 563).

9. *Vision of Ezra* (J.R. Mueller and G.A. Robbins). This work is quite closely related to the *Greek Apocalypse of Ezra*, but the relationship is not one of simple dependence in either direction. I would be inclined to date it later than the *Greek Apocalypse*, partly because the role of Ezra is further removed from his role in *4 Ezra*, which provided the original inspiration for this cycle of Ezra apocalypses. However, even the date which Mueller and Robbins suggest (between 350 and 600 CE) is, on present evidence, too precise: it might even be earlier, it could certainly be later.

As Mueller and Robbins recognize, this work's closest relationships (apart from with other works in the Ezra cycle) are with the apocalypses of Peter, Paul and the Virgin and the apocryphal *Apocalypse of John*. This raises an important issue about the criteria for inclusion in a collection of Old Testament pseudepigrapha. All these apocalypses, whether they bear Old Testament or New Testament pseudonyms, are Christian works which draw on Jewish apocalyptic sources and traditions. In fact, the *Apocalypses of Peter* and *Paul* are probably closer to ancient Jewish apocalyptic sources than are the *Greek Apocalypse of Ezra* and the *Vision of Ezra*. To distinguish here between Old Testament pseudepigrapha, which bear an Old Testament pseudonym, and New Testament apocrypha, which bear a New Testament pseudonym, is to draw a quite artificial distinction among works which are closely related to each other and are equally useful, but also equally problematic, means of access to Jewish apocalyptic traditions.

10. *Questions of Ezra* (M.E. Stone), of which Recension B is here published in translation for the first time, is an intriguing work, much of whose content must surely go back to ancient Jewish sources. But not even Stone can decide whether it originated in Armenian or not. This is an extreme case of the tantalizing character of so many of the ostensibly late pseudepigrapha, which seem to preserve early material but offer no clues to their time of origin.

11. *Apocalypse of Sedrach* (S. Agourides). It is annoying to find that this work has been given verse numbers which do not correspond to those in Wahl's edition (1977).[30] Although Agourides's work was completed without knowledge of Wahl's edition, the verse numbers could easily have been brought into line with what is likely to remain the standard edition of the Greek text.

This work is related to the apocalypses of the Ezra cycle, but presses further the theme of the seer's debate with God in relation to his compassion for sinners. Agourides's arguments for seeing it as a Jewish work which has been only superficially Christianized should be considered carefully, but do not carry complete conviction. The claim that much of its doctrinal content is 'atypical of medieval Christianity' (p. 606) is too broad a generalization to be useful. In the many centuries of Christian history during which the *Apocalypse of Sedrach* could, on present evidence, have originated, there is plenty of evidence of minority Christian viewpoints not dissimilar to those of the apocalypse. Its general doctrinal tendency is consistent, for example, with the views of some of the 'merciful' Christians (*misericordes*) reported by Augustine (*De civ. Dei* 21.17–27). Views less extreme but tending in the same direction are found in the *Apocalypse of Paul* and the *Apocalypse of the Virgin*, and even though their ideas about mercy for the damned probably derive from Jewish sources, the popularity of these apocalypses shows that there were Christian circles in which such ideas were welcomed and propagated.[31] Moreover, the apocalyptic genre of the seer's debate with God was attractive precisely to writers, whether Jewish or Christian, who

---

30. See n. 28 above.

31. On the place of the teaching of these apocalypses, as well as the *Apocalypses of Sedrach* and *Ezra*, in the early Christian tradition, see now E. Lupieri, '*Poena aeterna* nelle più antiche apocalissi cristiane apocrife non gnostiche', *Augustinianum* 23 (1983), pp. 361-72.

wanted a vehicle for some degree of protest against the official theology.

The attribution of the apocalypse to Sedrach is not easy to explain if it is Christian, but not much easier to explain if it is Jewish. The problem disappears if we accept the suggestion[32] that the name is a corruption of Ezra. This is not to deny that Jewish sources have undoubtedly been used (e.g. the substitution of Christ for Michael in ch. 9 is transparent), but the identification of Jewish material requires caution.

The intriguing possibility that 6.4-6 preserves a pre-Christian parable of the prodigal son, which Jesus deliberately adapted to make a different point, should not be dismissed without further consideration, but it is also possible that the author has deliberately used only the beginning of Jesus' parable (as he understood it), leaving open the possibility of the prodigal's repentance, which forms the theme of the later part of his work.

12. *2 Baruch* (A.F.J. Klijn). Klijn's introduction is largely a translation of his German introduction in JSHRZ. It is a commendably thorough treatment within its scope.

13. *3 Baruch* (H.E. Gaylord, Jr) is the most neglected of the apocalypses which were included in *APOT*, no doubt partly because it seems to have little relevance to New Testament studies. But this neglect is mistaken, arising as it does from the tendency to restrict relevance to the mere search for parallels. A proper understanding of early Christianity requires a rounded picture of the religious context in which it originated and grew, and in this sense it is as important for the student of the New Testament to understand aspects of contemporary Judaism which bear little resemblance to anything in the New Testament as it is for him or her to study those which influenced early Christianity. If early Christians did not share the concerns of *3 Baruch*, it is at least worth asking why they did not. Precisely because New Testament scholars are unlikely to find *3 Baruch* very interesting, they should make the effort to study it! It is a post-70 CE Jewish apocalypse which reacts very differently to the catastrophe from the way in which the authors of *4 Ezra* and *2 Baruch* reacted. Baruch's attention is turned away from the fate of the earthly Jerusalem and the problems of history and eschatology, and towards the mysteries of the heavenly realms. But this interest (which includes meteorological and astronomical topics as well as more obviously religious subjects) had always been a feature of the Jewish apocalypses, as we have recently been becoming more aware.

3 Baruch survives both in Greek and in a Slavonic version. As in

---

32. M.E. Stone, 'The Metamorphosis of Ezra', *JTS* 33 (1982), p. 6.

APOT, the translations of the two versions are here printed in parallel, since the differences between the two are such that any other treatment of them would be very misleading. By far the most important advance on *APOT* is in the textual basis for the translation of the Slavonic and in the resulting estimation of the value of the Slavonic for access to the original apocalypse. The translation is based on Gaylord's forthcoming edition of the Slavonic text, for which he has examined all known manuscripts of the Slavonic (though, unfortunately, in one respect the translation here is not as definitive as that in his forthcoming edition will be: see p. 655). From this it now becomes clear that where the Slavonic and the Greek diverge, it is the Slavonic that is frequently more original and represents a less Christianized version of the apocalypse than the extant Greek manuscripts do. Thus Gaylord's work on the Slavonic not only takes us closer to the original apocalypse; it also increases our confidence that *3 Baruch* is an originally Jewish work. (Gaylord himself is unwilling to assert this last conclusion, because he thinks that too sharp a distinction between Jewish and Christian works in the first two centuries CE may be artificial. He has a point.) Gaylord's work on *3 Baruch* is thus a striking instance of the great importance of work on the Slavonic versions of the pseudepigrapha.

Gaylord seems to me too cautious about identifying *3 Baruch* with the Baruch apocryphon known to Origen, especially since he concludes for other reasons that *3 Baruch* was written before Origen. The problem is that there were seven heavens in the work known to Origen, whereas in both our versions of *3 Baruch* Baruch gets no further than the fourth heaven. However, precisely Gaylord's vindication of the greater originality of the Slavonic indicates that both our versions of *3 Baruch* are abbreviated. 16.4-8 in the Slavonic must be an abbreviation of an originally longer ending in which Baruch travelled to higher heavens in order to view the punishments of the damned and the resting place of the righteous. An early abbreviation of *3 Baruch* by Christian copyists is easily explained, in that material on hell and paradise was readily available in well-known early Christian apocalypses such as those of Peter and Paul (the latter perhaps drew some of its material on these subjects from *3 Baruch*), whereas *3 Baruch* would have been copied and read for the sake of its more unusual material on the contents of the lower heavens.

14. *Apocalypse of Abraham* (R. Rubinkiewicz and H.G. Hunt). There can be no real doubt about the *Apocalypse of Abraham*'s place among

the ancient Jewish apocalypses: it should be the least controversial of *OTP*'s additions to the apocalypses in *APOT*. But since it has been pre-served only in Slavonic, there is room for doubt about the originality of everything in the Slavonic version. Rubinkiewicz's suggestions of Bogomil interpolations (p. 684)[33] probably go too far (23.5-11 seems to me the passage most likely to have been adapted under Bogomil influence), but in a Slavonic apocryphon they are always possible. Nor can we tell what might have been omitted as objectionable in Bogomil eyes (e.g. reference to bodily resurrection). However, most of the con-tents of the apocalypse have sufficient parallels in other early Jewish documents to give us confidence in their originality.

The translation offers few really major differences from that of Box and Landsman,[34] but it has a better textual basis, and it stays closer to the original, with the result that, so far from clearing up obscurities in Box and Landsman's translation, it extends obscurity to passages Box and Landsman had made relatively clear. It is as well that the English reader thereby gains a sense of the real difficulty of the Slavonic text. The French translation in the new edition by Philonenko-Sayor and Philonenko[35] (which appeared too late to be noticed here) quite often makes plausible sense of passages which Rubinkiewicz and Hunt deliber-ately leave obscure.[36] Scholars who cannot read Slavonic will probably have the best access they can have to the text by using these two new translations together.

The notes are purely textual. For help in understanding the text the reader must go to Box (whose notes are still very useful) and to Philonenko. The introduction is also disappointing: the work's relation to other Abraham traditions, its close affinity with the *Ladder of Jacob*, its important relationship to Merkabah mysticism, all go unmentioned. Its particular response to the fall of Jerusalem is hardly adequately characterized.

33. He discusses these at greater length in R. Rubinkiewicz, 'La vision de l'histoire dans l'Apocalypse d'Abraham', in *ANRW* 2.19.1 (1979), pp. 137-51.

34. G.H. Box and J.I. Landsman, *The Apocalypse of Abraham* (London: SPCK, 1918).

35. B. Philonenko-Sayor and M. Philonenko, *L'Apocalypse d'Abraham: Introduction, texte slave, traduction et notes* (= *Sem* 31 [Paris: Adrien-Maisonneuve, 1981]); see also B. Philonenko-Sayor and M. Philonenko, *Die Apokalypse Abrahams* (JSHRZ, 5.5; Gütersloh: Mohn, 1982).

36. E.g. their paraphrase of 10.12 (10.11 in *OTP*'s numbering) is clearly, in the light of the following verse, the correct interpretation.

15. *Apocalypse of Adam* (G. MacRae) is the only gnostic apocalypse included in *OTP*, chosen because of its arguably pre-Christian character.

16. *Apocalypse of Elijah* (O.S. Wintermute). There was an ancient Jewish *Apocalypse of Elijah*, probably existing as early as the first century CE, but this is not it. The ancient apocalypse survives probably in three reliably attributed quotations, the rather complex evidence for which has been collected in the edition by Stone and Strugnell.[37] These are more reliable evidence for the contents of the original apocalypse than anything in the Coptic *Apocalypse of Elijah*, which is translated here, and should certainly have been included in *OTP* (they are nearly as extensive as the fragments of the *Apocryphon of Ezekiel*). It seems that out of the original Jewish *Apocalypse of Elijah* developed two later works, whose precise relationship to it can only be guessed: the Coptic *Apocalypse of Elijah*, translated here, which in its present form is a Christian work of perhaps the fourth century, and the Hebrew *Apocalypse of Elijah*, which, although in its present form is later, is as likely as the Coptic *Apocalypse* to preserve material from the original apocalypse. It could well have been included in *OTP*, both for this reason and as a representative of the large body of medieval Hebrew apocalypses, in the same way as *3 Enoch* is included as a representative of the Hekalot literature.

The Coptic *Apocalypse* itself is an interesting work, for which Wintermute provides a thorough introduction and useful notes. He is wisely cautious about the identification of a Jewish stratum (though he is sure it exists) until much more work on this and related documents is done. It is not clear to me how his suggestion (plausible in itself) that the title *Apocalypse of Elijah* is only a secondary identification resulting from the Christian account of Elijah's martyrdom (p. 722) is consistent with his acceptance of the view that a common ancestor lies behind this and the Hebrew *Apocalypse of Elijah* (p. 729). He has not noticed the Coptic *Apocalypse*'s dependence on the *Apocalypse of Peter* (at 3.1-4; 5.26-29).

17. *Apocalypse of Daniel* (G.T. Zervos). Again it is an unnecessary inconvenience to have the text divided into chapters and verses different from those in Berger's edition,[38] which is bound to remain the standard edition of the text (despite some deficiencies: *OTP*, p. 756) and the fullest commentary on the work.

---

37. Stone and Strugnell, *Books of Elijah*.
38. K. Berger, *Die griechische Daniel-Diegese* (SPB, 27; Leiden: Brill, 1976).

Zervos follows Berger in dating the work to the early ninth century, on the basis of an alleged reference to the coronation of Charlemagne in 7.14. Even if this reference is not quite certain, the date is approximately correct. This is therefore one of the very large number of Byzantine apocalypses from the early medieval period, which include a confusingly large number of other Daniel apocalypses, the Armenian *Vision of Enoch*, and the several versions of Pseudo-Methodius. The fact that this text is attributed in one manuscript to Daniel and in another to Methodius is an indication of the fact that in the Byzantine period these were regarded as the two most appropriate pseudonyms for historical-eschatological apocalypses. Whether there is any particular justification for choosing this rather than other Byzantine apocalypses for inclusion in *OTP* I am not sure,[39] but it is an extremely interesting work, which illustrates rather well the way in which such late apocalypses do preserve early material. But Berger's commentary on this work (invaluable as an introduction to the whole field of later Christian apocalyptic) is an education in the vast complexity of the task of understanding how early traditions passed to and through such later apocalypses.

General Comments

It is likely that *OTP* will be criticized for including works which are too late and/or too Christian to be evidence for the Judaism of the period before 200 CE. There probably are some works which should not have been included. On the other hand, provided readers of *OTP* are fully aware of the character of the late works and of the problems of detecting early Jewish material in such works, inclusiveness can well be regarded as a virtue. Widening horizons is always better than restricting them. Many of the apocalyptic 'newcomers' in *OTP* merit at least further study, which may or may not vindicate their relevance to the study of the New Testament and early Judaism. While the question remains open, it is better to have them brought into the limelight for a time rather than left

---

39. An equally well qualified candidate for inclusion might be the Tiburtine Sybil, on which see P.J. Alexander, *The Oracle of Baalbek: The Tiburtine Sibyl in Greek Dress* (Dumbarton Oaks Studies, 10; Washington, DC: Dumbarton Oaks Centre for Byzantine Studies, 1967); D. Flusser, 'An Early Jewish-Christian Document in the Tiburtine Sibyl', in A. Benoit, M. Philonenko and C. Vogel (eds.), *Paganisme, Judaisme, Christianisme: Mélanges offerts à Marcel Simon* (Paris: Boccard, 1978), pp. 153-83.

in the shadows where they have been until now.

The real problem is whether *OTP*, in selecting apocalyptic works other than those which because of their undoubtedly early date and Jewish character must be included, has not made a quite arbitrary selection. I have already pointed out several examples of works which are excluded, but whose claim to inclusion is at least as good as that of some works which have been included. The point should not be pressed too far, lest we be in danger of regarding the limits of the pseudepigrapha as another 'canon' to be fixed. Rather than discussing what the limits should be, it would be more profitable to establish that the pseudepigrapha must remain an open and fluid collection, not to be closed and fixed by *OTP* any more than it should have been by *APOT*. Once the limits of the Old Testament pseudepigrapha have been opened to include works which are not even probably Jewish works of the period before 200 CE, then the limits can never be closed again, because the range of such works which may to some degree depend on early Jewish sources or preserve early Jewish traditions is very large indeed, and scholarly judgments about them will always vary.

However, there is one issue which may make the very concept of a collection of Old Testament pseudepigrapha, as *OTP* has conceived it, less than useful. A collection of 'Old Testament pseudepigrapha' can hardly include the *Apocalypse of Peter*, the *Apocalypse of Paul*, the apocryphal *Apocalypse of John*, or a host of other Christian apocalypses bearing New Testament pseudonyms. Yet, as I have already pointed out above, such apocalypses are closely related to the Christian apocalypses which bear Old Testament pseudonyms, some of which are included in *OTP*. The distinction, which the concept of the 'Old Testament pseudepigrapha' forces, is quite foreign to the nature of the literature itself. Charlesworth's claim that the New Testament apocrypha 'only infrequently were shaped by early Jewish tradition' (*OTP*, p. xxvii) may be more true of other categories of New Testament apocrypha, but it is quite untrue of apocalypses. The impression (which *OTP* is bound to propagate) that a Christian apocalypse written under the name of Ezra or Daniel is, in some undefined sense, more 'Jewish' than one written under the name of Thomas or the Virgin Mary, is wholly misleading. Both classes of apocalypse are equally likely to preserve early Jewish apocalyptic material. Moreover, the two classes can only be adequately studied together, as one class, as well as in relation to older apocalyptic writings. It is a further danger of the concept of 'Old Testament pseudepigrapha' that it tends to encourage the study of relatively late works primarily by means of their affinities with earlier works, whereas they also need to be very thoroughly related to the historical and literary context to which, in their present form, they belong. It will not advance our understanding of the Christian apocalypses which bear Old Testament pseudonyms if, by their inclusion in the Old Testament pseudepigrapha, they are artificially extracted from their place in the broader tradition of Christian apocalyptic literature.[40]

I would suggest that the student of ancient Jewish apocalyptic, especially in the New Testament period, really needs to be acquainted with four bodies of literature, which for practical purposes can be distinguished as follows:

1. Apocalypses which were written or probably written before 200 CE, and which have suffered no more than minor editing at a later date. This category will include both Jewish works (*1 Enoch, 2 Enoch?, Sib. Or.* 3–5, 11, *Apocryphon of Ezekiel, Apocalypse of Elijah* fragments, '*Apocalypse of Zephaniah*', *4 Ezra, 2 Baruch, 3 Baruch, Apocalypse of Abraham, Ladder of Jacob*) and Christian works (New Testament *Apocalypse of John, Shepherd of Hermas, Ascension of Isaiah, Apocalypse of Peter, Sib. Or.* 1–2, 7–8, *5 Ezra*), since in this period at least Christian apocalyptic was still in very close contact with Jewish apocalyptic. (With the exception of *Sib. Or.* 12–14, it is probable that no Jewish apocalypses from after 200 CE have been preserved outside categories [3] and [4] below.)

2. Christian apocalypses, whether bearing Old Testament or New Testament pseudonyms or others (e.g. Methodius), written during the period from 200 CE to at least 1000 CE. This is a very large body of literature.

3. The Hebrew Merkabah texts written from c. 300 CE onwards (see Alexander's list in *OTP*, pp. 250-51).

4. The Hebrew apocalypses, such as the *Hebrew Apocalypse of Elijah*, the *Book of Zerubbabel*, the *Secrets of Rabbi Simon ben Yohai*.[41]

---

40. I do not mean here to exclude their possible relationship also to later Jewish apocalyptic. Later Christian and later Jewish apocalyptic probably developed with more cross-fertilization than is often recognized.

41. A convenient, if not wholly satisfactory, collection of translations is in G.W. Buchanan, *Revelation and Redemption* (Dillsboro, NC: Western North Carolina Press, 1978). See also the listing and description of some of the works in categories (3) and (4) in A.J. Saldarini, 'Apocalypses and "Apocalyptic" in Rabbinic Literature

The apocalyptic tradition should be envisaged as essentially a continuous stream, which after c. 200 CE divided into the three streams (2), (3) and (4), which from then on produced distinct bodies of literature (though they were not without influence on each other).[42] But because the tradition was essentially continuous and also notably conservative, preserving and at the same time constantly reusing and adapting earlier material, all three later branches of the tradition are capable of illuminating ancient apocalyptic. They may throw light on the meaning of ancient material, they may preserve ancient traditions and reflect the contents of ancient apocalypses which as such are no longer extant, they may even contain as yet unidentified ancient documents. Because the apocalyptic literature we have from the period before 200 CE has almost exclusively been passed down to us via stream (2), the Christian stream, we have tended to look especially to this stream for further light on ancient apocalyptic. Recently, the light which stream (3) can throw on ancient apocalyptic has begun to be appreciated. The contribution of stream (4) has as yet been scarcely explored at all. It should be stressed that all three later streams can only contribute reliably to the study of ancient apocalyptic if they are first of all understood in their own right, as literature of their own period. If they are simply plundered for parallels or scoured for ancient-looking material, serious mistakes are likely to be made.

In relation to this classification of apocalyptic literature, it can be seen that *OTP* tends to distort the picture: it does not even include all of (1); it includes a fairly arbitrary selection of (2), one example, not the earliest, of (3), and no examples of (4). Even this, however, is probably better than a very narrowly defined collection of ancient Jewish apocalypses. For students of ancient apocalyptic must be encouraged to acquaint themselves with the later phases of the tradition. Otherwise they will not be able to perform even such necessary tasks as assessing arguments for a late date for *2 Enoch* or for the *Parables of Enoch*, or assessing the extent of Christian editing in a work such as *3 Baruch*. They will therefore have to venture into many unfamiliar areas, such as Byzantine history or Merkabah mysticism or Bogomil religion or Ethiopian Christianity, and will have to rely heavily on specialists in such areas. But this simply highlights once again the necessarily cooperative and interdisciplinary nature of pseudepigraphal studies.

and Mysticism', *Semeia* 14 (1979), pp. 187-205.

42. Of course, further divisions occur within (2): Ethiopia, for example, has its own apocalyptic tradition.

Finally, it is worth pointing out that serious attention to the collection of apocalypses in *OTP*, for all its deficiencies, ought to change our common impressions of Jewish apocalyptic and its relationship to the New Testament. Used with proper discrimination for the light they can shed on Jewish apocalyptic in New Testament times, these documents bring to light a concern with a very wide range of apocalyptic revelations: tours of the seven heavens with their various meteorological, astronomical and angelological secrets; tours of hell and paradise; revelations of the secrets of the creation and the primeval history; visions of the glory of God and his worship in heaven; anguished demands for answers to problems of theodicy; as well as interpretation of history and the events of the last days. Most of these themes go back in some form as far as the early parts of *1 Enoch*, and scholars such as Stone[43] and Rowland[44] have pointed out how mistaken it is to see eschatology as the only or even in every case the central concern of Jewish apocalyptic. But the prominence of some of these topics in some of the later apocalypses helps to focus our attention more carefully on their presence in the earlier literature too. What we have still to take full account of is the fact that most of the concerns of Jewish apocalyptic in New Testament times do not appear in the New Testament writings. Heavily influenced by apocalyptic as primitive Christianity undoubtedly was, it was also highly selective in the aspects of apocalyptic which it took over. This is a fact about the New Testament which can only be appreciated by diligent study of pseudepigraphal works which do not look at all relevant to the New Testament!

BIBLIOGRAPHICAL ADDENDA

Since this article was first published, the following literature of special relevance to the discussion of individual apocalypses has appeared:

2 Enoch
Böttrich, C., 'Recent Studies in the *Slavonic Book of Enoch*', *JSP* 9 (1991), pp. 35-42.

Apocryphon of Ezekiel
Bauckham, R., 'Early Jewish Visions of Hell', *JTS* 41 (1990), pp. 355-85.
—'The Parable of the Royal Wedding Feast (Matthew 22.1-14) and the Parable of the Lame Man and the Blind Man (*Apocryphon of Ezekiel*)', *JBL* 115 (1996), pp. 447-64.

43. M.E. Stone, *Scriptures, Sects and Visions* (Oxford: Blackwell, 1982).
44. Rowland, *Open Heaven*.

—'A Quotation from *4Q Second Ezekiel* in the *Apocalypse of Peter*', *RevQ* 59 (1992), pp. 437-46.

Meuller, J.R., *The Five Fragments of the Apocryphon of Ezekiel* (JSPSup, 5; Sheffield: Sheffield Academic Press, 1995). See review by R. Bauckham in *JTS* 47 (1996), pp. 192-94.

Apocalypse of Zephaniah

Bauckham, R., 'The *Apocalypse of Peter*: A Jewish Christian Apocalypse from the Time of Bar Kokhba', *Apocrypha* 5 (1994), pp. 7-111.

—'Descent to the Underworld', *ABD*, II, pp. 145-59.

—'Visiting the Places of the Dead in the Extra-Canonical Apocalypses', *Proceedings of the Irish Biblical Association* 18 (1995), pp. 78-93.

4 Ezra

Bergren, T.A., *Fifth Ezra: The Text Origin and Early History* (SBLSCS, 25; Atlanta: Scholars Press, 1990).

Apocalypse of Sedrach

Bauckham, R., 'The Conflict of Justice and Mercy: Attitudes to the Damned in Apocalyptic Literature', *Apocrypha* 1 (1990), pp. 181-96.

Perentidis, S., 'La Jonction de l'*Apocalypse de Sedrach* avec l'*Homélie sur l'Amour* d'Ephrem', *JTS* 36 (1985), pp. 393-96.

Apocalypse of Elijah

Bauckham, R., 'Early Jewish Visions of Hell', *JTS* 41 (1990), pp. 355-85.

Frankfurter, D., *Elijah in Upper Egypt: The Apocalypse of Elijah and Early Egyptian Christianity* (Minneapolis: Fortress Press, 1993). See review by R. Bauckham in *JEH* 46 (1995), pp. 488-90.

JSNT 42 (1991), pp. 45-67

DAVID DAUBE ON THE EUCHARIST AND THE PASSOVER SEDER

Deborah Bleicher Carmichael

David Daube

The work of the biblical and legal scholar, David Daube, has not been disseminated widely because a sizeable number of his papers are scattered in many different journals, often in out-of-the-way publications. This article focuses on Daube's ideas on the links between the bread and wine of the Passover celebration and the bread and wine which Jesus interpreted at the Last Supper.

A brief biographical sketch is first in order. Daube was born in 1909 in Freiburg. From an early age, David and his older brother Benjamin studied Hebrew, Aramaic and Talmud with a tutor who lived with the family. By the time David completed gymnasium he had mastered Latin and Greek as well. He had also rejected the idea, so basic to the orthodox Judaism of his background, that the Pentateuch was written by Moses. This combination of linguistic sophistication and scepticism toward conventional ideas characterizes the vast and imaginative scholarly output of Daube's long career. He has repeatedly formulated new questions and broken through to new insights concerning ancient material in the fields of Roman, Greek, biblical and Talmudic law and the Jewish background of the New Testament.

Daube studied Roman law at the University of Freiburg and biblical law at the University of Göttingen where he received his doctorate. It was his Roman law teacher, Otto Lenel, who, in the late 1930s, sent Daube out of Nazi Germany to W.W. Buckland, the Regius Professor of Civil Law at Cambridge. Here Daube became a Fellow of Gonville and Caius and received a second doctorate in Roman law. He was a lecturer in law at Cambridge, 1946–1951. During that time he also participated in C.H. Dodd's New Testament Seminar. In 1951 he was appointed

Professor of Jurisprudence at Aberdeen. In 1955 he was made Regius Professor of Civil Law at Oxford where he was a Fellow of All Souls. In 1970 Daube took an unusual step and relinquished his Regius Professorship to become Professor-in-Residence and Director of the Robbins Hebraic and Canon Law Collections at the Law School of the University of California, Berkeley. In July, 1990, he received his ninth honorary doctorate from the University of Aberdeen. He continues to teach at the Berkeley Law School and holds a position as visiting Professor of History at the University of Konstanz, Germany.

A project is under way, supported by the Oxford Centre for Postgraduate Hebrew Studies, the Robbins Collection of the Law School of the University of California, Berkeley, and the Max Planck Institut für Rechtsgeschichte in Frankfurt, whereby Daube's over 200 papers are being compiled for republication in collected form.[1] One volume will include the articles in which Daube works out how the Jewish Passover Haggadah influenced writers of the Gospels, a theme to which he has returned again and again over the past fifty years.

The focus of this paper is how the symbolic meanings attached to a piece of unleavened bread and, possibly, to the cups of wine at Passover formed the context in which Jesus spoke what are known as 'the words of interpretation' over bread and wine at the Last Supper. Daube's work opens up new questions about ideas long held in both Jewish and Christian circles: ideas about the significance of a broken-off piece of unleavened bread known as the *afikoman* eaten at Passover; and ideas about the words spoken by Jesus over bread and wine at the Last Supper.

The Afikoman

Early on in the Passover Eve service (the Seder), before reciting the exodus story, the leader breaks off and puts aside a piece of unleavened bread known as the *afikoman*. In current practice, at the end of the meal, someone, often a child, brings the *afikoman* to the leader who divides it among the company. Ideas about the significance of this morsel have varied. A commonly held view is that it is a game of hide and seek

---

1. See now D. Daube, *Collected Studies in Roman Law* (2 vols.; ed. D. Cohen and D. Simon; Frankfurt am Main: Klostermann, 1991) and *Collected Works of Daube: Talmudic Law*, I (ed. C.M. Carmichael; Berkeley: Robbins Collection Publication, 1992).

played with children to keep them awake during a long evening.[2] It is also understood as meaning dessert because the *afikoman* is to be eaten as the last bit of food that evening. One custom is to keep a crumb of it as a good luck charm. In each of these interpretations the term *afikoman* refers to a piece of unleavened bread. But in another view the word *afikoman* is interpreted as an exhortation to members of the company not to go on to other festivities after celebrating the Passover.[3]

In 1925 Robert Eisler published the first part of an article on the Last Supper in *ZNW*.[4] He argued that the *afikoman* was part of a messianic ritual at Passover and thus constituted the background for the words which Jesus spoke over a piece of bread at the Last Supper. In what seems to have been an unusually vehement episode of scholarly jousting, the Christian scholar, H. Lietzmann, and the Jewish scholar, A. Marmorstein,[5] published papers in the 1926 issue of the journal intended to refute Eisler's views decisively. The second part of Eisler's article was published in the same issue.[6] Lietzmann, then editor of the journal (and in the same year author of a book on the Last Supper[7]), inserted a note to the readers in the 1927 issue in which he reported how he had given in to pressure from Eisler's lawyer to publish the second part of Eisler's article, despite his judgment that Eisler's work did not meet standards for scientific quality. Lietzmann refused to publish Eisler's response to the two articles criticizing his work, and announced that henceforth he would have no further professional dealings with Eisler.[8] For the next forty years Eisler's views lay dormant until, in 1966, David Daube re-argued the key points in a lecture entitled 'He That Cometh' given at St Paul's Cathedral under the auspices of the London Diocesan Council for Christian–Jewish Understanding.[9]

---

2. '*afikoman*', *EncJud* (Jerusalem: Keter, 1972), II, p. 330.

3. For these meanings, see C. Roth (ed.), *Haggadah* (London: Soncino, 1934), pp. viii, 15.

4. 'Das Letzte Abendmahl', *ZNW* 24 (1925), pp. 161-92.

5. Respectively, 'Jüdische Passahsitten und der *aphikomenos*', and 'Miscellen', *ZNW* 25 (1926), pp. 1-5, 249-58.

6. 'Das Letzte Abendmahl', *ZNW* 25 (1926), pp. 5-37.

7. *Messe und Herrenmahl* (Bonn: Marcus und Weber, 1926).

8. 'Erklärung des Herausgebers über sein Verhalten gegen Herrn Dr Robert Eisler', *ZNW* 26 (1927), p. 96.

9. *He That Cometh* (London: Diocesan Council, 1966). Ernst Bammel draws attention to another instance in which Eisler's ideas are taken up and re-argued, namely, in the work of S.G.F. Brandon: 'The Revolution Theory from Reimarus to

In the era before the destruction of the Second Temple in Jerusalem, the Passover celebration would have included a distinctly messianic component. Symbolic interpretations of the elements of the Seder were linked both with the dramatic rescue from Egypt and with hopes for final redemption in the future. Rabbinic literature preserves eschatological interpretations of various parts of the Seder: for example, the four cups of wine, the psalms sung before and after the meal, and a prayer recited toward the end of the service asking God to remember the messiah. Indeed the Passover eve itself was thought to be the very night when the people would again be redeemed by the messiah.[10] In certain circles, then, the Passover celebration of Jesus' time would have included expressions both of grateful reminiscences about past events and of fervent expectations for a messianic future. Incidentally, like Daube, Joachim Jeremias places the Last Supper and the meaning of Jesus' words within the context of Passover.[11] However, while Jeremias concludes that the Last Supper actually took place at a Passover Seder, Daube prefers to leave the question open.[12]

A number of symbolic meanings linked to the exodus story are attributed in the Bible, and in rabbinic and later commentary, to the unleavened bread eaten at Passover. It is the 'bread of affliction'[13] representing the harsh rule of Egyptian slavemasters. It is the 'bread of poverty' eaten by impoverished Israelites during their slavery. It is also bread baked in haste by a people in flight. The ancient Aramaic description of unleavened bread is *lahma' 'anya'*, 'poor, afflicted bread'. Here the bread itself is personified. This personification of the bread becomes interesting when we note that in some ancient texts the Jewish people themselves could be similarly represented. Paul uses the symbol of the

Brandon', in *idem* and C.F.D. Moule (eds.), *Jesus and the Politics of his Day* (Cambridge: Cambridge University Press, 1984), pp. 11-68.

10. For these interpretations, see J. Jeremias, *Die Abendmahlsworte Jesu* (Göttingen: Vandenhoeck & Ruprecht, 1960); ET, *The Eucharistic Words of Jesus* (London: Charles Scribner's Sons, 1966), pp. 59, 206, 252, 256-62; D. Daube, 'The Earliest Structure of the Gospels', *NTS* 5 (1959), p. 175.

11. *Words*, p. 1-88.

12. Daube, *He That Cometh*, p. 19 n. 42.

13. Daube discusses the relevance to the virgin birth of the rabbinic comments on this affliction: 'And [God] saw our affliction: this refers to the separation of man from wife, as it is said: "And God saw the children of Israel, and God knew"' (*The New Testament and Rabbinic Judaism* [London: Athlone Press, 1956], pp. 5-9). See D.C. Allison, *The New Moses* (Minneapolis: Fortress Press, 1993), pp. 146-50.

people as bread when he writes, 'Cleanse out the old leaven that you may be a fresh dough' (1 Cor. 5.7).[14]

Eisler and Daube argue that in a future-oriented, messianic sense, the unleavened bread stood for the whole of the Jewish people. A broken-off piece of bread represented a longed-for redeemer who had not yet appeared. During the Passover celebration of redemption, this messianic figure was symbolically brought into the midst of the company and united with the Jewish people through a ritual involving the *afikoman*.

Such a ritual may not have been widely practised. Passover celebrations were not standardized and could vary greatly around a central core of stable ideas. Today's Haggadah, a composite of stories, interpretations, prayers, songs and instructions for the evening, preserves an ancient practice that was not universally accepted when it was first introduced by Hillel, who lived a generation or so before Jesus. Hillel ate unleavened bread, bitter herbs and paschal lamb, the three key symbolic foods of Passover, all together rather than each separately. In the Talmud (*b. Pes.* 115a) Hillel's peers did not agree to this practice, but his followers imitated it in his memory, as is still done to this day. The ritual involving the *afikoman* probably also originated as the practice of a small group.

As early as the Middle Ages, from when we have the first written Haggadah, the ritual of the *afikoman* bridged most of the celebration and comprised two of the fifteen orders of the Seder.[15] At the fourth step, called *yahats* ('let him divide'), a piece of unleavened bread is broken in half, the larger portion of which is called the *afikoman*. After the meal, at the twelfth step, called *tsafun* ('that which is hidden'), the leader divides and distributes the *afikoman*, which is to be the last morsel of food eaten that evening. Daube thinks that a telling sign that these two steps were considered unconventional by the compilers of the Haggadah is that no blessing is recited over either one. Nor, incidentally, is a blessing recited over the food eaten in memory of Hillel. In matters of ritual, silence can be revealing. For example, it may indicate that the rite in question is regarded as out of the mainstream.

In the Haggadah, the word *afikoman*, when it appears in instructions to the leader, designates the broken-off piece of unleavened bread. In the body of the Haggadah itself, in the Hebrew text, the word appears only in the reply given to a question posed by a wise son who asks about all

14. For these symbolic meanings, see Roth, *Haggadah*, pp. vi, 34, 35; Daube, *He That Cometh*, p. 7.

15. Roth, *Haggadah*, p. 5.

the laws of Passover. Two sets of questions are asked by sons or disciples during the Seder. The first set, centred on unusual aspects of the Passover meal, begins with a question familiar even in popular culture: 'Why is this night different from all other nights?' The second set of more general questions is asked by four sons. The first son is wise—he wants to know about all the rules of Passover. The second son is wicked—he scornfully excludes himself from the company. The third son is simply pious—he wants to know the plain, basic meaning. And the fourth son does not know how to ask—so the leader must take the initiative. Incidentally, elsewhere, Daube demonstrates how the Gospel writer Mark structures the presentation of certain material on the basis of this section of the Haggadah.[16]

The concluding sentence of the brief reply to the wise son's question ends with the word *afikoman*. Scholars throughout the ages have found the sentence difficult to translate, particularly the word *afikoman*. The sentence reads: *'ayn maftirin 'achar hapesach 'afikoman*. Daube's comment is that

> It is untranslatable. It may mean that one should not finish up after the Passover lamb with the *Aphiqoman*, or on the contrary that one should not dismiss the *Aphiqoman* after the Passover lamb, or goodness knows what. However we interpret it, it is contrary to regular Hebrew-Aramaic syntax. No attempt to translate it as it stands can be said to have succeeded.[17]

What one can say is that whatever the sentence means—its meaning may well have been secret—the information was to be communicated to the wise son or disciple. Moreover, the significance attributed to the *afikoman* by the early rabbis stands in sharp contrast to the later notion that the *afikoman* simply refers to a game to keep children awake. By the way, wakefulness on Passover Eve was a topic of interest to the rabbis. They did, in fact, have strategies for keeping children awake, but none involved the *afikoman*.[18]

---

16. 'Earliest Structure', pp. 174-87.

17. *He That Cometh*, p. 9.

18. 'But we distribute to them [children] parched ears of corn and nuts on the eve of Passover, so that they should not fall asleep, and ask [the questions]' (*b. Pes.* 108b); 'It was related of R. Akiba that he used to distribute parched ears of corn and nuts to children on the eve of Passover, so that they might not fall asleep but ask [the questions]. It was taught, R. Eliezer said: The *matzoth* are eaten hastily on the night of Passover, on account of the children, so that they should not fall asleep' (*b. Pes.*

The Babylonian Talmud preserves a lengthy but difficult discussion of the question, 'What does *afikoman* mean?' (*b. Pes.* 119b). The rabbis are concerned with what should constitute the last bite of food eaten at the Passover meal. The agreed-upon answer is, 'an olive[-sized piece] of unleavened bread'. While they are strikingly silent about the significance of this morsel, they do clarify a number of possible uncertainties. For example, they rule out foods which might constitute a final course at a normal meal, savoury dishes such as mushrooms, pigeons, dates, parched ears of corn, and nuts. The rabbis emphasize that even if one eats sweet desserts at the end of the meal one must nevertheless finish with a small piece of unleavened bread which is eaten for reasons other than appetite.

The puzzling precept, *'ayn maftirin 'achar hapesach 'afikoman*, is found verbatim in the most ancient rabbinic texts: in the Mishnah (the earliest rabbinic codification of Jewish law),[19] in the Tosefta (a supplement to the Mishnah),[20] in the Mekhilta (an early commentary on Exodus),[21] in the Talmud,[22] and in the oldest sections of the Passover Haggadah.[23] The word *afikoman* seems to be Greek, but translators have by no means agreed on the Greek *Vorlage*. M. Jastrow bases his

---

109a); 'R. Eleazar said, "They toss unleavened bread to children so that they won't fall asleep". R. Judah says, "Even if one has eaten only one small savoury, even if he has dipped only one piece of lettuce, they still toss unleavened bread to children, so that they won't fall asleep"' (*t. Pisha* 10.9). It was the concern of the rabbis that the children stay awake in order to ask the questions, presumably those which initiate the telling and discussion of the exodus story. Questions are asked by children early in the Seder and the story of the exodus is recounted before the meal is eaten. The rabbis do not appear to be concerned that the children stay awake all evening, but only long enough to perform their role of asking questions. The *afikoman* is consumed much later in the evening, at the end of the meal, and does not appear to have played a part in rabbinic strategies for keeping children awake. No mention of *afikoman* is made in any of these texts. It appears that children could be given unleavened bread early on in the proceedings, even before it would have normally been eaten by the company as part of the Seder.

For Daube's views on the issue of wakefulness at Passover as it relates to the scene at Gethsemane between Jesus and the disciples who fall asleep, see *New Testament*, pp. 332-35.

19. *M. Pes.* 10.8.

20. *T. Pisha* 10.11.

21. *Mek. Pisha* on Exod. 13.14.

22. *B. Pes.* 119b.

23. J. Freedman, *Polychrome Historical Haggadah for Passover* (Springfield: Shapolsky, 1974), p. 26.

translation, 'after-dinner entertainment',[24] on *epikomon*. H. Danby, the translators of the Soncino Babylonian Talmud and H. Lietzmann, basing their translations on *epi komon*, interpret *afikoman* to mean, respectively, 'revelry',[25] an exhortation, 'off to the entertainment!',[26] and 'off to a crawl (*auf den Bummel*)'.[27] H. Strack and P. Billerbeck cite two meanings in Jewish tradition: 'festal song' based on *epikomion*, and 'dessert'. They formulate the problem: 'The meaning of the word *afikoman* was forgotten early on. Already the Tosephta understands the word as "the dessert". This erroneous explanation then held its sway throughout the entire period of Jewish antiquity.'[28] One might note that both the traditional and some modern translations of *afikoman* bear no relationship to the broken-off piece of unleavened bread which the term designates within the context of the Passover celebration. In offering his interpretation, Eisler comments that the word always designates a piece of bread in the Passover ritual.[29]

Daube, agreeing with Eisler, translates the word *afikoman* as straight-forwardly derived from the Greek *afikomenos*, which means 'The Coming One', or 'He that has come'. Daube argues that the term refers to an awaited redeemer who, symbolically united with his people, makes them whole as they contemplate their past, and future, redemption. He comments that, 'But for the theological and historical consequences that follow, it is hard to believe that this obvious, philologically easiest, *naheliegendste* derivation would have been overlooked in favour of the most far-fetched, tortuous ones'.[30]

It seems that a ritual involving the *afikoman* was preserved but over time its meaning was, perhaps even deliberately, distorted. Already the discussions in the Babylonian Talmud, which purport explicitly to explain the meaning of *afikoman*, while detailed, are at best cryptic. Even so, an

24. '*afikoman*', in *Dictionary of the Targumim, the Talmud Babli and Yerushalmi, and the Midrashic Literature* (New York: Pardes Publishing House, 1950), p. 104.

25. H. Danby, *The Mishnah* (Oxford: Oxford University Press, 1933), p. 151.

26. *B. Pes.* 119b.

27. Lietzmann, 'Passahsitten', p. 4.

28. H. Strack and P. Billerbeck, *Kommentar zum Neuen Testament aus Talmud und Midrasch* (Munich: Beck, 1928), IV.1, p. 73.

29. 'Das Letzte Abendmahl' (1925), pp. 174-75. Roth (*Haggadah*, pp. 15, 44) gets around the problem in a curious way. He claims that the use of the word in the answer to the wise son, and the use in reference to the broken-off piece of unleavened bread, 'though derived from the same Greek words, mean something totally different'.

30. *He That Cometh*, p. 8.

aura of specialness about this fragment of unleavened bread shows up in these discussions. Such an aura has also been preserved in various folk traditions. For example, it is thought to bring good luck, longevity, protection from evil and safe childbirth. A custom close to the meaning argued by Eisler and Daube is one in which a member of the family ties the *afikoman* to his shoulder and visits neighbours to herald the coming of the messiah.[31]

How could such an important idea have been lost? It seems likely that as Christianity emerged from Judaism, Jewish ideas which had been taken up and developed by the followers of Jesus were played down or even suppressed by Jewish authorities. The notion that a human being could perform the divine function of redemption came to be eliminated from the Jewish community's annual meditation upon redemption.[32] For example, the figure of Moses is absent from the prayers, stories and biblical passages of the Passover Haggadah. Daube comments, 'What a *tour de force*: to weave legends, prayers, hymns around the Exodus without once making mention of the figure that dominates the biblical account'; and 'Think what it means. It is as if one were to spend annually a night commemorating Britain's rescue in the Second World War, rehearsing the main course of events as well as telling elaborate stories about them, without once mentioning Churchill.'[33]

The Last Supper and the Afikoman

With his view that a messianic ritual involving a piece of unleavened bread was a significant aspect of Passover, Daube turns his attention to the Last Supper. That meal is portrayed in the Synoptic Gospels as having taken place in a Passover setting. The participants would all have been familiar with the rituals and symbols of the festival. Matthew writes, 'Jesus took the bread, and blessed, and broke it, and gave it to the disciples and said, "Take, eat; this is my body"' (Mt. 26.26). Daube argues

31. '*afikoman*', *EncJud*, II, p. 330.

32. For Daube's discussion of the rabbinic views that the Israelites were redeemed by the personal action of God and not by the action of a messenger (or, in some variant texts, 'the messenger', namely, Jesus), see *New Testament*, pp. 325-29.

33. Respectively, 'The Significance of the *Afikoman*', *Pointer* (London, 1968), p. 5; and *He That Cometh*, p. 12. See also *New Testament*, pp. 170-95, for Daube's views on how the sequence of events at the Seder was altered to suppress open-ended questioning and discussion so that Christian ideas did not enter the Passover service.

that the context of Jesus' words is the ritual involving the *afikoman*. If we accept his proposition, we are in a position to explain two puzzling elements of the scene. How could a piece of bread be understood as standing for a person? And why were the disciples not shocked at the apparent crudity of the language? According to Daube, the disciples are likely to have been familiar with a ritual in which a piece of bread did indeed stand for a person, namely, the messiah. They would have understood Jesus to be associating himself with a messianic symbol which was eaten as part of a Passover meal.

If we had never before heard Jesus' words, and if we put aside the interpretations with which we are familiar, we would find his words bewildering, even shocking in their suggestion of cannibalism. Yet those who heard the words were given no explanation. Jesus does not explain his interpretation of the bread as extensively as he does his interpretation of the wine. If he were referring to the *afikoman*, his words over the bread, 'This is my body' (in Aramaic he could have said, 'This is me'), would have conveyed a message of self-revelation. The messiah with whom this Passover company had on previous occasions united itself symbolically by eating a piece of unleavened bread had, in Jesus, actually arrived.[34]

34. Daube ties the meaning of the *afikoman* more closely to the ancient Passover celebration than does Eisler. While Eisler expands rather lavishly on symbolic ideas about, for example, bread, or the middle *matsah* called the Levite, Daube is more restrained in his argumentation. Daube, moreover, addresses himself directly to possible counter-arguments, such as why the unusual term *afikomenos* would have been used instead of the more common *erchomenos*, or the fact that in some Talmudic passages a piece of lamb, not a piece of bread, was to be the last bite of the Passover meal. Eisler might appear to recognize problems in his own line of reasoning—for example, he comments that there is no Talmudic evidence for the classification of the three *matsoth* as representing the estates Kohen, Levi, and Israel ('Das Letzte Abendmahl' [1925], p. 163 n. 3)—but he goes on to develop his argument, in which he relates the *afikoman* to the three classifications, as though the problem did not exist.

Daube adds a number of points not found in Eisler's discussion: the observation that New Testament accounts of the Last Supper presuppose a ritual wherein a piece of bread is eaten as the messiah; indications of the Hellenized setting in which such a ritual might have developed; the esoteric nature of the ritual with its parallel in Hillel's unique way of eating unleavened bread; the unsuitability of responding to the wise son's question with a precept about the *afikoman* if the term refers simply to a trivial meal custom or a children's game; the unlikelihood that a Christian practice might have influenced a Jewish one; and the warning not to look for an exact parallel

Daube points out that there is another instance in which a Gospel writer uses the breaking of bread as the action by which Jesus reveals his identity.[35] Properly understood, the action can shed light on the mystical encounter on the road to Emmaus in Luke 24. On the first day of the week after his crucifixion Jesus encounters two of his followers, neither of whom was present at the Last Supper. He walks and speaks with them but they do not recognize him. Nevertheless they invite him to their village. They remain unaware of the identity of their guest until, 'When he was at the table with them, he took the bread and blessed, and broke it, and gave it to them. And their eyes were opened and they recognized him; and he vanished out of their sight' (Lk. 24.30-31). In reporting their encounter to the disciples in Jerusalem, the men state explicitly that 'he was known to them in the breaking of the bread' (Lk. 24.35). Here, as at the Last Supper, Jesus' identity is disclosed, this time in his resurrected state, by an act involving bread.

In Luke, Jesus offers no comment on the bread as he had done at the Last Supper, but the men comprehend his meaning immediately. Such ready understanding is puzzling—how does Jesus come to be associated with the breaking of bread so unmistakably so that no comment is necessary? Some scholars propose that the men recognized Jesus because, when he blessed and broke the bread, he did so in a way that was uniquely characteristic of him, or familiar to those who had seen him perform the miracle of the loaves and fishes.[36] But Jesus was not the only Jew in Israel to bless, break and distribute bread at mealtime. Such an act would have been customary. Why should the act be uniquely characteristic or emblematic of one individual, Jesus? Daube suggests that 'What enlightened them was his repetition—maybe slightly modified—of the self-revelation, "This is my body"'.[37]

We might pursue the matter further. Another element built into Luke's account may have contributed to the context within which the men correctly interpreted the actions of their guest. Although the meal was

between the ritual involving the *afikoman* and the Eucharist because of the fluidity of Passover practices in antiquity.

35. *Wine in the Bible* (London: Diocesan Council, 1974), p. 14.

36. For example, A. Plummer, *The Gospel according to St Luke* (ICC; Edinburgh: T. & T. Clark, 5th edn, 1901), p. 557; N. Geldenhuys, *Commentary on the Gospel of Luke* (London: Marshall, Morgan & Scott, 1950), p. 635; and J.M. Creed, *The Gospel according to St Luke* (London: Macmillan, 1930), p. 297.

37. *Wine*, p. 14.

an ordinary one, the setting had Passover features. The encounter took place during the week of Passover. Moreover, it was the stranger, not the host, who pronounced the blessing, then broke and distributed the bread. Such an initiative on the part of a guest would have gone against customary meal practice in which it was the host's responsibility to bless, break and distribute bread.[38] An honoured guest might be asked to say the grace after the meal, or might be permitted to be the first to take food,[39] but in Luke the stranger is accorded neither of these two honours. The guest, Jesus, does take the remarkable step of assuming the role of the host in a home that was not his.

There is, however, a situation in which his action would not be unusual. At Passover, if a distinguished teacher were part of the company, he would lead the Seder instead of the host.[40] In such a circumstance a guest could indeed take bread, bless, break and distribute it in place of the host. In Luke's episode, before sitting down to the meal, the stranger had clearly assumed the role of a teacher during the walk with his fellow travellers: 'And beginning with Moses and all the prophets, he interpreted to them in all the scriptures the things concerning himself' (Lk. 24.27).[41] Here, then, three men gathered for a meal during the week of Passover. The one who had demonstrated his superior learning had also appropriated the host's role and presided over the meal, as could well occur in a Passover setting. In so doing, Jesus assumed the same role as the one he had at the recent meal in Jerusalem, thereby setting the stage for his re-enactment of the central feature of that meal—the messianic ritual involving the piece of bread.

The two men knew of the events surrounding the crucifixion, though they had not attended the Last Supper. Earlier they had asked the stranger, 'Are you the only visitor to Jerusalem who does not know the things that have happened there these days?' (Lk. 24.18). It is a distinct possibility that the two men's knowledge of events extended to the events at the Last Supper, including Jesus' memorable pronouncement over the bread, his self-disclosure as the messiah. Now, at their own

---

38. Strack and Billerbeck, *Kommentar*, I, p. 687.

39. *B. Ber.* 46a, 47a.

40. Daube, 'Earliest Structure', p. 174.

41. 'The things concerning himself' cannot mean that the stranger, Jesus, referred to himself directly. It is more likely that he would have spoken in the third person of the messiah, as Lk. 24.26 indicates: 'Was it not necessary that the Christ should suffer these things and enter into his glory?' Cf. Lk. 24.44-46.

table, at a meal reminiscent of Passover, Jesus again performed the ritual which, certainly since the Last Supper, meant to his followers that the messiah was present—hence the men's recognition. There is a sense in which what Jesus did on this occasion was the first re-enactment of the Last Supper. Might this particular pericope in Luke have been written to explain and justify the institutionalization of the memorial rite? Since the master himself had repeated the act, all the more should his followers do so.

Melito of Sardis

Further linguistic evidence supports Daube's understanding of *afikoman* as the messianic 'He who has come'. This evidence originates in the time when Jewish and Christian religious practices were not yet disentangled. A Christian group known as the Quartodecimans continued to celebrate Passover alongside the Jews. Jeremias has gone into the matter. While the Jews ate the Passover meal, the Christian group fasted. During their fast they read and discussed the story of the exodus (Exod. 12). At about 3 a.m. the fast was broken with the meal and the celebration of the Eucharist. In Jeremias's description of the Quartodeciman rite we might note how close he comes to describing a ritual reminiscent of the one suggested by Daube. Jeremias writes:

> The unusual time of this celebration itself shows what the emphasis was at this early Christian passover: the primary concern was neither with the remembrance of the passion nor with the remembrance of the resurrection, but with the expectation of the Parousia! That the messiah would come on the night of passover was both a Jewish and a Christian hope. Each year, therefore, during the passover night the primitive community awaited until midnight, in prayer and fasting, for the return of the Lord. They prolonged the waiting into the hours after midnight. If he had not come bodily by cock-crow, then they united themselves with him in the celebration of table fellowship.[42]

A Quartodeciman manuscript called *Peri Pascha*, written by the second-century bishop of Sardis, Melito, was discovered in the 1930s. By 1960 the text was regarded by scholars such as F.L. Cross as 'nothing less than a Christian Passover Haggadah'.[43] In his translation and analysis

---

42. *Words*, p. 123.
43. *Early Christian Fathers* (London: Duckworth, 1960), p. 107.

of *Peri Pascha*, S.G. Hall divides the text into two sections.[44] The first section corresponds to a reading and discussion of Exodus 12. In this first section the author, Melito, works out a comparison between Jesus and the paschal lamb. In the second half of the text, Hall identifies specific parallels between the structure of *Peri Pascha* and the Passover exposition outlined in the Mishnah (*m. Pes.* 10). The parallels which Hall identifies include: a tale which, as the Mishnah requires, 'begins with the disgrace and ends with the glory'; the symbolic use of unleavened bread and bitter herbs; and ideas about God's personal presence and deeds on earth. Also, this second section of the text begins with a question, 'What is the Pascha?', just as the questions begin the tale of the exodus story in the Haggadah. But most interesting for the purposes of Daube's argument is a striking linguistic parallel. Melito uses the word *afikomenos* twice, in both instances to refer to Jesus as the messiah who has come. Hall comments, '*afikomenos* may allude to the Passover *afikoman*'.[45]

Bread and Wine as Symbols of Sacrificial Death

If we understand Jesus' words spoken over bread at the Last Supper not in the light of his death, but rather in terms of the *afikoman* at the time of the meal, we have to distinguish sharply the words spoken over the wine from those spoken over the bread. Jesus' words over wine in Matthew's text are, 'Drink of it all of you; for this is my blood of the covenant which is poured out for many for the forgiveness of sins'

44. *Melito of Sardis on Pascha and Fragments* (Oxford: Clarendon Press, 1979); see also his 'Melito in Light of the Passover Haggadah', *JTS* NS 22 (1971), pp. 29-46. There is also a critical edition of the text in B. Lohse, *Die Passa-Homilie des Bischofs Meliton von Sardes* (Leiden: Brill, 1958).

45. *Melito*, p. 35 n. 32. Hall makes his comment because of a suggestion by M. Werner ('Melito of Sardis, the First Poet of Deicide', *HUCA* 37 [1966], pp. 205-206) that *afikoman* in the Melito text is to be understood as meaning 'guest'. Werner overlooked the unmistakable messianic context of the *Peri Pascha* in which *afikomenos* does not refer simply to a guest, but specifically to Jesus as messiah. In his note Hall, without comment, refers the reader to Daube's *He That Cometh*.

J. Blank in his critical edition, *Meliton von Sardes Vom Passa* (Freiburg im Breisgau: Lambertus, 1963), gives translations of *afikomenos* comparable to Hall's: 'Dieser kam vom Himmel auf die Erde' (p. 118); 'Dieser ist der zu dir kam' (p. 124). Blank does not make a link to the Passover Haggadah, but he nonetheless comments, 'Bei Meliton schwingt stark das Moment der "Ankunft" (*aphikomenos*) Christi auf Erden mit' (p. 73).

(Mt. 26.27-28). The distinction between the words over bread and those over the wine can be a difficult one to maintain because from the earliest writing after the crucifixion, namely Paul's, the bread and wine appear to be interpreted together as signifying Jesus' death. Paul's is the predominant view in liturgical and scholarly writings to this day. He wrote, 'For as often as you eat this bread and drink the cup, you proclaim the Lord's death until he comes' (1 Cor. 11.26). One can understand how, from the earliest attempts at interpretation, the events of Jesus' last days were understood in these terms. His death alone must have been a watershed in the light of which the past would forever be viewed.

Jeremias remarks, 'Of all the influences of the liturgical usage on the text the most enduring was…the tendency to make parallel the word over the bread and the word over the cup'.[46] The problems that arise when the single idea of death is linked to both symbols of Passover must not be obscured. A problem might not appear to arise in the comparison of wine to blood. Words associating wine with blood do occur in biblical texts,[47] and might plausibly reflect anticipation of a violent death. One ought, however, to be puzzled by the idea, expressed so clearly in Matthew's text, that the wine, standing for blood, should be drunk rather than, say, poured out. For example, sacrificial blood from the paschal lamb would not have been drunk (not that there is any suggestion that the wine at the Seder ever represented the blood of the paschal lamb). One might wonder why the disciples were not shocked at the thought of drinking Jesus' blood. They had not been shocked at the thought of eating his body because there was a ritual in which a person was indeed symbolically eaten.[48]

The idea that unleavened bread could signify sacrificial death is problematic. The difficulty arises because unleavened bread was not associated with death or sacrifice in the tradition. Even so, Paul seems to formulate the link explicitly: 'For as often as you eat this bread and drink the cup, you proclaim the Lord's death until he comes' (1 Cor. 11.26). Jeremias attempts a line of reasoning to explain the shared symbolism of

46. *Words*, p. 114.
47. Gen. 49.11; Deut. 32.14; Isa. 63.3, 6.
48. For Daube's discussion of the comment in *b. Sanh*. 98b, 99a that there will be no messiah for Israel since they already enjoyed, literally ate, him in the days of Hezekiah, see *He That Cometh*, p. 2. E. Bammel attributes this comment to the Hillel of around 15 BCE and not to the Hillel of around 300 CE, 'Das Wort vom Apfelbäumchen', *NovT* 5 (1962), pp. 219-28.

bread and wine in terms of sacrificial death. He proposes that the words of interpretation at the Last Supper represent the second time during the Seder that the disciples heard Jesus give interpretations of Passover food. The first time would have been earlier in the evening, during the recital of the Haggadah, when it was required to explain unleavened bread, paschal lamb and bitter herbs in terms of the exodus from Egypt. Jeremias argues that in the second round of interpretations, namely, the words recorded in the Gospels, Jesus interprets the bread and the wine in terms of himself as a sacrifice. By speaking of bread as flesh and wine as blood, Jesus would have had in mind the flesh and blood that are separated when an animal such as the paschal lamb is slaughtered for sacrifice.

Jeremias maintains,

> Jesus had prepared the way for this comparison of himself with the sacrifice earlier, in the passover meditation... Since he [Jesus] interpreted the bread and wine in terms of himself...it is a likely assumption that in the preceding passover devotions he had also interpreted the passover lamb in terms of himself.[49]

If Jesus had indeed linked his own fate to that of the Passover lamb the comparison, in his terms, would have made sense. One wonders why, then, given the aptness of that comparison, Jesus would employ a less appropriate symbol, unleavened bread, to convey the same sacrificial message? Even Jeremias has to postulate a prior statement, in which Jesus would have used the more appropriate symbol of the paschal lamb, to establish a context within which Jesus' statement over bread could be interpreted in terms of death. Such arguments are unnecessary in the light of the role of the *afikoman*—it signified, not self-surrender, but self-revelation.[50]

---

49. *Words*, p. 222. Jeremias argues against a view found, for example, in R. Otto (*Reich Gottes und Menschensohn* [Munich: Beck, 1934]; ET, *The Kingdom of God and the Son of Man* [London: Lutterworth, 1943], pp. 296, 300, 302), that the significance of Jesus' use of the bread lies in the action of breaking it (*Words*, pp. 220-21). Contrary to Otto, Jeremias affirms that the Last Supper was a Passover meal. He observes that 'The interpretation of the special elements in the Jewish passover rite, which was the precedent for the form of Jesus' words of interpretation, is not concerned with any actions, but with the components of the meal themselves' (p. 221). He also observes that the early church had from the beginning understood Jesus to be referring to the bread and wine, not to any actions associated with them.

50. Interestingly, a few years before Eisler published 'Das Letzte Abendmahl', in

By demonstrating how the words over the bread and the words over the wine are rooted in quite different sections of the Passover Haggadah, Daube is able to tease out distinctions lost to the retrospective view as first expressed by Paul. In his second St Paul's Cathedral lecture in 1974 ('Wine in the Bible') he turns his attention to the wine. He considers, but rejects as too negative, proposals made by some scholars that wine was an unnecessary element of the ritual commemorating the Last Supper, or that Jesus might have attributed no particular importance to the wine. Daube does, however, notice a number of details which point to a different, indeed lesser, significance for the wine.

Daube analyses textual variations where wine is mentioned, where it is not mentioned, and where the requirements for commemorative action with bread and wine differ. In Luke (22.19a), the shorter variant reading of the words of interpretation does not mention wine at all. Jesus only comments on the bread, 'This is my body'. This shorter variant, moreover, does not include a prescription that bread be eaten in Jesus' memory. In the longer variant of the Lukan text (22.19b), Jesus does prescribe commemorative action, but again only for the bread, 'This is my body which is given for you. Do this in remembrance of me.' In this longer variant, Jesus does comment on the cup, 'This cup which is poured out for you is the new covenant in my blood' (Lk. 22.20), but the text does not include a requirement that wine be drunk in his memory.

Paul's version of the words of interpretation also differentiates between the bread and the wine. Paul recounts Jesus' prescription that bread should be eaten in his memory with the words, 'Do this in remembrance of me' (1 Cor. 11.24). The wording of Jesus' prescription that wine should be drunk in his memory is 'Do this, as often as you drink it, in remembrance of me' (1 Cor. 11.25). The formulation 'as often as you drink it' in 1 Corinthians, and the absence of any mention of commemorative drinking of wine in either of the two Lukan variants, suggest to

---

an article titled 'Jesus and the Blood-Sacrifice' (*The Quest: A Quarterly Review* 12.1 [1920], pp. 230-43), he argued that Jesus was among those who opposed sacrificial worship in the Temple. His argument led him to speculate, 'If we remember that Jesus certainly symbolized the impending sacrifice of the "suffering" Messiah's body and blood, not by any of the well-known Pauline allusions to the sacrifice of the passover-lamb, but simply by breaking a piece of unleavened bread and pouring out for his disciples a cup of wine, it becomes quite possible that really no passover-lamb was served on the table of the Last Supper' (p. 242). I am grateful to Dr E. Bammel for drawing my attention to this article.

Daube that there were times when either wine was not part of early Christian celebrations or its use was optional.[51]

After Jesus' death, when meal gatherings of his followers are depicted in early sources such as Acts (2.42, 46; 20.7), only bread is mentioned. Although wine may have been part of a meal that is described in the texts simply as 'breaking bread', wine receives no explicit mention in these passages. Surely had the wine played an important role in the memorial rite it would have been mentioned too. In two instances when Jesus reveals himself in his resurrected state, in the Lukan episode about the encounter on the road to Emmaus, and in an episode involving James the Just from the *Gospel according to the Hebrews* 8, Jesus discloses his identity through the medium of breaking bread—again wine has no part in either scene.

Daube explains the lack of centrality of wine in terms of the Passover Seder. Wine had a secondary significance at Passover. It was not unique to that festival but was used at other festivals as well. Rabbi Gamaliel (Paul's teacher) required that three of the foods eaten at Passover must be interpreted, namely, paschal lamb, unleavened bread and bitter herbs. There was no obligation to interpret the wine and, unlike unleavened bread, no time was set aside for comments to be made about wine. And certainly no rite such as that of the *afikoman*, the Coming One, existed with respect to the wine.

The evidence that suggests a secondary role for wine both in the Seder and in the New Testament might have some bearing on the significance of the wine at the Last Supper. The words spoken over the bread are reported with greater consistency than those spoken over the wine. The wine was given a lengthier explanation in each account of the Last Supper than the words over the bread. Since the symbolic meaning of bread would have been well understood, it required less of an explanation. Not so for the wine: more had to be said to establish and define its symbolic significance, and there was greater room for variation in its interpretation. Daube comments, 'A degree of uncertainty as to the wine

---

51. The two statements about bread and wine in 1 Cor. 11.24 and 25 ('Do this...') constitute Jesus' requirement for certain commemorative acts. The next sentence in 1 Cor. 11.26 ('For as often as you eat this bread and drink the cup, you proclaim the Lord's death until he comes') constitutes, by contrast, an interpretation of those commemorative acts, whenever they are performed. This sentence cannot be used as evidence that both bread and wine were always to be used together in commemorative rituals.

should be expected', and 'An utterance of Jesus' about the wine could be longer in taking root in the celebration and be subject to more varied treatment'.[52]

The idea that Jesus' words over wine are to be interpreted in terms of his death is accepted by Daube.[53] He also believes, as does Jeremias, that the words and ideas relating to bread and wine were made parallel. Daube sees a distinction between form and substance. In substance, the meaning of Jesus' words over bread, his self-revelation as messiah, became absorbed in the light of his crucifixion into the meaning of his words over wine, that is, his sacrificial death. In reverse fashion, the form of Jesus' words over the wine took on the form of his statement over the bread.

Where does this overview lead? An attempt has been made to discern in the various accounts of the Last Supper what Jesus might actually have intended when he interpreted bread and wine in terms of himself. A number of problems arise with the understanding of the bread and the wine as synonymous symbols of self-sacrifice. Unleavened bread was not associated with death nor with sacrificial symbolism. If we accept the argument that there was a ritual whereby a piece of unleavened bread represented the messiah who, as a broken-off portion of the Jewish people, was symbolically united with them during the Passover celebration, the notion that a piece of bread could stand for Jesus makes sense. With his words over bread he declared that the symbolic messiah was now actually present in his own person.

The words over the cup of wine are more difficult. Wine, described in biblical texts as the blood of grapes, can have a symbolic meaning as blood. Jesus, by making the comparison, might actually have talked of sacrificing his life. But there is a problem in asking his followers to drink the wine as his blood. Surely the idea is an alarming one. There is no

52. *Wine*, pp. 14, 15. Eisler takes up the wine in his second (1926) article, 'Das Letzte Abendmahl'. His interpretation of the wine is dependent upon links he makes between a blessing over wine in the *Didache*, where there is a reference to the vine of David, and Psalm 80, which Eisler thinks was interpreted messianically in Jesus' day. To Eisler, Jesus' words over the wine conveyed, among other ideas, a messianic self-revelation similar to the one in his words over the bread. Daube does not accept Eisler's views on wine (*He That Cometh*, p. 14).

53. In *New Testament*, pp. 330-31, and *Wine*, pp. 18-20, Daube discusses the Passover-related context of Jesus' vow to drink no wine until his 'father's kingdom' (Mt. 26.29), or until the 'kingdom of God' (Mk 14.25): Jesus postpones drinking the fourth cup of the Seder, which in the Haggadah celebrates the kingdom of God.

indication that there was a ritual, comparable to that of the *afikoman*, in which wine was drunk as blood.

Might the overall position be as follows? The self-revelation of Jesus as the messiah in the ritual of the *afikoman* was the central feature of the Last Supper. The new thing that he did with the *afikoman*, namely, declaring that the Coming One had come, was so profound that it invited memorialization after his death. With regard to the wine, Jesus himself did not in fact pronounce words of interpretation over it. However, his death influenced mightily the interpretation of events at the Last Supper. It was because of his death that the wine was brought into prominence and, because of its association with blood, was given sacrificial signifi-cance. The shocking element in the drinking of wine as blood—Daube does not address this point—arose inadvertently because that act was modelled upon the act of eating bread as Jesus' body, a notion which we saw as intelligible in the light of Jewish practice. The sacrificial meaning attributed to the wine in turn was transferred to the bread. Such was the power of this idea of sacrificial death, and such was the extent of the mutual influence of ideas relating to bread and wine, that the original use of these symbols by Jesus was transformed.

JSNT 38 (1990), pp. 13-27

THE SABBATH IN THE SYNOPTIC GOSPELS

Herold Weiss

New Testament scholarship has not achieved a consensus on Jesus' attitude toward the Sabbath. Whether by his actions he actually broke the Sabbath commandment remains a matter of dispute, even if, as R.E. Brown has said,[1] 'that Jesus violated the rules of the scribes for the observance of the Sabbath is one of the most certain of historical facts about his ministry'. Most studies have argued that he openly challenged what is designated as 'Jewish Sabbath observance' and some have further argued that by doing so he had declared the 'Jewish Law' obsolete.[2] This paper attempts to show that the evidence on the Sabbath in the Synoptic materials does not support this contention. To the contrary, the traditions preserved in the Synoptics[3] make clear that the early Christians who followed Jesus took for granted the validity of the Sabbath law. What the stories in the Synoptics show us is that they continued to debate which activities were permissible on the Sabbath. This basic observation, it will be suggested, could help us to refine the typologies we use for the reconstruction of early Christianity.

The kind of review of the Synoptic materials attempted here inevitably raises questions as to how what is of interest to us at the moment

1. R.E. Brown, *The Gospel according to John* (AB, 29; Garden City, NY: Doubleday, 1966), I, p. 210.

2. H. Braun, *Jesus of Nazareth: The Man and his Times* (Philadelphia: Fortress Press, 1979), pp. 58-61; W. Rordorf, *Sunday* (Philadelphia: Westminster Press, 1968), pp. 62-63; E. Stauffer, 'Neue Wege der Jesusforschung', in *Gottes ist der Orient* (Berlin: Töpelmann, 1959), p. 167; S. Schulz, *Die Stunde der Botschaft: Einführung in die Theologie der vier Evangelisten* (Hamburg: Furche, 1967), p. 85; E. Schweizer, *Good News according to Mark* (Richmond, VA: Knox, 1970), p.40.

3. For an analysis of the evidence in John, see H. Weiss, 'The Sabbath in the Fourth Gospel', *JBL* 110 (1991), pp. 311-21.

relates to other issues which are of particular interest to individual Gospels. My study will not altogether avoid dealing with some items in the agendas of single Gospels, but the focus will be on the question being asked.

I

Before we conduct an examination of the Sabbath in the Synoptic materials, it may be useful to set out the methodological constraints that have informed this issue thus far. Ever since Bultmann classified the controversy dialogues as apophthegms, the narrative elements of these pericopes have been understood as 'imaginary scenes'. He explained quite well what was methodologically involved in this by stating:

> We must keep away at first from the question whether Jesus sometimes healed on the Sabbath day, or whether he used a certain saying which we find in a Controversy Dialogue in a discussion with his opponents. Of course it is quite possible that he did; indeed, very probable; but the first question to be asked, methodologically speaking, must be about the literary form of the controversy dialogue, and its origin as a literary device. This is simply the question about the *Sitz im Leben*, which is not concerned with the origin of a particular report of a particular historical happening, but with the origin and affinity of a certain literary form in and with typical situations and attitudes of a community.[4]

Bultmann located the *Sitz im Leben* of the controversy dialogues about the Sabbath in the apologetic and polemical activities of the Palestinian church. Those who have accepted Bultmann's methodological limitation have also accepted his conclusion, with the exception of A. Hultgren, as will become clear below.

Since Bultmann's work, however, there has been no lack of those who have been asking the historical rather than the formal question. But their efforts and their conclusions have been uneven.

E. Lohse argued that the only report that could claim historical validity was the healing of the man with the withered hand at the synagogue.[5] But W. Rordorf defends the authenticity of the report of the conduct of Jesus' disciples in the wheat field.[6] M.J. Borg, after pointing out the difficulties connected with the appeal to David's conduct in this particular

4. R. Bultmann, *History of the Synoptic Tradition* (Oxford: Blackwell, 1963), p. 40.

5. E. Lohse, 'Jesu Worte über den Sabbat', in W. Eltester (ed.), *Judentum, Urchristentum und Kirche* (Berlin: Töpelmann, 1960), p. 85.

6. Rordorf, *Sunday*, pp. 60-67.

episode, as well as with the Markan Sabbath controversies generally, insisted that the story reflects 'an actual historical occurrence rather than...the imaginary faculty of the community'.[7] D. Flusser considered Jesus' Sabbath activities as permissible under the law, arguing that his healings were done by the power of the word and thus no law was broken.[8] To this G. Vermes countered that, in at least one case, Jesus did touch the sick person to effect the healing (Lk. 13.10-17).[9] A.E. Harvey and E.P. Sanders, on the other hand, reaffirmed that the stories of healing on the Sabbath reveal no instance in which Jesus transgressed the Sabbath law, since the imposition of the hand is not work.[10] H. Maccoby argued that the Pharisees specifically allowed healing on the Sabbath. Therefore Jesus' Sabbath conflicts must have been with the Sadducees or the Essenes, who had stricter views on Sabbath observance.[11]

Some have argued that Jesus by his conduct was reinterpreting the significance of the Sabbath law. Borg argued that Jesus was showing his preference for deeds of mercy over the personal quest for holiness.[12] Banks saw the issue as one of authority, rather than one of legality. Commenting specifically about the incident in the wheat field, he said that by defending the conduct of his disciples Jesus was not in open opposition to the law, but pointing out the overriding importance of the mission of the disciples.[13] H.C. Kee, however, considered that emphasizing the importance of the disciples' mission was the intent of the editor of Mark, rather than that of Jesus.[14] C.K. Barrett, commenting on

---

7. M.J. Borg, *Conflict, Holiness, and Politics in the Teachings of Jesus* (SBEC, 5; New York: Mellen, 1984), p. 152.

8. D. Flusser, *Jesus* (New York: Herder & Herder, 1969), pp. 49-50.

9. G. Vermes, *Jesus the Jew* (New York: Macmillan, 1973), pp. 25, 231.

10. A.E. Harvey, *Jesus and the Constraints of History* (Philadelphia: Fortress Press, 1985), p. 264.

11. H. Maccoby, *Early Rabbinic Writings* (Cambridge: Cambridge University Press, 1988), pp. 170-72. Maccoby explains that the Fourth Gospel, aware that the Pharisees did not consider healing among the 39 kinds of work forbidden on the Sabbath (*m. Šab.* 7.2), introduced into the traditional stories the carrying of a bed and the making of clay in order to make the conflict between Jesus and the Pharisees plausible. According to him Jesus was a Hasidic Pharisee (p. 123).

12. Borg, *Conflict*, pp. 148-50.

13. R. Banks, *Jesus and the Law in the Synoptic Tradition* (SNTSMS, 28; Cambridge and New York: Cambridge University Press, 1975), pp. 116-17.

14. H.C. Kee, *Community of the New Age* (Philadelphia: Westminster Press, 1977), pp. 38-40.

the healing of the man with the withered hand (Mk 3.1-6), argued that here the debate is not concerned with 'the conventional dispute about what is and what is not permitted on the Sabbath', but has shifted so as to allow Jesus to single out 'an egoism that is inconsistent with good Jewish piety'.[15]

As said above, Bultmann traced all these pericopes to the Palestinian church and its apologetic and polemical endeavors vis-à-vis the Jews. More recently A. Hultgren in a careful form-critical analysis of these narratives challenged Bultmann's conclusion that they share the rabbinic pattern of disputes about points of law and belong to a common *Sitz im Leben*. He distinguished between unitary and non-unitary stories and allowed for several different life settings. Some of them, according to Hultgren, originated in the missionary and catechetical activities of the church outside of Palestine. In terms of what concerns us here, it is to be noted that Hultgren assigned the controversy dialogues having to do with the Sabbath to the Christian apologetic response to Jewish criticisms. In this way they reflect a dispute Christians were having with 'outsiders'.[16]

G. Theissen, however, who studied these narratives in connection with his structuralist work on the miracles, classified the miracle stories that have become controversy dialogues about the Sabbath as 'rule miracles'.[17] That is, they argue for the adoption of the rule being proposed. Apparently this was not uncommon in Judaism before the rabbis agreed on the principle that 'Miracles are not to be mentioned',[18] which meant that halakah could not be established on the basis of confirmatory miracles, or charismatic visions.[19] Within the Christian communities, it would seem, this type of evidence continued to be valued.

II

A. We may begin our study of the Synoptic Sabbath evidence with the accounts of the burial and the resurrection of Jesus. Mark matter-of-

15. C.K. Barrett, *Jesus and the Gospel Tradition* (Philadelphia: Fortress Press, 1968), p. 63.

16. A. Hultgren, *Jesus and his Adversaries* (Minneapolis: Augsburg, 1979), pp. 50-51.

17. G. Theissen, *The Miracle Stories of the Early Christian Tradition* (Philadelphia: Fortress Press, 1983), pp. 106-11.

18. Theissen, *Miracle Stories*, p. 107.

19. See A. Guttmann, 'The Significance of Miracles for Talmudic Judaism', *HUCA* 20 (1947), pp. 363-406, cited by Theissen.

factly reports that on the evening of the Day of Preparation, identified as προσάββατον (15.42), Joseph of Arimathea arranged to have Jesus taken from the cross and placed in a tomb while two Marys watched. Then, when the Sabbath had passed (διαγενομένου τοῦ σαββάτου, 16.1), three women went to the tomb to anoint the body. Mark takes for granted that all readers would understand the necessity to postpone the anointing due to the Sabbath.

Matthew's account follows Mark rather closely in the burial scene, omitting Pilate's inquiry about Jesus' condition, and adding that the tomb belonged to Joseph. But he launches an argument against the slanderous rumor that the disciples stole the body. Thus he tells of the arrangements made by the Pharisees in order to have the tomb sealed and guarded (27.62). By this means he shows the Pharisees in flagrant violation of the Sabbath while, by contrast, the Christian women who were rather anxious to anoint Jesus' body wait until after the Sabbath to go about their business (28.1).

Luke also follows Mark in the details of the burial, pointing out that it was the Day of Preparation, and the Sabbath was beginning (ἐπέφωσκεν, 23.54), and then, somewhat to our surprise since usually he is reluctant to mention the law and the commandments, he reports that the women went home and prepared the spices and ointments but 'on the Sabbath they rested according to the commandment' (23.56).

Taken together, these three reports of the burial show no awareness of any Sabbath controversies. They reflect a community unaware that Sabbath observance is being questioned. It would seem, then, that when the story of the Sunday morning anointing came into prominence as part of the Christian Gospel the Christian communities saw no problem with Sabbath observance. In fact, it could be argued that these Christians wished to show the women (and themselves) as observant of the Sabbath.

B. Besides these references to the Sabbath with clear roots in the Christian tradition there are, at the other end of the spectrum, four references to the Sabbath which are clearly redactional. Mk 1.21 (// Lk. 4.31) reports the exorcism in the synagogue at Capernaum which took place on a Sabbath while Jesus was teaching there. Had the event taken place on any other day, it would not have made any difference. A second case occurs at Mk 6.2, where Jesus' teaching in the synagogue on a Sabbath gives rise to opposition and the saying 'A prophet is not without honor, except in his own country, and among his own kin, and in his own house'. This saying receives quite different settings in other Gospels (cf. Mt. 13.57; Lk. 4.24; Jn 4.44). Another example appears at Lk. 4.16, where Jesus' sermon in the synagogue at Nazareth is reported. Luke says here of Jesus what he repeatedly says of Paul in Acts: to be in the synagogue on the Sabbath 'was his custom'. Finally, there is the Matthean expansion of the apocalyptic saying, 'Pray that it may not happen in winter' (Mk 13.18). Mt. 24.20 reads, 'Pray that your flight may not be in winter or on a Sabbath'.[20] Luke, for reasons of his own, omits the saying altogether. We may conjecture that, if Luke was written about 90 CE, it was already well known that the Fall of Jerusalem did not take place in winter, thus what had concerned Mark was no longer problematic. Matthew, on the other hand, gave the saying a new lease of life by expressing concern for the sanctity of the Sabbath. That the Matthean redaction was concerned with the Sabbath, as noted already, is supported by Mt. 27.62.

The evidence presented thus far would seem to indicate that the Christian communities that sustained the Synoptic tradition did observe the Jewish Sabbath, and probably felt that they were doing it even better than the Pharisees. It does not appear from it that the Sabbath was a matter in dispute. On the contrary, all of it assumes that Christians agreed on the necessity to observe the Sabbath rest.

C. There are in the Synoptic Gospels, however, references to the Sabbath which show clearly that Sabbath observance was a controversial matter. Basic evidence is provided by the two stories placed together, and in the same order, by all three Synoptics. These are the incident of the disciples plucking grain while making their way through a wheat field (Mk 2.23-28 // Mt. 12.1-8 // Lk. 6.1-5), and the healing of the man with the withered hand at the synagogue (Mk 3.1-6 // Mt. 12.9-14 // Lk. 6.6-11). Bypassing for the moment the Markan account, let us review first how the stories are expanded by Matthew and Luke.

1.a. Matthew expands the story of the disciples in the wheat field by drawing a parallel with David's men at the tabernacle: both groups of men were hungry.[21] He also adds, 'Have you not read in the law how

---

20. Braun (*Jesus*, p. 58) says that Mt. 24.20 is the only text in the Synoptic Gospels that deals positively with Sabbath observance. He also assigns the saying to the Jewish-Christian community that continues to observe Sabbath regulations because it had found Jesus' radical rejection of all Sabbath casuistry unacceptable. In this he is correct in the description, even if not in the explication.

21. Kee (*Community*, p. 39) thinks that hunger provided a sufficient reason on account of the importance of their mission, but there is no evidence that such

on the Sabbath the priests in the Temple profane the Sabbath and are guiltless?' This second Old Testament precedent corresponds to an ordering of priorities known from the rabbinic literature, to which Matthew gives an appropriate christological twist by claiming: 'I tell you, something greater than the temple is here!' According to Rabbi Simeon ben Menasiah, Rabbi Akiba taught: 'If punishment for murder has precedence over Temple worship, which in turn has precedence over the Sabbath, how much more the safeguarding of life must have precedence over the Sabbath'.[22] Both Matthew and Akiba argued on the basis that the Temple had precedence over the Sabbath. However, while Akiba moves from this premise to point out that activities on behalf of those in peril have precedence over Temple activities, Matthew concludes that the activities of Jesus are those which have precedence over Temple activities. Matthew also appeals to Hos. 6.6, a text that also specifies activity that is preferable to Temple activity,[23] and which was used by early Christians in diverse contexts (cf. Mt. 9.13). For the moment it may be important to note the relative significance given to the Sabbath and the Temple in the Matthean expansion, one which apparently the rabbis also adopted later.

1.b. Luke gives the narrative a different tone by changing the charge made by the Pharisees. Rather than challenging the conduct of his disciples, the Pharisees challenge the action of Jesus himself: 'Why are you doing what is not lawful?' they ask. Like Matthew with his comparison of Jesus and the Temple, by singling out Jesus' activity as the one being questioned Luke is giving prominence to the story's secondary christological significance. This new emphasis is also evident in that both record the secondary affirmation that the Son of Man is Lord of the Sabbath.[24] In the process of expanding the secondary christological implications of the story, both leave out the central affirmation in Mark: 'The Sabbath was made for man, not man for the Sabbath'.[25] These

reasoning entered into any rabbinic discussion, apart from Matthew's own.

22. See Vermes, *Jesus*, p. 181, for full documentation.

23. Braun (*Jesus*, p. 60) says that the quotation from Hosea is to prove that casuistry is out, period, but here he seems to be claiming too much.

24. It is difficult to decide whether this development took place at the traditional or the redactional stage.

25. Clearly this is a radical statement, but the fact that it is found in neither Matthew nor Luke may not necessarily be due to its radicality. Their emphasis on christological considerations may have been a major factor. Since the two statements appearing side by side in Mark do not go together well, it is not difficult to see why

transformations of the account at the hands of Matthew and Luke show that with the passage of time these stories came to be used to establish the Lordship of Christ, something which is not quite apropos when practical questions of lawful Sabbath conduct are to be decided.

2.a. Matthew also alters the Markan story of the healing of the man with the withered hand with the introduction of material from Q. In the earlier Markan version Jesus takes the initiative and asks, 'Is it lawful on the Sabbath to do good or to do harm, to save life or to kill?' Bultmann understood this to be an 'organically complete apophthegm'[26] in which, following rabbinic ways of argumentation, the main saying had been turned into a rhetorical question.[27] Matthew takes this punch-line from the lips of Jesus and gives it to the Pharisees, a not uncommon phenomenon in the Synoptic tradition.[28] Then Jesus answers the Pharisees with a saying from Q, of which there are three versions. Besides being Jesus' answer in this narrative, it appears as a doublet in Luke, once at the healing of a man with dropsy (Lk. 14.1-6), and then at the healing of the woman who had been suffering eighteen years a spirit of infirmity (Lk. 13.10-17). The three versions of this Q saying read:

> What man of you if he has one sheep and it falls into a pit on the Sabbath, will not lay hold of it and lift it out? (Mt. 12.11)

> Which of you having a son or an ox that has fallen into a well, will not immediately pull him out on a Sabbath day? (Lk. 14.5)

> Does not each of you on the Sabbath untie his ox or his ass from the manger and lead it away to water it? (Lk. 13.15)

In the Matthean setting, the Q saying prompts the exclamation, 'Of how much more value is a man than a sheep!' and a direct answer to the original question put forth by the Pharisees: 'So it is lawful to do good on the Sabbath'.

both Matthew and Luke chose one of them.

26. Bultmann, *History*, p. 12.

27. Hultgren (*Adversaries*, pp. 50-51) argued against Bultmann and the early form critics who classified these stories as Pronouncement Sayings and centered the value of the story on the dominical saying, thereby ascribing the exchange between Jesus and his adversaries to typical rabbinic influences. He classifies the stories as conflict stories, wishing to give more value to the drama of the exchange between Jesus and his opponents.

28. One of the best examples, among many, is the Great Commandment in Lk. 10.27.

2.b. The Lukan version of the healing of the man with the withered hand preserves the Markan story almost word for word, with the exception of some christological twists. It omits reference to the fact that Jesus 'looked at them in anger', and instead records that Jesus 'knew their thoughts' (Lk. 6.8). Luke also links other healing miracles to the Sabbath controversies by means of doublets of the Q saying found in Matthew. One is the healing of the man with dropsy. In this account the Pharisees are present but silent throughout. Jesus opens fire with the question 'Is it lawful to heal on the Sabbath or not?' Then, after he had already healed the man, he justified his action with one version of the Q saying (Lk. 14.5).

The second Lukan miracle story with a version of this Q saying shows even more clearly the Lukan hand at work. The account itself of Jesus' healing of the woman with the spirit of infirmity does not include the Q saying. After the healing, faced by the fact, the ruler of the synagogue rebukes the people, saying: 'There are six days on which work ought to be done; come on those days to be healed, and not on the Sabbath day' (Lk. 13.14). To this directive Jesus responds: 'You hypocrites! Does not each of you on the Sabbath untie his ox or his ass from the manger, and lead it away to water it? And ought not this woman, a daughter of Abraham whom Satan bound for eighteen years, be loosed from this bond on the Sabbath day?'[29] The Lukan agenda is unmistakable here, and the following comment makes it explicit: 'As he said this, all his adversaries were put to shame; and all the people rejoiced at all the glorious things that were done by him' (Lk. 13.17). The story, quite obviously, conforms to the Lukan appropriation of the passage from Isaiah 61 which promises release to the captives on the acceptable year of the Lord, thus causing all the people to rejoice.[30]

We may assign the untying of the ox or the ass from the manger in Luke to his working with the motif of the release of captives. We may note that the specification of the actions of *taking a hold* and of *lifting*

29. This story clearly reflects the conflict of Christians with the ruler of a synagogue, rather than a discussion among Christians. This may account for the charge, 'You hypocrites', and the sarcastic reference to the Jew who is not mindful of the needs of a daughter of Abraham.

30. The centrality of the quotation from Isa. 61, given as the text for Jesus' sermon at Nazareth, is widely recognized. See J.A. Sanders, 'From Isaiah 61 to Luke 4', in J. Neusner (ed.), *Christianity, Judaism and Other Greco-Roman Cults* (SJLA, 12; Leiden: Brill, 1975), I, pp. 75-106.

out may reflect Matthew's involvement in a more direct confrontation with the specifics of the Oral Law. The Lukan doublet, which mentions a son or an ox, may be softening the scene by referring to less strenuous action for more valuable objects, or may be credited to Luke's humanitarian concerns. Irrespective of how the specifics of each version of the Q saying are explained, it must be recognized that it functioned to settle arguments as to what could or could not be done on the Sabbath on the part of those who accepted the validity of the Sabbath.[31]

In general, it could be said that by their redactional activity on the material Matthew and Luke exhibit quite different concerns. Matthew seems to be concerned to establish the relative value of the Sabbath versus the Temple. But this does not argue for his low estimation of either one. He has Jesus paying the Temple tax (Mt. 17.24-27) and advising people to make sure to offer their sacrifices at the Temple (Mt. 5.23-24), and also is quite positive about the validity of the Sabbath. Luke, on the other hand, who sees in the Temple what is best in human piety and depicts the early Christian community as spending the time of day at the Temple (Acts 2, 3), adapts the Sabbath controversies to serve more directly his christological interests.

3. We may now turn to the Markan accounts of our two basic Sabbath controversy stories. The story of the disciples plucking grain on the Sabbath (Mk 2.23-28), as has been noticed by many, is notorious for its artificiality.[32] It is not easy to imagine the Pharisees trailing Jesus and his disciples on the open fields on a Sabbath day. Moreover, the fact that what is being called into question is the behavior of the disciples is somewhat unusual.[33] Still, the account preserves three elements that are an integral part of the tradition: a reference to David's conduct, a Sabbath saying, and a Son of Man saying. On the last element, the christological affirmation 'The Son of Man is Lord of the Sabbath', there has been some debate as to whether it came to Mark from the tradition or is a Markan creation.[34] Everyone seems to agree, however, that, if it came from the tradition, Son of Man did not have titular connotations. This

---

31. Braun (*Jesus*, p. 60) argues that these rhetorical questions do away with casuistry, by arguing on the basis of common practice, but that is not the case. The question accepts the casuistic approach to the issue.

32. Cf. Hultgren, *Adversaries*, p. 112.

33. F.W. Beare, *Earliest Records of Jesus* (Oxford: Blackwell, 1962), pp. 91-92; Schweizer, *Mark*, p. 70; Hultgren, *Adversaries*, p. 114.

34. Bultmann (*History*, pp. 16-17) already raised the issue, but left it open.

makes its relation to the previous affirmation quite problematic. It would seem more likely, therefore, that it is a secondary development.[35]

In the appeal to the conduct of David and his men, as has been noticed,[36] the analogy is not quite relevant since the two activities being compared do not belong to the same order. One has to do with cultic matters and the realm of the sacred, while the other is a question of law. Thus, as Bultmann has said, 'It is a likely conjecture that the Scriptural proof was used apart from its present context in the controversies of the early Church'.[37] The introduction of this analogy, however, again shows an early interest on the part of the Christian communities to discuss the relative importance of the Sabbath and the Temple. Like Matthew later, Mark was already quite involved in a struggle with the Temple.[38]

At the core of the story, then, is found the remarkable saying, 'The Sabbath was made for man, not man for the Sabbath'. This claim apparently was so radical that both Matthew and Luke omitted it. There have been attempts to find a rabbinic context for it. The one suggested, 'The Sabbath was given to you, not you to the Sabbath', is the comment of a second-century teacher on Exod. 31.13, 'You shall observe my Sabbaths'. This baraitha, however, comes from a commentary written much later.[39] Besides the problem of the dating, it is quite clear that it is not the same to say that the Sabbath was given to humanity, and to say that it was given to the Jews. In fact, it may have been this aspect of it that prevented Matthew and Luke recording it. It would seem proper, in any

35. On the secondary character of Mk 2.28, see V. Taylor, *The Gospel according to Mark* (London: Macmillan, 1959), p. 220; C.E.B. Cranfield, *The Gospel according to Mark* (Cambridge: Cambridge University Press, 1959), p. 118; D.E. Nineham, *The Gospel of St Mark* (Baltimore: Penguin, 1963), p. 106; F.W. Beare, 'The Sabbath was Made for Man', *JBL* 79 (1960), p. 135; E. Klostermann, *Das Markusevangelium* (Tübingen: Mohr, 4th edn, 1950), p. 31; E. Lohmeyer, *Das Evangelium des Markus* (Göttingen: Vandenhoeck & Ruprecht, 2nd edn, 1963), p. 66; E. Haenchen, *Der Weg Jesu: Eine Erklärung des Markusevangelium und der kanonischen Parallelen* (Berlin: Töpelmann, 1966), p. 121; Hultgren, *Adversaries*, pp. 113-14. For a critical review of the case for inauthenticity, see M.D. Hooker, *The Son of Man in Mark* (London: SPCK, 1967), pp. 94, 175-77.

36. For comments on the relevance of the appeal to David, see Hultgren, *Adversaries*, pp. 111-12.

37. Bultmann, *History*, p. 16.

38. See W. Kelber, *Mark's Story of Jesus* (Philadelphia: Fortress Press, 1979), pp. 62-70.

39. *Mek. Exod.* 31.14, and *b. Yom.* 85b (Str-B II, 5). See Vermes, *Jesus*, p. 180.

case, to conclude that what the statement affirms is more significant than what it denies. As such, the statement clearly serves to stress the importance of the gift of the Sabbath.[40]

Of the Markan story of the man with the withered hand (Mk 3.1-6) we may point out that in this early version the apophthegm, here turned into a rhetorical question, is clearly at the center of the story. The matter in dispute is also well defined. It is not the validity of the Sabbath per se, but what kind of activity may be lawfully performed on the Sabbath day. That Mark should use the story as a mile post on the road to Calvary does not in any way change this fact about the story itself; and should not be used to read into the story Jesus' radical abrogation of the Sabbath law.

III

From the above analysis we may conclude that there are five different kinds of references to the Sabbath in the Synoptic tradition:

1. Well-grounded traditional stories and redactional statements that assume the obligations of the Sabbath rest among Christians.
2. The aphorism 'The Sabbath was made for man, not man for the Sabbath'.
3. The affirmation 'It is lawful to do good on the Sabbath', or versions of it in the form of a question.
4. The justification of a given activity by appeals to common sense in the care of domestic animals.
5. Old Testament testimonia quoted to defend activities some would judge unlawful. It is of note that these have to do with Temple matters.

Upon examination of the evidence, it is clear that within the early Christian communities Sabbath observance *per se* was not in question. They took for granted the legitimacy of the Sabbath. What was being debated were the kinds of activities which were to be considered lawful on that day. From this, it is also clear that the controversies preserved in the Synoptic tradition do not reflect attempts on the part of Christians, who had declared the Sabbath obsolete or who had found the Jewish way of observing it legalistic or unspiritual, to defend themselves from

40. A point also recognized by Maccoby, who considers the saying to come from a common Pharisaic stock of maxims (*Rabbinic Writings*, p. 170).

charges leveled at them by Jews, who insisted on the validity of the Sabbath legislation. These disputes were, rather, internal affairs within some Christian communities which were engaged, just like their Jewish counterparts, in determining what could be done lawfully on the Sabbath.

It would not be misleading to say that most interpreters have understood the disputes reflected in the tradition to involve non-Christian Jewish opponents. Lohse's words may be quoted as characteristic of the traditional interpretation. Commenting on the appeal to the example of David in Mark 2, he wrote, 'The practice of the community, which has freed itself from the Jewish Sabbath, is being supported and vindicated from Scripture'. The statement 'The Sabbath was made for man, not man for the Sabbath' is said to indicate that 'the absolute obligation of the commandment is...challenged'. Later, however, Lohse concedes, 'though its validity is not contested in principle'.[41] If the validity of the Sabbath commandment is not being contested in the most radical of all the traditional Sabbath pronouncements, how is it possible to argue that the Christian communities found themselves in conflict with their Jewish neighbors on account of the fact that they had freed themselves from the Jewish Sabbath because Jesus had declared Sabbath observances obsolete? Our review of the evidence has made clear which of Lohse's observations has the support of the texts. It has shown that there were controversies among Christians as to how to observe the Sabbath. In other words, at least some Christians, of Jewish and Gentile origin inside and outside Palestine, continued to carry on their worship services on the Sabbath, and, like all other Jews and God-fearers of the time, were engaged in defining what kinds of other activities could be performed lawfully on that day. Thus the Sabbath stories reflect a time when those who guided their lives by the Torah carried on an internal debate as to permissible Sabbath activities.

41. E. Lohse, 'Sabbaton', *TDNT*, VII, p. 22; Borg, who argues for a peculiar interpretation, already recognized that the text does not support what many have claimed when he says, 'These violations of Sabbath law as then understood seem to be programmatic flowing out of the alternative paradigim that Jesus taught: the Sabbath was a day for works of compassion. This change did not mean that the Sabbath was abrogated; rather it was subordinated to deeds of mercy rather than to the quest for holiness' (*Conflict*, p. 151). While arguing from the opposite perspective, Maccoby makes the same point. He writes, 'his insistence on the Pharisaic view that healing was permitted on the Sabbath does not imply that he wished to abolish the Sabbath' (*Rabbinic Writings*, p. 170).

IV

If the above is correct, it would seem that the attempt to classify these controversy dialogues in terms of a continuum along a Jewish to Gentile axis[42] is not very helpful and may in fact be misleading. R.E. Brown's proposal for a new grid to help us understand early Christian stratigraphy,[43] on the other hand, offers a more realistic alternative tool. In his proposal, however, Brown does not single out attitudes toward the Sabbath as a significant variant. He lists as significant criteria attitudes toward the Temple, food laws and circumcision. According to his typology, both Jews and Gentiles aligned themselves in four basic postures:

1.   Those who insisted on full compliance with the Mosaic law, including circumcision.
2.   Those who held on to some Jewish observances, but did not insist on circumcision.
3.   Those who did not require observance of any Jewish laws, but who could voluntarily participate in Temple rituals.
4.   Those who did not require observance of any Jewish laws and saw no abiding significance in the Temple rituals.

According to Brown, what needs to be given particular weight is how different Christian communities related themselves to the Law and the Temple. Our study of the Sabbath in the Synoptic tradition suggests that Brown's proposal may benefit by incorporating this element into the grid. Distinguishing Sabbath observance as another discrete feature of the early Christian communities which may be used to mark their development will allow us to have an even more nuanced understanding of their history. In the case of circumcision and Temple ritual Christians divided by being in favor of or against them, but in the case of the Sabbath, they were basically in favor of it. How to observe it, and on which day,[44] however, have been disputed issues that have divided them from very early times.

42. As done by Hultgren, *Adversaries*, pp. 175-80.
43. R.E. Brown and J.P. Meier, *Antioch and Rome* (New York: Paulist Press, 1983), Section I.
44. That Christians debated on which day to observe the Sabbath is in evidence in Rom. 14.5-6. See H. Weiss, 'Paul and the Judging of Days', *ZNW* 86 (1995), pp. 137-53.

In terms of Brown's grid, the Christian communities represented by the Synoptic tradition would seem to fit into either Group 1 or Group 2. While in full compliance with the Sabbath Mosaic legislation, they were trying to determine what was to be considered proper Sabbath behavior by appeals to words of Jesus, Old Testament testimonia and what common sense demanded in the care of domestic animals. As noted above, however, both Mark and Matthew used 'the argument from Temple ritual' in their Sabbath controversies connected with the plucking of grain. Since concern for Temple ritual appears only in Brown's Groups 3 and 4, the fact that here the lawfulness of certain activity on the Sabbath is defended by appeals to what has been the case in the Temple, while at the same time a polemic against the Temple is being carried on, means that the significance of the Temple also plays a part in Groups 1 and 2. It may be said, then, that Sabbath observance among early Christians was, like circumcision and Temple worship, part and parcel of their religious heritage and they did not reject it radically and abruptly under the leadership of Jesus himself. When, in time, Christians elaborated more concrete positions toward these three institutions in Judaism they were worked out independently of each other, and were conditioned as much by sociological as by theological considerations. The recognition of this requires that our attempts to understand the transitions be much more nuanced than they have been in the past.

JSNT 26 (1986), pp. 3-27

POPULAR PROPHETIC MOVEMENTS AT THE TIME OF JESUS:
THEIR PRINCIPAL FEATURES AND SOCIAL ORIGINS

Richard A. Horsley

Popular prophetic movements constituted one of the distinctive forms which social unrest assumed in Jewish Palestine in the first century CE. These movements are of special interest to New Testament studies because they provide important comparative material for Jesus and his social-historical context. As D. Hill pointed out, the similarities between these prophets and their movements and certain features of primitive portions of the Synoptic tradition can be used to understand the context of Jesus' eschatological prophecy. 'What is distinctive, as well as what is characteristic, in Jesus' ministry must be argued within this context, rather than (or at least as much as) in comparison with the expectations of messianic figures in Jewish apocalyptic literature.'[1]

Previous studies have focused narrowly on the leaders of these movements and have labelled them 'messianic prophets' or, more recently, 'sign prophets'.[2] The demise of 'the Zealots' concept and the social-historical vacuum it leaves, however, are now leading us into ever more precise socio-historical analysis of groups and leaders around the time of Jesus.[3] It is now discerned not only that Josephus clearly distinguished

1. D. Hill, 'Jesus and Josephus' "Messianic Prophets"', in E. Best and R.McL. Wilson (eds.), *Text and Interpretation: Studies in the New Testament Presented to M. Black* (Cambridge: Cambridge University Press, 1979), pp. 143-54.

2. R. Meyer, 'Prophētēs', *TDNT*, VI, p. 826; P.W. Barnett, 'The Jewish Sign Prophets—AD 40–70: Their Intentions and Origin', *NTS* 27 (1980–81), pp. 679-97.

3. M. Smith, 'Zealots and Sicarii: Their Origins and Relations', *HTR* 64 (1971), pp. 1-19; S. Zeitlin, 'Zealots and Sicarii', *JBL* 81 (1962), pp. 395-98; M. Stern, 'Sicarii and Zealots', in M. Avi-Yonah (ed.), *World History of the Jewish People, First Series: Ancient Times.* VIII. *Society and Religion in the Second Temple Period* (Jerusalem: Masada, 1977), pp. 263-301; R.A. Horsley, 'The Sicarii: Ancient

the Sicarii and the Zealots proper as two different groups, but also that the popular prophetic movements were quite different from the popular messianic movements as well as from the Sicarii and Zealots.[4] Having discerned *that* these various groups and movements were different, we can now move toward greater precision regarding *how* they were different, a clearer sense of the distinctive feature of each group or type of movement. By broadening the approach from a focus on the individual prophets to include their network of social relationships, however, it may be possible to glean more information from our limited sources on these prophets as well as to gain a more precise sense of their distinctive characteristics as leaders of significant movements in particular social circumstances. Furthermore, the reexamination of subjects such as these popular prophets in their network of social relationships leads us to take up suggestions made recently regarding the potential utility of certain sociological approaches to New Testament and related materials.[5]

Principal Features of the Popular Prophetic Movements

Sources Must be Taken Seriously but Not Uncritically

Josephus portrays these prophets as charlatans and 'false prophets'. Yet parallel to this pejorative labelling he uses language with reference to these prophets in ways which indicate the seriousness with which they were taken and the particular form that their message and movements must have assumed. First, he mentions that these leaders themselves (at least the 'Egyptian' and Theudas) claimed to be *prophets* (*Ant.* 20.97,

Jewish "Terrorists"', *JR* 59 (1979), pp. 433-38; *idem*, 'Josephus and the Bandits', *JSJ* 10 (1979), pp. 37-63; *idem*, 'Ancient Jewish Banditry and the Revolt against Rome, AD 66–70', *CBQ* 43 (1981), pp. 409-32. Many of the essays in E. Bammel and C.F.D. Moule (eds.), *Jesus and the Politics of his Day* (Cambridge: Cambridge University Press, 1984) were apparently written prior to the appearance of these articles, as indicated in the 'Foreword', p. xi; the essay by E. Bammel, 'The Revolutionary Theory from Reimarus to Brandon', pp. 11-68, is especially valuable.

4.   Besides the literature in the previous note, see now Barnett, 'The Jewish Sign Prophets'; and R.A. Horsley, 'Popular Messianic Movements around the Time of Jesus', *CBQ* 46 (1984), pp. 471-93; *idem*, '"Like One of the Prophets of Old": Two Types of Popular Prophets at the Time of Jesus', *CBQ* 47 (1983), pp. 435-63.

5.   E.g. R. Scroggs, 'The Sociological Interpretation of the New Testament: The Present State of Research', *NTS* 26 (1979–80), pp. 164-79 (esp. 177-79); H.C. Kee, *Christian Origins in Sociological Perspective* (Philadelphia: Westminster Press, 1980), chapter 3.

169). This is all the more striking because, as Blenkinsopp and others have noted, Josephus otherwise avoids the use of the term 'prophet', apparently out of the conviction, shared with the scribes/Pharisees, that the succession of truly inspired prophets had ceased with Haggai, Zechariah and Malachi.[6] He does not employ the term for the Essene seers, nor does he use it for himself or any other contemporary figure who, he may have thought, possessed true divine interpretation of events. Secondly, he portrays these prophets with the same language that he used for Moses. In his treatment of the exodus events he had labelled the Egyptian magicians as 'charlatans'; hence we might expect that he would have been tempted to treat these figures who were apparently imitating Moses but were really 'charlatans' or 'false prophets' in terms parallel to the Egyptian opponents of Moses. But Josephus does just the opposite.[7] He portrays the first-century prophets in exactly the same terms as he portrays Moses: just as Moses did signs of liberation (σημεῖα τῆς ἐλευθερίας) in accordance with God's providence (πρόνοια τοῦ θεοῦ) so did the first-century prophets (cf. *Ant.* 2.286, 327, and 20.168; *War* 2.259).

Josephus's histories cannot be used as if they were simply transcripts of figures and events in ancient Jewish society.[8] Often he is using written sources, even where he is not quoting or even following them closely. Like any other ancient historian, however, Josephus not only writes the speeches which he places in the mouths of certain main actors in his histories, but he himself portrays and characterizes actors and events according to his own point of view. Therefore, when we encounter (in Josephus's narrative) 'Exodus-Conquest imagery' and the 'synonymous terms' σωτηρία and ἐλευθερία, we are dealing with Josephus's *portrayal* of the prophets, not with the imagery employed by the prophets themselves or the very promises they themselves made.[9] Or, before we can make any judgment about the 'Egyptian' prophet, we must take into account that it is Josephus (not the prophet himself) who sets him

---

6. J. Blenkinsopp, 'Prophecy and Priesthood in Josephus', *JJS* 25 (1974), pp. 240, 250.

7. Contra Barnett, 'The Jewish Sign Prophets', p. 683.

8. Because Barnett's presuppositions about and approaches to the textual sources are different from those assumed by many in New Testament studies and Jewish history, his article also serves as a challenge to others to reexamine and refine their own presuppositions regarding what conclusions can justifiably be drawn from the evidence at our disposal.

9. Contra Barnett, 'The Jewish Sign Prophets', pp. 686, 685.

up in a 'deliberate almost stylized manner'.[10] The particular words in Josephus's text are probably chosen by Josephus; hence we should check his other usage of key words before speculating about their possible implications in a given passage.[11] Similarly, connections between events or figures may be due to Josephus's editorial activity or intentional interpretation of events. Thus it seems unwarranted to speculate that members of prophetic movements 'almost certainly interacted with' the Sicarii simply because they are placed in proximity in Josephus's presentation of events,[12] or to imagine that particular prophets saw themselves and their actions as a connected sequence (in imitation of the ancient biblical sequence).[13]

Not Intentions but Actions/Events

It would seem impossible, therefore, to deal with the *intentions* of the prophets.[14] Given the character of our principal sources, Josephus's histories, we simply cannot determine how the prophets presented themselves or their ideas and intentions *from* the accounts of Josephus. Our relationship with the prophets is more indirect. We can only work analytically *through* the accounts to the prophets and their movements. Because Josephus, no matter how stylized or hostile his narratives may be, is reporting on events and *actions* taken by these prophets, however, we are able to reconstruct the actions taken by these prophets and their movements. Then, insofar as we are able to place actions and events in a particular social-historical context and view them against a known cultural background, we can also interpret the actions of the prophets. Thus we can deal, not with the prophets' intentions, but with their actions and relationships.

Not Solitary Prophets but Leaders of Movements

The various prophetic figures mentioned by Josephus who appeared among the Jewish people in the first century CE can be seen to fall into two principal types.[15] The earlier prophet-like figures Menahem and

10. Contra Barnett, 'The Jewish Sign Prophets', p. 683.

11. Contra Barnett, 'The Jewish Sign Prophets', p. 683.

12. Contra Hill, 'Jesus and Josephus' "Messianic Prophets"', p. 148.

13. Contra Barnett, "The Jewish Sign Prophets', p. 683.

14. As attempted by Barnett, 'The Jewish Sign Prophets', pp. 686-88.

15. Argued more fully in Horsley, '"Like One of the Prophets of Old"'. The critical review of literature on 'The Charismatic', by S. Freyne in *Ideal Figures in*

Judas, who made predictions regarding the fate of Hasmonean rulers and Herod, belong to yet a third type (seers or predictors of future events) and were confined to the Essenes (*War* 1.78–80; *Ant.* 13.311; 15.373–78). All of the other prophets mentioned by Josephus as active in the first century were apparently from among the common people and were not associated with any particular literate group, Pharisees or Essenes. That these prophets were really of two distinctive types can be seen from close examination of reports about them in Josephus and the Gospels and by comparing them with prophetic phenomena earlier in Israelite-Jewish history. Jesus son of Hananiah and John the Baptist are primarily individual spokespersons for God, delivering oracles of divine judgment to their contemporary situation. These two figures, moreover, have certain features in common with the classical biblical (oracular) prophets such as Jeremiah, and can be seen as standing in the same Israelite-Jewish tradition of oracular prophets. During the Jewish Revolt against Rome of 66–70 there were other prophets who delivered oracles. Because the oracles of the latter concern the liberation of the people, they may appear different in type from Jesus or John. The distinctive role of both, however, is to deliver oracles. Moreover, the classical biblical oracular prophets, in whose messages oracles of judgment were indeed dominant, also delivered oracles of salvation. Hence we should follow the biblical tradition in our categorization, making delivery of oracles the distinguishing criterion, not judgment versus salvation, and view the salvation-prophets of 66–70 along with Jesus and John as individual oracular prophets.

The other prophets about whom Josephus reports—Theudas, the 'Egyptian', a Samaritan, and some unnamed figures—were all leaders of movements. They may also have been spokespersons for God. Josephus, however, mentioned not what they said as individual spokespersons, but rather that they inspired, organized and led sizeable groups of people in movements which were eventually suppressed by Roman military forces. Whether a given movement, such as that led by the 'Egyptian',

---

Ancient Judaism (Missoula, MT: Scholars Press, 1980), pp. 223-58, suggests that the 'charismatic' cannot be determined as a third type of popular prophet. The typologies in J. Becker, *Johannes der Täufer und Jesus von Nazareth* (Neukirchen–Vluyn: Neukirchener Verlag, 1972), pp. 44-54, and D. Aune, *Prophecy in Early Christianity and the Ancient Mediterranean World* (Grand Rapids: Eerdmans, 1983), chapter 5, esp. pp. 121-29, are overly complex and mix together literary phenomena with concrete prophetic figures.

was 30,000 strong (Josephus, *War* 2.261) or had only 4,000 participants (Acts 21.38), these prophets stood at the head of noteworthy movements of popular unrest. In dealing with these prophets, therefore, we must analyze their movements and not simply the individual figures themselves.

Not 'Messianic' Prophets, but Popular Prophetic Movements as Distinguished from Popular Messianic Movements

The distinctive character of these prophets and their movements may have been somewhat obscured by the label 'messianic prophets'.[16] This label, of course, comes from a period in New Testament study when we were using the term 'messianic' in a highly synthetic manner. An ideal synthesis of Jewish eschatology had been constructed in which salvation or the end-time was to be inaugurated by a messiah or some 'messianic' figure as the divine agent, whether 'prophet', 'Son of Man', or Davidic 'messiah'. Thus 'messianic' has been used as virtually synonymous with 'eschatological' or 'political' or both. Now that the field is developing more awareness of the concrete social-historical context and of the varying social forms actually operative in Jewish society, however, continuation of the label 'messianic prophets' would simply create confusion.

There were two distinctive forms of popular movements among the Jewish people headed by charismatic leaders, judging from Josephus's accounts. Movements headed by prophets constituted one of these types of movements. Popular movements of the other type were headed by 'kings' such as Judas, Simon and Athronges in 4 BCE and Simon bar Giora in 68–70 CE.[17] Insofar as the kings at the head of these movements had been popularly acclaimed by their followers (*War* 2.55, 57, 60; *Ant.* 17.274, 281, 285), the movements of this second type would appear to stand in (or to be reminiscent of) the ancient Israelite tradition of popular anointing or election of kings, from Saul and David to Jeroboam and Jehu (1 Sam. 11.14-15; 2 Sam. 2.4; 5.3; 1 Kgs 12.16-20; 2 Kgs 9.1-13).[18] Thus the term *messianic* should be applied to those movements headed by a popular king or messiah. The movements headed

16. Meyer, 'Prophētēs', pp. 826-27.

17. Josephus's accounts of these popular kings are analyzed in Horsley, 'Popular Messianic Movements'.

18. See Horsley, 'Popular Messianic Movements', pp. 475-78; F.M. Cross, *Canaanite Myth and Hebrew Epic* (Cambridge, MA: Harvard University Press, 1973), pp. 219-29.

by men who claimed to be (or were seen as) prophets should be labelled accordingly: popular *prophetic* movements.

Among the popular movements (and leaders) mentioned by Josephus there is no overlap or confusion between these two distinctive types of movements. Barnett claims that 'the Egyptian' 'is both a "prophet" and also a "king"'.[19] He bases this claim on (a misreading of) Josephus's phrase 'to rule the people' (τοῦ δήμου τυράννειν). This phrase hardly means, however, to 'set himself up as tyrant of the people' (i.e. in the sense of 'king'). In contemporary Greek usage, a tyrant was hardly a king, but rather a popular leader, generally of lower socio-economic strata, whose 'tyranny', similar to 'democracy', stood in contrast to 'aristocracy' or 'monarchy' as a form of government. Finally, a comparison of Josephus's account of 'the Egyptian' with his accounts of the popular 'kings' shows clearly that he used distinctive terminology of 'donning the diadem' and 'claiming the kingship' when he wanted to indicate this other type of movement and leadership.[20]

Not Signs but Actions as the Crucial Feature
of the Prophetic Movements
Can we affix a distinctive label to the leaders of the prophetic movements to distinguish them not just from the messianic movements but from the other type of popular prophets as well? At the very beginning of his article, Barnett almost arbitrarily labels these figures 'Sign Prophets, in the absence of existing descriptive titles'.[21] The title we use, however, should describe the phenomena accurately—and 'sign prophets' surely does not. Of the five accounts of prophets who clearly belong to the same type by virtue of the similarities in Josephus's descriptions, signs are mentioned in only one. Josephus's (only) other reference to signs comes in a case which is difficult to categorize by type, 'individual oracular' or 'movement' (*War* 6.285). Nor do the prophets in the other accounts take actions which could be construed as signs, so that we could legitimately infer an implicit pattern even where Josephus does not use the term 'signs' explicitly. Thus the signs are distinctive in only one of Josephus's five accounts, that of the anonymous 'deceivers and

19. Barnett, 'The Jewish Sign Prophets', p. 683.

20. J. Hanson, 'Diadem: Insignia of Popular Messiahs in Josephus' (unpublished paper).

21. Barnett, 'The Jewish Sign Prophets', p. 679.

imposters' who led their followers out into the wilderness (i.e. *War* 2.259; *Ant.* 20.167–68).[22]

The distinctive thing which all of these prophets had in common is that they all led their followers into (anticipated) participation in some great liberating action by God. The Samaritan led his followers up Mt Gerizim to the anticipated recovery of the sacred vessels which Moses had buried there—which in contemporary Samaritan belief would inaugurate a new age of restoration (*Ant.* 18.85–86). Theudas led his followers with their possessions to the Jordan River in anticipation that at his command the waters would be parted and afford them an easy passage to freedom (*Ant.* 20.97). Under Felix (52–60) unnamed 'deceivers and imposters' led their followers out into the wilderness in anticipation that God would give them 'signs of freedom' (*War* 2.259; *Ant.* 20.167–68). The 'Egyptian' prophet led his followers around Jerusalem anticipating that the walls of the city would fall down at his command, the Romans be overpowered and the people given entrance into the (liberated) city (*Ant.* 20.169–71; *War* 2.261–62). Lastly, under Festus (60–62) another unnamed 'imposter' led his followers into the wilderness in anticipation of liberation and rest from their troubles (*Ant.* 20.188). All of these movements focus upon some particular divine liberating action and the prophets led their followers out to participate in that anticipated action. Even in the case where 'signs' appear, they were subordinate to the liberation of which they were the tokens. Not signs, therefore, but the liberating acts of God were the distinctive focus which all of these prophetic movements had in common.

The similarity between these movements, however, goes even further into a distinctive pattern according to which the liberating acts of God were apparently conceived. Reconstruction of this pattern involves some speculation on our part in connection with biblical traditions in one or two cases. However, the basic pattern can be discerned which seems to underlie and inform all of these prophetic movements. Each of them appears to be a repetition of a great divine act of liberation from the past (biblical) history of the people. But they are not mere repetitions. The pattern appears to be one of a historical-eschatological typology. We are entirely familiar with this basic pattern as one of interpretation and expectation in biblical, especially prophetic, literature. Thus the return from Babylonian exile was interpreted by the Second 'Isaiah' in imagery

---

22. The portrayal of Jonathan in Cyrene in *War* 7.438 may indicate that the 'signs' terminology may be due to Josephus himself.

borrowed from the exodus as a *new* redemption, a *new* way through the wilderness and a *new* conquest. The basic pattern is vividly clear in the highly compact and mythologized poem of Isa. 51.9-11. The new (eschatological) exodus-conquest is anticipated according to the model of the original (historical) exodus.[23] As a pattern of interpretation and expectation, this historical-eschatological typology is also familiar to us from New Testament passages such as the 'sign of Jonah' and 'the Queen of the South', Lk. 11.29-32, and 1 Cor. 10.1-13.[24] In the prophetic movements of the first century, however, groups of people were *acting out* this pattern. Focusing on a new/eschatological act of God conceived after the pattern of great historical acts of deliverance, these prophets and their followers themselves took action in anticipation of the divine action.

Not Forcing, but Participating in God's Action

In acting out this pattern of liberation according to the historical-eschatological typology, these prophets and their followers were participating in the new divine action. Barnett suggests that the prophets were attempting to 'force God's hand', to force God's salvation into existence.[25] His suggestion, however, rests on the assumption that the signs were their distinctive feature. Once we recognize that the signs are mentioned in only one case, there is nothing left in the other cases which could have served as the 'levers' by which to activate God's action.

Such a 'lever' would have been superfluous to these prophetic movements in any case, for they were not forcing God's hand, but following God's lead. The very motivation for the formation of these movements, judging from their actions, was apparently the conviction that God was about to act and that they were called to participate in that action as the people about to be liberated. The Qumran community and the letters of Paul provide familiar examples of such participation in God's saving action. The Qumranites went out into the wilderness 'to prepare the way

23. Cross, *Canaanite Myth and Hebrew Epic*, pp. 136-37; B.W. Anderson, 'Exodus Typology in Second Isaiah', in *idem* and W. Harrelson (eds.), *Israel's Prophetic Heritage: Essays in Honor of James Muilenburg* (New York: Harper & Row, 1962), pp. 177-95.

24. See H.J. Schoeps, *Paul* (Philadelphia: Westminster Press, 1961), pp. 229-35; F.M. Cross, *The Ancient Library of Qumran* (Garden City, NY: Doubleday, rev. edn, 1961), p. 116; more generally, see E. Auerbach, 'Figura', in *Scenes from the Drama of European Literature* (New York: Meridian, 1959), pp. 11-76.

25. Barnett, 'The Jewish Sign Prophets', p. 688.

of the Lord', apparently seeing themselves as participating in the beginning of a new exodus and covenant community.[26] Paul understood the crucifixion and resurrection of Jesus as inaugurating the eschatological sequence of events in which he and others were called to participate (and in which his own ministry was a significant contribution).[27] 'Signs', of course, might be understood as indications or tokens that something great was about to happen, as seems to be the case with the Pharisees who seek a sign from Jesus in Lk. 17.20-21. But signs, in the Gospel tradition generally, are understood as *manifestations* of God's activity, not as *tokens* of future activity.[28] Thus, even in the case of the 'charlatans' leading their followers out into the wilderness to experience signs of liberation 'according to God's plan', they can be understood as anticipatory participation in God's liberating actions (and not as forcing God's salvation).

The Social Origins of the Prophetic Movements

That these prophetic movements involved thousands of people and fostered 'revolutionary changes', such that the Roman authorities suppressed them violently with massive military force, suggests that they were serious social movements, major manifestations of social unrest. In order to explore the significance of these movements it is necessary to move beyond the usual 'history of ideas' approach into more sociological approaches which are increasingly finding their way into New Testament studies.

In fact, precisely because our sources for the prophetic movements are so limited, some of the comparative approaches and theories which have recently been applied to early Christianity and ancient Jewish groups would also be helpful in understanding the character of these movements. For example, noting that the Jewish prophetic movements of the first century CE have certain principal features in common with what have been analyzed comparatively as 'millenarian movements', one could legitimately (if also speculatively!) reconstruct other features of the first-century Jewish movements by extrapolation and analogy. Or,

26. Cross, *Ancient Library of Qumran*, pp. 78-85.

27. Schoeps, *Paul*, pp. 88-110; J.C. Beker, *Paul the Apostle* (Philadelphia: Fortress Press, 1980), esp. chapters 8 and 14.

28. E.g. N. Perrin, *Rediscovering the Teachings of Jesus* (New York: Harper & Row, 1967), pp. 73-74.

similarly, one could apply Weber's concept of the charismatic leader to the Jewish prophets and their movements, noting (among other things) that: leaders arise in times of crisis and distress, appeal to those who are alienated, marginal, or suffering from 'relative deprivation', with a message of protest against the corrupt regime or intolerable situation, and promote a return to or a renewal of the people's proper tradition of life. As an attractive alternative to the intolerable or inept established institutional order, 'the holder of charisma seizes the task that is adequate for him and demands obedience and a following by virtue of his mission'.[29] Such approaches (concepts/theories) are indeed very useful for detecting 'the recurrent regularities of social events'.[30] They have been used to advantage in bringing new insights and perspective on Jewish groups and early Christianity.[31] Such approaches would also be useful in helping us determine what the popular prophetic movements had in common with other Jewish groups and movements. As one interpreter pointed out, all of the well-known Jewish groups (sects/philosophies) at the time of Jesus can be understood as millenarian groups.[32] Similarly, virtually all such Jewish groups, from the Essenes to the popular messianic and prophetic movements, can be interpreted in terms of charismatic leaders catalysing a following of discontented people in a situation of crisis or distress. Such approaches are less useful, however, for more precise sociological analysis, for making more precise distinctions among the Jewish groups and movements at the time.

In his review of recent sociological interpretation of the New Testament, Scroggs noted that one of the approaches which has been pursued vigorously with regard to early Christianity but not with regard to contemporary Jewish society is an analysis of class structure and the class

29. Kee, *Christian Origins*, pp. 54-56.

30. Y. Talmon, 'Pursuit of the Millennium: The Relation between Religious and Social Change', *Archives Européennes de Sociologie* 3 (1962), p. 126.

31. See the treatment of Pharisees, etc., in S.R. Isenberg, 'Millenarism in Greco-Roman Palestine', *Rel* 4 (1974), pp. 26-46; and that of 'earliest Christianity' in J. Gager, *Kingdom and Community* (Englewood Cliffs, NJ: Prentice-Hall, 1975), pp. 20-36.

32. Isenberg, 'Millenarism', pp. 35-39. Aune (*Prophecy*, pp. 125-28) subsumes virtually all movements under 'millenarian', and then must have subtypes, of which 'revolutionist' is clearly a misnomer for the popular prophetic movements. Cf. the critique of such use of sociological concepts by C.S. Rodd, 'On Applying a Sociological Theory to Biblical Studies', *JSOT* 19 (1981), p. 104.

composition of social movements.[33] Class analysis would seem appropriate to mass movements which were 'fostering revolutionary changes' and which were viewed as threats to the Roman order. Such analysis may help us understand the social origins of the prophetic movements, and how they were 'expressions of distress' as well as 'protests against distress'.

As Scroggs points out, however, 'Social dynamics may create the situation but may not determine the response to the situation'.[34] Thus we must supplement class analysis with an attempt to understand why the prophetic movements assumed their particular form. In his relational or 'interactionist' revision of Weber's theory of charisma, Worsley reminds us that any particular prophet's message and authority—and the very presuppositions and distresses and desires of those people among whom he catalyses a movement—are 'highly culturally conditioned'.[35] It is necessary therefore to explore the particular Jewish cultural traditions out of which the prophets and their followers may have been responding to their situation.

Class Analysis: The Social Location of the Prophetic Movements
The prophetic movements occurred basically among the common people, as distinguished not only from the priestly aristocracy but from the literate 'sects' as well. When Pharisees, Essenes or priests are involved in a group or an event, Josephus appears to make a point of it. For example, he mentions that the leaders of the 'Fourth Philosophy' were 'teachers' and 'Pharisees', and at one point he notes that two of the several leaders among the Zealots in 68–69 were 'priests' (*Ant.* 18.4; *War* 2.118; 4.225). Thus it is significant that he mentions no priests or members of one of the sects in connection with any of the prophetic movements.

That the prophetic movements were basically popular phenomena can be seen from (a) the social origins of the followers, (b) the content of the prophets' messages/actions, (c) the direction of their messages/ actions, and (d) the effects of their messages/actions.

(a) Most of Josephus's references to the followers of the prophets are in such vague general language (πλῆθος, *War* 2.259; *Ant.* 18.85; ὄχλος, *Ant.* 20.97, 167) that it is difficult to tell whether it was primarily the

33. Scroggs, 'Sociological Interpretation', pp. 169-70.
34. Scroggs, 'Sociological Interpretation', p. 167.
35. P. Worsley, *The Trumpet Shall Sound* (New York: Schocken Books, 2nd, augmented edn, 1968), pp. ix-xxi, xxxv-xxxix.

peasantry who were involved or perhaps the common people from Jerusalem as well. Josephus uses the terms 'multitude' and 'crowd' (even δῆμος) elsewhere indiscriminately, sometimes with reference to the city-people (δῆμος, *War* 1.55) and sometimes with reference to what are obviously country people from the towns and villages of Judea.[36] Unless otherwise indicated, one would assume that the crowd or multitude was from the countryside, for a very large movement would have had difficulty getting started under the watchful eye of the Jewish and Roman authorities in Jerusalem itself. Most important for determination of the issue are Josephus's parallel reports about the prophet who had come 'from Egypt'. In the *Antiquities* one might get the impression that the followers were city people. Josephus often uses δημοτικός with reference to Jerusalemites. And he suggests that the prophet had come to Jerusalem and then led his followers out to the Mount of Olives. However, Josephus also uses δημοτικός in a more general sense with reference to the Jews, hence Jerusalemites are not necessarily meant in this case. Most decisive, however, is the parallel passage in the *War*. Josephus says here explicitly that the prophet appeared *in the country*. Thus in the only case in which he uses a particular rather than a general term, Josephus indicates explicitly that the prophet recruited his followers from the peasant villages of the Judean countryside, and that the Jerusalem 'city-people' (δῆμος) fought *against* the prophet's followers. It appears justifiable to generalize from this explicit reference that the followers of these prophets generally came from the peasantry, which comprised the vast majority of the populace anyhow (90 per cent in any traditional peasant society). Whether the prophets themselves were 'peasants', that is, from the towns and villages, Josephus does not indicate.[37] It may be pertinent to note that the popular *oracular* prophet Jesus son of Hananiah was a 'crude peasant' according to Josephus (*War* 6.300).

(b) The 'content' of the prophetic movements indicates that they were movements of the discontented among the common people, certainly not of the comfortable. The quest for 'liberation' or 'freedom' and 'rest from trouble' suggests an implicit indictment of the established order of things and its replacement by a more egalitarian and just (liberated) social order. Judging simply from the size of the movements led by Theudas

---

36. On Josephus's use of these and related terms, see V.A. Tcherikover, 'Was Jerusalem a "Polis"?', *IEJ* 14 (1964), pp. 63-66.

37. Is the reference to the prophet 'from Egypt' a symbolic or a geographical one?

and the prophet 'from Egypt' their messages struck a responsive chord among the people. It is not surprising that the ruling groups, as represented in this case by the wealthy priest-historian Josephus, perceived that these prophets were fostering 'revolutionary changes'.

(c) Consistent with their 'revolutionary' content, moreover, the actions of the prophetic movements—or perhaps rather the actions they anticipated God as taking—were directed against the established order and ruling groups. This may seem more implicit than explicit in most of the cases, in which the prophets and their leaders appear simply to be *withdrawing* from an intolerable situation, participating in a new 'exodus' from bondage, as it were. The action is more explicit in the case of the 'Egyptian's' movement: he and his followers went out to participate in the divinely-led overthrow of the established order ensconced in Jerusalem (although it is not clear whether this focuses on the Roman rule or the high-priestly aristocracy or both). Again it may be pertinent to note the parallels among the popular oracular prophets. John the Baptist attacked Herod Antipas. Jesus son of Hananiah announced doom against Jerusalem and the Temple, the political-economic bases, as well as symbols, of the Jewish ruling order.

(d) The ruling groups' anxious and brutally repressive reactions, finally, further reveal the popular character and potentially revolutionary implications of the prophetic movements. Roman governors, dispatching cavalry and/or infantry, simply slaughtered or crucified the large numbers of disruptive elements in the countryside or, in the one case, outside the walls of Jerusalem (*Ant.* 18.87; 20.98–99, 171, 188; *War* 2.260, 263). Again the case of the oracular prophets appears parallel. The Jewish authorities, Antipas as well as the Jerusalem aristocracy, were anxious merely about the spoken word, perhaps because they were aware of the long tradition in their society of popular prophets who had spoken against oppressive royal and priestly rule. If they were thus aware of that tradition, it did not keep them from taking action to kill or suppress the popular prophets (*War* 6.302; Mk 6.17-29). Thus the effect of the prophetic movements in evoking a repressive reaction by the ruling groups further indicates their popular character.

The Cultural Background which Informed the Social Form of the Prophetic Movements
Several movements so similar in characteristics that we discern a particular social form do not spring up suddenly without some cultural back-

ground which informs the distinctive behavior of their leaders and participants. There is no obvious 'first' or immediate precedent for these movements. There are, however, biblical traditions of ancient prophetic movements which may have influenced the formation of such movements, and at least one striking, if somewhat distant historical precedent.

For the background of the prophetic movements we must reckon with the existence of a popular memory of traditions parallel to the scribal-intellectual cultivation of those same traditions in written form as Scripture. In most complex traditional societies there exists a popular or 'little' tradition alongside—and indeed interacting with—the official or 'great' tradition.[38] From Old Testament studies we are familiar with a variation of this distinction. Even after the official Yahwist epic was composed in court circles, the popular traditions of the stories of key formative events of the people continued in oral form. The same will have been true after the Priestly completion of the Torah in post-exilic times. Indeed, the Hasidim and then the Pharisees undertook, as part of their responsibility, to make sure the people were familiar with the scriptural traditions even though most of them were illiterate peasants.[39] The exodus tradition, of course, remained vivid in the people's mind through celebration of the feast of the Passover year after year. It is virtually certain that the common people cultivated a memory of the great formative events of exodus and conquest. Moreover, it would be reasonable to surmise that the people also kept alive a memory of earlier 'prophetic movements' such as those led by Gideon, Deborah, Samuel, and Elisha. Unless a passage such as Mk 6.15 can simply be dismissed as a composition by the evangelist, it indicates that a memory of such prophetic figures was alive among those attempting to interpret the actions of Jesus of Nazareth.

Barnett finds an immediate prototype for the prophetic movements in Jesus' feeding of the five thousand in John 6; but this is based on the unwarranted assumption that history can be reconstructed directly out of sentences of John's Gospel.[40] The Qumran community, to which

---

38. R. Redfield, *Peasant Society and Culture* (Chicago: University of Chicago Press, 1969), pp. 70-72; E.R. Wolf, *Anthropology* (New York: Norton, 1974), pp. 73-74.

39. See e.g. V. Tcherikover, *Hellenistic Civilization and the Jews* (New York: Atheneum, 1970), pp. 125-26, 220, 223, 253-56; J. Neusner, *First Century Judaism in Crisis* (Nashville: Abingdon Press, 1975), chapters 2 and 3.

40. Barnett, 'The Jewish Sign Prophets', pp. 689-93. See rather the more careful

Barnett makes virtually no reference (i.e. only to one image, not to the community), might provide at least a distant historical prototype for the later popular prophetic movements. Like Josephus, perhaps, we usually think of the Essenes at Qumran as one of the standard Jewish 'philosophies' or 'sects' of late Second Temple times. Sociologically speaking, however, in its origins the Qumran community appears to have been yet another prophetic movement. Although the group was probably composed largely of scribal Hasidim dominated by a strong priestly element, the original Qumranites were headed by a prophetic figure. The Righteous Teacher led the group in action designed to 'prepare the way of the Lord in the wilderness', in conscious imitation of ancient Israel led in the wilderness by Moses: a new exodus out into the wilderness to form a new covenant community in anticipation of eschatological deliverance.[41]

Did the Righteous Teacher and his scribal-priestly followers then originate this type of prophet and movement? Since there are such huge gaps in our sources for the Second Temple period in general, perhaps it would be prudent to say merely that they were the first instance of this type we know of. Of course, the typological pattern of thinking about deliverance in the immediate future was clearly used by the Qumran community. The *Testament of Moses*, moreover, provides evidence of a priestly-influenced group's interest in what 'Moses' revealed to his successor 'Joshua' regarding future salvation for the period of Hellenistic persecution just prior to the Maccabean Revolt.[42] Hence the idea was there for an inspired 'prophet' such as the Righteous Teacher to act upon.

It seems unlikely, however, that the Righteous Teacher and the Qumranites were the direct prototype upon which the popular prophetic movements were modelled. The long temporal distance (almost two centuries) of the exodus to Qumran led by the Teacher makes influence on the later prophetic movements unlikely. The more distinctive 'distance' between the Qumranites and the prophetic movements led by Theudas, the 'Egyptian', and others, however, may have been their social difference. The Qumran community had originated from priestly-scribal

critical treatment by E. Bammel, 'The Feeding of the Five Thousand', in *idem* and Moule (eds.), *Jesus and the Politics of his Day*, pp. 197-229.

41. Cross, *Ancient Library of Qumran*, pp. 78-85; G. Vermes, *The Dead Sea Scrolls in English* (New York: Penguin, 2nd edn, 1975), pp. 35-38.

42. G. Nickelsburg, *Jewish Literature between the Bible and the Mishnah* (Philadelphia: Fortress Press, 1981), pp. 80-83.

circles. Well before the time of the popular prophetic movements of the first century CE the Qumranites, while physically and mentally still in wilderness exile, had become one of the principal Jewish 'sects' (as Josephus explains, *War* 2.119–61; *Ant.* 18.11–23). The Qumran community, moreover, busily engaged in searching already recognized scriptural revelation for elucidation on the present, was no longer interested in any new prophetic action or oracles. Its distinctive product was literary interpretation, including scrolls of *pesharim* on authoritative prophecies from the past.[43] The prophetic movements of the mid-first century CE, on the other hand, were spontaneous movements among the Jewish peasantry. Considering what the Qumran community had become by that time, therefore, it is difficult to imagine how it could have provided a model for the popular movements. The typological pattern of expectation which apparently influenced the Hasidim in the second century BCE, however, was still alive in Jewish culture in the first century CE—still alive, that is, for less intellectually inclined popular movements to act out. It thus seems likely that, not the wilderness community at Qumran, but the popular memory of the glorious divine liberating actions of the past—those led by Moses and Joshua, perhaps also by Elijah and Elisha—provided the model that influenced the distinctive social form taken by the popular movements.

The Socio-Historical Context of the Prophetic Movements
It is evident that, despite the view which may have prevailed among the scribes and sages—that the succession of true prophets had been broken off in early post-exilic times—concrete popular prophetic phenomena continued or revived among the common people. Besides oracular prophets such as John the Baptist and Jesus son of Hananiah, several prophetic movements, all apparently with the same distinctive social form, occurred in the first century CE. The oracular prophets would appear to be a revival of the long (biblical) tradition of oracular prophets which, as indicated in Zech. 13.2-6, was still discernibly alive among the people as recently as the Persian period. The prophetic movements may not have been a revival of a continuing tradition of popular prophetic movements. The most recent prototype would have been those led by Elijah and Elisha. But the 'action' prophets and their followers were likely informed by the memory of the ancient liberation movements led

---

43. Cross, *Ancient Library of Qumran*, pp. 111-16; J.T. Milik, *Ten Years of Discovery in the Wilderness of Judaea* (London: SCM Press, 1963), pp. 40-41.

by Elijah and Elisha as well as by the great actions of the exodus and conquest. We must clearly reckon with the continuing influence of the ancient biblical traditions among the ordinary people as well as among the scribes and sages.

It has been generally recognized that biblical prophecy is usually a response to particular social-historical circumstances and, indeed, is often addressed to a particular historical situation. Like the oracles of their eighth-century BCE successors, the messages and movements of Elijah and Elisha, for example, were a response to and were directed against particular socio-political relations and the ruling class which fostered them.[44] It would thus appear appropriate, in approaching the popular prophets of the first century CE, to assume the same specific relationship between social-historical circumstances and prophetic words and actions.

It may not be possible to pursue such a method with any degree of precision, however, because we have so little material on particular prophets and movements. We have only a few words of John the Baptist (as transmitted and/or reshaped in Josephus and the Gospels), and only the most elementary sense of the basic actions of the prophets who led movements. It is highly unlikely that there would be any point, therefore, in attempting to draw very specific connections between political figures and events, on the one hand, and popular prophets' oracles or actions, on the other. The one notable exception is John the Baptist's admonition to Antipas regarding his marriage (already commented upon above). Otherwise, we can make only rough connections between the broad general social-historical situation and prophetic words and actions. This is illustrated, ironically, by Barnett's discussion. He sketches the 'context' for each of the 'sign prophets' but then apparently can make no specific connections between a given prophet and his 'context'. Barnett also focuses on what is happening at the top of the social ladder in the behavior of individual Roman governors and Jewish high priests, in what appears almost to be a personalization of historical relationships which were far more complex.[45] Moreover, he fails to inquire into the social stratum in which the 'sign prophets' occurred in order then to assess which events and relationships might have constituted the most relevant aspects of the historical context.

Designing our approach according to the limitation of our sources

44. H.B. Huffmon, 'The Origins of Prophecy', in F.M. Cross (ed.), *Magnalia Dei: The Mighty Acts of God* (Garden City, NY: Doubleday, 1976), pp. 176-84.

45. Barnett, 'The Jewish Sign Prophets', pp. 680-86, esp. 682.

means that we must deal primarily in terms of general social-historical conditions. If we are able to draw specific connections between prophetic actions and particular figures and events at all, it would be only on the basis of an understanding of the relevant general conditions. However, the importance of the general social conditions in this case is suggested precisely by the clear class division between the popular prophetic movements, on the one hand, and the ruling groups who suppressed them, on the other. Particularly relevant would be an inquiry into the kinds of conditions that would make thousands of peasants ready to follow a prophet in search of liberation. The following paragraphs are intended as a brief and only partial sketch of the circumstances of disruption, or of threatened disruption, among the traditional Palestinian Jewish peasantry in the first century CE.

The situation of Palestinian Jewish society was one of increasingly intense economic pressure on the peasantry. The fact that, in a peasant society where subsistence depended upon possession of a plot of land, large numbers of people were already displaced from their land (e.g. the number of laborers just waiting for work in Jesus' parable in Mt. 20) indicates that additional numbers were probably threatened with loss of their land by the political-economic pressures. Moreover, the ways in which and the reasons why the economic pressures were directed against the peasantry meant further disruption to the traditional way of life and values of the people. This can be illustrated with a few examples, some of which may be related indirectly and generally (but not necessarily directly) to particular popular prophets.

Intense economic pressures had been placed upon the Jewish peasantry for several decades by the multiple demands for tithes, taxes, and tribute.[46] The taxation extracted by the Herodian rulers served not simply to support an illegitimate government, with its mercenary troops for security forces and bureaucrats who spoke a foreign language. Herod's massive building projects within and outside of Palestine and his astounding munificence to foreign cities and imperial family members were continued by his descendants and successors. Antipas disrupted more than the religious sensibilities of his subjects by the building or refurbishing of Hellenistic cities such as Tiberias and Sepphoris (*Ant.* 18.27, 36–38). Agrippa I apparently attempted to imitate, if not match, Herod the Great in his

---

46. F.C. Grant, *The Economic Background of the Gospels* (London: Oxford University Press, 1926), pp. 87-91; S. Applebaum, 'Economic Life in Palestine', in *The Jewish People in the First Century* (Assen: Van Gorcum, 1976), pp. 661-64.

sponsorship of Hellenistic culture (buildings, munificence directed abroad) at the expense of his common Jewish subjects.[47] Heavy royal or imperial taxation on top of religious (Temple, etc.) taxation placed the still independent and productive peasantry in circumstances where many were forced to borrow to meet subsistence needs.

Surplus wealth flowed into and piled up in Jerusalem.[48] But there were no ways in which it could be channeled to the people most in need. Some of it was used to fund the building projects such as the Temple and paving the streets of the city. But such projects, including the feeding of the thousands of workmen, had basically to be supported by the heavy taxation of the peasantry. There are indications that besides being used on luxury goods or simply stored in the Temple treasury in the form of valuable metals and other objects (*War* 6.282), such surplus wealth (largely in the hands of the royal and priestly aristocracy) was 'invested' in land. The mechanism was, of course, loans at usurious rates to the needy peasantry. Many were forced eventually to forfeit their land.[49] Many others came heavily into debt and under the threat of expropriation (as in the parables of Jesus in Mt. 18.23-33 and Lk. 16.1-7). For many peasants already threatened with loss of their land, the prolonged drought and resultant famine of the late 40s must have meant acute distress. The fact that an already serious flight into banditry throughout the period escalated to epidemic proportions in the 50s and 60s may be as good an indication as we could find that there were pressures forcing people off the land.[50]

Finally, the priestly aristocracy, who supposedly represented the interests of the Jewish people, were behaving in an increasingly predatory manner against the very people who supported the Temple establishment with their tithes. This resulted in a serious loss of legitimacy for the high

47. Contra Barnett, 'The Jewish Sign Prophets', pp. 680-81, I cannot imagine that the passing of Agrippa I was a 'disappointment to the *people* of Judaea' (my emphasis). I assume we should base historical reconstructions not on Josephus's editorial generalization but rather on the information he provides which, in the case of Agrippa I, belies his own generalizations. Compare *Ant.* 19.335–37 and 351–52 with 19.328-31; and 19.343-50 with 19.331.

48. Some relevant documentation in J. Jeremias, *Jerusalem at the Time of Jesus* (Philadelphia: Fortress Press, 1975), pp. 54-57, 73-77, 87-99, 124-26, 138.

49. The very existence of the many large landed estates at this time is evidence. See, most recently, M. Goodman, 'The First Jewish Revolt: Social Conflict and the Problem of Debt', *JJS* 33 (1982), pp. 422-24.

50. References and discussion in Horsley, 'Ancient Jewish Banditry', pp. 412-20.

priesthood and priestly aristocracy generally. The fact that the Sicarii focused their terrorist activities against these collaborators with Roman rule may be a good indicator that lack of respect for the central religious-political authorities extended beyond these discontented members of the intelligentsia. The priestly aristocracy became so blatant in its predatory behavior that individual families would sponsor strong-armed gangs both for defense against each other and for raids upon the threshing floors to expropriate the tithes intended for the often poverty-stricken regular priests (*Ant.* 20.180–81; 20.206–207).[51]

Without making direct and overly precise connections between particular prophets and particular historical figures and circumstances, it is nevertheless possible to discern that the popular prophets were both reactions to and directed against the oppression of the Jewish peasantry in Roman-dominated Palestine. Heavy taxation compounded by the tendency of the wealthy to take advantage of marginalized peasant families and thepredatory behavior of the ruling families brought intense economic pressures on the previously independent and free-holding peasantry. The oracular prophets protested the situation, both John the Baptist and Jesus son of Hananiah apparently pronouncing divine judgment on the situation and its perpetrators. The action prophets, building their movements out of the threatened or already disrupted peasantry, led their followers into active participation in the 'revolutionary changes' they announced as imminent.

Implications for Understanding Jesus' Ministry

Much of the interpretation of Jesus as prophet has been done on the basis of a highly synthetic picture of expectations of an eschatological prophet in Jewish literature.[52] Even in very recent scholarship, this synthetic concept of 'prophecy' and 'eschatological prophet' has been presupposed not simply for early Christian interpretations of Jesus but for Jesus' own actions and sayings as well.[53] There is little solid evidence, however, for Jewish expectations of an eschatological prophet (whether 'a returning Elijah', 'a prophet like Moses', or 'the eschatological

51. The parallel passage, *War* 2.274–75, is misleadingly translated in the LCL edition.

52. E.g. O. Cullmann, *The Christology of the New Testament* (Philadelphia: Westminster Press, 1959), pp. 11-30; F. Hahn, *The Titles of Jesus in Christology* (New York: World, 1969), pp. 352-65.

53. E.g. Aune, *Prophecy*, for example in pp. 122-26.

prophet').[54] This makes all the more important Hill's suggestion that Jesus' ministry should be studied rather in comparison with the popular Palestinian prophets and their movements. Following Hill's suggestion, however, would mean not just a shift of comparative material, but a shift of focus as well. Instead of concentrating on prophetic concepts and expectations in Jewish apocalyptic literature which may have been used to interpret the significance of Jesus, we would focus on actual popular prophetic movements, which modern scholars can use, by comparison and contrast, to discern what is characteristic and distinctive about Jesus and his movement. By implication, parallel comparisons and contrasts could be made between Jesus and other distinctive types of popular leaders and movements as well (for example, the popular oracular prophets such as Jesus son of Hananiah and the popular messianic movements such as those which emerged after the death of Herod). Analysis of Jesus and his movement can thus be carried out in more precise terms. Instead of lumping all prophetic and messianic expectations into a synthetic picture which is then compared with early Christian literary evidence, we can make comparisons of particular features of Jesus and his movement with other popular figures and movements of distinctive types. Although comparisons between Jesus and the prophetic movements cannot be explored adequately in the confines of an article such as this, the implications of this shift of both focus and comparative material for understanding Jesus as prophet can at least be briefly delineated. It is important to note both similarities and differences.

Although Jesus of Nazareth may resemble the solitary popular oracular prophets such as Jesus son of Hananiah in some of his prophecies (e.g. the lament over Jerusalem, Lk. 13.34-35), he is similar to figures such as Theudas and the 'Egyptian' in being a leader of a sizeable movement. The crucial feature of Jesus' ministry, moreover, similar to those of the popular prophetic movements, is not miracles as signs of something else, but divine action, in Jesus' case the (imminent) presence of the rule of God. As with the other prophetic leaders of movements, furthermore, Jesus summons his followers to become participants in the saving action of God.

The social location and social-historical context of Jesus' ministry also appear to be much the same as those of the popular prophetic move-

54. Survey of the limited evidence in Horsley, '"Like One of the Prophets of Old"'; similar critical survey of limited evidence for the term 'messiah' prior to the time of Jesus in M. de Jonge, 'The Use of the Word "Anointed" in the Time of Jesus', *NovT* 8 (1966), pp. 132-48.

ments, except of course that Jesus was largely in Galilee instead of Judea. Although his career climaxed in Jerusalem (like the group led by the 'Egyptian') Jesus' ministry took place almost exclusively in rural villages, and his followers were basically from the common people. There are a number of indications in Jesus' parables and other sayings that debt and even landlessness were serious difficulties for the people addressed (e.g. Mt. 18.23-33; 20.1-7; Lk. 6.30; 16.18).

Besides the similarities, however, there were also some significant differences between Jesus and the popular prophetic movements. Both focused on the imminent (eschatological) action of God. Judging from the accounts of Josephus, however, prophets such as Theudas and the 'Egyptian' thought of this action in rather fantastic terms. The latter, for example, apparently expected the sudden miraculous fall of Jerusalem, analogous to the fall of Jericho in the biblical narrative. Although there were some visionary and other fantastic elements in the preaching of Jesus, the dominant note was one of 'prophetic realism', more like the popular oracular prophets. Leaving aside the climactic events in Jerusalem for a moment, Jesus' Galilean ministry focused on how the saving action of God was taking shape in concrete social relations (such as table fellowship, forgiveness of debts, etc.). There was little sense of a sudden 'supernatural' intervention by God in human affairs as appears to have been the case with Theudas, the 'Egyptian' and similar movements. The popular prophetic movements appear to have been somewhat oblivious to the concrete political situation. They may have been expecting 'revolutionary changes', as Josephus says, but they were surely not seriously revolutionary in the sense of building a broader social base and organization. Jesus of Nazareth and his movement must have been far more serious in this sense. Jesus, while announcing that God was taking the initiative (the kingdom of God was at hand), emphasized that the kingdom was a matter of people renewing their social relations in accordance with the will and in response to the enabling presence of God.

There is some question, finally, whether and to what extent the fundamental pattern which informs the popular prophetic movements can be found in Jesus' ministry. Treatment of this issue might focus on two kinds of material in particular: the sayings of Jesus which have been labelled 'eschatological correlatives' (such as Lk. 11.29-32; 17.26-30),[55]

---

55. R.A. Edwards, *The Sign of Jonah* (SBT, 2.18; London: SCM Press, 1971), pp. 47-58.

and what have been called Jesus' 'symbolic actions'.[56] From the 'eschatological correlative' sayings it is at least clear that at an early point followers of Jesus understood his ministry in terms of present (eschatological) events which corresponded to highly significant events in the history of Israel. The emphasis in these sayings, however, was less on the great events of liberation (exodus and conquest) under Moses and Joshua, than on crucial times of judgment (Noah and Jonah). The corresponding implication for the present, eschatological time: judgment was at hand and repentance was urgent. Nevertheless, in one of these correlatives (Lk. 11.31) there is also the highly positive implication that Jesus' ministry is far greater than the corresponding great historical time of salvation under Solomon. At least in the community which preserved and used the sayings gathered into Q, Jesus' ministry and God's imminent action appear to have been understood in terms of a historical-eschatological pattern similar to the one embodied in the popular prophetic movements.

A comparison with the popular prophetic movements might also lead us to reconsider whether a number of the significant actions of Jesus were simply 'symbolic'. Jesus' actions such as the healing miracles, the cursing of the fig tree, the 'cleansing of the Temple', and the selection of the Twelve are discussed in scholarly literature as being 'prophetic' or 'symbolic' dramatizations of what would be done by God in the future.[57] It has been argued above that it is misleading and reductive to conclude that 'signs' rather than saving divine actions were the principal feature of the popular prophetic movements. These prophets and their followers were not simply symbolizing in present dramatic 'demonstrations', as it were, what God would finally carry out at some time in the future, but were caught up in the keen conviction that God was acting in the present and that they were participating in the divine action. In comparison, how should we understand Jesus' dramatic actions? Surely the cursing of the fig tree was a 'symbolic action'. But are some of his other significant actions merely 'symbolic' or 'prophetic', like Jeremiah's wearing of yoke-bars around his neck or Isaiah's going around Jerusalem naked and barefoot?[58] In actions such as the appointing of the Twelve, the

56. Summary and references in Aune, *Prophecy*, pp. 161-63.
57. See Aune, *Prophecy*, pp. 161-63.
58. The 'triumphal entry' and the 'cleansing of the Temple' are problematic; they should perhaps be understood more as actions of a 'messiah', analogous to past actions by David, Hezekiah, or Josiah, rather than as the actions of a prophet (as in

institution of the new covenant at the last supper, and even healings and exorcisms, Jesus was not simply predicting or symbolizing, but manifesting the action of God. Judging from the occurrence of several popular prophetic movements, this pattern of understanding and action appears to have been current among the common people right around the time of Jesus.

Mal. 3). See B.D. Chilton, 'Jesus *ben David*: Reflections on the *Davidssohnfrage'*, *JSNT* 14 (1982), pp. 88-112, esp. pp. 102-105.

JSNT 8 (1980), pp. 24-45

STREAMS OF TRADITION EMERGING FROM ISAIAH 40.1-5
AND THEIR ADAPTATION IN THE NEW TESTAMENT

Klyne R. Snodgrass

The importance of the initial verses of Isaiah 40 in describing the gospel events is obvious on even a cursory reading of the evangelists' accounts. Similarly, one cannot proceed very far in analyzing the Gospels without realizing that midrashic activity must be investigated in order to understand the adaptation of the Old Testament by the New and specifically the use of Isa. 40.1-5 by Mark and Luke. Many people tend to look on midrashic studies, however, as a retreat into *esoterica* and have not been able to get excited about this discipline. Granted, midrashic studies have tended to focus on the meaning of the term 'midrash' and the techniques used in the formation of midrash more than the explanation of midrash in specific texts, whether in terms of the patterns evidenced, the borrowing of previous midrashic conclusions, or the formation of new midrash to convey the author's thought. In addition, not infrequently those involved in midrashic studies have made an appreciation for midrash more difficult by being overly technical, more imaginative than the facts will substantiate, or by seizing on one element in a whole stream of tradition and thereby causing distortion. A sane and holistic approach is required in which one is aware that material was used in a variety of ways over the centuries and which attempts to accumulate as much definite material as possible to establish both a 'feeling' for the use of the text and specific examples of what certain groups have done with it. The crucial factor about careful midrashic and related studies is that they provide an understanding of the tradition and heritage from which a text emerges. This information is significant for both scholar and proclaimer of the text and cannot be ignored.

Such is the case with the use of Isa. 40.1-5, since the New Testament attraction to these verses is paralleled sufficiently elsewhere, so that there is a 'stream of tradition' that gives assistance in interpreting the New

Testament passages. The order in which the various 'tributaries' are dealt with will not be chronological. The New Testament texts will be dealt with last because of the number of issues that need to be treated there.

The Old Testament

Before dealing with texts that attempt to explain or adapt Isa. 40.1-5, attention should be given to the Old Testament text itself and especially to the role that these verses play in Isaiah. Most of those analyzing Isaiah would view 40.1-11 as the prologue or overture to chs. 40–66. The themes of God's comfort and his restoration of his people run through the entire section (e.g. 49.8-13; 51.11-16; 52.7-10; 66.13-14). Of special interest is the reappearance of the phrase פַּנּוּ דֶרֶךְ from 40.3 in 57.14 and 62.10, although the latter both speak of preparation of the way of the people while 40.3 speaks of preparation of the way of God. Similarly, the idea of a highway in the desert as a New Exodus theme in 40.3-4, which is developed from 11.16 and 35.8, reappears in 43.19 and 49.11. Numerous other parallels can be shown as well.[1]

The impact of this section also on Mal. 3.1 merits consideration. In view of the fact that the *piel* of פנה does not appear outside Mal. 3.1 and the three texts mentioned in Isaiah (40.3; 57.14; and 62.10), and in view of the common theme of the appearance of the Lord, there is a good possibility that Mal. 3.1 was influenced by Isa. 40.3.

The Septuagint

[1]παρακαλεῖτε παρακαλεῖτε τὸν λαόν μου, λέγει ὁ θεός. [2]ἱερεῖς, λαλήσατε εἰς τὴν καρδίαν Ιερουσαλημ, παρακαλέσατε αὐτήν· ὅτι ἐπλήσθη ἡ ταπείνωσις αὐτῆς, λέλυται αὐτῆς ἡ ἁμαρτία· ὅτι ἐδέξατο ἐκ χειρὸς κυρίου διπλᾶ τὰ ἁμαρτήματα αὐτῆς.

[1]Comfort, comfort my people says God, [2]Priests, speak to the heart of Jerusalem, comfort her because her humiliation has been filled, her sin has been atoned for because she received from the hand of the Lord double for her sins.

---

1. Note for example the themes of 40.5 that are developed later, such as the theme of the effectiveness of the Word of God (55.11) or all flesh being affected by God's activity (66.23). On the role of Isa. 40.1-11, see C. Westermann, *Isaiah 40–66: A Commentary* (OTL; Philadelphia: Westminster Press, 1969), pp. 28-33; and R.F. Melugin, *The Formation of Isaiah 40–55* (BZAW, 141; Berlin: de Gruyter, 1976), although both focus only on chs. 40–55.

³φωνὴ βοῶντος ἐν τῇ ἐρήμῳ
ἑτοιμάσατε τὴν ὁδὸν κυρίου, εὐθείας
ποιεῖτε τὰς τρίβους τοῦ θεοῦ ἡμῶν·
⁴πᾶσα φάραγξ πληρωθήσεται καὶ πᾶν
ὄρος καὶ βουνὸς ταπεινωθήσεται, καὶ
ἔσται πάντα τὰ σκολιὰ εἰς εὐθεῖαν
καὶ ἡ τραχεῖα εἰς πεδία· ⁵καὶ
ὀφθήσεται ἡ δόξα κυρίου, καὶ ὄψεται
πᾶσα σὰρξ τὸ σωτήριον τοῦ θεοῦ· ὅτι
κύριος ἐλάλησεν.

³A voice of one crying in the wilderness,
'Prepare the way of the Lord; make
straight the paths of our God'.
⁴Every ravine will be filled and every
mountain and hill will be lowered and all
the crooked places will be straight and
the rugged level.
⁵And the glory of the Lord will be seen,
and all flesh will see the salvation of
God because the Lord spoke.

The translation of Isa. 40.1-5 in the Septuagint contains a few surprises. The difficulty of knowing to whom the words are addressed is alleviated by the insertion of ἱερεῖς. The insertion cannot be explained with certainty. It could have arisen from the conflict between priestly and political parties. Or, as R.R. Ottley suggested, since the pronoun of v. 1 was not rendered, כם might have suggested כהנים.[2] There is another possibility that deserves mention. If Mal. 3.1 were connected to Isa. 40.3 as it obviously is at a later date, then this identification may be due to the identification of the מלאך יהוה as the priest in Mal. 2.7.

Three other changes need to be mentioned. In v. 2 the idea of comfort is emphasized by the insertion of παρακαλέσατε. (Note also the insertion of παρακαλέσει in 40.11.) The phrase ἐν τῇ ἐρήμῳ in v. 3 has apparently been taken with φωνὴ βοῶντος instead of ἑτοιμάσατε and בערבה is not represented in the next clause at all.[3] In v. 5 new direction is given to the text by the insertion of τὸ σωτήριον τοῦ θεοῦ to specify what will be seen by all flesh. The phrase may have been influenced by Isa. 52.10.

The Targum

¹נבייא אתנבו תנחומין על ¹O you prophets, prophesy consolations
²עמי אמר אלהכון: מלו על concerning my people, says your God.
ליבה דירושלם ואתנבו עלה Speak to the heart of Jerusalem and

2.   R.R. Ottley, *The Book of Isaiah according to the Septuagint* (Cambridge: Cambridge University Press, 1906), II, p. 297.
3.   H. Kosmala ('Form and Structure in Ancient Hebrew Poetry', *VT* 14 [1964], pp. 441-43) argues for the possibility of an original *Vorlage* behind the Septuagint text in which במדבר went with קול. C.C. Torrey (*The Second Isaiah* [New York: Charles Scribner's Sons, 1928], p. 305) also argues for a metrical division in which the caesura follows במדבר.

ארי עתידא דתתמלי מעם   prophesy concerning her that she is
גלותהא ארי אשתביקו לה   about to be filled with the people of her
חובהא ארי קבילת כס   exiles, that her transgressions have been
תנחומין מן קדם יהוה   forgiven her, that she has received the
כאלו לקת על חד תרין בכל   cup of consolations from before the
חטאהא: ³קל דמכלי במדברא   Lord as if she had been smitten twice for
פנו אורחא קדם עמא דיהוה   all her sins. ³The voice of one crying,
כבישו במישרא כבשין קדם   'In the wilderness prepare a way before
כנשתא דאלהנא: ⁴כל חיליא   the people of the Lord; tread down in the
יראמון וכל טור ורמא   desert paths before the congregation of
ימאכון ויהי כפלא למישרא   our God'. All the valleys shall be raised
ובית גידודין לבקעא: up and every mountain and hill shall be
⁵ויתגלי יקרא דיהוה ויחזון   made low and the uneven shall become
כל בני בסרא כחדא ארי   a plain and the steep places a valley.
במימרא דיהוה גזיר כין: ⁵And the glory of the Lord shall be
revealed and all sons of flesh will see it
together for by the word of the Lord the
decree is thus.

The differences of the Targum and the Hebrew text are not numerous but the meaning of the text has been changed considerably. Where the Septuagint added ἱερεῖς in 40.2 to specify the addressees, the Targum adds נבייא אתנבו in 40.1 to achieve the same end. The addition of a reference to the prophet is fairly frequent in the *Targum of Isaiah* (e.g. 35.3, 5; 40.13; 41.27; 58.1, 3; 62.10). The most significant changes occur in vv. 2-3. Whereas the Old Testament says that Jerusalem's hard service has been filled, the Targum indicates that *she* is about to be filled with the people of her exiles. Accordingly, the way that is prepared in the wilderness in v. 3 is no longer in anticipation of Yahweh coming to his people but is for the people themselves as they return to Jerusalem. Lars Hartman has suggested the influence of Isaiah 35 on the *Targum of Isaiah* 40,[4] but one should note that in the two other texts of Isaiah with the phrase דרך פנו (57.14 and 62.10) the preparation of the way is for the people of God, and it appears that the rendering in the Targum of 40.3 is derived at least partly from these two texts. (Note also the insertion which deals with the wicked in *Targ. Isa.* 40.6-7 which may derive from Isa. 57.20-21.) One should note in passing that the statement that Jerusalem has received double for her sins has been diminished by 'as if' and that the content of revelation in the Targum is the Kingdom of God (40.9).

---

4. L. Hartman, *Prophecy Interpreted: The Formation of Some Jewish Apocalyptic Texts and of the Eschatological Discourse Mark 13 par* (ConBNT, 1; Lund: Gleerup, 1966), pp. 127-28.

The Dead Sea Scrolls

The suggestion that Isa. 40.3 inspires the faith and provides the philosophy of the Qumran movement[5] is no exaggeration even though the text is not quoted frequently. Certainly the designation of the community or at least community life as דרך (ה) in 1QS 9.9, 17-21 and 10.21 (and indeed the later Christian self-designation as ἡ ὁδός in Acts 9.2; 19.9, 23; 22.4; 24.14, and 22) was derived from Isa. 40.3. Allusions to the community in the wilderness also seem to be drawn from this Old Testament text. Note 1QM 1.3 which refers to returned exiles who pitch camp in the desert of Jerusalem in preparation for war (cf. 4QIsa[a] 1.5–6.1). 4QpPs 37 3.1 speaks of those who 'return from the wilderness and live for a thousand generations'.[6] Of primary significance, however, are two texts in 1QS that adapt Isa. 40.3 in describing the community.

1QS 8.12b-16a

ובהיות אלה ליחד בישראל	And when these become a community
בתכונים האלה יבדלו מתוך¹³	in Israel according to all these rules, they
מושב הנשי העול ללכת	will separate from the dwelling of
למדבר לפנות שם את דרך	perverse men *in order to go to the desert*
הואהא¹⁴כאשר כתוב	*to prepare there the way of Him*[7] even
במדבר פנו דרך...ישרו	as it has been written. 'In the wilderness
בערבה⁸מסלה לאלוהינו	prepare the way of...; make straight in
היאה¹⁵ מדרש התורה [אשר] צוה	the desert a highway for our God'. This
ביד מושה לעשות ככול	is the study of Torah which he
הנגלה עת בעת¹⁶וכאשר	commanded by the hand of Moses to do
גלו הנביאים ברוח קודשו	according to all that has been revealed
	time and again and even as the prophets
	revealed by the Holy Spirit.

5. See S.V. McCasland, 'The Way', *JBL* 77 (1958), p. 226. On 'the Way', see E. Repo, *Der 'Weg' als Selbstbezeichnung des Urchristentums* (Helsinki: Suomalainen Tiedeakatemia, 1964).

6. 1QS 4.2 also appears to allude to Isa. 40.3. Note also that 1QpHab 2.15 seems to allude to Isa. 40.2.

7. The translation at this point is purposely cumbersome to highlight the unusual way of making reference to God by substituting for יהוה. See H.P. Rüger, 'הואהא Er: Zur Deutung von 1QS 8, 13-14', *ZNW* 60 (1969), pp. 142-44.

8. The text at this point actually reads בערכה which most view as an error for בערבה. D. Barthélemy ('Notes en marge de publications recentes sur les Manuscripts de Qumran', *RB* 59 [1952], p. 198) sees the error as an allusion to

1QS 9.17b-20a

ולהוכיח דעת אמת ומשפט צדק	He will admonish with true knowledge
לבוחרי ¹⁸ דרך איש כרוחו	and righteous judgment those choosing
כתכון העת לדנחותם בדעה	the way, each according to his spirit
וכן להשכילם ברזי פלא ואמת	according to the norm of the time to lead
בתוך ¹⁹ אנשי היחד להלך	them in knowledge and thus to instruct
תמים איש את רעהו בכול	them in the mysteries of wonder and
הנגלה להם היאה עת פנות	truth in the midst of the men of the
²⁰ הדרך למדבר	community so that a man may walk

He will admonish with true knowledge and righteous judgment those choosing the way, each according to his spirit according to the norm of the time to lead them in knowledge and thus to instruct them in the mysteries of wonder and truth in the midst of the men of the community so that a man may walk perfectly with his neighbor in all that has been revealed to them. *This is the time for preparing the way to the wilderness...*

Clearly Isa. 40.3 has been programmatic for the community's self-understanding. No emphasis is placed on the voice crying, but the reference to the wilderness has been understood literally. This is not surprising given the theological understanding of the wilderness as a place of eschatological testing and from which deliverance will come.[9] The words 'prepare the way...make straight...a highway' have been interpreted figuratively. The preparation in 1QS 8.15 is understood explicitly as study of the Torah (מדרש התורה) and in 9.19 as the observance of Torah, but there is no difference, since the content in 8.12-13 expects the study to be lived out in community.[10]

J. de Waard has suggested that the interpretation in 1QS 8.15 arises from the rabbinic technique of אל תקרי ('Do not read'—i.e. read a different word or another word in addition to) so that מדרש arises from ישרו.[11] He also goes on to suggest that the interpretation here is derived

---

Pirke Abot 6.5 with the meaning 'Rectifiez soigneusement la voi pour notre Dieu'.

9.   Note Hos. 2.14 and the motif of the exodus as an image of salvation (e.g. Isa. 11.15-16). See W.R. Stegner, 'Wilderness and Testing in the Scrolls and in Mt. 4.1-11', *BR* 12 (1967), pp. 18-27; U. Mauser, *Christ in the Wilderness* (SBT, 39; London: SCM Press, 1963); and S. Talmon, 'The Desert Motif in the Bible and in the Qumran Literature', in A. Altmann (ed.), *Biblical Motifs* (Cambridge, MA: Harvard University Press, 1966), pp. 31-63.

10.   O. Betz, *Offenbarung und Schriftforschung in der Qumransekte* (Tübingen: Mohr [Paul Siebeck], 1960), p. 157.

11.   J. de Waard, *A Comparative Study of the Old Testament Text in the Dead Sea Scrolls and in the New Testament* (STDJ, 4; Leiden: Brill, 1965), pp. 52-53. Betz (*Offenbarung*, p. 157) suggests that the similarity of דרך and דרש may have encouraged the combination, although he recognizes that this is not necessary.

from the reading of *Targ. Isa.* 40.3 so that כבישו ('tread down') there is
understood as 'make clear', מישרא ('desert' or 'plain') is understood as
'camp', and כבשין ('paths') is understood as כבשן ('secret'). Therefore
de Waard suggests that the text was understood as 'Make clear in the
camp the secrets before the people of our God', an interpretation to
which he sees an allusion in 8.11-12. Neither of these suggestions has
much merit. It is not impossible that the *Targum of Isaiah* was known in
Qumran, but the suggestion that Isa. 40.3 was understood as 'Make
clear in the camp the secrets before the people of our God' is overly
imaginative and without basis in the text. The fact that the quotation in
1QS reads מסלה לאלוהינו instead of כבשן לעם אלוהינו or something
similar makes it clear that the preparation is for the coming of God. Nor
is it necessary to suggest the rabbinic device אל תקרי to arrive at the
emphasis on studying and living תורה. Words like דרך and ישר had a
long history of being used metaphorically of proper living before God.
Note especially Isa. 35.8; 45.13; Prov. 3.6; 9.15; 11.5; 15.21; and Jer.
31.9. Similar to the interpretation here is that in *Mek. Exod.* 18.20: 'And
you shall show them the Way (הדרך); that is the study (תלמוד) of
Torah'. It is the history of the word rather than the similarity of radicals
that leads to the interpretation of פנו דרך by מדרש התורה. One should
note as well that other passages mentioning preparation of the way have
been interpreted ethically in *Targ. Isa.* 57.14-15 and 62.10.

It is clear in both these texts that the Qumran community viewed their
right living in the wilderness as the means of preparation for the soon
coming of God. John A.T. Robinson views these passages as pointing to
a future eschatological time which in the present is only an ideal.[12] His
argument is far from convincing, but at least the community viewed
itself as fulfilling what was necessary to prepare the way for God's
redemption, and they did so because of their interpretation of Isa. 40.3.

There is an additional use of Isa. 40.1-5 that has received virtually no
attention. 4Q176, which has been entitled 'Tanḥumim', is essentially a
series of quotations nearly all of which are taken from Isaiah 40–54.
Allegro has described column I as quotations of Ps. 79.2-3; Isa. 40.1-5;
41.8-9 and *pesher*, and column II as quotations of Isa. 49.7, 13-17; 43.1-2;
43.4-6; 51.22-23; 52.1-3; 54.4-10 and *pesher* and Zech. 13.9.[13] The

12. J.A.T. Robinson, 'The Baptism of John and the Qumran Community', in his
Twelve New Testament Studies (SBT, 34; London: SCM Press, 1972), pp. 14-15.
13. J.M. Allegro, *Qumran Cave 4* (DJD, 5; Oxford: Clarendon Press, 1968),
pp. 60-67.

order is debatable depending on how one arranges the fragments and there are numerous other fragments too small to identify. The description of column I is misleading, however. The first lines are not a quotation of Ps. 79.2-3 and there is no *pesher*, unless Allegro has taken these first lines as a *pesher*. Lines 1-3 are apparently a prayer concerning, or a prophecy of, God acting to defeat the nations and reverse the calamity of his people. The words were styled on Psalm 79. Line 4 begins with two words from Ps. 79.3 (קובר ואין) and there are themes and words that are common to lines 1-3 and Psalm 79: holy place, Jerusalem, dead bodies (but 'servants' in Ps. 79.2 has been changed to 'priests' in line 3). The important point for our purposes is that immediately following the picture described via Psalm 79 'consolations from the Book of Isaiah' are given and Isa. 40.15 is quoted first. The other texts that are quoted continue the theme of consolation and deliverance.[14]

This text also forces attention onto the sociological context of the community and the reasons why the words of comfort are so important. That the community felt oppressed and sought comfort in these words seems fairly clear, especially with the change of 'servants' to 'priests' in line 3. Presumably the oppression was due to foreign domination and probably to social ostracization as well. Their inadequate existence and longing for salvation made the words of Isa. 40.1-5 so meaningful.

The results of the investigation so far show that Isa. 40.1-5 was important for two reasons: (1) it was a classic statement of the consolation that comes from God and was understood specifically in the context of God's eschatological comfort; (2) the focus on the preparation of the way gave specific focus to the eschatological orientation by being interpreted of the return of the exiles or by being understood specifically of a group that viewed themselves eschatologically and expected their ethical behavior to prepare the way of God's coming. The remaining occurrences of the use of these verses will verify these conclusions.

---

14. J. Strugnell ('Notes en marge du volume V des "Discoveries in the Judaean Desert of Jordan"', *RevQ* 7 [1970], p. 229) is hesitant to apply the title 'Tanḥumim' to the whole work, but he does describe it as a 'chaîne de mots consonants tirés du Livre du Deutéro-Isaie'. The extent to which the other verses are included because of similarities to Isa. 40.1-5 is uncertain. For example, has the appearance of העקב in Isa. 40.4 led to the attraction of 41.8 with its occurrence of יעקב or is the similarity merely coincidental while the attraction is to the concept of election? The latter is probably the case. At any rate the theme of consolation is the common bond bringing the quotations together.

Apocrypha and Pseudepigrapha

The references here are not numerous but they will help to round out the picture. Bar. 5.7 adapts Isa. 40.4 to describe the redemption of Israel: 'For God ordered every high mountain and the eternal hills to be lowered and the ravines to be filled to make a smooth land in order that Israel may walk securely in the glory of God'. As in some texts before, the preparation is of a way in which the people are to walk. However, *Ass. Mos.* 10.1-5 seems to borrow ideas from Isa. 40.4-5 and here the high mountains are made low before the coming of God (cf. *1 En.* 1.6).[15]

The Rabbinic Literature

The use of Isa. 40.1-5 as a classic statement on the comfort of God and as descriptive of God's activity at the end of the age is evident in the rabbinic material. The most significant treatment of these verses is that which appears in *Pes. R.* 29/30a, 29/30b, 30, and 33. The first three in their entirety are a commentary on Isa. 40.1-2. They stress the certainty of God's coming to comfort his people and demonstrate both the rationale for and the nature of the comfort. *Pes. R.* 33, which deals more generally with the comfort of God on the basis of Isa. 51.12, makes reference to Isa. 40.1 in sections 3 and 11 and to Isa. 40.2 and 5 in section 13. The extended treatment on Isa. 40.1-2 in *Pesikta Rabbati* is due to the fact that Isaiah 40 is read as the haftarah on the first Sabbath following the ninth of *Av*, one of the fasts commemorating the destruction of the Temple. This fact alone demonstrates the extent to which the passage was viewed as a major statement on God's comfort. This conclusion is so obvious that it is unnecessary to treat other rabbinic passages in support.[16]

The eschatological orientation given to this text is clear in some of the rabbinic passages referred to above in that they point to God's eschatological comfort. A different eschatological orientation is also revealed.

15. Note that *Pss. Sol.* 8.16(18)-17(19) adapts the imagery of Isa. 40.3-4 by placing it, with a good dose of irony, in the mouths of the princes of the land who go out 'to make the rough ways even' for Pompey as he captures Jerusalem.

16. The following texts should be cited: *Gen. R.* 100.9; *Lev. R.* 10.2; 21.7; *Lam. R.* 1.2.23; 1.22.57; *Midr. Ps.* 4.8; 22.27; and 23.7. See also Sir. 48.24 and *Tanḥ. on Deut.* 1.1§1 (ed. Horeb, p. 617) which is quoted by O. Schmitz and G. Stahlin, 'παρακαλέω, παράκλησις', *TDNT*, V, p. 792.

Lev. R. 1.14 interprets Isa. 40.5 of the age to come: 'In this world the *Shechinah* manifests itself only to chosen individuals; in the Time to Come, however, "The glory of the Lord shall be revealed, and all flesh shall see it together, for the mouth of the Lord has spoken it"'. *Deut. R.* 4.11 adapts Isa. 40.4 to interpret literally 'the time when the Lord shall enlarge Palestine's borders' (Deut. 12.20). Only when the valleys are literally lifted up and the hills leveled will the full extent of Palestine be known. Significantly, the explanation of 'enlarging the borders' which concludes this chapter offers quotations of Mal. 3.4, 23; Zech. 1.16-17 and 9.9 to provide a note of comfort and hope.[17]

There is another use of Isa. 40.3-4 which deserves attention. Several rabbinic texts in commenting on God's leading Israel with a cloud (Exod. 13.21) enumerate seven clouds, one of which went before Israel to prepare the way by raising the depressions and lowering the elevations.[18] The activity of this cloud was drawn from Isa. 40.3-4, but the use of this text is based on the assumption that what is true concerning Israel in the future was also true in the exodus. W.S. Towner has shown that the link between the Isaiah 40 passage and the exodus narrative is explicitly based in *Mekilta de Rabbi Simeon* on Isa. 11.16 where the exodus narrative was used to describe God's redemptive activity.[19] Even with the focus on the historical exodus, the place of Isaiah 40 to explain God's future work is apparent.

The New Testament

The New Testament adaptation of Isa. 40.1-5 is unique in certain respects, and it opens up several areas of investigation. Isa. 40.3 is one of the few quotations that appear in all four Gospels and the only formula quotation in all four. In each case the words are applied to John the Baptist, but in Jn 1.23 the words are a self-identification by the Baptist whereas in the Synoptics the identification comes as a comment of the evangelists. It is well known that Mark has attributed an additional quotation to Isaiah, which is usually identified as Mal. 3.1 and/or Exod. 23.20, whereas

17. Also *Lekah Tov* on Num. 24.17 (See Str–B, I, 96).

18. *Num. R.* 1.2; 19.16; *Mek.*, Besh. I. 178-92; *Mek. SbY* (ed. Epstein-Melamed), p. 47; *Sifre Num.* 83 (on Num. 10.34); *t. Soṭ.* 4.2.

19. W.S. Towner, *The Rabbinic 'Enumeration of Scriptural Examples'* (SPB, 22; Leiden: Brill, 1973), pp. 155-59. It should be added that *b. 'Erub.* 54a understands the exalting of the low places as the result of repentance.

Matthew and Luke use this quotation in later discussions about the Baptist (11.10 and 7.27 respectively). At first glance it appears that John does not include this second quotation, but there is the possibility that 3.28b (ἀπεσταλμένος εἰμὶ ἔμπροσθεν ἐκείνου) reflects the conflated tradition recorded in the Synoptics. Certainly these words are not drawn from Jn 1.23. Jn 1.6 refers to the Baptist as ἄνθρωπος ἀπεσταλμένος παρὰ θεοῦ and 1.30 to one who comes after him, which could account for the words in 3.28, but it is more likely that these expressions are a result of the same interpretive tradition that is reflected in the Synoptics by the conflated quotation. One should also notice that whereas Matthew and Mark use only v. 3 from Isaiah 40, Lk. 3.4-6 quotes Isa. 40.3-5.

Each of the Gospels either assumes or states explicitly in addition to quoting Isa. 40.3 that the Baptist preached in the wilderness. The Synoptics emphasize the ethical content of his message by emphasizing the theme of repentance, and Mt. 3.8-10 and especially Lk. 3.8-14 stress the necessity of good works. This ethical interpretation of Isa. 40.3 obviously parallels the understanding of 1QS 8.12-13 and 9.17-18. The only allusions to this ethical emphasis in John, however, appear in the mention of cleansing and fasting in 3.25-26. The concern is much more to present John as a witness to the identity of Jesus.

The passages in Matthew and John do not show evidence of midrashic activity other than that which stands behind the adaptation of Isa. 40.3 directly to John the Baptist. The passages in Matthew and John will therefore occupy our attention only to the extent that they relate to Mark and Luke. The latter will have to be examined more closely because the use of more extended midrash has been suggested for both.

Mark 1.2-3

The problem of the form of the quotation in these two verses deserves more serious attention than it usually receives. The origin of the quotation in v. 2b is not easily determined. Usually Mal. 3.1 is mentioned but the wording, at least in the Septuagint, is not the same. The Septuagint includes ἐγώ (as does Matthew), has ἐξαποστέλλω instead of ἀποστέλλω, has μου instead of σου, uses ἐπιβλέψεται instead of κατασκευάσει, omits the article before ὁδόν and places πρὸ προσώπου μου with the second clause instead of the first. (Notice, however, that Matthew and Luke agree against Mark in including ἔμπροσθεν in the second clause.) Consequently many would point to Exod. 23.20, where the first clause is identical to what is found in the Synoptics. However, the second clause goes in a different direction from the Markan text. The suggestion that a conflation of Exod. 23.20 and Mal. 3.1 lies behind the quotation has merit particularly because פנה דרך probably lies behind κατασκευάσει τὴν ὁδόν. In addition there is evidence that Exod. 23.20 and Mal. 3.1 were connected in Judaism.[20] However, one must recognize that the form of the quotation here is unknown elsewhere.

The quotation of Isa. 40.3 in the Synoptics is identical to the Septuagint except that all three have αὐτοῦ instead of τοῦ θεοῦ ἡμῶν. The usual explanation that the Synoptists have made the change because they understand the text to refer to Jesus is not certain. Regardless of how the evangelists understood the text, αὐτοῦ could easily have arisen from an attempt to avoid the divine name. 1QS 8.13 substituted for the divine name an intensification of the third person pronoun: ללכת למדבר לפנות... שם את דרך הואהא ('to go to the desert to prepare there the way of him').[21] The antecedent of the pronouns in vv. 2-3 is uncertain on a ny reading. The author announces the beginning of the Gospel and immediately presents the composite quotation which he attributes to Isaiah. If one says that the speaker is obviously recognized as God, does σου then refer to the people, as in Exod. 23.20, or to Jesus? Do αὐτοῦ and κυρίου refer to Jesus or to God? At least in Mark one can make a case that the terms refer to God since κύριος is usually used of Jesus only in the vocative.[22]

Now that the difficulty of the form of the text has been set before us, we may inquire further about the origin of the text. Some would attribute Mk 1.2b to an interpolator and be finished with the problem, but as we will see there is good reason to accept the text as original.[23] Before that, however, attention must be given to an elaborate theory which has been proposed by C.T. Ruddick and which is relevant to midrashic studies.[24]

20. *Exod. R.* 32.9 and *Deut. R.* 11.9 connect Exod. 23.20 and Mal. 3.23. J. Mann (*The Bible as Read and Preached in the Old Synagogue* [Cincinnati: Hebrew Union College, 1940], I, p. 479) indicates that when Exod. 23.20 was the reading (Seder 61a) for the synagogue service, the sermon was given on Mal. 3.1-8 and 23-24.

21. See n. 6.

22. De Waard, *Comparative Study*, pp. 50-51.

23. There is confusion in the manuscript evidence over whether the quotation should be attributed to 'Isaiah the prophet' or just to 'the prophets'. The latter is almost certainly a scribal attempt to avoid ascribing 1.2b to Isaiah.

24. C.T. Ruddick, Jr, 'Behold, I Send My Messenger', *JBL* 88 (1969), pp. 381-417.

On his view vv. 1-3 and 7-8 are attributed to the evangelist and the messenger motif is derived from Genesis 31–32. The whole picture of John and Jesus is viewed as molded from the story of Jacob and Esau. Jacob is a type of Jesus who supplants the elder Esau/John (both of whom are characterized by a wilderness lifestyle). The one coming after who is mightier is Laban. Verbal parallels are seen in ὁδός, ἀποστέλλω, ἔμπροσθεν αὐτοῦ/πρὸ προσώπου σου, ἁμάρτημα/ἁμαρτία, ἰσχύει/ἰσχυρότερος, ὀπίσω μου. Mk 1.2 and 1.7 originate from the Genesis passage, and the baptism of Jesus is modeled on Jacob meeting Esau in that there is a theophany in both accounts and Esau is well pleased with Jacob as God is well pleased with Jesus. In fact, the whole of Mark is treated this way. The resultant view is that Mark is a liturgical lectionary following the triennial cycle of the Jewish year. Quite apart from the lectionary hypothesis, the whole theory has little to support it. It appears that *any* correspondence between Mark and Genesis, no matter how incidental, is grasped to support the theory. The differences between the texts are enormous. Only with difficulty can one overlook that it is Laban who is mighty in Gen. 31.29 and who comes after Jacob in 31.36 or that it is Esau who is well pleased in Gen. 33.10 as opposed to God in the baptismal account. The verbal parallels are superficial and coincidental. That similar words (especially common ones) appear in two different accounts does not establish a genetic relationship between the two or suggest that the latter is a midrash on the former. The method used here is unacceptable.

A more reasonable explanation for the origin of Mk 1.2 and indeed of the use of both parts of the citation would build on what can be observed about 'the stream of tradition' emerging from Old Testament texts. The role of Isa. 40.3 and its context in describing God's comfort and eschatological deliverance is clear in the material presented above. To that should be added the fact that Mal. 3.1 (and 23) was interpreted in the same way. (E.g. *Exod. R.* 32.9 on Exod. 23.20: 'Wherever the angel appeared, the Shechinah appeared... In the millennium, likewise, when he [the angel] will reveal himself salvation will come to Israel, as it says, "Behold, I send My messenger, and he shall clear the way before me".'[25]) There is even slight evidence that Isa. 40.1-5 and Malachi 3 were connected in Judaism,[26] and as we will see the connection is obvious

25. See also *Num. R.* 16.11; *Deut. R.* 4.11.
26. *Deut. R.* 4.11; *Pes. R.* 33, which provides commentary on Isa. 51.12 and the theme of comfort, in section 8 also quotes Mal. 3.23. Sir. 48.10 in describing Elijah

in Luke. It is this traditional understanding of these verses that makes them so important for Mark that they can be used *without explanation* at the beginning of the Gospel. The question of the antecedent of the pronouns is probably irrelevant to the author's purpose. The two quotations stand as eschatological pointers showing that the Old Testament promises are fulfilled and salvation has come to God's people. The wording in Mk 1.2 and the attribution of these words to Isaiah probably result from traditional usage. Whether one wishes to explain these phenomena by referring to a testimonia hypothesis is relatively unimportant. What is clear is that Mark has adopted a stream of tradition which will summarize immediately what his Gospel is about and which will provide the direction for the explanation that follows. There is another factor that shows the importance of these texts for Mark and adds to the already convincing argument against 1.2 being an interpolation. ὁδός in Mark is an important redactional motif. Jesus not only teaches the 'way of God' (12.14) but his disciples 'follow in the way' (10.52).[27] If so, the composite quotation not only provides a link with the Old Testament, but also establishes a theme that is integral in Mark's explanation of discipleship.

Luke

The use of Isa. 40.3-5 in Luke seems unimportant at first glance. It appears that Luke is just like Matthew and Mark with the one exception that for some unknown reason he has expanded the quotation to include Isa. 40.3-5. The expansion, however, is quite deliberate and a closer examination will reveal that the longer citation tips the author's hand as to how important this text has been for him, particularly in the birth narratives. It has long been recognized that various Old Testament passages provide the framework for the birth narratives,[28] but rarely has sufficient attention been paid to the place of Isa. 40.3-5. The following texts owe at least part of their wording to Isa. 40.3-5 and will be considered individually: Lk. 1.17; 1.76-79; 2.30-31; 3.3-6; and 9.52. In addition, if Isa. 40.3-5 is so important for the writer, the use of παράκλησις

---

in terms of Mal. 3.23-24 also uses words from Isa. 49.6. See the discussion by J. Jeremias, 'παῖς θεοῦ', *TDNT*, V, pp. 686-87. *4 Ezra* 6.19 speaks of the time when the humiliation of Zion is complete and 6.25-26 speaks of those who see God's salvation and who are changed and converted to a different spirit (Isa. 40.5 and Mal. 3.23-24?).

27. I owe this observation to Ernest Best. See also possibly 4.15 and 10.46.

28. See R. Laurentin, *Structure et théologie de Luc I–II* (Paris: Gabalda, 1957).

τοῦ Ἰσραήλ in 2.25 and ἕτερα παρακαλῶν in 3.18 may also have been derived from Isa. 40.1-2 and its understanding in Judaism.[29]

Luke 1.17. The wording in this verse is not a quotation, but rather is the weaving together of several phrases or paraphrases from Old Testament texts. The words are taken primarily from Mal. 3.1 and 23 (in a non-Septuagint form), but as we will see, there is indication that the same conflation of Mal. 3.1 and Isa. 40.3, which is in Mk 1.2-3, is present here. Several items require comment. The antecedent of the pronoun αὐτοῦ presents no problem. By necessity it refers to God since Jesus has not even been mentioned previously.[30] The use of κατεσκευασμένον is especially noteworthy since it appears elsewhere in the Gospels only at the quotation of Mal. 3.1 (in Mt. 11.10; Mk 1.2; Lk. 7.27). Here, however, it is not the way that is prepared at all; it is the *people* who are prepared. In addition this preparation is emphasized by the use of ἑτοιμάσαι which demonstrates the influence of Isa. 40.3.[31] The task of the child is to go before God in the spirit and power of Elijah to prepare for the Lord a pre-pared people. The phrase 'a prepared people' is not explicitly paralleled elsewhere,[32] but the idea is implicit in the kind of ethical interpretation of Isa. 40.3 that is found in 1QS 8.12-13 and 9.17-18. The expectation of the preparation of the way usually carried with it an ethical interpretation[33] and the transition to a 'prepared people' would not be difficult.

Luke 1.76-79. The description of what John the Baptist will be that is given in these verses is to some degree an expansion of 1.17. The same

29. O. Schmitz, 'παρακαλέω, παράκλησις', *TDNT*, V, pp. 792-93, 798; esp. note *Tanh. on Deut.* 1.1§1 quoted in *TDNT*, V, p. 792 n. See also Str–B, II, pp. 124-26.

30. See I.H. Marshall, *The Gospel of Luke* (NIGTC; Exeter: Paternoster Press, 1978), p. 58; H. Schürmann (*Das Lukasevangelium: Erster Teil* [HTKNT, 3; Freiburg: Herder, 1969], p. 36), however, sees the reference of αὐτοῦ as ambiguous, but understands it to refer to Jesus.

31. R.E. Brown, *The Birth of the Messiah* (Garden City, NY: Doubleday, 1977), p. 277; W. Wink, *John the Baptist in the Gospel Tradition* (SNTSMS, 7; Cambridge: Cambridge University Press, 1968), p. 69; P. Benoît, 'L'enfance de Jean-Baptiste selon Luc. I', *NTS* 3 (1956–57), p. 181.

32. Note 2 Kgdms 7.24: καὶ ἡτοίμασας σεαυτῷ τὸν λαόν σου Ἰσραήλ; Wis. 7.27: φίλους θεοῦ καὶ προφήτας κατασκευάζει; Josephus, *Apion* 11.188: παντὸς μὲν τοῦ πλήθους κατεσκευασμένον πρὸς τὴν εὐσέβειαν.

33. Note also *Targ. Isa.* 57.14 and 62.10.

combination of Mal. 3.1 and Isa. 40.3 is evidenced here.[34] The role of
Isa. 40.3 is ignored by some,[35] but in view of the use of κατασκευάζειν
in the quotation of Mal. 3.1 in 7.27 and in the allusion in 1.17, the use of
ἑτοιμάσαι here is almost certainly from Isa. 40.3. The preparation of
the way is defined in vv. 77-79. Depending on the way that the clauses
are seen in relation to each other, at least two ideas are included: (1) giving
knowledge of salvation and what it entails; (2) the ethical instruction that
will 'direct our feet in the way of peace'. The use of κατευθῦναι is
reminiscent of εὐθύνατε in the quotation of Isa. 40.3 in Jn 1.23, but the
language seems to be derived from the general ethical interpretation
applied to the concept ὁδός (which indeed may stand behind the
Johannine form of the quotation). Specifically, 'the way of peace' may
be derived from Isa. 59.8. The focus on the knowledge of salvation in
vv. 77-78 is not an insertion of ideas from elsewhere but is also drawn
from Isa. 40.5 (cf. Lk. 3.6). The combination of Mal. 3.1 and Isa. 40.3
was used by Mark as an eschatological pointer to indicate what the Gospel
was about. The same combination appears in Luke and is interpreted
soteriologically and ethically. The formative role of Isa. 40.3-5 for this
section of Luke is obvious.

At this point, however, mention of another approach must be made.
M. Gertner has suggested that Lk. 1.76-79 is a 'covert midrash' on the
priestly blessing found in Num. 6.24-26 which Luke has borrowed from
Judaism and reworked.[36] The importance of the priestly blessing (which
Gertner does demonstrate) and the fact that Christians borrowed Jewish
interpretations are both obvious. It is not enough, however, to view the
Benedictus as a midrashic paraphrase on the priestly blessing with the
claim that the concepts of blessing, keeping, shining, granting, lifting,
face, and peace all appear. That 'keeping' is understood in *Num. R.* 11.5
to refer to protection and deliverance from the enemy does not demonstrate that salvation and deliverance in Lk. 1.71 and 74 respectively are
based on the blessing. The assumption that פניו ('his face') in the
blessing ('Yahweh make his face shine on you') is contained in ἐνώπιον
in Lk. 1.75 and 76 is unconvincing, as is the further suggestion of a
word-play with פנה. The words ἐπιφᾶναι and εἰρήνη are paralleled in
the blessing, but these, like many of the words in question, are common

34. Brown, *Birth of the Messiah*, p. 389; Wink, *John the Baptist*, p. 66.
35. M. Rese, *Alttestamentliche Motive in der Christologie des Lukas* (Gütersloh:
Gütersloher Verlagshaus Gerd Mohn, 1969), p. 180.
36. M. Gertner, 'Midrashim in the New Testament', *JSS* 7 (1962), pp. 267-92.

in biblical language and do not constitute proof of dependence on the priestly blessing. While ἐπιφᾶναι does not appear in the Septuagint in Isa. 9.2 and while σκότος καὶ σκιὰ θανάτου is a fairly traditional phrase, Lk. 1.79a seems to be a non-Septuagintal allusion to Isa. 9.2. (Ps. 107[106].10 is actually closer but does not have the 'enlightening' theme.) At any rate the crucial phrase of the priestly blessing of Yahweh making his *face shine* is not present, and ἐπιφᾶναι by itself is not clearly drawn from Num. 6.25. I can only conclude that if this is a covert midrash on Num. 6.24-26, it has been hidden so well that the origin cannot be objectively determined.

The role of Isa. 40.3-5 on the other hand is quite clear. This text along with Mal. 3.1 has provided the basis for Lk. 1.76-79. Just as the two passages have been programmatic for Mark's Gospel, they are for Luke's, and Lk. 1.77-79 provides commentary on 1.76 by expounding on its soteriological and ethical significance.

Luke 2.30-31. The influence of Isa. 40.3-5 on these verses seems fairly clear although one could point to passages like Isa. 52.10 for the same theme of seeing God's salvation. The combination, however, of seeing God's salvation, the salvation prepared before the people, and the mention of παράκλησις in 2.25 likely reflects the quotation of Isa. 40.3-5 in Lk. 3.4-6.[37] One major difference obviously is that here the reference is to God's preparation rather than the people's preparation for God. There is an interplay between the preparation for God and the preparation for the people (note Isa. 57.14 and 62.10 and *Targ. Isa.* 40.3), and the idea here is not far removed. Cf. 1 Cor. 2.9.

Luke 3.3-6. Enough has been said about the role of the extended quotation in Luke that comments here will be abbreviated. The quotation is like the Septuagint except for αὐτοῦ instead of τοῦ θεοῦ ἡμῶν in v. 4, the omission of πάντα and the use of ὁδοὺς λείας instead of πεδία in v. 5, and the omission of ὀφθήσεται ἡ δόξα κυρίου and ὅτι κύριος ἐλάλησεν in v. 6. There is disagreement over whether Luke himself expanded the citation or whether he received it in the tradition. Schürmann argues the latter since an expansion by Luke cannot be demonstrated elsewhere,[38] but the importance of the verses for Luke

37. Schürmann, *Das Lukasevangelium*, p. 126; Brown, *Birth of the Messiah*, pp. 439 and 458.
38. Schürmann, *Das Lukasevangelium*, p. 161. However, T. Holtz (*Untersuch-*

makes the suggestion all the more plausible here. The ethical interpretation of the preparation of the way is clear in vv. 10-14. It is also possible
that vv. 5-6 are to be understood metaphorically, so that ταπεινωθήσεται
is used of the humbling of the proud and σκολιά of crooked men[39] (cf.
Acts 2.40), but this is by no means necessary. It appears that the primary clause Luke wanted to include was καὶ ὄψεται πᾶσα σὰρξ τὸ
σωτήριον τοῦ θεοῦ, for this encapsulates what he understands concerning the Christ event and its universal proclamation (cf. Acts 13.23-
26, which also interprets Isa. 40.3-5, and Acts 28.28).

Luke 9.52. The words that we are accustomed to by now seem to be
out of place within this context. The messengers who are sent before the
face of Jesus to prepare for him are clearly his disciples. At first glance it
may look like a coincidence, but as I. de la Potterie has suggested,[40] it
seems that the words of Mal. 3.1 and Isa. 40.3 have been combined
again and used suggestively by Luke. These words are placed at the
beginning of the journey to Jerusalem and the task of preparation for the
coming one is still taking place even though John the Baptist is dead.
The disciples now fulfill a role that was previously filled by him. The
same theme is continued in 10.1. The disciples go before to make ready
for the eschatological appearing of their Lord.

The hermeneutical implications of this use of Isa. 40.3 are rather far
reaching. Even though Lk. 3.4-6 had explicitly quoted three verses
'written in the book of the words of Isaiah the prophet' as descriptive of
the ministry of John the Baptist, surprisingly now they are adapted to
the role of the disciples. The interpretive principle of 'correspondence in
history'[41] is not merely seen when specific New Testament events are
viewed as corresponding with Old Testament works, but correspondence
between an event in Jesus' life and the Old Testament is sometimes
extended further, so that what is said of Christians corresponds both to
Jesus' life and to the Old Testament. (Other examples would include the

ungen über die alttestamentlichen Zitate bei Lukas [Berlin: Akademie Verlag, 1968],
p. 37) sees the addition as from Luke.

39. Marshall, *The Gospel of Luke*, p. 137.

40. I. de la Potterie, 'Le titre ΚΥΡΙΟΣ appliqué à Jesus dans l'évangile de Luc',
in A. Descamps (ed.), *Mélanges bibliques en hommage au R.P. Béda Rigaux*
(Gembloux: Duculot, 1970), p. 128.

41. R.N. Longenecker, *Biblical Exegesis in the Apostolic Period* (Grand Rapids:
Eerdmans, 1975), p. 94.

righteous sufferer theme, the ministry of the suffering servant, the stone testimonia, and the theme of the hardening of Israel.) This is not the context to carry on the discussion of hermeneutics, but this phenomenon should not be viewed as precedent for a 'new hermeneutic' which sets the text free to become something new for a modern reader. Rather, it represents the author's understanding of God's working with his chosen people and is similar to the attempt of modern scholars to find the principle of theology operative in a text.[42]

Conclusion

Two concerns have been present from the outset of this study: (1) to trace the use and interpretation of Isa. 40.1-5; (2) to view midrash as a process in which streams of tradition develop and enrich or intensify later adaptation of Old Testament texts. The place of Isa. 40.1-5 as a major text pointing to God's eschatological comfort seems beyond question. That was probably never in doubt, but the way the text is used and adapted at various points and the way that it is interpreted ethically need to receive attention if the significance of the New Testament texts is to be appreciated. The formative role that these verses have particularly in Mark and Luke can be appreciated only in light of previous usage. Such previous usage is demonstrated in the Qumran material presented above and the further development of the rabbinic traditions is in keeping with this. No doubt there was previous Christian adaptation of the verses prior to their use in the Synoptics even though the explicit examples do not exist. The way that Mark employs the material without explanation as an eschatological indicator, however, is evidence enough. Consequently an adequate understanding will deal with both the Jewish and Synoptic midrashic activity. In particular the midrashic activity of Luke in using Isa. 40.3-5 to summarize the gospel events needs more attention than it has received in the past.

The concern to view midrashic activity as part of a stream of tradition is not doubted in theory. In practice, however, it becomes easy to isolate one's attention on a particular text and make suggestions that are unlikely (as we have seen) when the whole stream is viewed. The concern for the development of a tradition is more ponderous and at times even pedestrian, but in the end the results seem much more dependable.

---

42. J. Bright, *The Authority of the Old Testament* (Nashville: Abingdon Press, 1967), pp. 143-60.

Questions are automatically raised in such an endeavor as to whether a text is midrash (implying explicit exegetical activity) or merely reflects traditional language, but those questions need to be treated anyway if 'midrash' is to be a meaningful term at all.

JSNT 29 (1987), pp. 101-21

JESUS AS MEDIATOR

D.R. de Lacey

1. *Is Jesus a Mediator?*

We begin by asking: does Paul believe that Jesus is mediator? An immediate way to find an answer would seem to be to look at his usage of the word μεσίτης. True, it is applied to Jesus in 1 Tim. 2.5, though not necessarily in a titular sense: but the more obvious occurrence, especially for those doubtful of the authorship of the pastorals, is in Gal. 3.19-20. This is the only other in the Pauline corpus, and here it is applied to Moses in an apparently pejorative sense. A mediator is a 'bad thing': the fact that the old covenant was mediated at all is a black mark against it. Surely, to say then that Jesus is a μεσίτης would be to deny the point that Paul is making: and this is, for some, adequate basis for denying that Paul saw Jesus as mediator. Thus Cullmann sees the concept of mediation as 'only a variant of the concept of High Priest',[1] and restricts his discussion to Hebrews: while Guthrie limits his attention exclusively to 1 Timothy 2.[2] Becker doubts whether we see anywhere in the New Testament the idea of Jesus as the fulfilment of a mediator concept.[3] Discussing 'other passages where the same thought [viz. mediation] finds expression in other terms' he comes up only with Jn 14.6 and Mt. 11.25-30.[4]

This to me highlights the difficulties of proceeding by means of word studies, venerable though the method is. It raises major problems of

1. O. Cullmann, *The Christology of the New Testament* (London: SCM Press, 1959), p. 89.
2. D. Guthrie, *New Testament Theology* (Leicester: IVP, 1981).
3. O. Becker, 'μεσίτης', *NIDNTT*, I, p. 374.
4. And concludes with a 'paradox' which I can only see as a nonsense: 'He has emptied all our preconceived ideas of mediation' ('μεσίτης', p. 375).

method, resting as it does on at least two fallacies.

The first is that the form of an isolated piece of discourse is deter-minative of its meaning. This is nonsense, even supposing that there were objective criteria by which 'form' could be abstracted from total understanding. The clearest demonstration of this, I suppose, is in cases of irony, where form and content are deliberately set against each other.[5] A corollary is that it is not necessary for there to be a formal 'title' for a particular christological belief to be present and even expressed.

The second is that clear definition of words and their meanings is an essential prerequisite to understanding. But beyond a very minimal level, this becomes a vain and counter-productive exercise. It is clearly impor-tant that we understand each other; that in some reasonably objective sense our terms, for each of us, do refer to the same thing. But different words mean different things to different people, different things at differ-ent times and places, different things in different contexts;[6] they may even have widely differing connotations in different contexts.

Back to the Bible, then, with this in mind. For the Old Testament, it is a singular fact that there is no simple term which could be translated by 'mediator'; wherefore O. Becker actually claims that 'we cannot find the concept of mediatorship in the Old Testament';[7] despite the fact that

---

5. There is an excellent example in E.D. Hirsch, *Aims of Interpretation* (Chicago: University of Chicago Press, 1976), p. 24.

6. In a recent High Court case the jury needed to understand one of the Judge's words:

> After an absence of over five hours, they returned to ask Mr Justice Comyn if they could have a dictionary. He told them that, in law, he must refuse.
>
> The foreman then asked him to define the word 'imputation', which he had used in his direction to them.
>
> After consultation with counsel on both sides, the judge ruled that it meant 'meaning' (*The Daily Telegraph*, 1 March 1984, p. 3).

This might strike some as extraordinary. The *OED* defines 'imputation' as 'The act of imputing or attributing something, usually a fault, crime, etc., to a person... The attributing to believers of the righteousness of Christ... Attribution of merit (to oneself); the making a merit of a thing'; and my *Roget* gives as synonyms 'attribution, assignment, reference to, ascription, aetiology, inquiry, basis, reason why, rationale, apparentation...' or 'slur, reproach, censure...' It is unlikely that any dictionary would regard 'imputation' and 'meaning' as synonyms; but that is not significant here. What is significant is that, *in this context*, those involved in this piece of communication agree that this is what the word was used to mean. Well indeed that the learned Judge refused the jury a dictionary.

7. 'μεσίτης', p. 373.

he proceeds immediately to point out that prophets and priests, as well
as Moses and the Servant of Deutero-Isaiah, were all seen as mediators.
The position of Oepke in *TDNT* is surely more plausible: 'Though the
word is not used, mediatorship is at the heart of Old Testament religion'.[8]
This paper argues that the same is true for Paul; that the concept of
Jesus Christ as mediator is a central and powerful one for him. Christians
come to God 'through him';[9] and act 'through him';[10] God comes to
Christians and acts in them 'through him';[11] and also acts in the world
'through him'.[12] Further, he is seen as the medium of Christian
experience: Christians live 'in him', as part of his body, of his image.[13]
Admittedly, at times he is himself seen as the goal of Christian experience:
the church is (or is to be) the bride of Christ, to be presented to *him* at
the eschaton.[14] Yet Paul never forgets that ultimately the goal is the
Father—even if this actually needs defending in 1 Cor. 15.24-28.

Rather, then, than making Gal. 3.19-20 the keystone of our approach
to Paul, perhaps we should look again at this passage in the light of more
general considerations.

2. *The Central Question*

I begin with what seems to me to be one of the major issues of Pauline
Christology (or Pauline theology). Why did he think it 'good' news to
present Judaism with a mediator? From all that we know of Judaism, we
get the impression that however much the majesty of God may be
exalted and his transcendence stressed, it was always perfectly clear that
God was *im*mediately and directly approachable. The humblest petitioner could penetrate the ranks upon ranks of heavenly attendants of
the divine throne, and be heard by God himself. Although the prophetic
Spirit had departed from Israel, the בת קול was still sometimes given,
and the קול was the קול יהוה. How would an early Christian be heard,

---

8. 'μεσίτης κτλ.', *TDNT*, IV, p. 614.
9. Rom. 1.8; 7.25; 16.27; 2 Cor. 1.20; 3.4-5.
10. Rom. 8.37; 1 Cor. 8.6; 2 Cor. 1.5(?); 1 Thess. 4.2; 5.9.
11. Rom. 1.5; 5.1, 9, 12, 16; 1 Cor. 15.57; 2 Cor. 1.5; 5.18; Gal. 1.1; Phil. 1.11.
12. Rom. 2.16 (judgment); 1 Cor. 8.6; Col. 1.16 (creation); 1 Cor. 15.21
(eschaton); Col. 1.20 (reconciliation).
13. See my unpublished dissertation, 'The Form of God in the Likeness of Men'
(doctoral thesis, University of Cambridge, 1974), chapter 4.
14. 2 Cor. 11.2; cf. Eph. 5.26-27.

who came to such a society and proclaimed the good news that Jews could no longer approach God directly, but must come via Jesus Christ?

Only in the light of Jewish and early Christian understandings of mediators in general, I deem, will it be possible to reach a satisfactory answer to this question.

It would be possible in principle to distinguish a number of different sorts of mediators in first-century Judaism: earthly or heavenly, personal or impersonal, and so forth. Perhaps the most useful distinction is that between the personal (including angels and various sorts of human mediator) and the non-personal (the various attributes of God such as his Wisdom or Word). Admittedly, any such distinction is pretty rough and ready. Philo in particular is happy to identify Wisdom or the Logos with the Angel of the Lord or with the primal Man of Gen. 1.26-27. In Gen. 48.16 המלאך can even be used as a designation for God himself.[15] Yet in general I think the distinction is valid and useful, and that the groups function in significantly different ways.

It is the question of the relationship between function and status which I think most interesting in studying these figures. In many christological studies a wedge is driven between 'function' and 'status': Cullmann's *Christology* is unashamedly functional (Jesus' status is of secondary significance) while to Pannenberg status is all important (a focus on function would lead to 'subjectivism').[16] In fact in the development of new ideas the two are likely to go hand in hand, and we cannot decide *a priori* which will take the lead in any particular situation.

To focus on mediation is, clearly, to focus on a function. My question may be reformulated: was Jesus viewed as mediator because of what he was perceived to be, or did the experience of his mediation lead to a new evaluation of who he must be? The answer to that will, I believe, depend on where we see him fitting into the schema of first-century mediators.

---

15. Clearly the passage (Gen. 48.15-16) is picking up previous references to the מלאך יהוה in earlier chapters; but equally clearly the parallelism here (האלהים אשר התהלכו אבתי לפני...האלהים הרעה אתי...המלאך הגאל) removes the possibility of any ambiguity such as may be present in those earlier chapters.

16. See my forthcoming paper 'On Debating about the Christ' for a critique of such approaches.

3. *Mediators in Judaism*

a. *The Need for Mediation*
There is a repeated refrain in the Old Testament that God can be known, personally and individually. Superficially, this would seem to make redundant the concept of mediation. However, this is actually qualified in important ways. Despite a belief in his omnipresent activity in the world, God was seen as dwelling specifically in Zion, and indeed in the Temple there,[17] where he was experienced through the mediation of priest and offering. This is itself only one aspect of the universal Old Testament stress on the transcendence of God: that no one can see him and live. Hence in some sense[18] mediation is essential. The important thing is that it never functions in such a way as to make God remote. The various sorts of mediator, and the ways in which they were seen to operate, need further investigation, and meanwhile I deliberately leave the idea of 'mediation' as vague as possible.

b. *Types of Mediator*
In terms of the distinction drawn above, the group of 'personal' mediators is relatively unproblematic, though it embraces a wide diversity of sorts of being, from the thousands which are created for an instant's labour and then annihilated, to figures like Michael and Metatron and the מלאך יהוה who is more or less identified with יהוה himself, and who perhaps stand outside this schema in a special category. Human mediators too cover a wide range, from institutional mediators such as priest or prophet to great heroes of the past like Enoch or Moses, or contemporary martyrs. Melchizedek, perhaps, would be hard to classify! But of any particular figure both function and status are readily open to investigation (again, excepting perhaps Metatron or the מלאך יהוה). But it is the other group which I think is likely to cause greater problems: what I called divine characteristics. What do we mean when we talk of the wisdom, the word, or the spirit of God mediating his work in the world? Are these truly intermediary figures (that is, more or less, inde-

17. R.J. McKelvey (*The New Temple* [Oxford: Oxford University Press, 1969]) is wrong to suggest that the two were therefore in any sense identified. This is simply an example of metonymy.

18. We are back to the problem noted above; 'mediation' may have acceptable or unacceptable connotations depending entirely on the context in which it is applied. So there is no incongruity in Isa. 57.15.

pendent hypostases); or simply ways of speaking about God himself (so that the wisdom of God simply *means* 'God in his wisdom' just as 'the face of the glory' [פני הכבוד] simply means יהוה in the Angelic Liturgy)?[19] In what sense do they mediate between God and his world? What is the relation between their status and their function? These, it seems to me, are important questions too often overlooked in the literature. And I suspect that they are overlooked primarily because they are not the easiest questions to answer! Neither their function nor their status is immediately apparent.

1. *Angels*. No systematic conception of angels is to be found in the Old Testament. Linguistically מלאך retains its secular meaning of 'messenger' throughout the Old Testament period, while also being used as a technical term for the heavenly entourage.[20] Conceptually there was fluidity in thought between the stars and angels (both are 'the host of heaven') at least until the time of Nehemiah.[21] However, the Old Testament itself witnesses to a growing interest in the denizens of heaven; and by the beginning of the first century CE beliefs in angels had developed widely, though the majority of angels appear to have been thought of as nothing more than heavenly bell-boys, and not particularly intelligent ones at that.[22]

There was a great variety of beliefs about angels in the first century, as can be seen from the polemical nature of many statements concerning them. Moore affirms that 'in orthodox Judaism they [angels] were not intermediaries between man and God'.[23] But this is too simple. This very attitude of 'orthodoxy' is likely to have developed in the face of beliefs to the contrary, as G.H. Box claims:

19. J. Strugnell, 'The Angelic Liturgy at Qumran', in *Congress Volume, Oxford* (VTSup, 7; Leiden: Brill, 1960), pp. 318-45.

20. Details in *TDNT*, I, s.v. ἄγγελος.

21. See S.F. Noll, 'Angelology in the Qumran Texts' (doctoral thesis, Manchester University, 1979), p. 15.

22. Cf. the tradition that prayers should be in Hebrew because otherwise the angel who transmitted them to God would misunderstand and garble them; *b. Šab.* 12b. On the other hand, they had greater knowledge than mere humans: *b. Ḥag.* 16a.

23. G.F. Moore, *Judaism* (Cambridge, MA: Harvard University Press, 1927), I, p. 411. Cf. J. Goldin, 'Not By Means of an Angel and Not By Means of a Messenger', in J. Neusner (ed.), *Religions in Antiquity* (NumenSup, 14; Leiden: Brill, 1968), pp. 412-24, and the refrain from which Goldin takes his title. Note also *y. Ber.* 13a and *4 Ezra* 7.102-15.

It seems clear that such ideas were implicit in some forms of popular Judaism, which are reflected in certain phenomena of the Targums, and which the Rabbis had every reason to regard as highly dangerous to the pure conception of God.[24]

Noll even goes so far as to say that

An important emphasis in post-exilic angelology is placed upon the idea of angels as mediators. The idea is rooted in the Old Testament (Gen. 28.12), but its increased importance may be due to a certain 'spiritualizing' of the functions of human mediators—prophets, priests, and scribes,[25]— as well as a certain 'distancing' of God from the world in the thought of this period.[26]

The second part of the latter statement may need modification: God does not in general become remote to Judaism. Nor is it clear what Noll means by angels functioning as 'prophets': presumably he means that 'The most important intermediary function of angels is revelation of secret knowledge' (p. 30). But it is the priestly aspect which may be the most interesting. In the 'Angelic Liturgy' of Qumran the leading angels are said to have clearly priestly functions;[27] and to my mind it is likely (though I am open to correction) that Melchizedek = Michael, while still retaining some links with Genesis and Psalm 110. But it must be remembered that this is not any angel, but a special figure who is only called 'angel' in a slightly ambivalent way. Certain specific angels, then, might be seen as more or less equivalent to God. But ontologically or functionally, or what? I confess that I am not sure.

24. 'The Idea of Intermediation in Jewish Theology', *JQR* 23 (1932–33), pp. 103-19 (105). It is seen for instance in *b. Šab.* 12b; 1QH 3.18ff.; Tob. 12.12-15; *2 Bar.* 6.7; *3 Bar.* 11–17; *1 En.* 9.10; 15.2; 40.9; 47.2; 99.3, 16; *T. Levi* 3.5; 5.6-7.

25. 'E.g., Malachi uses *ml'k* for a prophet (1.1; 3.1b, 23), priests (2.4, 7) or an angel (3.1a?)...' (*Angelology*, p. 28).

26. *Angelology*, pp. 28-29: but Noll refers to H.J. Wicks, *The Doctrine of God in the Jewish Apocryphal and Apocalyptic Literature* (London: Hunter & Longhurst, 1915) for a caution over the last statement. This goes back to Ezek. 40.4; Job 5.1; Zech. 1.12; 4.6-10; etc.; see R. Le Déaut, 'Aspects de l'intercession dans le Judaïsme ancien', *JSJ* 1 (1970), pp. 35-57 (29). See Tob. 12.12-15. 'The most important intermediary function of angels is revelation of secret knowledge' (*Angelology*, p. 30).

27. Noll, *Angelology*, p. 122, citing Strugnell. Strugnell suggests that this is because the idea of heaven as a temple came into prominence when the earthly temple was no longer available, though a rival expectation focused on a new or cleansed temple in Jerusalem: see also E.P. Sanders, *Jesus and Judaism* (London: SCM Press, 1985), chapter 2.

It is also claimed that at Qumran 'the presence of angels…is a substitute for the presence of the Lord himself'[28] though this may be a rather unfair way of putting it. It might be better to say, as Noll does later, that the sectarians joined with the angels in the worship of God.[29] Further, the existence of 'a principal angelic creature' was not in question in the rabbinic period, according to Segal; only his 'identity, title and function'.[30] This figure was clearly of greater significance in first-century Judaism than a casual reading of the rabbis might suggest, as their embarrassment itself indicates. This area needs further investigation.

What is it that angels mediate? It may be easier to say what they do not.

> One final word. It may be of some significance that the emphasis of 'not by an angel and not by a messenger' occurs in the following contexts: (1) God's redemption of Israel from Egyptian bondage; (2) God's punishment of Israel; (3) God's providing for Israel on its land; (4) God's revelation of the Law to Moses at Sinai; (5) Moses' communication to Israel of the Sabbath as covenant-sign… Let the theologians make what they can of that.[31]

Well, here is one theologian's attempt. First, I think it is overschematic. Segal acknowledges that angels *do* redeem[32] and punish:

> R. Hilfi (PA2)…reports that R. Judah (PA2) felt that the repetition [of YHWH in Gen. 19.24] meant that the divine punishment was carried out by the angel Gabriel. Thus he must believe that one of the 'YHWH's in that passage refers to Gabriel. While Gabriel was not considered a separate, independent power by the rabbis, the tradition attests to the existence of exegesis which allowed the tetragrammaton to signify a being other than Israel's one God.[33]

But this only where the boundary between God and angels has already become at the least blurred, as is the case with Melchizedek/Michael at Qumran, or Enoch/Metatron in *3 Enoch*.[34] That is not to say that one

---

28. Noll, *Angelology*, p. 55. Cf. P. Schäfer, *Rivalität zwischen Engeln und Menschen* (Berlin: de Gruyter, 1975), p. 36.

29. Noll, *Angelology*, pp. 192-93.

30. A.F. Segal, *Two Powers in Heaven* (SJLA, 25; Leiden: Brill, 1977), p. 187.

31. Goldin, 'Not By Means of an Angel', p. 424.

32. 'Heavenly Ascent in Hellenistic Judaism, Early Christianity and their Environment', *ANRW* 2.23.2 (1980), p. 1336.

33. Segal, *Two Powers*, p. 131.

34. See my article 'One Lord in Pauline Christology', in H.H. Rowden (ed.), *Christ the Lord* (Leicester: IVP, 1982), pp. 191-203, for further discussion.

could not tell the difference between God and an angel. It would be better to say that ἄγγελος/מלאך has become polyvalent, and can function as a designation for a mediator who does not, as it were, *stand between* God and humanity but actually manifests the transcendent God. Hence function leads to greatly increased status.

What does all this add up to? I suggest the following points:

1. Belief in angels was not a carefully developed 'system', designed to 'explain' God's dealings with the world. It developed largely folkloristically as a means of dilating on the glory of God, of spiritualizing valued qualities (e.g. priesthood) and no doubt of satisfying vulgar curiosity about the sparse references in the Old Testament.

2. Correspondingly, angel mediators were not permitted to obscure the direct relationship between God and his people. There was a constant and unresolved tension, I suspect, between the model of the oriental emperor, whose work is all done by his minions, and the model of a God who acts directly. At least for the important things, the latter won hands down, as the refrain 'Not by means of an angel...' shows.

3. Because this is true even for the greatest angels—the four (or six, or seven)—we may have here an explanation of why angel Christologies never caught on in the earliest Christianity. What, I suspect, early Christianity did get from this area of speculation was an ambivalence over their mediatorial value, or to put it another way, that mediation may be seen in two ways, either focusing on the thing or person being mediated, or on the mediator.

4. But at the top of the hiererchy, so to speak, was a small group of figures[35] who stood outside this speculation, functioning in a very different way.

2. *Human Mediators*. Here there is a wide range of possible areas of study, but because I suspect that their relevance to our study is minimal, I shall restrict myself to some desultory remarks only. In what senses could human beings be intermediary figures? From the literature, it would appear that there might be several options. In the apocalypses, the man becomes the vehicle for new revelations; and in one (*Ethiopic Enoch*) he appears to be given a new role (as Son of Man); alas, we cannot know what significance this had.[36] The apocalyptic seer (notably Enoch or similar ancient worthy) mediates new revelations of God, as in

35. Perhaps only one for each individual community.
36. See my 'Form of God', pp. 72-80, for discussion.

their own way did the prophets of old. Their major function in the literature is that of keeping the faith alive in times of crisis, and encouraging
belief in the presence and reality of God. Priests clearly have a different
mediating role which needs to be explored further. But neither priest nor
Temple is essential to communion with God in the first century. Moses'
unique role merits him a section by himself, but first I want to look
briefly at the various ways in which human beings might be said to
mediate redemption.

(a) *Mediators of Redemption.* 'The most consistent earthly redeemer
figure in Judaism is the messiah', says Segal[37]—and no clear pre-Christian
consensus emerges as to his nature or functions. But even in the Old
Testament the anointed king is clearly representative of the people of
God, and this fact continues through the inter-testamental period.[38] But
the sense in which he mediates the redemption is minimal, and is probably not tied to the *status* of the messiah (other than his status *as*
messiah). That is, reflection on the nature of redemption does not seem
to have resulted in the developing of new understandings of the nature
of the redeemer-figure.

The same is true of other mediators, such as the merits of the fathers[39]
or the *Aqedah Yitzhaq.* In 1QpHab 8.1-3 the faithful are saved 'because
of their faith in the Teacher of Righteousness', according to Vermes's
translation (p. 237); but I suspect that the phrase [ב]אמונתם במורה העדק
(Lohse: 'um...ihrer Treue willen zum Lehrer der Gerechtigkeit') indicates
their faithfulness to his teachings, not their trust in him personally. He is
not evidently a redeemer figure, nor is his status shaped by redeemer
ideas. For our purposes in exploring what it means for Jesus to be seen
as mediator, such figures seem relatively unimportant.

Since Jesus dies a violent death, martyr-figures may be relevant.
There is certainly evidence that martyrs were seen as mediators: the
classic text is *4 Macc.* 6.27-29: 'Let our punishment be a satisfaction in
their behalf. Make my blood their purification, and take my soul to
ransom their souls.'[40] But again their act does not affect their status.

---

37. 'Heavenly Ascent', p. 1336.
38. See N.T. Wright, 'The Messiah and the People of God' (doctoral thesis,
Oxford University, 1980). But see also C.C. Rowland, *Christian Origins* (London:
SPCK, 1985), pp. 92ff. for caution here.
39. Or one's own merits, as Aher's in *b. Ḥag* 15a.
40. More examples in J.C. O'Neill, *Messiah* (Cambridge: Cochrane, 1980), lec-

(b) *Moses*. Nowhere in the Old Testament is Moses called a mediator (not surprisingly, since as we have noted the term does not seem to have been developed); but the term becomes at least a quasi-title in the inter-testamental period.[41] It is so used in the Samaritan *Memar Marqah*.[42] And it is a commonplace in the rabbinic literature.[43] But this need not necessarily denigrate Moses: quite the converse. However, one strand of Jewish interpretation does seem to see this mediation as implying inferior status. Here of course the primary point is that aspect of Jewish belief with which we began: that God has spoken directly to his people; 'not by means of an angel, and not by means of a messenger'. There is evidence that other first-century Jews beside Paul had to wrestle with this apparent contradiction. Josephus (*Ant.* 3.89) argues that the people were obliged to hear God himself immediately before the giving of the decalogue (through the mediator!) so that 'the excellence of the things said might not be impaired'. Callan comments: 'This suggests that the mere fact of Moses' mediation diminishes the power of the words he speaks';[44] but it is not so clear that this is what Josephus had in mind. Moses says 'it is not Moses, son of Amaram and Jochabed, but he who...opened for you a path through the sea...he it is who favours you with these commandments, using me for interpreter'. We may couple this with Philo's distinction between Moses speaking as God's interpreter things too great to be lauded by human lips and his speaking as an inspired prophet, possessed by God and carried away out of himself.[45] R. Judah, in *Cant. R.* 1.2.4, is even more outspoken: when Moses became the people's mediator, they tended to forget what they learned. Just as the human Moses is transitory, so is his teaching. The fact that this is

ture 4, and his paper in W. Horbury and B. McNeil (eds.), *Suffering and Martyrdom in the New Testament* (Cambridge: Cambridge University Press, 1981), pp. 9-27.

41. E.R. Goodenough argued that Philo portrays Moses as 'a perfect example of hellenism's ideal king' and Meeks goes further, linking the title with the tradition that Moses is clothed with the name of God. Philo three times uses it so: *Vit. Mos.* 2.166; *T. Mos.* 1.14; 3.12. See W.A. Meeks, 'Moses as God and King', in Neusner (ed.), *Religions in Antiquity*, pp. 354-71.

42. So S. Liebermann, *Hellenism in Jewish Palestine* (New York: Jewish Theological Seminary, 1950), pp. 81-82. It does not so occur elsewhere in the Samaritan literature, it would seem.

43. References in T. Callan, 'Pauline Midrash', *JBL* 99 (1980), pp. 549-67 (555), from which the above references are also drawn.

44. 'Midrash', p. 557.

45. *Vit. Mos.* 2.188.

elsewhere also explicitly denied (e.g. *b. Šab.* 30a) indicates the problems seen in this approach. All these writers, in their different ways, want to have their cake and eat it; and this is a constant problem with the idea of mediation in the inter-testamental literature.

There are two specific occasions with reference to which Moses is called the mediator of the people. The less obvious one is at the incident of the Golden Calf. According to Philo (*Vit. Mos.* 2.166):

> [when he heard of their disloyalty he] took the part of mediator and reconciler...begging that their sins might be forgiven. Then when this protector and intercessor had softened the wrath of the Ruler he wended his way back[.]

In other traditions Moses breaks the tables of the Law, precisely because he knows that the Torah condemns the people. In *ARN* 2 it is because it would condemn them to death at the hands of God, for the Torah contains the words 'Thou shalt have no other gods before me'. R. Jose the Galilean claims this was done on Moses' own initiative, and compares a betrothed maiden who is unfaithful: by tearing up the betrothal certificate the offence is diminished. But *ARN* is not unproblematic here: Jose's position is strongly opposed by Judah b. Bathyra, Eleazar b. Azariah, Aqibah and Meir, who all affirm that the tablets were broken by the direct command of God. Callan comments, 'In these traditions the law is seen as something which worsens the human situation', and has no difficulty in seeing a comparable, but more comprehensively negative, attitude in Paul's mind.

The other occasion is of course that of the giving of the Law itself, when the people themselves request that God speak only through a mediator. This is not particularly problematic to Jewish exegetes, since Deut. 5.28 explicitly approves this attitude. But insofar as it suggests fault or weakness, that is on the part of the people or of Moses, not on the part of God or the Law. If anything, it magnifies the greatness of the Law, too great for gross human hearing.[46]

4. *Divine Attributes as Mediators*

> In spite of the dearth of specific Hebrew texts implying intermediation between earth and heaven by figures other than God, the Greek intellectual and philosophical atmosphere virtually necessitated such an idea.[47]

---

46. Philo, *Poster C.* 143; *Somn.* 1.143; *Exod. R.* 29.4[?].
47. Segal, 'Heavenly Ascent', p. 1354.

This is particularly true for Philo. But what part do divine attributes play in Palestinian Judaism? Lack of both time and competence preclude a coherent investigation. I select at random some relevant details. I suspect that the development of such concepts as the wisdom, word, name, glory, spirit and shekhinah of God were attempts to comprehend the relationship between a transcendent deity and the world. I rather doubt that Judaism favoured the sort of metaphysical speculation which was the bread and butter of the Greek philosophical schools. But insofar as the questions were raised, such terms became useful as tools in developing an answer.

Clearly each derives from a different area of thought, different problems, perhaps different mind-sets. And that itself is not insignificant. Take for instance the shekhinah. Clearly, in origin, the shekhinah of God was unlikely to be in any sense distinguishable from God himself: the shekhinah of God *was* God—God with us. But we then see a development; we are told that it becomes first a periphrasis for the ineffable Name, then in some sense a hypostasis. But the language of hypostasis is slippery in the extreme. What does it mean to think of the shekhinah of God, *as distinct from* God himself? Does it make sense to think of the shekhinah as a creature? And how much can one transfer the answers we give to these questions to the other terms: to word and wisdom and spirit?

I have wandered from mediation; but only because I think these are fundamental questions to bear in mind. How then did these things (for want of a better word!) function as mediators? Were they attempts to explain *how* God interacts with the world, or only to stress the *dass*?

We need to be very careful in our analysis of this language. There is clearly a distinction between identifying Jesus with a heavenly *person*[48] and identifying him with an attribute of God.[49] We therefore need to be clear about what Jews thought they were doing when they used this language.

Unfortunately, no one uses such language self-consciously; no one actually states that Wisdom or Word is just a periphrasis or a piece of

48. Perhaps a parallel to the identification of Enoch with the Son of Man in *1 En.* 71.14?

49. 'Word', 'wisdom' and 'spirit' are clearly important terms for the early church. Indeed, it is generally held that a wisdom Christology was the basis for several other christological developments, for instance the belief that Christ was the mediator of creation.

metonymy.[50] My hunch is that in this language we are not dealing with independent hypostases, or attributes of God.[51] The words are indirect ways of referring to God himself: the Wisdom of God is God's own wise act; or better God himself acting wisely. The Spirit of God is God acting among human beings;[52] the Dwelling of God is his own presence with his people.

We need also to investigate the question of why, if all these were functioning as periphrases for God himself, some but not others were transferred to Jesus. Why not Power, Kingdom, Spirit, and so forth?

a. *The Word*
As far as I am aware no one has persuasively overturned the conclusions of G.F. Moore in his 1922 study:

> It may not be superfluous to correct at the outset any notion that Onkelos and the others in their versions systematically, if not altogether consistently, eliminate or neutralise the anthropomorphisms of the original.[53]

מימרא 'seems to serve only the purpose of a buffer…but it is always a buffer-*word*, not a buffer-idea; still less a buffer person' (p. 53). Indeed, according to Moore, it is 'a phenomenon of translation, not a creature of speculation' (p. 54).

No doubt the situation was not identical in Hellenistic Judaism, but even there one needs caution in assessing the data. Wis. 18.15ff. describes the Word of God in terminology clearly borrowed from the Old Testament description of the מלאך יהוה and Ringgren in *RGG* (3rd edn, 1959) therefore argues that this implies that what he calls 'the philo-

---

50. And yet it would appear that that is how this language functioned in Jewish thought. The evidence for this claim is as follows. (1) In the Targums and midrash, and other Jewish literature, these terms are used in place of the Name of God; or to denote the presence of God. I have already discussed the suggestion that this stems from a desire to minimize God's direct action: I do not find it cogent. (2) These terms are used to denote the authors of actions which the writers clearly believe are the works of God himself. (3) No clear distinctions are drawn by the writers between the various terms; they act in the main interchangeably. (4) No clear distinction can be drawn between the referent of these terms and God himself.

51. So also J.D.G. Dunn, *Christology in the Making* (London: SCM Press, 1980), pp. 132ff. But 'Spirit' (and indeed the other terms too) is a much less fixed idea than Dunn suggests. *A* Spirit and *the* Spirit may turn out to be very different things!

52. Though with specific eschatological overtones.

53. 'Intermediaries' in Jewish Theology', *HTR* 15 (1922), pp. 41-85 (45). Assertions to the contrary are still made, though with no attempt to answer Moore.

sophy of hypostatization cannot conceive of abstract concepts without a concrete base or carrier, and thus not without individualization and personification'. On this J.E. Fossum comments:

> The aim of the hypostatization process in the Jewish religion obviously is to safeguard the transcendence of God and weaken a too vivid anthropomorphism. In *Ps.* viii...it is said that God's name is glorious over all the earth...; hereby, it is implied that God in his essence does not work in nature.[54]

But this is nonsense. The context of Wisdom 18 is precisely a retelling of the death of the firstborn—little wonder the language is similar. Is 'word' here translationese, or is it roughly equal to 'command'? Either way, Fossum's conclusions are a long way off target.[55]

Because Paul does not use it, I shall skip here any discussion of the λόγος in Hellenistic Judaism, though I realize that it is relevant to the whole picture I am trying to reconstruct.

b. *The Spirit*

Moore points out that Spirit and Presence (Shekhinah) are used equivalently, except that Spirit has connotations of revelation which Presence lacks. Wherefore Schäfer sees Spirit as 'not author but mediator of the revelation effected by God'—prophetic experience comes ברוח and the ב is 'through, by means of'. But this may be an example of that overtidy mind which Caird gently ridiculed in *Language and Imagery*. Because we can define two different categories, it does not follow that we shall be able to squeeze all phenomena into them.

Even Dunn finds it difficult to see an independent hypostasis here and instead concentrates on the relative lack of interest in the Spirit in the inter-testamental period.[56] He surmises that this is because 'very few (if any) were prepared to lay claim in their own right to such experience [i.e. of divine immanence and inspiration to prophesy]',[57] or because of the danger of confusion with Greek conceptions of spirit. The former is unlikely since direct experience of the immanence of God *did* occur in

---

54. J.E. Fossum, *The Name of God and the Angel of the Lord* (Proefschrift, Utrecht: Elinkwijk Bv., 1982), p. 76.

55. With the LXX of Wis. 18.15 ὁ παντοδύναμός σου λόγος ἀπ᾽ οὐρανῶν ἐκ θρόνων βασιλείων ἀπότομος πολεμιστὴς εἰς μέσον τῆς ὀλεθρίας ἥλατο γῆς ξίφος ὀξὺ τὴν ἀνυπόκριτον ἐπιταγήν σου φέρων compare the MT of Exod. 12.23: ועבר יהוה לנגף את־מצרים...ופסח יהוה על־הפתח ולא יתן המשחית לבא אל־בתיכם לנגף.

56. *Christology*, pp. 134-36.

57. *Christology*, p. 136.

the first century, though it was expressed in other ways. Danger of misunderstanding is likely to make people more careful in their use of language, but hardly to abandon it altogether. More probably, it was because the Spirit was already linked with Age-to-Come beliefs that it was thought inappropriate as a way of expressing individual experience, its place being taken[58] by other expressions like the בת קול. Yet both in those experiences, and in the expressions of hope for the Spirit in the last days, it is clear that what is experienced is God himself.

c. *Wisdom*

Dunn begins his chapter on Wisdom with four options: Wisdom is

1. a *divine* being, an independent deity;
2. a *hypostasis*;
3. a *personification* of a divine attribute;
4. the personification of *cosmic* order.

He then suggests a *development* from Job 28[59] to the Wisdom of Solomon[60] from an undeveloped to a highly developed use.[61]

But all of this is linguistic confusion worse compounded. It assumes that the word always refers to the same concept, and that that concept must fit into one of the four classes offered.[62] I reject both assumptions. Clearly Philo (to take one example) can talk of human wisdom very much as we might, without any reference to the 'concept' of the Wisdom of God. So when Jews like Ben Sira identify Wisdom with the Torah, but also see Wisdom as 'a poetic personification for God's nearness'[63] this should occasion no surprise. It is, as Marböck says, poetic; and that is a category which theologians are notoriously bad at dealing with.[64]

---

58. Though not consistently; both Philo and Josephus use the idea of Spirit-inspiration of their own day.

59. 'Surely there is a mine for silver, and a place for gold which they refine... But where shall Wisdom be found?'

60. 'Wisdom...sits beside God's throne' (9.4); she is 'a pure emanation of the glory of the Almighty' (7.22ff.); etc.

61. Dunn, *Christology*, pp. 168-69.

62. Dunn actually acknowledges that the 'concept' is 'fluid'.

63. J. Marböck, *Weisheit im Wandel: Untersuchungen zur Weisheitstheologie bei ben Sira* (BBB, 37; Bonn: Hanstein, 1971), pp. 65-66, 129-30, cited by Dunn, *Christology*, p. 327 n. 37.

64. Dunn uses the phrase 'a kaleidoscope of imagery' but fails to see the significance of this for his thesis.

Wisdom can mean a lot of things; and *inter alia* it can act as a periphrasis for God's name.

5. *Jesus and Paul on Mediators*

For completeness I shall mention the few cases in the Gospels and in the Pauline corpus where mediators seem to be in view. The very fact that they are so few is itself significant, though in themselves they add little to our search.

a. *Jesus*

In any discussion of the Gospels we immediately run into the problem of distinguishing the various layers of tradition of which they are composed. This is not the place for an exhaustive discussion; nor is that necessary here. For our purposes it is adequate to note what may have been regarded as reasonably consonant with Jesus' own *Umwelt*.

The Pharisees' efforts to act as the guardians (and so, implicitly, mediators) of salvation (or the 'kingdom of heaven') are condemned in Matthew 23—but not, it appears, on principle. The problem is not so much that they had no right to open (or shut) the gate of the kingdom, but rather that they abused that right: they themselves will not practise what they preach (v. 3). Jesus implicitly accepts (or at least does not contest) that they do indeed shut the kingdom to others. The argument is of course heavily *ad hominem*, yet their authority is implicitly accepted as being real, if not authorized by God.

In the same vein, perhaps, is the use made of the 'shepherd' motif; though this is clearly a motif of the evangelists rather than of Jesus himself. It is interesting that in Mk 6.34 Jesus' response to the lack of a shepherd (in the Old Testament generally a king-figure) is to *teach*: to convey (or mediate) knowledge of God.

In the parable of the Pharisee and the publican Jesus pronounces justification upon the latter solely on the basis of his penitence. The cultus seems oddly irrelevant. Although the two are in the Temple, they might as well have been in a provincial synagogue. Is this because the story was preserved by a community which had severed its links with the Jerusalem Temple, or does it preserve an authentic reminiscence of Jesus' attitude to the cultus?

Matthew's Jesus also acknowledges the existence of guardian angels in a completely incidental reference.

b. *Paul*

Angels seem rather unimportant for Paul—perhaps because of controversy about their relationship to Jesus. It is God himself, not an angel,
who rescues him from dangers. Indeed, angelic mediators seem to get
rather a bad press from Paul; and human mediators are not significant
for him.

6. *Jesus as Mediator*

Clearly the early church was attracted by the paralleling, if not the
identification, of Jesus with certain intermediaries of Jewish thought—
and primarily those which, I have argued, were developed precisely to
explain God's dealings with the world. Thus Elijah, and the new Moses,
though present, are not very important, and angel Christologies are con-
spicuous by their absence. But Jesus as divine wisdom is by no means
incidental to Paul's thought, and Dunn acknowledges that this might
indeed be problematical, compromising pure monotheism:

> The exegetical answer seems to be that the first Christians were to some
> extent conscious of this danger... Thus when Paul attributes Wisdom's
> role in creation to Christ in 1 Cor. 8.6, he has already prefaced it with the
> strong Jewish confession that God is one. Thus he must mean that the
> creative and redemptive role of Sophia-Christ is nothing other than the
> creative and redemptive activity of this one God. That is to say, insofar as
> we can speak of the pre-existence of Christ, the deity of Christ at this
> point, it is the pre-existence and deity of the one God acting in and through
> Christ of which we are actually speaking. Christ is divine in no other
> sense than as God immanent, God himself acting to redeem as he did to
> create.[65]

But the straw at which Dunn grasps to save his thesis may turn out
eventually to break its back, if the blend of strawy metaphors may be
forgiven. For I have already argued (in an article of which Dunn himself
has written warmly!)[66] that 1 Cor. 8.6, far from establishing a premise of
uncompromising monotheism, in fact does the contrary. Paul cannot but
be thinking of the שמע, and he radically Christianizes it. He splits it into
two parts, as did the rabbis, but to very different effect. For him the one
God is the father, but the one Lord turns out to be Jesus himself, who

---

65. J.D.G. Dunn, 'Was Christianity a Monotheistic Faith from the Beginning?',
SJT 35 (1982), pp. 303-36 (330).

66. 'One Lord'; reviewed by Dunn in *SJT* 37 (1984), pp. 403-405.

thus turns out to be the means of creation. The link with wisdom is actually secondary in my opinion. And the mediating role is absolute: δι' οὗ πάντα is strong enough, but ἡμεῖς δι' αὐτοῦ must at least include Paul's awareness that all of Christian life is lived and experienced in Jesus Christ. Having said that, whether or not one adds a *title* of Mediator is largely irrelevant. Except, of course, that Galatians 3 suggests that mediation had such negative connotations for Paul, and so we must end with at least a footnote on that passage.

7. *Galatians 3.19-20*

So finally, we return to that problem passage which so easily throws researchers off the scent: Gal. 3.19-20. Could one who really thought of Jesus as a mediator have penned it? Could one who penned it really have thought of Jesus as a mediator?

The passage presents a multitude of problems, and we shall tackle only a few. The first is whether the ὁ δὲ μεσίτης is generic or specific. Harald Riesenfeld argues what I have long believed anyway: that the article before μεσίτης in v. 20 makes the statement specific, and that the sentence is elliptic: we need to supply another μεσίτης. Paul's statement then becomes ὁ δὲ μεσίτης μεσίτης ἑνὸς οὐκ ἔστιν: 'now this mediator is not the mediator of one [party]'.[67] Riesenfeld takes this to mean that Moses does not represent God, but only the angels;[68] but this is unlikely. We need to assume that Paul expected to be both comprehensible and persuasive. Any opponent clever enough to see this meaning in Paul's words would simply retort: Moses *did* represent God; Scripture plainly says so. Lightfoot argued that the thrust was that a mediator implies two equal parties, whereas the sovereign God alone gave the promise. Betz takes this further:

> Paul argues that anything that stands in contrast to the oneness of God is inferior. Since the concept of mediation presupposes by definition a plurality of parties, it is inferior and, consequently, renders the Torah

67. H. Riesenfeld, 'The Misinterpreted Mediator in Gal 3.19-20', in W.C. Weinrich (ed.), *The New Testament Era* (Macon, GA: Mercer, 1984), II, pp. 405-12; a position advocated at least as long ago as 1888 in an article by W.L. Davidson ('The Mediator Argument of Gal. III.19,20', *The Expositor* Third Series, 7 [1888], pp. 377-86). I am grateful to W.L. Kynes for this reference.

68. See also E.D. Burton, *Galatians* (ICC; Edinburgh: T. & T. Clark, 1921), pp. 190-92.

inferior. The true revelation of the one God does not need this concept…
in the revelation of the Gospel, Christ does not figure for Paul as a
'mediator'. Cf. 1 Tim. 2.5; Heb. 8.6; 9.15; 12.24.[69]

But again this is hardly likely to persuade the sceptic, especially one who
may think already that Christianity is inferior precisely in having a
mediator at all.

If we return to the Old Testament text which Paul is using, how can
we make sense of ὁ δὲ μεσίτης ἑνὸς οὐκ ἔστιν?[70] I suggest that the
most likely way is to stress the fact that in the text this mediator is
actually *appointed by both sides*: it is the *people*, not just God, who ask
him to mediate.[71] This, it seems to me, is adequate to provide a comprehensible and persuasive argument: God alone must choose, and not just
approve, the way in which his presence is to be experienced. The problem is not just that of a mediator, but of a mediator who is as it were a
third party.

Judaism itself displays an ambivalent attitude to mediation. On the one
hand it may be regarded as high honour to be a mediator; so that
μεσίτης/שרשׁוֹ becomes a quasi-title for Moses; yet on the other hand
the immediacy of God must never be compromised: direct dealing is
clearly superior to mediated transactions, and God deals directly with his
people. Perhaps one could say that the idea of mediation, then, can be
applied in two ways: we could talk of a mediator$_1$, who acts as a go-
between so that the principals do not meet; and a mediator^2 who simply
brings the two together.

Herein, perhaps, lies a solution to the problem of Gal. 3.19-20. Paul
plays on the dual connotations of the term. Moses was a mediator$_1$: he
stood between the two parties, appointed by both of them as a third
party so that the people did not see God face to face. I suspect therefore
that there is something of a play on words in v. 20. A single party could
act as his own agent; but *this* mediator[72] is not just mediating between
God and human beings (though that might be enough) but is appointed

69. H.D. Betz, *Galatians* (Hermeneia; Philadelphia: Fortress Press, 1979),
pp. 171-72 and n. 86.
70. Grammatically it would be reasonable to suppose that the order of ἑνὸς οὐκ
ἔστιν suggests a translation such as 'now there is no such thing as a mediator
of [only] one [party]'; but it is difficult to see how then to make sense of Paul's
argument.
71. Exod. 20.19; Deut. 5.27.
72. So Riesenfeld, 'Mediator', rightly I think.

by human beings to do so—and there is the angel-host as well, whatever that might imply. Now Jesus acts as mediator$_2$: he is the means by which we enter the presence of God himself. It was left to the later systematicians to see that the only one who could properly be a mediator$_2$ was one who was himself both God and a man; the Man Christ Jesus.

. *JSNT* 32 (1988), pp. 3-15

χάριν ἀντὶ χάριτος (JOHN 1.16):
GRACE AND THE LAW IN THE JOHANNINE PROLOGUE

Ruth B. Edwards

The interpretation of the phrase χάριν ἀντὶ χάριτος in the Johannine Prologue (Jn 1.16) is a notorious crux. The word χάρις, grace, occurs only four times in the Gospel, all four occurrences being in the Prologue and two in this very phrase. ἀντί is a *hapax legomenon* in the Gospel. The nub of the problem is the meaning of the preposition, since none of its regular senses leaps out as the obvious one for this context. It will be helpful to begin by reviewing the ways in which the preposition is regularly used and various conjectures that have been made for its possible meaning here.

1.   In origin the Greek preposition ἀντί, like Latin *ante*, appears to have meant 'in front of', 'opposite' in a strictly local sense; there are traces of this meaning in Classical Greek and in one or two Hellenistic papyri,[1] but it is never found in the New Testament or Septuagint, and I think we can rule it out here.

2.   The most common usage at all periods is in the sense 'instead of', 'in the place of'. According to J. Schreiner,[2] this is by far the most frequent meaning in the Septuagint, corresponding to Hebrew תַּחַת. Examples are Gen. 22.13: Abraham offered the ram *instead* of his son; and the succession formula, 'X died and Y reigned *in his stead*'. This usage is found also in the New Testament: e.g. Mt. 2.22, Ἀρχέλαος βασιλεύει ἀντὶ τοῦ πατρὸς αὐτοῦ, and Lk. 11.11, ἀντὶ ἰχθύος ὄφιν,

1.   LSJ, *s.v.* ἀντί A.I.; J.H. Moulton and G. Milligan, *The Vocabulary of the Greek Testament Illustrated from the Papyri and Other Non-Literary Sources* (London: Hodder & Stoughton, 1929), *s.v.*

2.   'Anti in der Septuaginta', in *idem* (ed.), *Wort, Lied, und Gottesspruch* (Festschrift für Joseph Ziegler; Würzburg, 1972), pp. 172-76.

'a snake *instead* of a fish'. According to Moulton and Milligan the meaning 'instead of' is also by far the most common in the Hellenistic papyri. I shall confine myself to one example: *P. Tebt.* II 343.24 (second century CE): ἀντὶ ἐλαιῶνος... ἄρουραι, '*instead of* an oliveyard ploughed fields'.[3] Few commentators in recent years have proposed an interpretation of the Johannine phrase taking ἀντί in this sense, but we shall come back to it later when we have examined the various alternatives.

3. Another very common meaning of ἀντί in our literature is 'in return for', occurring most notably in the biblical references to the *lex talionis*: Exod. 21.22-23, ψυχὴν ἀντὶ ψυχῆς, ὀφθαλμὸν ἀντὶ ὀφθαλμοῦ, ὀδόντα ἀντὶ ὀδόντος, 'life for life, eye for eye, tooth for tooth'. This usage is found several times in the New Testament not only in echoes of the *lex talionis* (e.g. Mt. 5.38), but also with reference to Christian teaching about not returning evil for evil: κακὸν ἀντὶ κακοῦ ἀποδίδοντες (Rom. 12.17; cf. 1 Thess. 5.15; 1 Pet. 3.9). This meaning 'in return for' appears in the only two other occurrences of the phrase χάριν ἀντὶ χάριτος that have been noted by those discussing the preposition,[4] namely: Euripides, *Helen* 1234: χάρις ἀντὶ χάριτος ἐλθέτω, 'Let there come one favour in return for another', or, roughly, 'one good turn deserves another'; and Dionysius of Antioch, *Ep.* 40: χάριν ἀντὶ χάριτος ἀπαιτήσαντες,[5] 'asking for one favour in exchange for another' (where χάρις has a more concrete sense of 'gift', the reference being to a suitable *quid pro quo* in return for a consignment of wine).

But the meaning 'a gift or favour in return for one already given by the recipient' hardly seems consistent with the Christian understanding of God's grace, which is universally seen in the New Testament as something freely given by God to those who do not merit it. Nor would it harmonize with the special Johannine emphasis on new birth, the Spirit, and eternal life as God's free gift to humankind. Augustine tried to get round this problem by suggesting that the first χάρις meant 'eternal life' and the second 'faith': he translates χάριν ἀντὶ χάριτος as 'gratiam pro gratia', explaining the phrase as follows: 'pro hac gratia in qua ex fide vivimus, recepturi sumus aliam'—'instead of this grace in

3.   Other examples are cited by Moulton and Milligan, *Vocabulary*, pp. 46-47.

4.   E.g. I. de la Potterie, *La Vérité dans Saint Jean* (AnBib, 73; Rome: Biblical Institute Press, 1977), I, p. 147.

5.   Ed. R. Hercher, *Epistolographi Graeci* (Scriptorum graecorum bibliotheca, 47; Paris: Ambrosio Firmin Didot, 1873), p. 266.

which we live by faith we shall receive another [i.e. immortality]'.[6] But it is obvious that Augustine is here forcing the text to fit the Pauline doctrine (so dear to him) of justification by faith through grace. His future tense, 'recepturi sumus', gives the game away! John is not talking about some future χάρις—nor even one we have partially begun to experience—but about grace we have already received: ἐκ τοῦ πληρώματος αὐτοῦ ἡμεῖς πάντες ἐλάβομεν, καὶ χάριν ἀντὶ χάριτος. Others have suggested that perhaps the second χάρις means 'thanks'; but this would involve a totally un-Johannine notion that God's grace could be given in return for human gratitude, and in any case χάρις only means 'thanks' in certain set contexts and formulae.

4.   A more subtle understanding is to suggest that ἀντί here means, rather more loosely, 'corresponding to', as effect corresponds to cause. This interpretation, which goes back to Thomas Aquinas, has been supported in modern times by Robinson, Bover, Joüon, Bernard and others.[7] The idea is that grace, that is, the grace which the Christian receives, in some sense *corresponds* to the grace of Christ. But this interpretation runs into the major difficulty that ἀντί never actually means 'corresponding to', except possibly in certain compounds such as ἀντίτυπος, literally 'counterblow', hence 'antitype', or ἀντιφόρτον, 'a load balancing another one'; but it should be emphasized that in most of the examples cited by commentators in support of this view ἀντί does not in fact mean 'corresponding to' but 'in exchange' (e.g. ἀντιχαίρειν, 'to rejoice in response to someone else', and ἀντίφωνος, 'sounding in answer'). There is nothing in the context to support this obscure meaning, which must fall on linguistic grounds.

5.   By far the most popular interpretation today is that adopted by a host of modern commentators, including Bultmann, Schnackenburg, Lindars, Barrett, Gnilka and Bruce,[8] namely that ἀντί here means

6.   Augustine, *In Johan. Tract.* 3.8 (*PL* XXXV, 1401).

7.   J.A. Robinson, *St Paul's Epistle to the Ephesians* (London: Macmillan, 1903), p. 223; J.M. Bover, 'Χάριν ἀντὶ χάριτος (Joh. 1. 16)', *Bib* 6 (1925), pp. 454-60, esp. 458; J.H. Bernard, *The Gospel according to St John* (ICC; Edinburgh: T. & T. Clark, 1928), I, p. 29; P. Joüon, 'Jean 1.16: καὶ χάριν ἀντὶ χάριτος', *RSR* 22 (1932), p. 206; cf. also M.-E. Boismard, *St John's Prologue* (Westminster, MD: Newman, 1957), p. 61.

8.   R. Bultmann, *The Gospel of John* (ET Oxford: Blackwell, 1971); R. Schnackenburg, *The Gospel according to St. John*, I (ET London: Burns and Oates, 1968); B. Lindars, *The Gospel of John* (NCB; London: Marshall, Morgan and Scott, 1972); C.K. Barrett, *The Gospel according to St. John* (London: SPCK, 2nd

'upon', 'in addition to', referring to the inexhaustible bounty of God's gifts, resulting in a constant stream of graces. This understanding has also been adopted in many modern translations—e.g. RSV and NEB: 'grace upon grace'; GNB and NIV: 'one blessing after another'. Theologically there is nothing objectionable in this view, which fits the context well. But it falls for one very good reason: there is no parallel to this usage in all Greek literature, which uses for this sense not ἀντί, but ἐπί—e.g. Sir. 26.15: χάρις ἐπὶ χάριτι γυνὴ αἰσχυντήρα, 'a shamefast woman is grace upon grace' (RV). But if John meant ἐπί, why did he not write ἐπί like Ben Sirach? Why coin a new usage? Naturally, those who adopt this translation try to find some parallels; almost all of them refer to a particular passage in Philo (*Poster. C.* 145) which is literally translated:

> Therefore God, having always held back (ἐπισχών) his first gifts, before those who received them became glutted and insolent, and having husbanded (ταμιευσάμενος) them, distributes others instead of them (ἀντ᾿ ἐκείνων) and a third supply instead of (ἀντί) the second, and continually new gifts instead of (ἀντί) older ones, sometimes different, sometimes the same.[9]

But there are serious problems with the use of this passage to interpret John: (1) Philo speaks of 'graces', χάριτες, in the plural; John of χάρις in the singular; (2) Philo is not in fact talking about an accumulation of gifts, that is, one gift on top of another, but the *replacement* or *substitution* of one kind of gift for another; in fact, ἀντί has its normal sense, 'in place of'; (3) the whole thought of Philo is very different from that proposed for the Gospel Prologue: John, on this interpretation, is emphasizing the superabundance of God's grace, while Philo is stressing God's wisdom in dispensing it carefully and not giving to people more than they can cope with. Leon Morris tries to make the Philo passage relevant by suggesting that what John means is that 'as one piece of

edn, 1978); J. Gnilka, *Johannesevangelium* (Würzburg: Echter Verlag, 1983); F.F. Bruce, *The Gospel of John* (Basingstoke: Pickering & Inglis, 1983). This meaning is also supported by W. Hendriksen, *John* (Grand Rapids: Baker, 1953), pp. 88-89, referring to his unpublished Princeton dissertation, 'The Meaning of the Preposition ἀντί in the New Testament', and by A. Hanson, 'John i. 14-18 and Exodus XXXIV', *NTS* 23 (1976), pp. 90-101 (97).

9. Philo, *Poster. C.* 145: Διὸ τὰς πρώτας αἰεὶ χάριτας, πρὶν κορεσθέντας ἐξυβρίσαι τοὺς λαχόντας, ἐπισχὼν καὶ ταμιευσάμενος εἰσαῦθις ἑτέρας ἀντ᾿ ἐκείνων καὶ τρίτας ἀντὶ τῶν δευτέρων καὶ αἰεὶ νέας ἀντὶ παλαιοτέρων, τοτὲ μὲν διαφερούσας, τοτὲ δ᾿ αὖ καὶ τὰς αὐτὰς ἐπιδίδωσι.

divine grace (so to speak) recedes it is replaced by another',[10] although this leads him theologically into deep water: in what sense can we speak of God's grace receding? Would John have ever used χάρις in such a concrete way? But the real fault lies in postulating an unattested meaning for ἀντί.

Apart from this isolated example from Philo, there is only one other significant passage which has been used to support the rendering 'upon' for ἀντί and that is Theognis 344, cited among others by Bauer in his standard New Testament Lexicon.[11] Here the phrase ἀντ' ἀνιῶν ἀνίας is cited as if it meant 'pain upon pain'. But one glance at the phrase in its context makes it quite clear that Theognis, also, is using ἀντί with its common meaning, (3) above, 'in return for'. He is complaining of his sufferings and asking Zeus for vengeance that he may inflict pain for (i.e. in return for) pain on those who wronged him. He uses ἀντί twice in the space of a few lines, first with the meaning 'instead of' (sense [2] above), and then with the meaning 'in return for' (sense [3]):

> Olympian Zeus, fulfil my timely prayer,
> Grant me some good instead of (ἀντί) troubles;
> May I die if I don't find some respite from cares,
> And pay back vexation for (ἀντί) vexation.
> For such is justice.[12]

Thus neither the Philo nor the Theognis passage offers any support for rendering ἀντί as 'upon', 'in addition to', and this interpretation must therefore be rejected.

All this suggests that perhaps we should take another look at the most common meaning of ἀντί, namely 'instead of', to see if there is not some possible solution here. Most of the interpretations suggested on these lines are highly implausible: in 1919 A. d'Alès suggested that the phrase χάριν ἀντὶ χάριτος referred to the replacement of grace received

10. L. Morris, *The Gospel according to John* (NICNT; Grand Rapids: Eerdmans, 1971), p. 110.

11. BAGD, *s.v.* ἀντί 2.

12. Theognis 341-45 in *Elegy and Iambus* (ed. J.M. Edmonds; LCL; London: Heinemann, 1931), I, p. 270:

ἀλλὰ Ζεῦ τέλεσόν μοι Ὀλύμπιε καίριον εὐχήν,
δὸς δέ μοι ἀντὶ κακῶν καί τι παθεῖν ἀγαθόν·
τεθναίην δ' εἰ μή τι κακῶν ἄμπαυμα μεριμνέων
εὑροίμην, δοίην τ' ἀντ' ἀνιῶν ἀνίας.
αἶσα γὰρ οὕτως ἐστί...

through Christ by the grace received, after his physical departure from this earth, by the Holy Spirit.[13] But this seems very forced: the whole passage is precisely about Jesus Christ as the incarnate Logos, full of grace and truth. More subtly M. Black suggested that there could have been a misunderstanding of an Aramaic original, which might have contained a word-play: אסְדָּא חֲלָף חִסְוּדָא, 'grace instead of shame', with reference to the gospel grace replacing the Law.[14] But, as Barrett and others have pointed out, there is no real evidence for an Aramaic origin for the Prologue, and in any case no Jew or even Jewish Christian would refer to the Law as a 'shame'. Black's conjecture has not met with any support, and it is interesting to see that he omitted it from his own major work, *An Aramaic Approach to the Gospels and Acts*.[15] Yet the relation of the gospel to the Law may in fact be the clue to this enigmatic phrase.

Several leading Fathers of the Greek church all thought that χάριν ἀντὶ χάριτος referred to the replacement of the Mosaic Law by the gospel—an interpretation found in Chrysostom,[16] Cyril of Alexandria,[17] Origen[18] and Theophylact,[19] and also adopted by Jerome,[20] linguistically

13. A. d'Alès, 'ΧΑΡΙΝ ΑΝΤΙ ΧΑΡΙΤΟΣ (Ioan, 1.16)', *RSR* 9 (1919), pp. 384-86; cf. M.J. Harris, 'Appendix: Prepositions and Theology in the Greek New Testament', *NIDNTT*, III, p. 1180.

14. M. Black, 'Does an Aramaic Tradition Underlie John 1.16?', *JTS* 42 (1941), pp. 64-65.

15. Oxford, 3rd edn, 1967.

16. Chrysostom, *Hom. in Jo.* 14 (*PG*, LI, 93), stressing that the Law itself had the nature of a gift: καὶ γὰρ τὰ τοῦ νόμου καὶ αὐτὰ χάριτος ἦν.

17. Cyril of Alexandria, *In Jo. Ev. Lib.* I, 101 (*PG*, LXXIII, 172-73), explaining that the grace of the Gospel (χάρις εὐαγγελική) replaces the grace of the law (χάρις νομική): Cyril readily recognizes the superiority of the new grace, but nevertheless affirms that the Law did impart a gift of grace to humankind: καὶ χάριν μὲν ἀνθρώποις καὶ ὁ νόμος ἐδίδου, καλῶν ὅλως εἰς θεογνωσίαν.

18. Origen, *Comm. in Jo.* 6.6 (*PG*, XIV, 200). The views of Origen are complicated and perhaps not entirely consistent: see further de la Potterie, *La Vérité*, I, pp. 19-20, with further references.

19. Theophylact, *Enarr. in Jo.* 1.518-19 (*PG*, CXXIII, 1164), understanding the grace of the new covenant as replacing that of the old lawgiving—καὶ χάριν δὲ ἐλάβομεν, τὴν τῆς καινῆς δηλαδὴ διαθήκης, ἀντὶ τῆς χάριτος, τῆς παλαιᾶς νομοθεσίας. He goes on to contrast the greatness of the gift of grace through Jesus Christ with the lesser gift of grace through the Law (χάριν μεγίστην ἀντὶ μικρᾶς χάριτος).

20. Jerome, *Ep.* 112.14 (CSEL 55, p. 383). Similar interpretations can also be

the most learned of the Latin Fathers. Most modern scholars have rejected this view[21] on the grounds that grace in the New Testament is generally opposed to Law—cf. Paul, 'You are not under law but under grace' (Rom. 6.14)—and that no New Testament writer would ever have referred to the Mosaic Law as χάρις. It is further argued that this antithesis or opposition between grace and Law is explicitly mentioned by John in v. 17, 'For the law was given through Moses: grace and truth came through Jesus Christ'. It is widely assumed that the author is here referring to a Pauline contrast or even opposition between gospel and Law. Thus W. Zimmerli writes, 'Paul's antithesis of grace and Law is adopted';[22] Gnilka describes v. 17 as 'a polemical- and Pauline-sounding statement';[23] Haenchen sees it as setting grace and truth 'in opposition' to the law;[24] Esser, Richardson, and many others all make the same point.[25]

But are we not here in danger of reading John with Pauline spectacles? Surely we must let John be himself.[26] It is true that the New Testament contains a substantial number of places where grace and the Law are

found in Ambrose, and in the Syrian Fathers: see de la Potterie, *La Vérité*, I, p. 120 n. 11.

21. E.g. Barrett, *St John*, p. 169. J. Moffatt (*Grace in the New Testament* [London: Hodder & Stoughton, 1931], p. 368) just dismisses this possibility as 'unnatural' without discussion.

22. 'χάρις, κτλ.', *TDNT*, IX, p. 399.

23. *Johannesevangelium*, p. 16.

24. E. Haenchen and U. Busse, *Das Johannesevangelium: Ein Kommentar* (Tübingen: Mohr–Siebeck, 13th edn, 1980), p. 131 (ET *John* [Hermeneia; Philadelphia: Fortress Press, 1984], I, p. 120). In his 'Probleme des Johanneischen Prologs' (in *Gott und Mensch* [Tübingen: Mohr–Siebeck, 1965], p. 132), Haenchen similarly writes: 'Dieser Gegensatz von Gesetz und Gnade ist dem vierten Evangelium fremd'; but why postulate an antithesis alien to the thought of the evangelist if the passage can satisfactorily be interpreted in a way consistent with his thought?

25. H.-H. Esser, 'Grace', *NIDNTT*, II, p. 119: 'The antithesis of law and grace (1.17) is typically Pauline'; A. Richardson, *An Introduction to the Theology of the New Testament* (London: SCM Press, 1958), pp. 283-84. D'Alès ('ΧΑΡΙΝ ΑΝΤΙ ΧΑΡΙΤΟΣ', p. 385) sees v. 17 as excluding the possibility that the Law could be referred to as grace: 'En opposant la grâce à la loi de Moïse, ce verset 17 paraît exclure l'idée qu'à la ligne précédente la loi de Moïse ait pu être désignée par le même nom de grâce'. The supposed opposition between Law and grace is also emphasized by S. Pancaro, *The Law in the Fourth Gospel* (NovTSup, 42; Leiden: Brill, 1975), p. 541.

26. 'Letting John be John' is the basic theme of J.A.T. Robinson's book, *The Priority of John* (Cambridge, 1985).

contrasted, but this is because the majority of occurrences of χάρις are in the writings of Paul, who was himself particularly preoccupied with this relationship. But nowhere else in John or the Gospels do we find a direct contrast between 'grace and truth' and the Law such as has been suggested for v. 17. The majority of commentators seem to assume that we have a case of *antithetic parallelism*; but there is no adversative—no ἀλλά or δέ in the Greek. Grammatically and structurally the two halves of the verse are exactly balanced: each consists of a nominative noun or noun-pair, a modifying prepositional phrase with διά, and a main verb in the aorist tense.

Noun Phrase	Prepositional Phrase	Verb
ὅτι ὁ νόμος	διὰ Μωϋσέως	ἐδόθη,
ἡ χάρις καὶ ἡ ἀλήθεια	διὰ Ἰησοῦ	ἐγένετο

As Barnabas Lindars and others have pointed out,[27] the clause might well be translated: 'Just as the law was given through Moses, so grace and truth came through Jesus Christ'. Such an interpretation would give ὅτι, 'for', its full weight, with v. 17 explaining the force of the previous verse. To say all this is not to suggest for one moment that the Law and 'grace and truth' are synonymous, or that Moses and Christ are one and the same, or even that ἐδόθη has exactly the same meaning as ἐγένετο.[28] In spite of the strict parallelism in form, there is a progression of thought in the second part of the verse which could not readily have been predicted from its first half. Jeremias and others have suggested that, rather than choosing between synonymous and antithetic parallelism for this verse, we should classify it as 'synthetic' or 'progressive'.[29] The new grace is superior to the old, as the Church Fathers strongly emphasized in their comments on this text; but the old covenant was still a gift of grace, that is, a mark of God's gracious favour to his people.

That John understood the Law in this way is further borne out by an examination of his other allusions to it. In contrast to his references to 'the Jews' (οἱ Ἰουδαῖοι), which are nearly always hostile, John invari-

27. Lindars, *The Gospel of John*, p. 98; J. Jeremias, 'Μωυσῆς', *TDNT*, IV, p. 873.

28. The word ἐγένετο may well have been chosen deliberately to echo v. 14 with its reference to the incarnation.

29. For the various types of Hebrew parallelism, see W.G.E. Watson, *Classical Hebrew Poetry: A Guide to its Techniques* (JSOTSup, 26; Sheffield: JSOT Press, 1984). For antithetic parallelism, see in more detail J. Krašovec, *Antithetic Structure in Biblical Hebrew Poetry* (VTSup, 35; Leiden: Brill, 1984).

ably alludes to Moses and the Law in a neutral or clearly affirmative manner. Thus later in this chapter we find the disciple Nathanael saying, 'We have found him of whom Moses wrote in the law and of whom the prophets wrote also' (1.45). In ch. 6 Jesus is seemingly identified with the prophet like Moses of Deuteronomy 18; in ch. 5 he reproaches unbelieving Jews: 'If you believed in Moses, you would believe in me; for he wrote of me' (5.45-47). In all these cases Moses is clearly seen as pointing towards Jesus. In ch. 7 the Jews are actually reproached for not believing Moses (7.19; cf. 7.22-23); in 10.34 Jesus refers to the Law as the word of God, saying that Scripture cannot be broken. In 8.17 he uses the Mosaic dictum that the testimony of two men is true to argue for the truth of his own testimony and that of the Father.[30] In Jn 3.14 Moses' lifting up of the serpent in the wilderness is seen as a type of Jesus' own lifting up on the cross. In ch. 6, Jesus' gift of himself as the bread of life is compared with God's gift of manna to the Israelites through Moses in the wilderness. Naturally, Christ's gift is immeasurably greater (that is the point of the passage), but the manna was still a gracious gift. Indeed the Moses/Christ typology runs far deeper than the explicit references to Moses himself. As scholars such as Glasson and Jeremias have pointed out,[31] behind the frequent references in the Fourth Gospel to Christ as the 'light' or the giver of 'living water' there are constant implicit allusions to the claims made in developed Judaism for the Law. These allusions do not deny that the Law was in its own day a light to those to whom it was given, a source of life and nourishment to God's people. But this former manifestation of God's gracious love and favour has now been replaced by a new, personal and unique manifestation through his Son. God's old methods of dealing with his people—the Temple, the sacrificial system, and all the rituals of Judaism—have now been replaced by the sending of his Son in love, in short by the good news of the gospel. (Such a lesson should be drawn from both the Temple cleansing and the miracle at Cana.) None of this implies that

30. In 8.17 and in 10.34 the phrase 'in your law' has been taken as implying some sort of distancing, but even here it would be wrong to infer that the evangelist's attitude was negative. In a recent article W.J. Dumbrell has written, 'In the fourth gospel, outside of the prologue the use of *nomos* is always pejorative' ('Law and Grace: The Nature of the Contrast in John 1.17', *EvQ* 58 [1986], p. 34). But such a generalization is not borne out by the references already cited.

31. T.F. Glasson, *Moses in the Fourth Gospel* (SBT, 40; London: SCM Press, 1963); Jeremias, 'Μωυσῆς', pp. 872-73.

the old manifestation through Moses was not also a gracious act. We may compare the role of John the Baptist: he was a burning light in his generation, but he was superseded by the 'real' light in the incarnation of Jesus Christ.

Earlier in this paper I was critical of some of the interpretations that have been suggested for χάριν ἀντὶ χάριτος. Can this one bear close scrutiny? It seems to me that for any interpretation to be convincing it must (a) be in accord with an attested meaning for ἀντί; (b) adopt a plausible interpretation for χάρις; and (c) be in keeping with the thought of the rest of the Prologue, and, if possible, with the theology of the Gospel as a whole, since, even if—as many scholars believe—the Prologue is based on a pre-existing hymn composed by someone else, the Gospel author is not likely to have incorporated anything blatantly inconsistent with his own theology.

I would like to suggest that the interpretation argued here meets all these criteria:[32] (a) it adopts one of the most widely attested meanings for ἀντί in Hellenistic Greek (in contrast to the most popular interpretation 'upon' which involves postulating a new usage); (b) it adopts a sensible interpretation for χάρις (unlike, for example, M. Black's ingenious, but unconvincing conjecture[33]); and (c) it fits excellently with the context of the phrase in the Prologue and in particular with v. 17; it also picks up and supports the other echoes of Exodus 34–35 which have been detected in the Prologue, including the motifs of 'seeing God', of his presence or *shekhinah* (symbolized by the pillar of cloud), and of his glory as he partially reveals himself on Mount Sinai to his servant Moses, who had found favour with him.[34] It is also completely in keeping with the theology of the rest of the Fourth Gospel.

There remain some further implications of this interpretation which are worth bringing out briefly. First, and most obviously, it reinforces

32. In recent years the interpretation of ἀντί as 'instead of' has been supported most notably by de la Potterie (*La Vérité*, esp. I, pp. 142-44) and by R.E. Brown (*The Gospel according to St John*, I [AB; Garden City, NY: Doubleday, 1966], p. 15), who, however, regards this as only one of three possible interpretations. For older scholars who have also supported this view, see de la Potterie, *La Vérité*, I, p. 142 n. 60.

33. 'Does an Aramaic Tradition Underlie John 1.16?'

34. See esp. A. Hanson, 'John I. 14-18 and Exodus 34', *NTS* 23 (1977), pp. 90-101: and H. Mowvley, 'John 1.14-18 in the light of Exodus 33.7–34.35', *ExpTim* 95 (1984), pp. 135-37. It is striking that the word חֵן, 'gracious favour', occurs frequently in this Exodus narrative.

the view, gaining in popularity today, of the essential Jewishness of John's Gospel. Earlier this century scholars like E.F. Scott and R.H. Strachan[35] sought to interpret the Gospel against a Hellenistic background, emphasizing, for example, the links between John's *logos* doctrine and that of Hellenistic Stoicism; C.H. Dodd continued in this tradition when he explored possible links with the Hermetic Corpus and with Philo.[36] More recently Johannine scholars have looked increasingly to the Jewish background as an aid to the interpretation of the Gospel. Similarities have been found to the thought and language of the Qumran texts; much work has been done on a possible relationship to Jewish liturgy (including lectionary readings in the synagogue); and links have been identified with rabbinic exegesis and ways of thought.[37] Some of this work has been rightly criticized as speculative; but it does seem to be established beyond doubt that the Fourth Evangelist was thoroughly steeped in Jewish tradition. Jn 1.16, on the interpretation argued here, offers further support to those who stress the Jewishness of John. Indeed, if I am right that this verse refers to the Law itself as God's gracious gift,[38] then the Fourth Evangelist may be seen to be offering a more positive view of the Law than is often supposed.[39]

35. E.F. Scott, *The Fourth Gospel: Its Purpose and Theology* (Edinburgh: T. & T. Clark, 1906); R.H. Strachan, *The Fourth Gospel: Its Significance and Environment* (London: SCM Press, 1917).

36. *The Interpretation of the Fourth Gospel* (Cambridge: Cambridge University Press, 1953); Bultmann (*The Gospel of John*) also draws heavily on the Hellenistic background in his interpretation of the Gospel.

37. See esp. B. Gärtner, *John 6 and the Jewish Passover* (Lund: Gleerup, 1959); A. Guilding, *The Fourth Gospel and Jewish Worship* (Oxford: Clarendon Press, 1960); P. Borgen, *Bread from Heaven* (NovTSup, 10; Leiden: Brill, 1965); *idem*, 'Observations on the Targumic Character of the Prologue of John', *NTS* 16 (1969–70), pp. 288-95.

38. For the Law, מַתַּן תּוֹרָה, as God's gift par excellence, see de la Potterie, *La Vérité*, I, p. 156; II, p. 687, with further references; C.G. Montefiore and H. Loewe, *A Rabbinic Anthology* (London: Macmillan, 1938), pp. 117-73 *passim*, esp. p. 121; cf. Josephus, *Ant.* 4.318, where the laws of God are called his 'finest gift' (δώρημα τὸ κάλλιστον). This very Jewish way of referring to the Law would be particularly appropriate if we were (along with many Church Fathers) to regard Jn 1.16 as intended by the Evangelist as the continuation of the words of John the Baptist, v. 17 then being his own comment.

39. John's attitude is positive in that he sees the Law as pointing to Christ, and as fulfilled in him; not, of course, in the sense that he expects its precepts still to be kept in all their details by Christians. We may compare the attitude of Paul, as discussed

This is not to suggest that John could be described as a 'Judaizer'. He both recognizes the immense value of God's revelation to the Jews, and realizes that there is a sense in which this has been superseded. That is the point of ἀντί ('instead of') in v. 16; and may also lie behind that much discussed phrase, χάρις καὶ ἀλήθεια, in v. 17. Scholars have long drawn attention to the correspondence between John's phrase here and the familiar Old Testament concept of חֶסֶד וֶאֱמֶת—in Hebrew a hendiadys meaning 'faithful (or enduring) love'.[40] But I think we must also allow for John giving a fresh nuance to the familiar phrase: the coming of Jesus Christ is not just God's χάρις (gracious gift); it is the *true* χάρις, just as Christ is the true vine, the true or real bread from heaven. The Old Testament symbols of God's gracious acts have been appropriated and Christianized.

This leads to a second and more general point: in interpreting the Fourth Gospel, as indeed any other part of Scripture, we need always to be sensitive to the form and manner of the author's message. All too often we seek to impose on the biblical writers modern ideas of what is an appropriate structure or method of exposition. The results are often theories of multiple authorship, confusion of sources, dislocation of texts.[41] While there is no need to disparage such methods of literary analysis, we have to bear in mind that ancient writers did not always think or compose in the ways that we expect. John has a particularly distinctive method of composition. He does not set out his work like a student's 'ideal' lecture, with his points neatly packaged and labelled. Rather he loves to

by R. Badenas, *Christ, The End of the Law* (JSNTSup, 10; Sheffield: JSOT Press, 1985), esp. pp. 144-51.

40. Brown, *St John*, p. 16; see further J.A. Montgomery, 'Hebrew *hesed* and Greek *charis*', *HTR* 32 (1939), pp. 97-102; L.J. Kuyper, 'Grace and Truth: An Old Testament Description of God and its Use in the Johannine Gospel', *Int* 18 (1964), pp. 3-19; on the meaning of חֶסֶד in the Old Testament, see further H.J. Stoebe, 'Die Bedeutung des Wortes Häsäd im Alten Testament', *VT* 2 (1952), pp. 244-54, esp. 248; N. Gluech, *Hesed in the Bible* (ET Cincinnati: Hebrew Union College, 1967), together with H.-J. Zobel, 'חֶסֶד', *TDOT*, V, pp. 44-64, esp. 53.

41. For example, Jn 1.19-34 has sometimes been seen as containing two recensions of the same material; Jn 3.22-30 has been thought to interrupt the flow of thought; chs. 5 and 6 have often been transposed. John's method of composition in these and similar places has been helpfully characterized by O. Cullmann, *The Johannine Circle* (ET London: SCM Press, 1976), p. 4, where he comments on the early Christian habit of considering the same truth more than once from different perspectives.

allude, at first enigmatically and poetically, to images and ideas, which he later repeats and expounds in different ways, often through the medium of dialogue. This can sometimes give the impression of loose construction or meandering thought. But again and again, if we are open in our response to what he is saying, we find that his work is in fact both logical and skilfully structured, with the more enigmatic phrases sowing seeds of thought, which prepare the reader for what is to come. Sometimes his ambiguous phrases seem to be deliberately obscure, just to make his readers think.

It may be so also with χάριν ἀντὶ χάριτος. The phrase is not immediately intelligible on its own; but, like *logos* at the start of the Prologue, it raises questions in the minds of readers, alerting them for what follows. Though it has a stereotyped ring about it, it is not used here in precisely the same way as elsewhere. Possibly John composed the phrase (or took it over from existing tradition) because he liked the sound of it, without having thought out exactly what he was implying by it; more probably he chose it quite deliberately because of its ambiguous quality. Whatever his motivation for using the phrase in v. 16, he quickly clarified his meaning in v. 17 by a direct reference to Moses and the Law. Thus these two verses together, along with the rest of his Prologue, form a splendid spiritual appetizer for the main meat of his message, the manifestation of God's love in Jesus Christ—a message set out so magnificently in the rest of his Gospel.

JSNT 23 (1985), pp. 69-72

THE βασιλικός IN JOHN 4.46-53

A.H. Mead

The healing miracle of Jn 4.46-53 is generally assumed to describe the same incident as do Mt. 8.5-13 and Lk. 7.1-10, although there are a number of differences. One of these is that the father (or master in Luke) of the person who is cured is described in Matthew and Luke as a centurion (ἑκατόνταρχος) but in John as a βασιλικός (the reading βασιλισκός, whence AV's 'nobleman', has weak textual support).

What does βασιλικός mean? NEB translates 'an officer in the royal service'. Commentators are, as far as I know, unanimous in taking him to be in the service of Herod Antipas, tetrarch of Galilee, who was never officially a king, but is given the title in Mk 6.14. Matthew and Luke correct this to 'tetrarch', but Matthew does not bother to do so later on (14.9 = Mk 6.26). Westcott[1] mentioned conjectural identifications— Chuza, Herod's steward (Lk. 8.3) or Manaen (Acts 13.1) ('who had been brought up with him'—his σύντροφος). The term βασιλικός is used also in Acts 12.20-21, where it describes the territory and robes of Herod Agrippa; but he was a real king.

A 'centurion' suggests a Roman legionary 'non-commissioned' officer. But the centurions in the Gospels are unlikely to have been legionaries; all or almost all the Roman troops in Judaea were auxiliaries, provincial non-citizens.[2] Greek versions of Roman military titles are found in non-Roman courts and armies: at Antipas's court there are χιλίαρχοι (*tribuni militum*) and a σπεκουλάτωρ.[3] σπεχουλάτωρ, a transliteration, is the

1. *Gospel according to St John* (London: Murray, 1908), I, p. 171.
2. E. Schürer, *History of the Jewish People in the Age of Jesus Christ* (ed. G. Vermes and F. Millar; Edinburgh: T. & T. Clark, new edn, 1973), I, p. 362.
3. Mk 6.27.

correct technical term: *speculatores* were employed as executioners.[4] It is possible that the Herodians deliberately imitated Roman usage; several members of the family spent long periods at Rome. But troops in Syria seem to have been shuttled fairly easily between the service of local rulers and that of Rome. Herod the Great had Thracian, German and Gallic (Galatian?) troops;[5] on his death his best troops were employed by the Romans, then by Archelaus, then by the Romans, then by Agrippa, then (from 44 CE) by the Romans again.[6] The Jews were exempt from service in the Roman army, but it need not follow that there were no Jews among the units just discussed, or at any rate no Galileans, no Samaritans, no more or less hellenized Jews. However, that the centurion in question was not a Jew is strongly indicated in Matthew, and quite clear in Luke. There is probably no more than stylistic significance in their preference for the Greek equivalent ἑκατόνταρχος for κεντυρίων (which only occurs once in the New Testament, at Mk 15.39ff.).

It is possible then, as is generally assumed, that John is thinking of an official of Antipas's court, and Matthew and Luke of a Roman officer, provincial rather than Roman, but certainly Gentile. Some critics also assume that the Johannine βασιλικός must have been a Jew: so Goguel, who thought that 'a Gentile officer would have been out of place in Capernaum, part of Herod's domain'. Yet Herod Antipas was a favourite of Tiberius, had named a city after him, and had populated it with 'strangers';[7] it is really not at all clear that a Gentile would have been out of place at his court, and arguments about whether John has changed a Gentile into a Jew or Q has changed a Jewish nobleman into a Gentile centurion[8] are unsoundly based. Barnabas Lindars accepts that the βασιλικός, who he thinks is an official of 'King Herod', may be either a Jew or a Gentile. He thinks that the Synoptic centurion, though certainly a Gentile, was in Herodian service too.[9] Here he agrees with Sherwin-White: 'this centurion cannot be a Roman soldier', because Capernaum

4.   G. Webster, *The Roman Imperial Army of the First and Second Centuries A.D.* (New York: Barnes & Noble; 2nd edn, 1979), p. 263.

5.   Josephus, *War* 1.33.

6.   Schürer, *History of the Jewish People*, p. 363.

7.   Josephus, *Ant.* 18.2.

8.   R.T. Fortna, *The Gospel of Signs* (SNTSMS, 11; Cambridge: Cambridge University Press, 1970), p. 45, citing Bultmann and disagreeing with him. Fortna is also my source for the reference to Goguel, *Introduction au Nouveau Testament*, II (Paris: Leroux, 1923).

9.   *Gospel of John* (London: Marshall, Morgan & Scott, 1972).

was not part of a Roman province until 44 CE.[10]

While there is always the possibility that we are dealing with two incidents whose details have interpenetrated,[11] rather than one whose details have diverged, there is another possibility, which does not seem to have been considered, which is that all three Gospels are describing an officer in the Roman service, though probably a provincial officer of auxiliary, not legionary, troops. The term βασιλικός, which had been used for the Hellenistic kings, was widely used in the Greek-speaking world for the Roman emperors, long before it became their official designation. In the New Testament it presumably refers to them in 1 Tim. 2.2, and must do so in 1 Pet. 2.13, 17.

> As early as the reign of Augustus a Greek poet could refer to him in an epigram as a *basileus*, and…from the second century onwards, as we have seen from numerous examples, *basileus*, *basileia*, and cognate terms were frequently used both in public documents and in literary works, including those addressed to him, to refer to the emperor and his rule.[12]

οὐκ ἔχομεν βασιλέα εἰ μὴ καίσαρα, shout the Jews in Jn 19.15. Caesar, unlike Antipas (who according to Luke was in Jerusalem at the time), was a real βασιλεύς. It is perhaps too easy to remember the Roman hatred of the title 'Rex', and forget how quickly and naturally, in the Eastern provinces, the Roman emperor acquired the attributes of Near Eastern kings.

But what was a Roman centurion doing in a semi-independent state? Roman regiments were normally only quartered in provinces, and client states were expected to contribute to imperial defence, not to have security provided for them. However, according to G.H. Stevenson (who cites Tacitus, *Annals* 12.15), a small garrison was stationed in the Kingdom of Bosphorus in Claudius's reign; more to the point Herod the Great 'at one time had the support of a legion'.[13] Josephus (*War* 1.20) has Caesar

10. A.N. Sherwin-White, *Roman Society and Roman Law in the New Testament* (Oxford: Clarendon Press, 1963), p. 124.

11. C.H. Dodd points out that this episode is in some respects closer to the story of the Syro-Phoenician woman than to the healing of the centurion's boy, and believes it to be influenced by the experience of the Gentile mission, as described in Acts. Yet he also notes that 'it is not said that the man was a Gentile' (*Historical Tradition in the Fourth Gospel* [Cambridge: Cambridge University Press, 1963], p. 193).

12. F. Millar, *The Emperor in the Roman World (31 B.C.–A.D. 337)* (London: Duckworth, 1977), p. 613.

13. *Roman Provincial Administration* (Oxford: Oxford University Press, 1939), pp. 46, 51.

make a present to Herod the Great of four hundred Galatians, previously in the service of Cleopatra, as a bodyguard. We have seen already how easily, after Herod's death, troops could be transferred between the service of the Romans and that of his family. Roman troops had to pass through client states when travelling between Syria and Judaea. They may have been employed on diplomatic missions to Herodian courts. They may even have visited them on leave.

There is, then, no need at all to suppose that the βασιλικός of Jn 4.46-53 is a Jew,[14] or that there is any contradiction between John and Matthew and Luke on his identity. He is a Gentile officer, perhaps in the service of Herod Antipas, but quite probably, I would suggest, in the service of Rome. The distinction may not have been so easy to make as is generally assumed; one might compare the forces of the Indian Empire, which included the Indian Army, the British Army in India, and the Indian princes' armies, with secondment of British officers possible among all three. The mission of our Lord expands: in ch. 3 new life is offered to the Jews, in 4.1-42, to the Samaritans; in these last few verses of ch. 4, with great brevity and a dramatic sign of power, it is brought to the Gentiles. The royal officer enters the Kingdom.

14. J.A.T. Robinson (*On Redating the New Testament* [London: SCM Press, 1976], esp. p. 265) argues that there is no mention at all of Gentiles, as such, in John. But it is surely possible to accept his general picture of the Gospel, as early and based on knowledge of Palestine, without insisting that Jesus' mission was entirely to the Jews.

JSNT 25 (1985), pp. 49-60

HELLENISTIC PARALLELS TO THE ACTS OF THE APOSTLES (2.1-47)

Pieter W. van der Horst

This collection of comparative materials to the second chapter of the book of Acts is, like the previous instalment (*ZNW* 74 [1983], pp. 17-26), based upon earlier compilations of the so-called *Observationes* literature of the seventeenth and eighteenth centuries, upon other secondary literature, upon the files of the Corpus Hellenisticum Novi Testamenti project in Utrecht, and upon my own research. I want to emphasize that the purpose of this collection is not to deny or doubt the fundamentally Jewish character of the New Testament writings. Its modest aim is to show how much (or little) these basically Jewish writings have in common with pagan literary documents of antiquity. It might also help to gauge how much first-century Jewish (and hence Christian) thought and diction have been influenced by Hellenistic ideas and modes of expression. In the case of Acts this influence is stronger than in most other New Testament books.

2.2-3: Wind and especially fire (often on the head) are frequently regarded as signs of divine presence. Iamblichus, *De mysteriis* 3.2: καὶ ποτε μὲν ἀναφὲς καὶ ἀσώματον πνεῦμα περιέχει κύκλῳ τοὺς κατακειμένους, ὡς ὅρασιν μὲν αὐτοῦ μὴ παρεῖναι, τὴν δὲ ἄλλην συναίσθησιν καὶ παρακολούθησιν ὑπάρχειν, ῥοιζομένου τε ἐν τῷ εἰσιέναι, καὶ περικεχυμένου πανταχόθεν ἄνευ τινὸς ἐπαφῆς, θαυμαστά τε ἔργα ἀπεργαζομένου πρὸς ἀπαλλαγὴν παθῶν ψυχῆς τε καὶ σώματος. *Ibid.* 3.6: ὁρᾶται δὲ καὶ τῷ δεχομένῳ τὸ τοῦ πυρὸς εἶδος πρὸ τοῦ δέχεσθαι, *scil.* τὸ πνεῦμα. Homer, *Iliad* 18.225-27: ἡνίοχοι δ᾽ ἔκπληγεν, ἐπεὶ ἴδον ἀκάματον πῦρ, | δεινὸν ὑπὲρ κεφαλῆς μεγαθύμου Πηλείωνος | δαιόμενον. Euripides, *Bacchae* 757-58 (on the maenads): ἐπὶ δὲ βοστρύχοις | πῦρ ἔφερον, οὐδ᾽

ἔκαιεν. Cicero, *De divinatione* 1.53.121: caput arsisse Servio Tullio dormienti quae historia non prodidit? (A.S. Pease *ad loc.* gives several parallels). Ovid, *Fasti* 6.634-36: Servius a caelo semina gentis habet. | signa dedit genitor tunc, cum caput igne corusco | contigit, inque comis flammeus arsit apex. Vergil, *Aeneid* 2.680-84 (on Anchises' son Julus) ...subitum dictuque oritur mirabile monstrum | namque manus inter maestorumque ora parentum | ecce levis summo de vertice visus Iuli | fundere lumen apex, tactuque innoxia mollis | lambere flamma comas et circum tempora pasci. *Ibid.* 8.680-81 (on Augustus): ...geminas cui tempora flammas | laeta vomunt. Cf. 7.71ff. Livy 1.39.2 (on Servius Tullius): puero dormienti...caput arsisse ferunt multorum in conspectu... mox cum somno et flammam abisse. *Ibid.* 25.39.16 (on L. Marcius): apud omnis magnum nomen Marcii ducis est; et verae gloriae eius etiam miracula addunt, flammam ei contionanti fusam e capite sine ipsius sensu cum magno pavore circumstantium militum. See also Valerius Maximus 1.6.1-2. Silius Italicus 16.118-21 (on Massinissa): huic fesso, quos dura fuga et nox suaserat atra, | carpenti somnos subitus rutilante coruscum | vertice fulsit apex, crispamque involvere visa est | mitis flamma comam atque hirta se spargere fronte. Pliny, *Naturalis historia* 2.241:...Servio Tullio dormienti in pueritia ex capite flammam emicuisse, L. Marcio in Hispania interemptis Scipionibus contionanti et milites ad ultionem exhortanti arsisse simili modo Valerius Antias narrat. Apuleius, *De Deo Socratis* 7: ...ut nonnullis regni futuri signa praecurrant, ut Tarquinius Priscus aquila obumbretur ab apice, Servius Tullius flamma conluminetur a capite. Plutarch, *Caesar* 63.2: Στράβων δὲ ὁ φιλόσοφος ἱστορεῖ πολλοὺς μὲν ἀνθρώπους διαπύρους ἐπιφερομένους φανῆναι, στρατιώτου δὲ ἀνδρὸς οἰκέτην ἐκ τῆς χειρὸς ἐκβαλεῖν πολλὴν φλόγα καὶ δοκεῖν καίεσθαι τοῖς ὁρῶσιν, ὡς δὲ ἐπαύσατο, μηδὲν ἔχειν κακὸν τὸν ἄνθρωπον. Dio Cassius 48.33.2 (on an unknown shepherd): αὐτῷ ἡ κεφαλὴ ποιμαίνοντι φλόγα ἀνέδωκεν. Cf. Aelius Aristides 28.110 (= 49, p. 527 Dindorf): λόγων δ᾽ αὕτη πηγὴ μία, τὸ ὡς ἀληθῶς ἱερὸν καὶ θεῖον πῦρ τὸ ἐκ Διὸς ἑστίας.

2.4: Divinely inspired speech was often discussed and described in pagan antiquity. Some examples suffice: Plutarch, *De defectu oraculorum* 40, 432D-E: τὸ δὲ μαντικὸν ῥεῦμα καὶ πνεῦμα θειότατόν ἐστι καὶ ὁσιώτατον, ἄν τε καθ᾽ ἑαυτὸ δι᾽ ἀέρος ἄν τε μεθ᾽ ὑγροῦ νάματος ἀπερᾶται. καταμειγνύμενον γὰρ εἰς τὸ σῶμα κρᾶσιν ἐμποιεῖ ταῖς ψυχαῖς ἀήθη καὶ ἄτοπον, ἧς τὴν ἰδιότητα χαλεπὸν εἰπεῖν σαφῶς, εἰκάσαι δὲ πολλαχῶς ὁ λόγος δίδωσι. θερμότητι γὰρ καὶ διαχύσει πόρους τινὰς ἀνοίγειν φανταστικοὺς τοῦ μέλλοντος εἰκός ἐστιν, ὡς οἶνος ἀναθυμιαθεὶς ἕτερα πολλὰ κινήματα καὶ λόγους ἀποκειμένους καὶ λανθάνοντας ἀποκαλύπτει· ΄τὸ γὰρ βακχεύσιμον καὶ τὸ μανιῶδες μαντικὴν πολλὴν ἔχει΄, κατ᾽ Εὐριπίδην. Plutarch, *Amatorius* 11, 755E: ἔοικε θεία τις ὄντως εἰληφέναι τὴν ἄνθρωπον ἐπίπνοια καὶ κρείττων ἀνθρωπίνου λογισμοῦ. Pollux, *Onomasticon* 1.15–16: εἰ δέ που καὶ πνεῦμα εἴη μαντικόν, ὁ μὲν τόπος ἔνθεος καὶ ἐπίπνους καὶ κάτοχος καὶ ἐπιτεθειασμένος καὶ κατειλημμένος ἐκ θεοῦ, ὥσπερ καὶ ὁ χρῶν ἀνήρ. οὗτος δὲ καὶ ἐνθουσιῶν, καὶ κεκινημένος ἐκ θεοῦ, καὶ ἀναβεβακχευμένος, καὶ πλήρης θεοῦ, καὶ παραλλάττων ἐκ θεοῦ. τὸ δὲ πνεῦμα εἴποις ἂν καὶ ἀτμὸν μαντικόν, καὶ ἆσθμα δαιμόνιον, καὶ θείαν αὖραν, καὶ ἄνεμον μαντικόν, καὶ φωνὴν προαγορευτικήν. τὰ δὲ ῥήματα τῶν τῷ ἀνδρὶ συμβαινόντων κατασχεθῆναι, καταληφθῆναι, ἐνθουσιάσαι, ἐπιθειάσαι, ἀναβακχεῦσαι, πληρωθῆναι θεοῦ. τὸ γὰρ ἐπιπνευσθῆναι κακόφωνον. τὰ δὲ ὀνόματα τοῦ πράγματος κατακωχή, κάθοδος θεοῦ, καταβολή, κατοχή, ἐπιθειασμὸς ἐπίπνοια, βακχεία, κίνησις ἐκ θεοῦ, κατάληψις, ἐνθουσιασμός. Justinus, *Epitoma Historiarum Philippicarum Pompei Trogi* 43.1.8: Fauno uxor fuit nomine Fatua, quae adsidue divino spiritu impleta veluti per furorem futura praemonebat. Cicero, *De divinatione* 1.6.12: aliquo instinctu inflatuque divino futura praenuntiat. Cf. similar expressions in 1.18.34; 1.19.38; 1.31.66. Livy 5.15.10: cecinerit divino spiritu instinctus. Dio Chrysostom 72.12: τῶν χρησμῶν...οὓς ἡ Πυθία ἔχρα καθίζουσα ἐπὶ τοῦ τρίποδος ἐμπιμπλαμένη τοῦ πνεύματος. Aelius Aristides 42.11 (6, p. 68 Dindorf); Asclepius λόγους ὑπέθηκε καὶ πρὸς τούτοις ἐννοήματα αὐτὰ καὶ τὴν λέξιν. 45.16 (8, p. 88 Dindorf); Sarapis δίδωσι λέγειν αὐτός. Cf. also 45.14 and, on Zeus, 43.1 and 31; 28.114–15 (49, p. 528 Dindorf) contains a long description of speaking under divine inspiration. Compare also his definition of inspiration in 2.53 (45, p. 17 Dindorf), μανία τίς ἐστιν ἀμείνων σωφροσύνης καὶ παρὰ θεῶν ἀνθρώποις γιγνομένη, with the one by Ps.-Galen, *Definitiones* 487 (19, 462 Kühn), ἔκστασίς ἐστιν ὀλιγοχρόνιος μανία. Two important Hellenistic-Jewish parallels are Josephus, *Ant.* 4.119, where Balaam says to Balak: δοκεῖς ἐφ᾽ ἡμῖν εἶναί τι περὶ τῶν τοιούτων σιγᾶν ἢ λέγειν ὅταν ἡμᾶς τὸ τοῦ θεοῦ λάβῃ πνεῦμα; φωνὰς γὰρ ἃς βούλεται τοῦτο καὶ λόγους οὐδὲν ἡμῶν εἰδότων ἀφίησιν, and a long passage in *T. Job* 48-52 where the daughters of Job speak in the language of the angels: 48 (first daughter) ἀπεφθέγξατο δὲ τῇ ἀγγελικῇ διαλέκτῳ, ὕμνον ἀναπέμψασα τῷ θεῷ κατὰ τὴν ἀγγέλων ὑμνολογίαν. (...) 49 (second daughter) τὸ μὲν στόμα αὐτῆς ἀνέλαβεν τὴν διάλεκτον τῶν ἀρχῶν, ἐδοξολόγησεν δὲ τοῦ ὑψηλοῦ τόπου τὸ ποίημα. (...) 50 (third daughter) ἔσχεν τὸ στόμα ἀποφθεγγόμενον ἐν τῇ διαλέκτῳ τῶν ἐν ὕψει (...) λελάληκεν γὰρ ἐν τῇ διαλέκτῳ τῶν χερουβιμ δοξολογοῦσα τὸν δεσπότην τῶν ἀρετῶν. (...) 51 καὶ ἀνεγραψάμην τὸ βιβλίον ὅλον πλείστων σημειώσεως τῶν ὕμνων παρὰ τῶν τριῶν θυγατέρων τοῦ ἀδελφοῦ μου, σωτήριον ταῦτα εἶναι, ὅτι ταῦτά ἐστιν τὰ μεγαλεῖα τοῦ θεοῦ. Note the parallels in this passage not only to v. 4 but also to vv. 8 and 11. Discussions of these and other passages can be found in F. Pfister, 'Ekstase', *RAC* 4 (1959), pp. 944-87 (with the supplementary remarks *s.v.* 'Enthusiasmos', *RAC* 5 [1962], pp. 455-57) and in G. Dautzenberg, 'Glossolalie', *RAC* 11 (1981), pp. 22-46.

2.5: For the expression ὑπὸ τὸν οὐρανόν cf. Plato, *Timaeus* 23c: ...κάλλισται πασῶν ὁπόσων ὑπὸ τὸν οὐρανὸν ἡμεῖς ἀκοὴν παρεδεξάμεθα. Plato, *Epistula* 7.326c: ἐκ γὰρ τούτων τῶν ἐθῶν οὔτ᾽ ἂν φρόνιμος οὐδείς ποτε γενέσθαι τῶν ὑπὸ τὸν οὐρανὸν ἀνθρώπων... δύναιτο.

2.6: To the idea that each one present heard the apostles talking in his or her own language, sometimes the following passage from the Homeric *Hymn to Apollo* has been adduced as a parallel, vv. 156-64:

πρὸς δὲ τόδε μέγα θαῦμα, ὅου κλέος οὔποτ᾽ ὀλεῖται,
κοῦραι Δηλιάδες, Ἑκατηβελέταο Θεράπναι·
αἵ τ᾽ ἐπεὶ ἄρ πρῶτον μὲν Ἀπόλλων᾽ ὑμνήσωσιν,
αὗτις δ᾽ αὖ Λητώ τε καὶ Ἄρτεμιν ἰοχέαιραν
μνησάμεναι ἀνδρῶν τε παλαιῶν ἠδὲ γυναικῶν
ὕμνον ἀείδουσιν, θέλγουσι δὲ φῦλ᾽ ἀνθρώπων.
πάντων δ᾽ ἀνθρώπων φωνὰς καὶ κρεμβαλιαστὺν
μιμεῖσθ᾽ ἴσασιν· φαίη δέ κεν αὐτὸς ἕκαστος
φθέγγεσθ᾽· οὕτω σφιν καλὴ συνάρηρεν ἀοιδή.

The theory that this text refers to the same phenomenon as Acts 2.6 was first proposed by E. Kalinka, *Das Pfingstwunder* (Commentationes Aenipontanae, 10; Innsbrück: Wagner, 1924), p. 17, and has again been defended by H.J. Tschiedel, 'Ein Pfingstwunder im Apollonhymnos', *ZRGG* 27 (1975), pp. 22-39. But it is much more probable that 'the accomplishment ascribed to the Deliades is that of singing in dialect' (thus T.W. Allen, W.R. Halliday and E.E. Sikes, *The Homeric Hymns* [Oxford: Clarendon Press, 1936], p. 225).

2.7: To the instances of ἐξίσταμαι used absolutely which are mentioned in Bauer's *Wörterbuch* add now the examples adduced by Pfister, 'Ektase', p. 947; e.g. Sophocles, *Antigone* 564; Menander, fr. 149; Plato, *Menexenus* 235a. Pfister gives other examples of ἔκστασις as a reaction to something miraculous (pp. 966-67).

2.9-11: To the geographical catalogue in these verses many more or less similar listings have been compared. E.g., S. Weinstock ('The Geographical Catalogue of Acts II 9-11', *JRS* 38 [1948], pp. 43-46) drew attention to a list of countries in Paulus Alexandrinus, *Elementa Apotelesmatica* 2 (p. 10 ed. A. Boer; second half of the fourth century CE): προσπαθεῖ δὲ ταῖς χώραις τὰ ζῴδια. ὁ μὲν Κριὸς τῇ Περσίδι, ὁ δὲ Ταῦρος τῇ Βαβυλῶνι, οἱ δὲ Δίδυμοι τῇ Καππαδοκίᾳ, ὁ δὲ Καρκίνος τῇ Ἀρμενίᾳ, ὁ δὲ Λέων τῇ Ἀσίᾳ, ἡ δὲ Παρθένος τῇ Ἑλλάδι, ὁ δὲ Ζυγὸς τῇ Λιβύῃ, ὁ δὲ Σκορπίος τῇ Ἰταλίᾳ, ὁ δὲ Τοξότης τῇ Κρήτῃ, τοῦ Αἰγοκέρωτος τῇ Συρίᾳ ἀπονενεμημένου, τοῦ Ὑδροχόου τὴν Αἴγυπτον λαχόντος, τῶν Ἰχθύων τὴν Ἰνδικὴν χώραν προσῳκειωμένων. Since in this list countries and lands are assigned to the several signs of the zodiac, Weinstock argued that the author of Acts intended to say that all nations who live under the twelve signs of the zodiac, that is, the whole world, received the gift to understand the apostles' preaching. But B.M. Metzger ('Ancient Astrological Geography and Acts 2.9-11', in *New Testament Studies, Philological, Versional, Patristic* [NTTS, 10; Leiden: Brill, 1980], pp. 46-56) rightly pointed out the paucity of actual similarities; only five names are identical. Interesting in this connection is Macrobius's remark on the catalogue of nations in the second book of Homer's *Iliad*, in *Saturnalia* 5.15.3: progrediens modo mediterranea, modo maritima iuncta describit, inde rursus ad utrumque situm cohaerentium locorum disciplina describentis velut iter agentis accedit, nec ullo saltu cohaerentiam regionum in libro suo hiare permittit, sed hoc viandi more procedens redit unde digressus est. Whether there was any principle or method behind the list in Acts comparable to the one here described by Macrobius remains obscure as before. As further examples see, for example, Curtius Rufus 6.3.3: Cariam, Lydiam, Cappadociam, Phrygiam, Paphlagoniam, Pamphyliam, Pisidas, Ciliciam,

Syriam, Phoenicen, Armeniam, Persidem, Medos, Parthenien habemus in potestate. Cf. also the letter in Ps.-Callisthenes 2.11.2 (ed. Kroll): Βασιλεὺς Ἀλέξανδρος σατράπαις τοῖς ὑποτεταγμένοις μοι Συρίας καὶ Κιλικίας καὶ Καππαδοκίας καὶ Παφλαγονίας καὶ Ἀραβίας καὶ τοῖς ἑτέροις ἔθνεσι χαίρειν. Other lists in Xenophon, *Cyropaedia* 6.2.10; Dio Chrysostom 9.5, 12 and 33.40; Arrianus, in *Die Fragmente der griechischen Historiker* 156 F1, 5-6; Darius's Behistun inscription 1.6 and Xerxes' Daiva inscription 19-28. Of special interest is Philo's list in *Leg. Gai.* 281 since it indicates the degree of dispersion of the Jews in the middle of the first century CE: (Jerusalem...) ἐμὴ μέν ἐστι πατρίς, μητρόπολις δὲ οὐ μιᾶς χώρας Ἰουδαίας ἀλλὰ καὶ τῶν πλείστων, διὰ τὰς ἀποικίας ἃς ἐξέπεμψεν ἐπὶ καιρῶν εἰς μὲν τοὺς ὁμόρους, Αἴγυπτον, Φοινίκην, Συρίαν τήν τε ἄλλην καὶ τὴν Κοίλην προσαγορευομένην, εἰς δὲ τὰς πόρρω διῳκισμένας, Παμφυλίαν, Κιλικίαν, τὰ πολλὰ τῆς Ἀσίας ἄχρι Βιθυνίας καὶ τῶν τοῦ Πόντου μυχῶν, τὸν αὐτὸν τρόπον καὶ εἰς Εὐρώπην, Θετταλίαν, Βοιωτίαν, Μακεδονίαν, κτλ. To the expression οἱ κατοικοῦντες (τὴν Μεσοποταμίαν...καὶ) τὴν Ἀσίαν cf. Plutarch, *Regum et imperatorum apophthegmata, Agesilaos* 1, 190F: Ἀγησίλαος ἔλεγε τοὺς τὴν Ἀσίαν κατοικοῦντας ἐλευθέρους μὲν κακοὺς εἶναι, δούλους δ' ἀγαθούς. The expression λαλεῖν τὰ μεγαλεῖα τοῦ θεοῦ is paralleled in *T. Job* 51 quoted above *ad* 2.4, but cf. also Aelius Aristides 40.12 (5, p. 59 Dindorf) καταλέγειν...δυνάμεις ἐμφανεῖς (sc. of Heracles) and 37.27 (2, p. 27 Dindorf) εἰπεῖν εἰς τὸ μέσον τὰ τῆς θεοῦ (sc. Athena).

2.12: To the motif of perplexity after hearing an unexpected language one might compare Herodotus 8.135 which describes the reaction to an utterance of a *promantis* in the sanctuary of Apollo in Copae, Boeotia: τοὺς μὲν ἑπομένους τῶν Θηβαίων ἐν θώματι ἔχεσθαι ἀκούοντας βαρβάρου γλώσσης ἀντὶ Ἑλλάδος, οὐδὲ ἔχειν ὅ τι χρήσωνται τῷ παρεόντι πρήγματι. The expression τί θέλει τοῦτο εἶναι reminds one of more or less similar locutions as in Aelian, *Varia Historia* 3.20: τί βούλεται τὸ πέμμα τοῦτο εἶναι; *ibid.* 4.9: τί δὲ ἐβούλετο αὐτῷ τὸ ὄνομα ἐκεῖνο; Aristophanes, *Ecclesiazusae* 753: τί τὰ σκευάρια ταυτὶ βούλεται; Herodotus 1.78: τί θελει σημαίνειν τὸ τέρας; cf. Maximus Tyrius 22.226.

2.13: ἕτεροι δὲ κτλ. looks strange after ἐξίσταντο δὲ πάντες in v. 12, but the πάντες are divided into two groups, the division being only indicated in the second half. So the meaning is: 'all reacted: some were perplexed, others mocked'. This construction does not occur often but there are some parallels: Plato, *Leges* 828c: ἀγῶνας μουσικούς, τοὺς δὲ γυμνικούς. Andocides 1.38: ἑστάναι δὲ κύκλῳ ἀνὰ πέντε καὶ δέκα ἄνδρας, τοὺς δὲ ἀνὰ εἴκοσι. *Ibid.* 1.105: εἰ αὐτοῖς ἐξέσται ἀδέως συκοφαντεῖν καὶ γράφεσθαι, τοὺς δὲ ἐνδεικνύναι, τοὺς δὲ ἀπάγειν... Lucian, *Lexiphanes* 2: κατέλαβον γὰρ τοὺς ἐργάτας λιγυρίζοντας τὴν θερινὴν ᾠδήν, τοὺς δὲ τάφον τῷ ἐμῷ πατρὶ κατασκευάζοντας.

Reactions of mockery or contempt in a similar context: *Corpus Hermeticum* 1.29 (after a religious discourse): οἱ μὲν αὐτῶν καταφλυαρήσαντες ἀπέστησαν, τῇ τοῦ θανάτου ὁδῷ ἑαυτοὺς ἐκδεδωκότες, οἱ δὲ παρεκάλουν διδαχθῆναι κτλ. *Ibid.* 9.4 (on those who know God): μεμηνέναι δὲ δοκοῦσι, καὶ γέλωτα ὀφλισκάνουσι, μισούμενοί τε καὶ καταφρονούμενοι καὶ τάχα που καὶ φονευόμενοι. Plutarch, *De defectu oraculorum* 42, 433C: νομέως τινὸς ἐμπεσόντος κατὰ τύχην, εἶτα φωνὰς ἀναφέροντος ἐνθουσιώδεις, ὧν τὸ μὲν πρῶτον οἱ παραγενόμενοι κατεφρόνουν.

Comparisons of drunkenness and ecstasy occur often, for example, Plutarch, *Quaestiones Romanae* 112, 291B (on ivy): ἄοινον ἐπάγει μέθην καὶ χαρὰν τοῖς ἐπισφαλῶς πρὸς ἐνθουσιασμὸν ἔχουσι; *De defectu oraculorum* 40, 432E (the subject is the divine pneuma which enters a human being): θερμότητι γὰρ καὶ διαχύσει πόρους τινὰς ἀνοίγειν φανταστικοὺς τοῦ μέλλοντος εἰκός ἐστιν, ὡς οἶνος ἀναθυμιαθεὶς ἕτερα πολλὰ κινήματα καὶ λόγους ἀποκειμένους καὶ λανθάνοντας ἀποκαλύπτει; *Septem sapientium convivium* 4, 150C, where someone who is drunk is called θεοῦ μεστός, sc. of Dionysus (cf. μεμεστωμένοι in Acts 2.13). Lucian, *Nigrinus* 5: ...καὶ αὐτὸς ἔνθεος καὶ μεθύων ὑπὸ τῶν λόγων περιέρχομαι. Iamblichus, *De mysteriis* 3.25: τὸ δὲ ἐπὶ τούτοις ἀπὸ τῆς ἐνθέου παραφορᾶς ἐπὶ τὴν ἔκστασιν τῆς διανοίας τὴν ἐπὶ τὸ χεῖρον ἀποπίπτει, τήν τε ἐν τοῖς νοσήμασι συμπίπτουσαν μανίαν παραλόγως αἰτίαν εἶναί φησι τῆς μαντικῆς. χολῆς γὰρ πλεονασμοῖς ὡς ἔστιν εἰκάσαι τῆς μελαίνης καὶ μέθης παρατροπαῖς καὶ τῇ λύσσῃ τῇ ἀπὸ λυσσώντων κυνῶν συμβαινούσῃ τὸν ἐνθουσιασμὸν ἀπεικάζει. Cf. Philo, *De ebrietate* 146: the soul filled with grace βεβάκχευται (...), ὡς πολλοῖς τῶν ἀνοργιάστων μεθύειν καὶ παρακινεῖν καὶ ἐξιστάναι ἂν δόξαι. That wine could induce a state of ecstasy is said in Euripides, fr. 265 Nauck: νῦν δ' οἶνος ἐξέστησέ με, and in Macrobius, *Saturnalia* 1.18.1:

Aristoteles (…) Apollinem et Liberum patrem unum eundemque deum esse cum multis aliis argumentis adserat, etiam apud Ligyreos ait in Thracia esse adytum Libero consecratum ex quo redduntur oracula. sed in hoc adyto vaticinaturi plurimo mero sumpto, uti apud Clarium aqua pota, effantur oracula.

2.14-36: E. Plümacher (*Lukas als hellenistischer Schriftsteller* [Göttingen: Vandenhoeck & Ruprecht, 1972], pp. 38-72) makes an interesting comparison between the purposeful 'Septuagintanachahmung' in several speeches in Acts and the intentional mimesis of the great classical examples in speeches in historiographical works of the Hellenistic-Roman period, for example, the imitations of Thucydides, Demosthenes, Xenophon, and others in Dionysius of Halicarnassus and Dio Cassius.

2.15: For the shameful idea of drinking at the third hour of the day, see Cicero, *Philippica* 2.41.104: et quam multos dies in ea villa turpissime es perbacchatus! ab hora tertia bibebatur, ludebatur, vomebatur.

2.17: Pfister ('Ekstase', pp. 969-74) gives many references for the idea that gods are the authors of ecstasy and for the phenomenon of visions as a concomitant of ecstasy.

2.19: For the juxtaposition of τέρατα and σημεῖα (also in vv. 22 and 43 *et passim*), cf. Plutarch, *Septem sapientium convivium* 3, 149C: ἤ τι σημεῖόν ἐστι καὶ τέρας.

2.20: The idea that an eclipse is a sign of impending doom is attacked as superstitious by Plutarch, *De superstitione* 8, 169B.

2.22: To the instances of δύναμις in the meaning of 'miracle', 'mighty deed' mentioned by Bauer (*Wörterbuch*, *s.v.* 4) add Aelius Aristides 23.18; 37.17; 41.7; 42.4; 48.30.

2.23: Bauer (*Wörterbuch*, *s.v.* βουλή 2b) gives some instances of βουλὴ θεοῦ/Διός in *Poimandres* and Quintus Smyrnaeus; add Aelius Aristides 43.25 (1, p. 9 Dindorf) Διὸς…βουλήν.

2.29: A parallel to the expression ἐξὸν εἰπεῖν μετὰ παρρησίας is found in Aristophanes, *Thesmophoriazusae* 540-42: εἰ γὰρ οὔσης | παρρησίας

κἀξὸν λέγειν ὅσαι πάρεσμεν ἀσταί, | εἶτ᾽ εἶπον ἀγίγνωσκον...
Aelius Aristides 6.2 (30, p. 571 Dindorf): ἀξιῶ δὲ γενέσθαι μοι μετὰ
παρρησίας εἰπεῖν. On David's tomb in Jerusalem in the first century,
see Josephus, *Ant.* 7.392–94.

2.31: As David *foresaw* Christ's resurrection, so Homer foresaw
Rome's future rule, according to Aelius Aristides 26.106 (14, p. 368
Dindorf): δοκεῖ δέ μοι καὶ Ἡσίοδος, εἰ ὁμοίως Ὁμήρῳ τέλειος ἦν
τὰ ποιητικὰ καὶ μαντικός, ὥσπερ ἐκεῖνος οὐκ ἠγνόησεν τὴν
ὑμετέραν ἀρχὴν ἐσομένην, ἀλλὰ προεῖδεν καὶ ἀνεφθέγξατο ἐν
τοῖς ἔπεσιν, οὕτως καὶ αὐτὸς κτλ.

2.33: The idea that the exalted Christ receives things from his Father
is paralleled in what Aelius Aristides says about the goddess Athena
and her father Zeus: 37.4-7 (2, p. 15 Dindorf): ...αἰεὶ πάρεστί τε καὶ
συνδιαιτᾶται (sc. Διί)...καὶ σύνεστι μόνη μόνῳ... (7) παρὰ τοῦ
πατρὸς παραλαμβάνουσα...

2.35: The image of enemies being used as a footstool is current in
Hellenistic-Roman literature; for example, Ovid, *Fasti* 4.857-58: urbs
oritur... victorem terris inpositura pedem. *Tristia* 4.2.44: et ducis invicti
sub pede maesta sedet. Ovid, *Epistulae* 9.12-13: haec humilis sub pede
colla tenet. Vergil, *Aeneid* 10.495-96: et laevo pressit pede talia fatus |
exanimem. For other instances, see F. Bömer, *P. Ovidius Naso: Die
Fasten II* (Heidelberg: Kerle, 1958), pp. 282-83.

2.37-38: After Peter's speech the hearers ask: τί ποιήσωμεν; Peter
answers with an imperative. Similarly, in *Corpus Hermeticum* 13.7, after
a speech by Hermes Trismegistus, his son Tat asks: ἀδύνατος οὖν εἰμι,
ὦ πάτερ; And Hermes answers: μὴ γένοιτο, ὦ τέκνον, ἐπίσπασαι κτλ.

2.39: *Ad* προσκαλέσηται...ὁ θεός, cf. Aelius Aristides 23.15 (42, p. 772
Dindorf): παρὰ τοῦ θεοῦ καλοῦντος τε ὡς αὐτόν. *Ad* κύριος ὁ θεὸς
ἡμῶν, cf. *P. Yale* inv. 1394V (120 CE), edited by G.M. Parassoglou in
ZPE 13 (1974), pp. 21-37, and reprinted by H.A. Rupprecht in
Sammelbuch griechischer Urkunden aus Ägypten, XII.2 (Wiesbaden:
Harrassowitz, 1977), no. 11236: ὁ κύριος ἡμῶν καὶ θεὸς ἐνφανέστατος
αὐτοκράτωρ Καῖσαρ Τραϊανὸς Ἀδριανὸς Σεβαστός. Whereas here
the titles 'Lord and God' are applied to the emperor, in *P. Mich.* III,

209.11-13 (c. 200 CE) the writer applies them to his own brother!: οἶδας γάρ, ἄδελφε, ὅτει οὐ μόνον ὡς ἀδελφόν σε ἔχω ἀλλὰ καὶ ὡς πατέρα καὶ κύριον καὶ θεόν (from G.H.R. Horsley, *New Documents Illustrating Early Christianity*, II [North Ryde: Macquarie University, 1982], p. 69).

2.40: ἑτέριος τε λόγοις πλείοσιν διεμαρτύρατο is a well-known stylistic abbreviatory device; see for example Xenophon, *Hellenica* 2.4.42 (after a speech): εἰπὼν δὲ ταῦτα καὶ ἄλλα τοιαῦτα κτλ. Polybius 21.14.4 πολλὰ δὲ καὶ ἔτερα πρὸς ταύτην ὑπόθεσιν διελέχθη. 3.111.11 ταῦτα δὲ καὶ τούτοις παραπλήσια διαλεχθεὶς κτλ.

2.41: ἀποδέχεσθαι τὸν λόγον occurs also in Plato, *Symposium* 194D; *Leges* 642D; *Theaetetus* 162E; etc.; cf. *Timaeus* 29D: τὸν μῦθον... ἀποδεχομένους. Lucian, *De dea Syria* 22: ὁ δὲ τόν τε λόγον ἀπηνέως ἀπεδέκετο. In our verse many late manuscripts read: οἱ μὲν οὖν ἀσμένως ἀποδεξάμενοι τὸν λόγον... This probably was a current combination; see for example Diodorus Siculus 12.54.1: ἀσμένως προσδεξάμενοι τοὺς τοῦ Γοργίου λόγους. 12.57.2: ἀσμένως... προσδεξαμένων τοὺς λόγους. Dionysius of Halicarnassus, *Antiquitates* 1.82.1: ἀσμένως δὲ ὑποδεξαμένου τὸν λόγον τοῦ μειρακίου... Cf. Josephus, *Ant.* 12.382: οἱ δὲ ἀσμένως δεξάμενοι τοὺς λόγους κτλ.

To Bauer's instances of ψυχαί in the meaning of 'persons' add Euripides, *Andromache* 611: ψυχὰς δὲ πολλὰς κἀγαθὰς ἀπώλεσας κτλ. *Helena* 52-53: ψυχαὶ δὲ πολλαὶ δι' ἐμ' ἐπὶ Σκαμανδρίοις | ῥοαῖσιν ἔθανον. An identical use of *anima* is found in, for example, Valerius Flaccus, *Argonautica* 7.274; 8.389.

For the overwhelming success of Peter's preaching (ὡσεὶ τρισχίλιαι) there is a nice parallel in what Porphyry says about Pythagoras, *Vita Pythagorae* 20: οὕτως δὲ πάντας εἰς ἑαυτὸν ἐπέστρεψεν ὥστε μιᾷ μόνον ἀκροάσει, ὡς φησὶ Νικόμαχος, ἣν ἐπιβὰς τῆς Ἰταλίας πεποίηται, πλέον ἢ δισχιλίους ἑλεῖν τοῖς λόγοις.

2.42-47: These verses contain a highly idealized picture of the life of the early Christian community and are as such one of the examples from late antiquity of idealizing descriptions of religious brotherhoods like the Essenes, Therapeutae, Brahmans, Gymnosophists, Egyptian priests, Pythagorean communities, etc., of which examples have been collected by A.-J. Festugière, 'Sur une nouvelle edition du "De Vita Pythagorica" de Jamblique', *Revue des études grecques* 50 (1937), pp. 47-94; see also his *La révélation d'Hermès Trismégiste I: L'astrologie et les sciences occultes* (Paris: Gabalda, 2nd edn, 1950), pp. 19-44; P.W. van der Horst, *Chaeremon, Egyptian Priest and Stoic Philosopher* (Leiden: Brill, 1984), pp. 56ff.; K. Berger, 'Hellenistische Gattungen im Neuen Testament', *ANRW* 2.25.2 (1984), p. 1280. By way of example suffice it to quote Iamblichus, *De vita Pythagorica* 30, which is part of a more elaborate description of the way of life of the Pythagorean community in chs. 29–32: ἐν μιᾷ μόνον ἀκροάσει, ὥς φασιν, ἣν πρωτίστην καὶ πάνδημον ἐπιβὰς τῆς Ἰταλίας ὁ ἄνθρωπος (sc. Pyth.) ἐποιήσατο, πλέονες ἢ δισχίλιοι τοῖς ἐνεσχέθησαν (cf. v. 41), αἱρεθέντες αὐτοὶ κατὰ κράτος οὕτως, ὥστε οὐκέτι οἴκαδε ἀπέστησαν, ἀλλὰ ὁμοῦ παισὶ καὶ γυναιξὶν ὁμακεῖόν τι παμμέγεθες ἱδρυσάμενοι (...), νόμους τε παρ' αὐτοῦ δεξάμενοι καὶ προστάγματα ὡσανεὶ θείας ὑποθήκας, ὧν ἐκτὸς οὐδὲν ἔπραττον, παρέμειναν ὁμονοοῦντες ὅλῳ τῷ τῶν ὁμιλητῶν ἀθροίσματι (cf. v. 46), εὐφημούμενοι καὶ παρὰ τῶν πέριξ μακαριζόμενοι (cf. v. 47), τάς τε οὐσίας κοινὰς ἔθεντο (cf. v. 44), ὡς προελέχθη, καὶ μετὰ τῶν θεῶν τὸν Πυθαγόραν λοιπὸν κατηρίθμουν κτλ.

2.44: The idea of collective property (εἶχον ἅπαντα κοινά) has a long history in ancient Greek and Latin literature; see M. Wacht, 'Gütergemeinschaft', *RAC* 13, Lieferung 97 (1984), pp. 1-59. Mostly it figures as an ideal realized only in primeval times, in the Golden Age or the Age of Kronos, or in Utopias ('Also here are the extolled, ideal conditions, which for the most part are a reflection of society's wishful thinking' [Wacht, 'Gütergemeinschaft', pp. 11-12]). Wacht gives many pertinent references in his full and useful survey. Very often this ideal is claimed to have been realized again in the earliest Pythagorean community (about which we know very little for certain). Also the community of the Essenes is said by some authors to have had everything in common: Philo, *Quod omnis probus liber sit* 86; *Apologia* 11.4; 11.12 (= Eusebius, *Praep. Evang.* 8.11.4, 12); Josephus, *War* 2.122–23; *Ant.* 18.20; Pliny, *Naturalis historia* 5.73; see further H.J. Klauck, 'Gütergemeinschaft in der klassischen Antike, in Qumran und im Neuen Testament', *RevQ* 11 (1982–83), pp. 47-79. It is in this light that Acts 2.44 should be seen, although it cannot be denied that besides this Hellenistic motif the idea that Deut. 15.4 has been fulfilled in the early Christian community plays a role here. From the many passages which could be quoted here I give only a selection.

Pythagoras, *Sententia* 24 (in Mullach, *Philosophorum graecorum fragmenta* 1.501): τὰ τῶν φίλων κοινά. Zenobius, *Proverbia* 4.79 (in Leutsch, *Paroemiographi* 106): κοινὰ τὰ φίλων· Τίμαιος φησὶν ὅτι προσιόντας Πυθαγόρᾳ μαθητὰς περὶ τὴν Ἰταλίαν ἔπειθεν ὁ φιλόσοφος κοινὰς τὰς οὐσίας ποιεῖσθαι. ὅθεν εἰς παροιμίαν ἡ συμβουλὴ τοῦ Πυθαγόρου ἦλθεν. Iamblichus, *De vita Pythagorica* 81: τῶν μὲν οὖν Πυθαγορείων κοινὴν εἶναι τὴν οὐσίαν διέταξε, sc. Pythagoras; *ibid.* 168: κοινὰ πᾶσι πάντα καὶ ταῦτα ἦν, ἴδιον δὲ οὐδεὶς οὐδὲν ἐκέκτητο. Cf. also Porphyry, *Vita Pythagorica* 20. Euripides, *Orestes* 735: κοινὰ γὰρ τὰ τῶν φίλων. *Andromache* 376-77: φίλων γὰρ οὐδὲν ἴδιον οἵτινες φίλοι | ὀρθῶς πεφύκασ', ἀλλὰ κοινὰ χρήματα. Cf. also *Phoenissae* 243. Plato, *Respublica* 424A: κατὰ τὴν παροιμίαν πάντα (...) κοινὰ τὰ φίλων ποιεῖσθαι. Cf. *ibid.* 449C and *Phaedrus* 279C. Aristotle, *Ethica Nicomacheia* 8.9, 1159b31: ἡ παροιμία 'κοινὰ τὰ φίλων'. Cf. *ibid.* 9.8, 1168b78; Terence, *Adelphi* 803-804: nam vetus verbum hoc quidem ait | communia esse amicorum inter se omnia. Cicero, *De officiis* 1.16.51: ut in Graecorum proverbio est: amicorum esse omnia communia. Justinus (Pompeius Trogus) 43.1.5: ... rex Saturnus tantae iustitiae fuisse dicitur, ut neque servierit quisquam sub illo neque quicquam privatae rei habuerit sed omnia communia et indivisa omnibus fuerint, veluti unum cunctis patrimonium esset. Compare the long passage in Seneca, *Epistula* 90.36-41, which probably goes back to Posidonius. Dio Chrysostom 3.110: παλαιός ἐστιν ὁ λόγος ὁ κοινὰ ἀποφαίνων τὰ τῶν φίλων (cf. 37.7). Lucian, *Saturnalia* 19: ἐχρῆν γάρ σε, ὦ ἄριστε Κρόνε, τὸ ἄνισον τοῦτο ἀφελόντα καὶ τὰ ἀγαθὰ ἐς τὸ μέσον ἅπασι καταθέντα ἔπειτα κελεύειν ἑορτάζειν. Aelius Aristides 27.24 (16, p. 392 Dindorf): M. Antoninus and L. Verus εἰσιν οἱ τὴν παροιμίαν ἐπὶ πλεῖστον ἄραντες καὶ διὰ τῶν μεγίστων ἔργων ὅρον δείξαντες ὅτι τῷ ὄντι κοινὰ τὰ φίλων (cf. 24.42 = 44, p. 837 Dindorf). Diogenes Laertius 8.10 also mentions Pythagoras as the author of the saying κοινὰ τὰ φίλων and in 10.11 he mentions Epicurus's opposition to this maxim (fr. 543 Usener): τόν τ' Ἐπίκουρον μὴ ἀξιοῦν εἰς τὸ κοινὸν κατατίθεσθαι τὰς οὐσίας καθάπερ τὸν Πυθαγόραν κοινὰ τὰ φίλων λέγοντα· ἀπιστούντων γὰρ εἶναι τὸ τοιοῦτον· εἰ δ' ἀπίστων οὐδὲ φίλων. Cf. the syllogism of Diogenes of Sinope in Diogenes Laertius 6.72: πάντα τῶν θεῶν ἐστι· φίλοι δὲ τοῖς σοφοῖς οἱ θεοί· κοινὰ δὲ τὰ φίλων· πάντα ἄρα τῶν σοφῶν. Varro *ap.* Macrobius, *Saturnalia* 1.8.3: ideo apud eum (sc. the temple of

Saturnus) locaretur populi pecunia communis, sub quo fuissent cunctis universa communia.

2.46-47: For the motif of the daily praise of God cf. Aelius Aristides 40.1 (5, p. 53 Dindorf): μέγιστον δὲ ὁ καθ᾽ ἡμέραν ὑπὸ πάντων ἔπαινος ἐπὶ πάσης τῆς παραπιπτούσης προφάσεως αἰεὶ γιγνόμενος. Also Chaeremon Stoicus, fr. 10 (p. 20 ed. van der Horst).

2.47: For the motif of the favour of the outsiders, cf. the passage quoted above from Iamblichus, *De vita Pythagorica* 30 (*ad* 2.42-47).

JSNT 35 (1989), pp. 37-46

HELLENISTIC PARALLELS TO ACTS
(CHAPTERS 3 AND 4)

Pieter W. van der Horst

For preliminary remarks on the aim of these contributions to the Corpus Hellenisticum Novi Testamenti project the reader is referred to the previous instalments in this series: *ZNW* 74 (1983), pp. 17-26 and *JSNT* 25 (1985), pp. 49-60 [reprinted above].

3.1: *Urkunden der Ptolemäerzeit* 42.4: ἀναβαίνειν εἰς τὸ ἱερὸν θυσιάσαι, cf. 70.19-20. Josephus, *Ant.* 12.164: ἀναβὰς εἰς τὸ ἱερὸν κτλ. For the 'ninth hour' cf. also Josephus, *Ant.* 14.65: ...δὶς τῆς ἡμέρας πρωΐ τε καὶ περὶ ἐνάτην ὥραν ἱερουργούντων ἐπὶ τοῦ βωμοῦ κτλ.

3.2: χωλός has to be distinguished from παραλυτικός and παραλελυμένος more clearly than is sometimes done in translations, commentaries or even dictionaries (e.g. Bauer has 'gelähmt' for both). Apart from the passages referred to in the Lexica, it is useful to compare the usage in the *Iamata* of Epidaurus and in the Hippocratic corpus, where it is made abundantly clear that χωλότης is always an affection of the feet, ankles, knees or hips, never a complete paralysis or paresis. Hence in 3.7 it is said that the man's feet and ankles grew strong again. In *Iamata* 16 and 35 (R. Herzog, *Die Wunderheilungen von Epidauros* [Leipzig: Dieterichsche Verlagsbuchhandlung, 1931], pp. 14 and 22) there are reports about healings of a χωλός by Asclepius; in both cases there is mention of a staff or walking-stick, which makes it certain that crippled persons are meant. This is also confirmed by *Iama* 36 (Herzog, *Wunderheilungen*, p. 22): Καφισίας (...) τοῖς τοῦ Ἀσκλαπιοῦ θεραπεύμασιν ἐπιγελῶν 'χωλούς',ἔφα, 'ἰάσασθαι ὁ θεὸς ψεύδεται λέγων· ὥς, εἰ δύναμιν εἶχε, τί οὐ τὸν Ἅφαιστον ἰάσατο;' ὁ δὲ θεὸς τὰς ὕβριος ποινὰς λαμβάνων οὐκ ἔλαθε· ἱππεύων γὰρ ὁ Καφισίας ὑπὸ τοῦ Βουκεφάλα (a wild Thessalian racing horse) ἐν τᾶι ἔδραι γαργαλισθέντος ἐπλάγη ὥστε πηρωθῆμεν (or τρωθῆμεν) τὸμ πόδα παραχρῆμα καὶ φοράδαν εἰς τὸ ἱαρὸν ἀγκομισθῆμεν. ὕστερον δὲ πολλὰ καθικετεύσαντα αὐτὸν ὁ θεὸς ὑγιῆ ἐποίησε. In *Iamata* 37, 38, 57, 64 and 70, real paralytics are called ἀκρατεῖς τοῦ σώματος/ τῶν σκελέων/τῶν γονάτων. On the miraculous healings of these para- lytics, see Herzog, *Wunderheilungen*, pp. 98-105. From the Hippocratic corpus cf. *De fractionibus* 19: σκέλος δὲ βραχύτερον γενόμενον χωλὸν ἀποδείξειε τὸν ἄνθρωπον. All other instances relate χωλότης to γούνατα, πόδες, ἰσχία, ἄρθρα (also rheumatism is called χωλότης!): *Art.* 53.63.82; *Progn.* 18; *Mochl.* 26.33.40; *Morb.* 1.3; *Loc. hom.* 7; *Int.* 18.41.51; *Nat. mul.* 14. In *Muliebria* 38 it is said that the non-treatment of some women's diseases may make the woman χωλὴν καὶ ἀκρατέα τῶν μελέων γενέσθαι τοῦ σώματος, that is, she may become a cripple or even a paralyzed woman. (I owe these and some other references to Dr Anastassiou of the *Thesaurus Linguae Graecae* project in Hamburg.)

3.2: Although we have no unambiguous other evidence for begging at temple gates, there are two passages that seem to indicate some conn- ection between begging and synagogues. Cleomedes, *De motu circulari* 2.1, 91 (on Epicurus's bad Greek) τὰ μὲν ἐκ χαμαιτυπείων ἄν τις εἶναι φήσειε, τὰ δὲ ὅμοια τοῖς λεγομένοις ἐν τοῖς Δημητρίοις ὑπὸ τῶν θεσμοφοριαζουσῶν γυναικῶν, τὰ δὲ ἀπὸ μέσης τῆς προσευχῆς (synagogue) καὶ τῶν ἐπ' αὐλαῖς προσαιτούντων, Ἰουδαϊκά τινα καὶ παρακεχαραγμένα καὶ κατὰ πολὺ τῶν ἑρπετῶν ταπεινότερα. Artemidorus, *Onirocritica* 3.53: προσευχὴ καὶ μεταῖται καὶ πάντες ἄνθρωποι προΐκται καὶ οἰκτροὶ καὶ πτωχοὶ λύπην καὶ φροντίδα καὶ τηκεδόνα τῆς ψυχῆς καὶ ἀνδρὶ καὶ γυναικὶ προαγορεύουσι.

3.3: With the expression ἐρωτᾶν...λαβεῖν for 'to beg' cf. Aristophanes, *Plutus* 240: αἰτῶν λαβεῖν τι μικρὸν ἀργυρίδιον. Aelianus, *De natura animalium* 2.48: κόρακες...ἐοίκασιν ἱκέται εἶναι, λαβεῖν τι αἰτοῦντες.

3.6: For the importance of the use of a powerful name at healings cf. Lucian, *Philopseudes* 9–10: ἢν γοῦν μὴ πείσῃς πρότερον ἐπάγων τῷ λόγῳ διότι φύσιν ἔχει οὕτω γίγνεσθαι, τοῦ τε πυρετοῦ καὶ τοῦ οἰδήματος δεδιότος ἢ ὄνομα θεσπέσιον ἢ ῥῆσιν βαρβαρικὴν καὶ διὰ τοῦτο ἐκ τοῦ βουβῶνος δραπετεύοντος, ἔτι σοι γραῶν μῦθοι (cf. 1 Tim. 4.7) τὰ λεγόμενά ἐστι. (...) 10 (...) εἴ γε μὴ οἴει τὰς ἰάσεις οἷόν τε εἶναι ὑπὸ ἱερῶν ὀνομάτων γίγνεσθαι. There are numerous parallels in the Greek Magical Papyri (*PGM*; see esp. T. Hopfner, *Griechisch-ägyptischer Offenbarungszauber*, I [Leipzig: Haessel, 1921; repr. Amsterdam: Hakkert, 1974], pp. 411ff. = parr. 680ff.). For example, *PGM* 4.216-17: ἐδυναμώθην τῷ ἱερῷ σου ὀνόματι. *Ibid.* p. 357: τοῦ ὀνόματος τοῦ φοβεροῦ καὶ τρομεροῦ (...) οὗ οἱ δαίμονες ἀκούσαντες (...) ἔμφοβοι φοβηθήσονται. *PGM* 12.118-19: τὸ μέγα ὄνομα Θώθ, ὃ (...) πᾶς δαίμων φρίσσει (cf. Jas 2.19).

3.7: Examples of healing by touching need not be given since a great many of them can be found in O. Weinreich, *Antike Heilungswunder* (Giessen: Töpelmann, 1909). Cf. also H. Wagenvoort, 'Contactus', *RAC* 3 (1957), pp. 404-21. At pp. 33ff. Weinreich has instances of healing by the right hand (very curious is Artemidorous 5.89: ἔδοξέ τις νοσῶν τὸν στόμαχον [...] παρὰ τοῦ Ἀσκληπιοῦ εἰς τὸ ἱερόν τοῦ θεοῦ εἰσιέναι, καὶ τὸν θεὸν ἐκτείναντα τῆς δεξιᾶς ἑαυτοῦ χειρὸς τοὺς δακτύλους παρέχειν αὐτῷ ἐσθίειν), but in Acts 3.7 the right hand is not the hand of the healer but of the healed. The motif of πιάζειν/πιέζειν is also found in Antoninus Liberalis, *Metamorphoses* 6.3: Ζεὺς δὲ νεμεσήσας (...). ἐλθὼν δ' εἰς τα οἰκία τοῦ Περίφαντος καὶ καταλαβὼν ὁμιλοῦντα τῇ γυναικί, πιέσας ἀμφοτέρους ταῖς χερσὶν αὐτὸν μὲν ἐποίησεν ὄρνιθα αἰετόν, τὴν δὲ γυναῖκα αὐτοῦ (...) ἐποίησε φήνην. Here the πιέζειν is a measure of punishment, not of healing. A nice parallel to the story as a whole is Philostratus, *Vita Apollonii* 3.39: καὶ μὴν καὶ χωλεύων τις ἀφίκετο, γεγονὼς μὲν ἤδη τριάκοντα ἔτη, (...) καὶ τοῦ σκέλους ἑτέρως εἶχεν. ἀλλ᾽ αἱ χεῖρες αὐτῷ καταφῶσαι τὸν γλουτόν, ἐς ὀρθὸν τοῦ βαδίσματος ὁ νεανίας ἦλθε.

3.7: The immediacy of miraculous healings is often stressed; see Weinreich, *Antike Heilungswunder*, pp. 197-98. For example, Diodorus Siculus 4.24.5: παραχρῆμα ἀποκαθίστασθαί φασι τοὺς τῇ προειρημένῃ νόσῳ κατεχομένους. Plutarch, *Pericles* 13.8 (the goddess Athena advises Pericles how to treat a man who has been given up by the doctors; when Pericles acts accordingly): ταχὺ καὶ ῥαδίως ἰάσατο τὸν ἄνθρωπον. Lucian, *Philopseudes* 7: αὐτίκα παύεται τὸ ἄλγημα. Lucian, *Lexiphanes* 12: ἡ δὲ αὐτίκα ἐπένευσεν καὶ σῶς ἦν. Cf. Asinarius 14 *et al.*

Tacitus, *Historiae* 4.81.3: statim conversa ad usum manus. Macrobius, *Saturnalia* 1.11.4: ...et vix consuminato sermone, sine mora recuperata bona valitudine, curia pedibus egressus est.

3.8: The element of demonstration is prominent in the often told story about Titus Latimus who had been punished with illness by a deity because of his disobedience; when finally he obeys the god, he is healed. For example, Dionysius Halicarnassus 7.68.6: καὶ ἐπειδὴ πάντα διεξῆλθεν, ἀναστὰς ἐκ τοῦ κλινιδίου καὶ τὸν θεὸν ἀναβοήσας ἀπήει τοῖς ἑαυτοῦ ποσὶ διὰ τῆς πόλεως οἴκαδε ὑγιής. Livy 2.36.8: ...qui captus omnibus membris delatus in curiam esset, eum functum officio pedibus suis domum redisse traditum memoriae est. See for the same story Plutarch, *Coriolanus* 13; Macrobius, *Saturnalia* 1.11.4 (partly quoted *sub* 3.7).

3.14: For the expression ἄνδρα φονέα cf. Sophocles, *Oedipus Colonus* 944: ἄνδρα (...) πατροκτόνον and *Oedipus Rex* 842: λῃστὰς (...) ἄνδρας. Cf. Maximus Tyr. 14.4: οἶκον ἀνδρὸς βασιλέως.

3.15: Add to the dossier of P.G. Mueller, ΧΡΙΣΤΟΣ ΑΡΧΗΓΟΣ (Bern and Frankfurt: Lang, 1973), the following instances: Cornutus, *Theol. Graeca* 6: Rhea is the ἀρχηγὸς (...) τῆς πρώτης καὶ ἀρχετύπου πόλεως, τοῦ κόσμου. *Ibid.*, 28: Demeter is ἀρχηγὸς νόμων καὶ θεσμῶν. Iamblichus, *De vita Pythagorica* 2: Pythagoras is ἀρχηγὸς τῆς θείας φιλοσοφίας. Cf. Aelius Aristides 30.1 (10, p. 113 Dindorf): Asclepius as τοῦ βίου καθηγεμών.

3.16: ὁλόκληρος and ὁλοκληρία in connection with healing and health is also attested in Plato, *Timaeus* 44C: ...ὁλόκληρος ὑγιής τε παντελῶς, τὴν μεγίστην ἀποφυγὼν νόσον, γίγνεται. Plutarch, *Stoicorum repugnantia* 30, 1047E: Chrysippus says that those are mad who set at naught τὴν ὑγιείαν καὶ τὴν ἀπονίαν καὶ τὴν ὁλοκληρίαν τοῦ σώματος (cf. 17, 1041E); *Communes notiones* 11, 1063F: it is irrational to give up happiness and virtue (εὐδαιμονία and ἀρετή) ἀνθ᾽ ὑγιείας καὶ ὁλοκληρίας.

3.17 (+19): That ignorance is the source of sin is a current idea in Greek literature, for example, Euripides, *Hippolytus* 1334-35: τὴν δὲ σὴν ἁμαρτίαν τὸ μὴ εἰδέναι μὲν πρῶτον ἐκλύει κακῆς. Xenophon,

Cyropaedia 3.1.38: ὁπόσα δὲ ἀγνοίᾳ ἄνθρωποι ἐξαμαρτάνουσι, πάντ᾽ ἀκούσια ταῦτ᾽ ἔγωγε νομίζω. Epictetus 1.26.6: τί οὖν εστι τὸ αἴτιον τοῦ ἁμαρτάνειν με; ἡ ἄγνοια. Plutarch, *De sera numinis vindicta* 6, 551E: ...οἷς δὲ ὑπ᾽ ἄγνοιας τοῦ καλοῦ μᾶλλον ἢ προαιρέσει τοῦ αἰσχροῦ τὸ ἁμαρτητικὸν εἰκὸς ἐγγεγονέναι δίδωσι μεταβάλλεσθαι χρόνον. Cf. further Sextus Empiricus, *Adversus grammaticos* 1.267; Dio Chrysostom 6.46; Aelian, *Varia Historia* 2.39; Ps.-Apuleius, *Asclepius* 22.

3.19: For the metaphorical use of ἐξαλείφειν add the following instances to Bauer's lemma: Lysias, *Adversus Andocidem* 39: δεινὸν ἂν εἴη εἰ περὶ Ἀνδοκίδου... ἐπεμελήθημεν, ὅπως ἐξαλειφθείη αὐτῷ τὰ ἁμαρτήματα ἄλλα. Plutarch, *De sera numinis vindicta* 20, 562B: ... ἡ δ᾽ ἀνθρώπων φύσις...κρύπτει τὰ φαῦλα καὶ τὰ καλὰ μιμεῖται πολλάκις, ὥστε (...) παντάπασιν ἐξαλεῖψαι καὶ διαφυγεῖν ἐγγενῆ κηλῖδα τῆς κακίας.

3.21: (ὃν δεῖ οὐρανὸν μὲν δέξασθαι): Plato, *Theaetetus* 177A: ἂν μὴ ἀπαλλαγῶσι τῆς δεινότητος, τελευτήσαντας αὐτοὺς ἐκεῖνος ὁ μὲν τῶν κακῶν καθαρὸς τόπος οὐ δέξεται. Virgil, *Aeneid* 7.209-11: hinc illum (...) | aurea nunc solio stellantis regia caeli | accipit. Achilles Tatius 5.5.8: καὶ ἐπὶ τὰς γυναῖκας τρέχει, ἃς δέχεται ὁ ἀήρ. Macrobius, *Commentarius in somnium Scipionis* 1.9.9: rectores quondam urbium recepti in caelum.

3.21: For ἀπ᾽ αἰῶνος cf. the honorific inscription from first-century CE Lycia about the doctor Heraclitus who is called πρῶτον ἀπ᾽ αἰῶνος ἰατρὸν καὶ συγγραφέα καὶ ποιήτην κτλ. in *Titulae Asiae Minoris* 2 (1944) 910.12-14.

3.24: Bauer *s.vv.* καί and δέ fails to mention the discussion on the combination καί...δέ in J.D. Denniston, *The Greek Particles* (Oxford: Clarendon Press, 2nd edn, 1954), pp. 200-203, and in R. Kühner and B. Gerth, *Ausführliche Grammatik der griechischen Sprache: Satzlehre*, II.2 (Hanover and Leipzig: Hahnsche, 1904), p. 253.

4.7: For the close interrelation of 'name' and 'power', see the passages quoted *ad* 3.6, and also the remarks in H. Betz, *Lukian von Samosata und das Neue Testament* (TU, 76; Berlin: Akademie Verlag, 1961), pp. 153ff.

4.9: For ἐν τίνι οὗτος σέσωται cf., for example, Sophocles, *Ajax* 519: ἐν σοὶ πᾶς ἔγωγε σῴζομαι. Euripides, *Heraclides* 499: ἐν τῷδε κἀχόμεσθα σωθῆναι λόγῳ; Aristophanes, *Lysistrata* 30: ἐν ταῖς γυναιξίν ἐστιν ἡ σωτηρία. Herodotus 8.108: ἐν ὑμῖν γὰρ ἔοικε εἶναι ἐμοὶ ἡ σωτηρίη (cf. Acts 4.12).

4.9: For εὐεργεσία as used in the context of healing miracles, see the passages quoted from Aelius Aristides in my *Aelius Aristides and the New Testament* (Leiden: Brill, 1980), pp. 35-36, e.g. 42.5 (6, p. 65 Dindorf); 38.15 (7, p. 75 Dindorf); 39.4 (18, p. 409 Dindorf) on Asclepius's healings: ταῖς εὐεργεσίαις παρ' αὐτοῦ πεποίηκεν ἁπάντων ἐκφανέστατον (sc. χωρίον).

4.11: When in their defence speech the apostles quote the Bible, that may be compared to Diogenes Laertius 6.63 and 66 where Diogenes the Cynic, when asked critical questions or being reproached, answers by quoting from Homer.

4.12: A contrast-parallel is Macrobius, *Commentarius* 1.8.3: solae faciunt virtutes beatum, nullaque alia quisquam via hoc nomen adipiscitur.

4.13: For ἀγράμματοι...καὶ ἰδιῶται cf. Lucilius 26.2 (649): quid ni et tu idem inlitteratum me atque idiotam diceres? Plutarch, *Apophthegmata regium* 186A: ἄνθρωπος ἀγράμματος καὶ ἄγροικος (cf. Celsus in Origen, *Contra Celsum* 1.27 where he calls Jesus ἰδιώτης καὶ ἀγροικότερος). Athenaeus, *Deipnosophistae* 10.80 (454), where it is said in a discussion on the *agrammatos*: καὶ Θεοδέκτης δ' ὁ Φασηλίτης ἄγροικόν τινα ἀγράμματον παράγει. Suda *s.v.* ἰδιώτης (122): ὁ ἀγράμματος. Although not a parallel, Lucian, *Vitarum auctio* 11 is a nice illustrative passage: οὐ γάρ σοι δεήσει παιδείας καὶ λόγων (...). κἂν ἰδιώτης ᾖς ἤτοι σκυτοδέψης ἢ ταριχοπώλης ἢ τέκτων ἢ τραπεζίτης, οὐδέν σε κωλύσει θαυμαστὸν εἶναι κτλ.

4.14: (οὐδὲν εἶχον ἀντειπεῖν): Aristophanes, *Plutus* 485: ἢ τι γ' ἂν Ι ἔχοι τις ἂν δίκαιον ἀντειπεῖν ἔτι; Achilles Tatius 5.6.1: καὶ ἡμεῖς αἰδεσθέντες ἀντιλέγειν οὐκ εἴχομεν.

4.19 (cf. 5.29): Plato, *Apologia* 29D: πείσομαι δὲ μᾶλλον τῷ θεῷ ἢ ὑμῖν. Herodotus 5.63: τὰ γὰρ τοῦ θεοῦ πρεσβύτερα ἐποιεῦντο ἢ τὰ τῶν ἀνδρῶν. Not strictly parallel but thematically related is Sophocles, *Antigone* 450ff. Epictetus 1.30: ἐκείνῳ (sc. θεῷ) σε δεῖ μᾶλλον ἀρέσκειν ἢ τούτῳ (sc. τινὶ τῶν ὑπερεχόντων). Athenaeus, *Deipnosophistae* 12.18 (520b): οὐδέποτε γὰρ τιμήσειν ἄνθρωπον μᾶλλον θεοῦ. Diodorus Siculus 9.26.4: δικαιότερον εἶναι χρῆσθαι τοῖς τοῦ θεοῦ ἢ τοῖς τῶν ἀνθρώπων εὑρήμασιν. Livy 39.37.17: veremur quidem vos, Romani, et si vultis, etiam timemus, sed plus et veremur et timemus deos immortales. For more formal parallels see K. Berger, 'Hellenistische Gattungen im Neuen Testament', *ANRW* 2.25.2 (1984), p. 1061.

4.20: With οὐ δυνάμεθα...μὴ λαλεῖν cf. Iamblichus, *Historia Babyloniaca* fr. 35 (p. 27 ed. E. Habrich): παραιτοῦμαι δὲ συγγνώμην ἔχειν μοι οὐ κατηγορεῖν βεβουλευμένῳ ἀλλὰ σιγᾶν μὴ δυναμένῳ, κτλ.

4.22: With the syntactical construction in ἐτῶν γὰρ ἦν πλειόνων τεσσαράκοντα cf. Plato, *Apologia* 17D: νῦν ἐγὼ πρῶτον ἐπὶ δικαστήριον ἀναβέβηκα ἔτη γεγονὼς πλείω ἑβδομήκοντα (Stallbaum *ad locum*: non opus est ut ἢ post πλείω addatur). For the motif of indicating the age of the healed person, see Philostratus, *Vita Apollonii* 3.38: καὶ παρῆγε γύναιον ἱκετεῦον ὑπὲρ παιδός, ὃν ἔφασκε μὲν ἑκκαίδεκα ἔτη γεγονέναι, δαιμονᾶν δὲ δύο ἔτη.

4.24 (δέσποτα): Euripides, *Hippolytus* 88: θεοὺς...δεσπότας καλεῖν χρεών. Xenophon, *Anabasis* 3.2.13: οὐδένα γὰρ ἄνθρωπον δεσπότην ἀλλὰ τοὺς θεοὺς προσκυνεῖτε. Chariton 3.2.12: ταῦτα εἶπε πρὸς τὴν θεόν· δεσποῖνα Ἀφροδίτη... The same way of addressing in 2.6.3 and 8.4. Aelius Aristides 42.1 (6, p. 63 Dindorf): Ἀσκληπιὲ δέσποτα κτλ., cf. 37.1 (2, p. 12 Dindorf). Josephus, *Ant.* 4.46: δέσποτα τῶν ὅλων, κτλ.

4.24: In σὺ ὁ ποιήσας we have a combination of 'Du-Stil' and 'Partizipialstil' (Norden), for which there are several parallels, for example, *PGM* 3.549-50: δεῦρο σύ, παντὸς κτίστα, θεῶν θεέ, κοίρανε παντός, Πᾶν, ὁ διαστήσας τὸν κόσμον πνεύματι θείῳ. For 'Du-Stil' cf. *3 Macc.* 6.2-7, a long prayer of Eleazar in which almost every phrase begins with σύ. Cf. also Aelius Aristides 43.1 (1, p. 1 Dindorf): τάδε σοὶ κατ' εὐχήν, Ζεῦ βασιλεῦ τε καὶ σῶτερ, δῶρα ἀνάγομεν, σὺ δὲ δέξαι, κτλ. A long and beautiful instance of 'Partizipialstil' is Josephus, *Ant.* 4.43–46, a long prayer of Moses with a whole series of participles which describe activities of the deity. See further *PGM* 4.2522ff., 12.248ff. and other instances mentioned by Eduard Norden in his *Agnostos Theos* (Leipzig: Tübner, 1913), Index *s.vv.*

4.27: With the expression σὺν ἔθνεσιν καὶ λαοῖς one might compare the similar but not completely parallel expression *gens et populus* or *populus et natio* in, for example, Livy 45.31; Justinus 3.1.12; 7.1.4; Pliny, *Naturalis Historia* 6.8 (23); Virgil, *Aeneid* 6.706; 10.202; Pomponius Mela 1.19; etc.

4.29: Regarding καὶ τὰ νῦν Berger ('Hellenistische Gattungen', p. 1169) remarks that in hymns often the 'Überleitung' to prayer is often indicated by (καὶ) νῦν (δέ). See for instance the above mentioned prayers of Moses and Eleazar in Josephus and *3 Maccabees* where this moment of transition is marked by νῦν οὖν in *Ant.* 4.43 and by καὶ νῦν in *3 Macc.* 6.9. Cf. also the hymn to Helios in E. Heitsch, *Die griechischen Dichterfragmente der römischen Kaiserzeit* (2 vols.; Göttingen: Vandenhoeck & Ruprecht, 1961–64), I, no. LIX 4: καὶ δὴ νῦν λίτομαι, μάκαρ ἄφθιτε, δέσποτα κόσμου.

4.29: The imperatives δός and δίδου often occur in ancient prayers (cf. also both versions of the Lord's Prayer); see, for example, Homer, *Iliad* 3.351: Ζεῦ ἄνα, δὸς τίσασθαι κτλ. A graffito in Ostia reads: Ἑρμῆ δίκαιε, κέρδος ...δίδου (in R. Meiggs, *Roman Ostia* [Oxford: Clarendon Press, 1960], p. 231); cf. Ovid, *Fasti* 5.689: da modo lucra mihi. With δὸς τοῖς δούλοις σου μετὰ παρρησίας πάσης λαλεῖν τὸν λόγον σου cf. Aelius Aristides 23.61 (42, p. 788 Dindorf): καί μοι πρὸς Διὸς δοθήτω τι παρρησίας ἤδη. 6.2 (30, p. 571 Dindorf): ἀξιῶ δὲ γενέσθαι μοι μετὰ παρρησίας εἰπεῖν. Lucian, *Deorum concilium* 2: ἀξιῶ δέ, ὦ Ζεῦ, μετὰ παρρησίας μοι δοῦναι εἰπεῖν.

4.31: That the earth or a building is shaken as a sign of the deity's assent or advent is a frequently occurring motif in ancient, both Jewish and pagan, literature. One of the many instances from the Septuagint is Ps. 17.7-8: ἐπεκαλεσάμην τὸν κύριον (...) ἤκουσεν ἐκ ναοῦ ἁγίου αὐτοῦ φωνῆς μου (...). καὶ ἐσαλεύθη...ἡ γῆ. *T. Levi* 3.9: ὅταν οὖν ἐπιβλέψῃ (cf. ἔπιδε in Acts 4.29!) κύριος ἐφ᾽ ἡμᾶς πάντες ἡμεῖς σαλευόμεθα· καὶ οἱ οὐρανοι καὶ ἡ γῆ καὶ αἱ ἄβυσσοι... σαλεύονται. Cf. further Ps.-Philo, *LAB* 9.5; *4 Ezra* 6.14ff. Josephus,

Ant. 7.76-77 (David consults the high priest about the outcome of an impending battle against the Philistines. The high priest tells him to wait at the 'Weeping Groves' and not to start the battle): πρὶν ἢ τὰ ἄλση σαλεύεσθαι μὴ πνέοντος ἀνέμου. ὡς δ᾽ ἐσαλεύθη τὰ ἄλση καὶ ὁ καιρὸς ὃν αὐτῷ προεῖπεν ὁ θεὸς παρῆν, οὐδὲν ἐπισχὼν ἐφ᾽ ἑτοίμην ἤδη καὶ φανερὰν ἐξῆλθεν τὴν νίκην. Plutarch, *Vita Publicolae* 9.6 (101d) (after a description of a heavy battle): ἐπελθούσης δὲ νυκτὸς οἵαν εἰκὸς οὕτω μεμαχημένοις καὶ γενομένων ἐν ἡσυχίᾳ τῶν στρατοπέδων, λέγουσι σεισθῆναι τὸ ἄλσος, ἐκ δ᾽ αὐτοῦ φωνὴν ἐκπεσεῖν μεγάλην, φράζουσαν ὡς ἑνὶ πλείους ἐν τῇ μάχῃ τεθνήκασι Τυρρηνῶν ἢ Ῥωμαίων. ἦν δ᾽ ἄρα θεῖόν τι τὸ φθεγξάμενον. Lucian, *Menippus* 9–10: ὁ δὲ μάγος ἐν τοσούτῳ δᾷδα καιομένην ἔχων οὐκέτ᾽ ἠρεμαίᾳ τῇ φωνῇ, παμμέγεθες δέ, ὡς οἷός τε ἦν ἀνακραγών, δαίμονάς τε ὁμοῦ πάντας ἐπεβοᾶτο καὶ Ποινὰς καὶ Ἐρινύας καὶ νυχίαν Ἑκάτην καὶ ἐπαινὴν Περσεφόνειαν (*Iliad* 9.457), παραμιγνὺς ἅμα καὶ βαρβαρικά τινα καὶ ἄσημα ὀνόματα καὶ πολυσύλλαβα. (10) εὐθὺς οὖν ἅπαντα ἐκεῖνα ἐσαλεύετο καὶ ὑπὸ τῆς ἐπῳδῆς τοὔδαφος ἀνερρήγνυτο καὶ ὑλακὴ τοῦ Κερβέρου πόρρωθεν ἠκούετο (a similar story in Lucian's *Philopseudes* 22). Iamblichus, *De Mysteriis* 2.4 (75.11-15): τὸ μέγεθος τῶν ἐπιφανειῶν παρὰ μὲν τοῖς θεοῖς τοσοῦτον ἐπιδείκνυται ὡς καὶ τὸν οὐρανὸν ὅλον ἐνίοτε ἀποκρύπτειν καὶ τὸν ἥλιον καὶ τὴν σελήνην, τήν τε γῆν μηκέτι δύνασθαι ἑστάναι αὐτῶν κατιόντων. Statius, *Thebais* 4.331-32: mirabar cur templa mihi tremuisse Dianae | …visa. Catullus 64.205-207: annuit invicto caelestum numine rector, | quo nutu tellus atque horrida contremuerunt | aequora concussit micantia sidera mundus. These lines from Catullus and also Virgil, *Aeneid* 9.106: adnuit et totum nutu tremefecit Olympum, have been inspired by Homer, *Iliad* 1.528-30: νεῦσε Κρονίων·…μέγαν δ᾽ ἐλέλιξεν Ὄλυμπον. On the lines in *Aeneid* 3.90-92: tremere omnia visa repente, | liminaque laurusque dei, totuaque moveri | mons circum, the commentator Servius remarks: adventu deorum moveri templa. Ovid, *Metamorphoses* 1.179-80: (Jupiter) terrificam capitis concussit terque quaterque | caesariem, cum qua terram, mare, sidera movit. 9.782-84: visa dea est movisse suas (et moverat) aras, | et templi tremuere fores imitataque lunam | cornua fulserunt crepuitque sonabile sistrum (the goddess is Isis). 15.671-72: …adventuque suo signumque arasque foresque | marmoreumque solum fastigiaque aurea movit.

4.32: The expression ψυχὴ μία, like *animus unus* or *mens una* or *spiritus unus* in Latin literature, was proverbial and mostly used to indicate real friendship. Diogenes Cynicus in Stobaeus 2.33.8: Διογένης ἐρωτηθεὶς τί ἐστι φίλος, 'μία ψυχή', ἔφη, 'ἐν δυσὶ σώμασι κειμένη'. Aristotle, *Ethica Nicomacheia* 9.8.2, 1168b6ff.: καὶ αἱ παροιμίαι δὲ πᾶσαι ὁμογνωμονοῦσιν, οἷον τὸ 'μία ψυχή' καὶ 'κοινὰ τὰ φίλων' κτλ. Plutarch, *De fraterno amore* 1.478C: ...τὸ χρῆσθαι μίαν ψυχὴν δυεῖν σωμάτων χερσὶ καὶ ποσὶ καὶ ὀφθαλμοῖς. Cicero, *De amicitia* 25.92: ...ut unus quasi animus flat ex pluribus. Cf. *De officiis* 1.17.56 and numerous other instances collected by A. Otto, *Die Sprichwörter und sprichwörtlichen Redensarten der Römer* (Hildesheim: Olms, 1962 [1880]), pp. 25-26, and R. Häusler (ed.), *Nachträge zu A. Otto, Sprichwörter und sprichwörtliche Redensarten der Römer* (Hildesheim: Olms, 1968), pp. 52, 69, 95, 133-34, 232, 261. Like the motif of community of goods (see my parallels to Acts 2.44 in *JSNT* 25 [1985], pp. 59-60 [pp. 207-19 above]) this theme also seems to be of Pythagorean origin: Iamblichus, *Vita Pythagorica* 167: ἀρχὴ τοίνυν ἐστὶ δικαιοσύνης μὲν τὸ καὶ ἴσον καὶ τὸ ἐγγυτάτω ἑνὸς σώματος καὶ μιᾶς ψυχῆς ὁμοπαθεῖν πάντας, καὶ ἐπὶ τὸ αὐτὸ τὸ ἐμὸν φθέγγεσθαι καὶ τὸ ἀλλότριον, ὥσπερ δὴ καὶ Πλάτων μαθὼν παρὰ τῶν Πυθαγορείων συμμαρτυρεῖ (cf. Plato, *Respublica* 462c and *Leges* 739b-d).

4.34a: In an idealizing description of Athens of earlier times Isocrates 7.83 (*Aereopagiticus*) says: τὸ δὲ μέγιστον· τότε μὲν οὐδεὶς ἦν τῶν πολιτῶν ἐνδεὴς τῶν ἀναγκαίων.

4.35a: Lucian, *Dialogus meretricum* 14.3: οὐχὶ δραχμὴν ἔθηκα πρὸ τοῖν ποδοῖν τῆς Ἀφροδίτης; *Philopseudes* 20: πολλοὶ...ἔκειντο ὀβολοὶ πρὸ τοῖν ποδοῖν αὐτοῦ.

JSNT 12 (1981), pp. 27-52

MOSES TYPOLOGY AND THE SECTARIAN NATURE
OF EARLY CHRISTIAN ANTI-JUDAISM: A STUDY IN ACTS 7

T.L. Donaldson

1. *Introduction*

The awful events of the Holocaust visited on the Jewish people during
the last war have forced Christians to a painful re-examination of the
origin, nature, and role of anti-Judaism in the Christian tradition.[1] Though
it has generally been agreed that the seed-bed of later Christian anti-
Semitism is to be found in the *adversus Judaeos* tradition of the Ante-
Nicene Gentile church,[2] the nature of New Testament anti-Judaism and
the extent to which it offers support for anti-Semitic attitudes have been
variously assessed. Some have seen the roots of anti-Semitism inextricably
bound up with the central christological message of the New Testament;[3]
others have argued that the basic message of Christianity was free of
anti-Semitism but that the New Testament has been tainted to a greater
or lesser degree;[4] still others have maintained that the New Testament is

1.   It was the sensitive and disturbing book by Jules Isaac—*Jésus et Israël* (Paris:
A. Michel, 1948)—which, more than anything else, precipitated this work of re-
examination, though Isaac's work was anticipated to a great extent by that of James
Parkes: e.g. *The Conflict of the Church and the Synagogue* (Philadelphia: Jewish
Publication Society of America, 1961 [1936]).

2.   The work of Parkes and Isaac, and more recently R. Ruether's *Faith and
Fratricide* (New York: Seabury Press, 1974), have been decisive in this regard.

3.   E.g. H.J. Schoeps, *The Jewish–Christian Argument: A History of Theologies
in Conflict* (trans. D.S. Green; London: Faber & Faber, 1963); B.Z. Bokser, *Judaism
and the Christian Predicament* (New York: Alfred A. Knopf, 1967), p. 17; F.G.
Bratton, *The Crime of Christendom* (Boston: Beacon Press, 1969); and Ruether,
Faith and Fratricide.

4.   This was essentially the position of Isaac, and Parkes has developed a similar
view in two books, *Jesus, Paul and the Jews* (London: SCM Press, 1936), and

anti-Semitic only in a false and anachronistic reading which ignores its Jewish setting.[5]

It is not my purpose here to review this discussion in any detail. I propose rather to contribute to the study of the origin and nature of the anti-Judaism of the New Testament by investigating one of its most sharply worded polemical passages—Stephen's speech in Acts 7— focusing particularly on the use made of Moses typology: Jesus is the eschatological prophet like Moses promised in Deut. 18.15-18 in that, like Moses and all the prophets, he was rejected and persecuted by his own people.

2. *The Polemic of Acts 7 in Current Discussion*

Though the speech recorded in Acts 7 has received much scholarly attention in recent years,[6] the question of the provenance and nature of

Judaism and Christianity (Chicago: University of Chicago Press, 1948), pp. 41-111. Parkes and Isaac have been followed by many others; e.g. F.C. Grant, *Introduction to New Testament Thought* (Nashville: Abingdon Press; New York: Cokesbury Press, 1950), pp. 94-97; and *idem, Ancient Judaism and the New Testament* (New York: Macmillan, 1959), p. 14; *idem, John Knox, Criticism and Faith* (Nashville: Abingdon Press; New York: Cokesbury Press, 1952), pp. 75-76; A.R. Eckardt, *Elder and Younger Brothers: The Encounter of Christians and Jews* (New York: Scribner's, 1967), and *idem, Your People, My People: The Meeting of Jews and Christians* (New York: New York Times Book Co., 1974); R.E. Willis, 'A Perennial Outrage: Anti-Semitism in the New Testament', *Christian Century* 87 (1970), pp. 990-92; among others.

5.   An early example of this approach was Walter W. Sikes's objection to the use made of John's Gospel in Nazi propaganda: 'The Anti-Semitism of the Fourth Gospel', *JR* 21 (1941), pp. 23-30. The first full-scale treatment of the anti-Judaism of the New Testament was that of P.O. Deever, 'The Anti-Judaism of the New Testament in Light of its Biblical and Hellenistic Background' (doctoral dissertation, Union Theological Seminary, 1958). This was closely followed by G. Baum, *The Jews and the Gospel* (London: Bloomsbury, 1961), reprinted as *Is the New Testament Anti-Semitic?* (Green Rock, NJ: Paulist Press, 1965). More recently, Baum has renounced the position taken in this book in favour of that of Ruether; see his introduction to her *Faith and Fratricide*, pp. 1-22. See also M. Hay, *Europe and the Jews: The Pressure of Christendom on the People of Israel for 1900 Years* (Boston: Beacon Press, 1960), p. 12; E. Flannery, *The Anguish of the Jews* (New York: Macmillan, 1964), pp. 27-35; F.H. Littell, *The Crucifixion of the Jews* (New York: Harper and Row, 1975); and W.D. Davies, 'Paul and the People of Israel', *NTS* 24 (1977–78), pp. 4-39.

6.   For thorough bibliographies, see M.H. Scharlemann, *Stephen: A Singular*

its anti-Jewish polemic has been generally treated as a minor adjunct to the more major concerns of sources, redaction and theology. Nevertheless, three main approaches to the polemic of the speech can be found in current discussion.

The first of these is found in Dibelius's seminal work, 'The Speeches in Acts and Ancient Historiography'.[7] In his view, the speeches are to be seen not as actual summaries of earlier speeches but as Lukan compositions, to be interpreted not with respect to the historical context in which Luke places them, but with respect to his purposes in the unfolding of his narrative. Acts 7 stands as somewhat of an exception to this general perspective, according to Dibelius. Because of the abruptness with which the speech is inserted into the narrative, the irrelevance of much of its content to the charges brought against Stephen, and the impartial tone of much of the recitation of history, Dibelius decided that Luke depended on a source for the neutral historical review (vv. 20-34) . As far as the polemical passage (vv. 35-53) is concerned, however, he felt that this was from Luke's own hand. He has been followed in this approach by Conzelmann[8] and Haenchen,[9] both of whom define the polemical insertions more precisely as consisting of vv. 35, 37, 39-43 (Conzelmann vv. 39-42), and 48-53.

Thus, though Luke depended on a source for some of the speech, the

Saint (Rome: Biblical Institute Press, 1968), and J. Kilgallen, *The Stephen Speech: A Literary and Redactional Study of Acts vii 2-53* (Rome: Biblical Institute Press, 1976). Add this literature since 1974: T.C.G. Thornton, 'Stephen's Use of Isaiah lxvi 1', *JTS* 25 (1974), pp. 432-34; R. Pummer, 'The Samaritan Pentateuch and the New Testament', *NTS* 22 (1975–76), pp. 441-43; E. Richard, 'Acts vii: An Investigation of the Samaritan Evidence', *CBQ* 39 (1977), pp. 190-208; *idem, Acts vi 1–viii 4: The Author's Method of Composition* (SBLDS, 41; Ann Arbor, MI: SBL, 1978); M.H. Scharlemann, 'Acts vii 2-53. Stephen's Speech: A Lucan Creation?', *Concordia Journal* 4 (1978), pp. 52-57; R.W. Thurston, 'Midrash and "Magnet" Words in the New Testament', *EvQ* 51 (1979), pp. 22-39; E. Richard, 'The Polemical Character of the Joseph Episode in Acts vii', *JBL* 98 (1979), pp. 255-67; and C.H.H. Scobie, 'The Use of Source Material in the Speeches of Acts iii and vii', *NTS* 25 (1978–79), pp. 399-421.

7.　　Found in *Studies in the Acts of the Apostles* (trans. M. Ling; ed. H. Greeven; London: SCM Press, 1956), pp. 138-85.

8.　　H. Conzelmann, *Die Apostelgeschichte* (Tübingen: Mohr [Paul Siebeck], 1963), pp. 50-51.

9.　　E. Haenchen, *The Acts of the Apostles: A Commentary* (trans. B. Noble, G. Shinn, and R.McL. Wilson; Philadelphia: Westminster Press, 1971), pp. 286-90.

polemic is his own insertion.[10] It has its origin not in the earlier movement centred around Stephen, but in the experience of Luke's own Gentile community,[11] and the speech as a whole is used by Luke to introduce the passage of the gospel into the Gentile world.[12]

This attempt to see the anti-Judaic polemic of Acts 7 as arising from and characteristic of the Gentile Christian community of Luke's own day must be judged to be inadequate. First, as will be outlined in more detail below, Stephen's survey of *Heilsgeschichte* contains many details and exegetical traditions not found in the Septuagint or Masoretic Text, but common within other textual and religious traditions in Palestinian Judaism. As Scobie has remarked,

> the more one envisages Luke as a Gentile Christian, writing in the last quarter of the first century and dependent on the LXX for his knowledge of the Old Testament, the more these discrepancies in vii 2-53 suggest the use at this point of some kind of special source.[13]

Moreover, since these variant traditions appear in both halves of the speech, it is probable that Luke is depending on a source for his polemic as well as for his neutral history.

Secondly, it is open to question whether there is any section of purely 'neutral history' in Acts 7 at all. As Richard has shown,[14] the first half of the speech displays the same mixture of reverence for one part of Israel's tradition and polemic against another part as is found in the rest of the speech: just as the people of Moses' day rejected him as ruler and judge, so the patriarchs, jealous of Joseph, sold him into Egypt. If this is the case, the speech must be seen as more of a unity than Dibelius would allow, which would imply that the considerations which would

10. Those few scholars who see the whole speech as a Lukan creation would, of course, also ascribe the polemic to Luke; see Kilgallen, *The Stephen Speech*, p. 163, and Richard, 'The Polemical Character of the Joseph Episode in Acts vii'.

11. 'What Luke is here depicting is the constant experience of his own community... At the time when Luke wrote, the Jews were the Christians' mighty and irreconcilable enemies; Jewry humbly open to receive the Word had become the dwindling exception, a merely theoretical possibility' (Haenchen, *The Acts of the Apostles*, pp. 289-90).

12. Dibelius, *Studies in the Acts of the Apostles*, p. 169. Richard calls Acts 7 Luke's 'farewell speech to Judaism' ('The Polemical Character of the Joseph Episode in Acts vii', p. 265).

13. 'The Use of Source Material in the Speeches of Acts iii and vii', p. 401.

14. 'The Polemical Character of the Joseph Episode in Acts vii'.

lead Dibelius to assume a source for part of the speech should apply to the speech as a whole.[15]

Finally, nowhere does the polemic of Acts 7 show evidence of a Gentile Christian standpoint. Gentiles are nowhere in view in the passage. The polemic against Stephen's hearers is carried out not for the benefit of Gentile Christians, but for the benefit of those Jewish Christians who desire to trace their lineage through Abraham, Joseph, Moses, David, and Jesus 'the Righteous One'. Furthermore, it is to be noted that in Luke's purposes Stephen's speech does not serve as the introduction to the Gentile mission, but to a mission to the Samaritans and Diaspora Judaism. As Klijn has observed,

> In Stephen's speech we are dealing with problems still arising within a Jewish community where a minority holds opinions different from the rest. The speech is an introduction to a (Jewish) Christianity outside Jerusalem and its temple.[16]

To find Luke's own attitude towards unbelieving Israel one would do better to look at the thrice-repeated statement of the rejection of the Jews in favour of the Gentiles (13.46-48; 18.6; 28.25-28).[17] But Stephen's speech must be judged to represent a pre-Lukan, and probably a pre-Gentile mission, standpoint.

A second approach to the polemic of Acts 7 has been to view the speech as characteristic of the theology of Stephen and the pre-Pauline Hellenistic Jewish church, but to interpret that theology as based on a radical and final rejection of Judaism, its history, traditions, and institutions. This position has been most fully worked out by Simon,[18] though similar approaches can be found in the earlier work of Bacon[19] and Jones.[20] Simon has interpreted Stephen as saying that because of Israel's

15. It should be mentioned, though, that Richard drew the opposite conclusion: the speech as a whole is the work of Luke himself.

16. A.F.J. Klijn, 'Stephen's Speech—Acts vii 2-53', *NTS* 4 (1957–58), p. 26.

17. It is to be noted, however, that all of these passages are ascribed to Paul, and that Luke gives an important place in salvation history to the Jewish Christian remnant; see J. Jervell, *Luke and the People of God* (Minneapolis: Augsburg, 1972).

18. M. Simon, *St Stephen and the Hellenists* (London: Longmans, Green, 1958).

19. B.W. Bacon, 'Stephen's Speech: Its Argument and Doctrinal Relationship', in *Biblical and Semitic Studies* (Yale Bicentennial Publications; New York: Scribner's, 1901), pp. 213-76.

20. M. Jones, 'The Significance of St Stephen in the History of the Primitive Christian Church', *The Expositor* 8th Series, 13 (1917), pp. 161-78.

lapse into the idolatrous worship of the golden calf, the "living oracles" (v. 38) which God had intended for Israel were not given at all. In fact, the Torah to which Israel held fast, together with the cultic rituals and sacrifices of the temple, had little to do with pure Mosaic worship. Stephen 'draws a distinction between the divinely ordered "living oracles", i.e. the authentic Law of Moses, and the ordinances concerning sacrifice and Temple, which were invented by the Jews'.[21] In Stephen's view, 'what the Jews...practise, and what their forefathers have practised since the making of the calf, is not divine Law, but just idolatrous distortion of it'.[22] Jesus' role as the 'prophet like Moses' according to Stephen was, Simon affirmed, to restore that pure Mosaic worship which had been forfeited at Sinai. Stephen is thus pictured as taking a position that was extreme, even in Christian circles, and Simon would find Stephen's spiritual descendants in Alexandrian Christianity and in such writings as the *Epistle of Barnabas*. Simon has been followed to a large extent by Barnard[23] and Ruether.[24]

Thus in this view the polemic of Acts 7 has its origin in the primitive Hellenistic Jewish-Christian church, and is characterized by a radical rejection of Judaism. While this approach is no doubt correct in its estimation of the origin of the speech, its interpretation of the theological nature of the polemic is open to question.

First of all, the theme of the speech is not a radical rejection of law and temple. Law and temple come into the discussion only as illustrations of the real theme, that Israel has consistently resisted and rejected both God's will and his messengers. As far as the law is concerned, it is unlikely that Stephen viewed the Torah as an inferior substitute for the 'living oracles'. The notion that the originally intended oracles were withheld rests on a wrong reading of v. 38, a reading that is directly contradicted by v. 39 which says, not that 'our fathers refused to *receive them*', but that 'our fathers refused to *obey him*'. Stephen's real point with respect to the law is that Israel has constantly broken it, a charge which reappears at the end of the speech: 'you who received the law as delivered by angels and did not keep it'. As this verse makes clear, Stephen's polemic was directed not towards the nature of the law, but

21. *St Stephen and the Hellenists*, p. 48.

22. *St Stephen and the Hellenists*, p. 46.

23. L.W. Barnard, 'Saint Stephen and Early Alexandrian Christianity', *NTS* 7 (1960–61), pp. 31-45.

24. *Faith and Fratricide*, p. 76.

towards the manner in which it had been disobeyed.

Stephen's remarks about the temple fall within a similar framework. There can be no doubt that Stephen is opposed to current temple worship. But as can be seen from his glorification of tabernacle worship (vv. 44-45), it cannot be said that he was against the Aaronic cult *per se*, dismissing it as mere idolatry. His opposition to the temple seems to be directed against the localization of worship, not primarily its form. In Stephen's recitation of *Heilsgeschichte*, emphasis is given to important divine encounters that have taken place outside Judea: Abraham's call in Mesopotamia, Joseph's reception of divine favour in Egypt, the burial of the fathers in Shechem, Moses' deliverance of the people from Egypt, and the tabernacle worship in the wilderness. Stephen's attack seems to be against Jerusalem-centred religion and hence, by inference, against the authority of the Torah—and temple-oriented movements of the Pharisees and Sadducees, movements which Stephen aligns with earlier examples of rebellion against God's will. I concur with Scroggs: 'The speech in no way rejects the Pentateuch or attacks the sacrificial cult contained in it. What is attacked here, as always in the speech, is Israel's rejection of God.'[25]

Secondly, far from taking a position radically opposed to Judaism, the author of this speech shows great reverence towards and identifies strongly with the people, institutions and events in Israel's history, even recognizing up to a point that Stephen and his hearers share a common heritage. This fraternal note is sounded in the introduction when Stephen addresses his hearers as ἄνδρες ἀδελφοί. He goes on to speak of 'our father Abraham' (v. 2), and repeatedly refers to 'our fathers' in a manner that does not explicitly exclude his listeners (vv. 11, 12, 15, 19, 39, 44, 45). If he begins to speak of 'your fathers' in vv. 51, 52, it is not because he wishes to dissociate himself from the Jewish tradition, but because he feels that his hearers have, by their actions, shown themselves to be heirs of that stream of Jewish history that was in opposition to the purposes of God. In addition, Stephen wholeheartedly accepts and affirms the Jewish institutions of the covenant with Abraham (v. 8), circumcision (v. 8), and the tabernacle (vv. 44-45). To characterize the polemic of Acts 7 as radically anti-Judaistic is to miss its point.

The third approach to Stephen's speech has been the attempt to discover links between the thought of Acts 7 and that of various dissenting

25. R. Scroggs, 'The Earliest Hellenistic Christianity', in J. Neusner (ed.), *Religions in Antiquity* (Leiden: Brill, 1968), p. 187.

sectarian groups within pre-70 CE Judaism. The discoveries at Qumran have drawn attention to the multi-faceted nature of Second Temple Judaism, spurred interest in the study of the various parties, sects and movements of the period, and provided us with primary information about a pre-war sect.

Klijn has attempted to find a relationship between the Hellenists of Acts 7 and the Dead Sea Covenanters, noting particularly the characterization of Israel's history under the twofold aspect of grace and rebellion (1QS 1.21-23), and the anti-temple stance.[26]

More attention has been paid, however, to possible links between Acts 7 and Samaritan thought. It was A. Spiro who first drew attention to the possibility of Samaritan features in Stephen's speech, in a brief appendix to Munck's Anchor Bible commentary on Acts.[27] Though his rather eccentric attempt to interpret the Ἐβραῖοι of Acts 6.1 as Samaritan Christians has won little hearing, he has been followed in his main point by a number of scholars.[28] From this evidence of Samaritan influence a

26. 'Stephen's Speech: Acts vii 2-53'.

27. A. Spiro, 'Stephen's Samaritan Background', Appendix V, in J. Munck, *The Acts of the Apostles* (AB, 31; Garden City, NY: Doubleday, 1967), pp. 285-300. Not all of the supposed links between Acts 7 and Samaritanism listed by Spiro, or by Scharlemann (*Stephen: A Singular Saint*, pp. 50-51), are equally convincing. The most significant parallels, however, are the following:

(a) The use of Deut. 18.15, not only because it is a passage of supreme importance to Samaritan thought, but also because the use of this verse in a context dealing with the giving of the law (Acts 7.35-38) closely parallels the Samaritan Decalogue where the Deuteronomy passage is included as part of the tenth commandment.

(b) The emphasis on Shechem, which because of its proximity to Mt Gerizim became a sacred Samaritan site. In Acts 7.16, Jacob is depicted as being buried in Shechem along with Joseph (Josh. 24.32), rather than in Hebron as is recorded in Gen. 50.12-14.

(c) The glorification of the tabernacle and the devaluation of the temple.

(d) The replacement of 'Damascus' by 'Babylon' in the citation of Amos 5.25-27 in v. 43, a replacement which turns this into an anti-Judah/Jerusalem rather than an anti-Israel/Samaria prophecy.

(e) The interest in Joseph; cf. *Memar Marqah* 4.2: 'There is none like Joseph the king, and there is none like Moses the prophet. Each of them possessed high status; Moses possessed prophethood, Joseph possessed the Goodly Mount. There is none greater than either of them.'

28. Including Scharlemann, *Stephen: A Singular Saint*; Scroggs, 'The Earliest Hellenistic Christianity'; Scobie, 'The Use of Source Material in the Speeches of Acts iii and vii'; and O. Cullmann, 'Samaria and the Origins of the Christian Mission', in *The Early Church* (trans. A.J.B. Higgins; London: SCM Press, 1976), pp. 183-92;

variety of conclusions have been drawn: Stephen was a Samaritan Christian (Spiro); he was a Jewish Christian with a unique interest in the Samaritan question (Scharlemann); Acts 7 was drawn from a source developed in the Hellenistic Jewish-Christian mission to Samaria (Scroggs); Acts 7 depends on a Samaritan source reworked into a Samaritan-Christian tract (Scobie); the Hellenists had affinities both with Qumran and with the Samaritans (Cullmann).

With respect to our interest in the origin of the polemic of Acts 7, it is necessary to exercise caution in the matter of Qumran and Samaritan parallels. It is not possible to see Acts 7 as just a Christianization of ideas found at Qumran or in Samaria, and it is not at all certain that early Christianity drew an inordinate number of its converts from these groups, as Cullmann maintains. The links with Qumran, in particular, are rather tenuous: the opposition to the temple in Acts 7 and in Qumran were based on decidedly divergent considerations. With respect to Samaritan influence, it is to be noted that the reference to David, the quotations from the prophets, and the opposition to any form of localized centre of worship would all be out of place in a Samaritan context.[29] Moreover, in view of the varieties of Old Testament textual tradition in Palestine in the first century, the features of Acts 7 which diverge from the Masoretic Text and the Septuagint may reflect the wider textual situation rather than a more particular Samaritan milieu.[30]

Nevertheless, the pattern of similarities—a similar opposition to Jerusalem-centred worship, similar attempts to show that Jerusalem-centred Judaism was no longer in the stream of authentic Old Testament religion, and a common stock of exegetical traditions (e.g. the interest in the prophet like Moses)—suggests that these groups were to be found in a similar non-conformist milieu within the Judaism of the Second Temple period. The primitive Hellenistic Jewish Christianity represented by Acts 7, then, is to be seen as originating within a Christian movement

idem, *The Johannine Circle* (trans. J. Bowden; London: SCM Press, 1976). For rejections of the Samaritan hypothesis, see Richard, 'Acts vii: An Investigation of the Samaritan Evidence', and W.H. Mare, 'Acts vii: Jewish or Samaritan in Character?', *WTJ* 34 (1971–72), pp. 1-21.

29. Cf. Scroggs, 'The Earliest Hellenistic Christianity', pp. 195-97.

30. See the articles by Richard, 'Acts vii: An Investigation of the Samaritan Evidence', and Mare, 'Acts vii: Jewish or Samaritan in Character?'. In my opinion, the Samaritan evidence, particularly the Shechem interest, is strong enough to imply some Samaritan connection, perhaps that Luke drew on a source developed or preserved in a Samaritan-Christian milieu.

that can be categorized as one of a number of dissenting sects within a wider Judaism, rejecting the central authority structure and nurturing a remnant mentality which characterized its relations with the rest of Judaism. In short, the polemic of Acts 7 is sectarian polemic.

3. *Stephen's Speech as Sectarian Polemic*

a. *Definition of 'Sectarian Polemic'*
Before turning to a more thorough study of this polemic, it is necessary to define our terms more exactly. What do we mean by the term 'sectarian'? What are the features of sectarian polemic?

To answer these questions it is necessary to consider the wider issue of unity and diversity within first-century Judaism. Investigation of the Judaism of the period 200 BCE–100 CE reveals both striking unity and marked diversity. On the one hand, common devotion to the law and the temple was great enough not only to sustain Jewish identity within a far-flung Diaspora, but also to rally the tiny nation twice within this period to fight for national and religious survival against overwhelming odds. On the other hand, the sources from the period provide evidence for a great variety of religious groups and movements, often engaged in hostilities and in bitter rivalries for power and influence, rivalries that did not diminish even in the face of a common enemy.[31] It is true that after the war with Rome, Judaism under the leadership of the Pharisees was characterized by a greater measure of unity. But this fact only serves to underscore the fundamental question: what understanding is there of the phenomena of unity and diversity that will also account for the eventual triumph of rabbinic Judaism?

Three separate approaches have been taken to the problem. One approach has been to transfer from Christian tradition the concepts of orthodoxy and heterodoxy. These terms are sometimes used loosely in discussions of first-century Judaism,[32] but recently McEleney has argued strenuously that 'there existed a firmly accepted Jewish orthodoxy in the first century and that this was even then a *definable* belief...which was accepted by all who called themselves Israelites'.[33] In his view, first-

---

31. Cf. Josephus's account of the power struggles in Jerusalem during the war with Rome: *War* 4.121–365.

32. E.g. Cullmann, *The Johannine Circle*, pp. 31-32; he uses the term 'heterodox' interchangeably with 'marginal' or 'non-conformist'.

33. N.J. McEleney, 'Orthodoxy in Judaism of the First Christian Century', *JSJ* 4 (1973), pp. 19-42.

century Jewish orthodoxy, expressed in part by the *Shema*, contained three elements—belief in the God of Israel, belief in the concept of the people of God, and the practice of the law.

This approach cannot be said to be helpful. Some measure of assent may be given to his contention that the distinction between orthodoxy and orthopraxy has often been drawn too sharply. And he is certainly correct in drawing attention to the fact that there were common elements in and similarities between all strands of Judaism, as Sanders has also demonstrated.[34] But he is definitely mistaken in seeing these common elements as comprising an orthodoxy,[35] for he has failed to distinguish between formal similarity and functional unity. Orthodoxy is a functional concept; it assumes a system where unity is founded on the acceptance of a common set of beliefs and where there is an authority structure competent to maintain this unity by means of discipline and, if required, exclusion.

Neither of these elements is to be found in first-century Judaism. No doubt both the Teacher of Righteousness and the 'Wicked Priest' would be in agreement with the three doctrines cited by McEleney, but neither would be prepared to admit the other to the company of the faithful. Nor did the Sanhedrin, with its uneasy compromise between the divergent religious attitudes of the Pharisees and Sadducees, exist to maintain unity in this way. The measure of unity that did exist in first-century Judaism was provided by a common infrastructure within which national and religious life was lived (the calendar of festivals, pilgrimages, temple tax system, synagogue worship, etc.), built on the foundation provided by the religious institutions of Jerusalem (temple, Sanhedrin), a foundation supporting and in turn supported by the dominant religious groups, the Pharisees and Sadducees. But the radical opposition of these two groups means that the concepts of orthodoxy and heterodoxy are of little help in characterizing the unity and diversity of first-century Judaism.

A second approach has been the attempt to describe unity and diversity by distinguishing between a dominant 'normative' Judaism and the marginal and insignificant sects. In this approach, best exemplified by

---

34. E.P. Sanders, *Paul and Palestinian Judaism* (London: SCM Press, 1977).

35. For criticisms of McEleney's position, see D.E. Aune, 'Orthodoxy in First Century Judaism? A Response to N.J. McEleney', *JSJ* 7 (1976), pp. 1-10, and L.L. Grabbe, 'Orthodoxy in First Century Judaism: What are the Issues?', *JSJ* 8 (1977), pp. 149-53; cf. N.J. McEleney, 'Replies to David E. Aune and Lester L. Grabbe', *JSJ* 9 (1978), pp. 83-88.

the majesty synthesis of George Foot Moore,[36] the Tannaitic literature is
seen as the embodiment of a unified system of religion which is the end
product of a long but inexorable process of development. In this picture
the existence of sects and parties is taken to be just a marginal note to
this linear process of development. This approach has been widely
judged to be inadequate,[37] both because it was not sensitive enough to
the variety of strands within even Tannaitic Judaism,[38] and also because
it read this picture of Judaism, derived from post-70 CE sources, back
into a period to which it did not apply, a period in which Pharisaism was
by no means normative and in which non-Pharisaic groups played roles
that in no way could be termed marginal.[39]

The most promising approach has been that of Sanders and others[40]
in which the importance of the existence of diverse groups for first-
century Judaism is recognized, but a distinction is made between parties
and sects. For Sanders, a party is defined, on the analogy of a political
party, as an interest group which takes its place within the wider community and attempts to influence the whole in the direction of its own
particular beliefs. A sect, by contrast, defines itself as the true community, cuts itself off from wider participation, and denies salvation to all
who do not join its group. While Josephus used the one term αἵρεσις of
all four Jewish groups, the term 'sect' in this definition could not be
applied to the Pharisees and Sadducees.

This approach is helpful, but only if it is immediately added that there

36. *Judaism in the First Three Centuries of the Christian Era* (3 vols.;
Cambridge, MA: Harvard University Press, 1927, 1930).

37. See, e.g., J. Neusner, 'The Demise of "Normative Judaism": A Review
Essay', in *Early Rabbinic Judaism* (Leiden: Brill, 1975), pp. 139-51; cf. M. Smith,
'The Dead Sea Sect in Relation to Ancient Judaism', *NTS* 7 (1960–61), pp. 355-56,
and Sanders, *Paul and Palestinian Judaism*, pp. 33-36. Sanders points out, rightly,
that Moore's achievement is to be judged by taking into account the context in which
he wrote, where Christian scholars had at best a second-hand acquaintance with those
texts that are 'normative' for contemporary Judaism.

38. See Neusner, 'The Demise of "Normative Judaism"', and G.C. Scholem,
Jewish Gnosticism, Merkabah Mysticism, and Talmudic Tradition (New York:
Jewish Theological Seminary of America, 1960).

39. A similar reading-back often characterizes the recent work edited by S. Safrai
and M. Stern, *Jewish People in the First Century* (2 vols.; Philadelphia: Fortress
Press, 1974, 1976).

40. *Paul and Palestinian Judaism*, pp. 425-26; cf. Smith, 'The Dead Sea Sect in
Relation to Ancient Judaism', pp. 347-60, and M. Simon, *Les sectes juives au temps
de Jésus* (Paris: Presses Universitaires de France, 1960), pp. 3-16.

is an important difference between a party such as the Pharisees and a modern political party. The Progressive Conservative party in Canada (Sanders's example) is not at all concerned with questions of 'getting in and staying in' as they apply to Canadian citizenship. It presents its policies as ones which would be of benefit to all Canadians, but is quite content with the current legislative definition of the body of people to whom the term 'Canadian' applies.

As far as a party like the Pharisees is concerned, however, it is quite probable that their 'policies' as a party were indeed linked to a distinct definition of the body of the people to whom the term 'Israel' applied. A party, no less than a sect, was aware of the presence within the nation of sinners who had forfeited their claim to be part of Israel. In contrast to a modern political party, the sects and parties of Judaism had in common the belief that it was necessary to draw a line between the sinners and the righteous within Israel, and that the covenant community was to be found within the narrower circle of the righteous rather than the nation as a whole. Unlike a sect, a party did not view itself as the remnant; it would not draw the line tightly around its own group. But like a sect, it was influenced by a remnant mentality, a belief that the old definition of Israel had broken down and that it was necessary to define new lines of demarcation.

Because he begins with rabbinic Judaism, that is, with materials produced when Judaism had become much more unified, Sanders downplays the presence of a remnant mentality within the Pharisaic movement. But if one begins at the other end, with the period following the Hellenizing crisis precipitated by Antiochus IV, a pervasive remnant mentality can be more clearly seen in the factionalism which developed in Judaism at this time. Indeed, this period was the seed-bed for most of the sects and parties of first-century Judaism. The deep social division leading up to this crisis, and the ensuing struggle in which Jew fought Jew to the death for the sake of the law, etched itself deeply into the religious consciousness of the nation.[41] Literature of the period shows a marked tendency to think of Israel in terms of the 'wicked' and the

---

41. E.g. *Jub.* 23.16-22, especially v. 19: 'And they shall strive with one another, the young with the old and the old with the young, the poor with the rich, the lowly with the great, and the beggar with the prince, on account of the law and the covenant'. See also the description of the final priesthood of the Seleucid era in *T. Levi* 17.11, as well as the description of the 'wicked men' who were advocates of Hellenism in Jerusalem; 1 Macc. 1.11-15; cf. 2 Macc. 4.12-17.

'righteous', or of the 'sinners' and the 'elect',[42] and Israelite sinners are declared to be worse than the Gentiles (*Jub.* 6.35-38; *Pss. Sol.* 1.8).

The struggle against the Hellenizing threat drew together a diverse group with a variety of concerns—priestly purity, the ḥasidic emphasis on the law, national liberation, and apocalyptic speculation, to name only the most obvious. Though differences were forgotten when confronted with a common enemy, once the initial struggle had been won, these differences reappeared and the coalition began to split apart, leading to the emergence of the Pharisees and Sadducees,[43] the Qumran sect[44] and others. The various groups within Israel, then, emerged from a milieu in which the hostility towards Israelite sinners was very keenly felt, with the result that when the coalition did begin to split apart, each of the splinter groups transferred their tradition of hostility very quickly to those other groups which, in their view, had 'betrayed the revolution' and aligned themselves with the sinners. This process can be seen very clearly in *Ass. Mos.* 5.1–6.1, where an anti-Hasmonaean group, which appears to identify positively with the Maccabean movement, sees the Hasmonaean era as a direct continuation of the pollution of the holy place by the Seleucids and their wicked Jewish allies.

It is beyond the scope of this paper to give full documentation of the continuation and development of this remnant mentality within the religious parties and sects of the late Second Temple period. And such documentation of the self-understanding of these groups is not an easy matter, both because of the incomplete nature of our sources and because of the difficulty in determining the provenance of many of the sources which are extant. The broad outlines, however, are clear. Of the two major parties, it would appear that remnant thinking became more attenuated among the Sadducees, the group which probably came to resemble most closely a modern political party. Among the Pharisees, it seems apparent that remnant ideas continued to play a role. As their name probably implies,[45] they were a party that began as a purity sect.

---

42. E.g. *1 En.* 1–5; *Ass. Mos.* 12.10-12; *4 Ezra* 8.19-30; *Pss. Sol.* 1, 3, 4, 8, 12, 13, 15, 17.

43. First mentioned by Josephus in connection with the reign of John Hyrcanus: *Ant.* 13.288–89.

44. This group was most probably formed in reaction to the assumption of the high priesthood by Jonathan or Simon; cf. G. Vermes, *The Dead Sea Scrolls: Qumran in Perspective* (London: Collins, 1977), pp. 150-52.

45. See H.F. Weiss, 'φαρισαῖος', *TDNT*, IX, pp. 12-16.

And in their attempts to exclude the Sadducees from national life during the reign of Alexandra Salome, in their later attempts to exclude the *minim* from Israel in the post-war period, and perhaps in the 'righteous–sinners' antithesis which pervades the quasi-Pharisaic *Psalms of Solomon*, one can see the continuation of a party form of remnant mentality.

Thus there was an identity crisis in first-century Judaism. The various parties, sects and movements shared a common mentality that a division was to be made between the righteous and sinners within Israel, and each felt that its group was at the heart of the true people of God. The distinction between party and sect in the first instance, then, has to do with the question of where and how the line is to be drawn. A sect is a religious group which draws the line very sharply around its own community: all Israelites are in this case to be classed as sinners except those who are members of the group. A party is a group that would draw the line much more loosely: though identification with the group is desirable, all Israelites are to be classed as righteous except those who make it evident that they are sinners. In the former case, everyone is excluded unless they deliberately include themselves; in the latter, everyone is included unless they demonstrate that they should be excluded.

The second distinguishing mark of a sect, which is really a corollary of the first, is a refusal to accept the central authority structure of the two main parties, the Sadducees and the Pharisees. This is definitely the case with the Qumran community, and it is on this basis that Samaritanism can be included as one of the sects within a wider Jerusalem.[46]

Thus the Hellenizing crisis precipitated by Antiochus IV created the

---

46. It is increasingly being recognized that it was in the period between the Maccabean revolt and the fall of Jerusalem that Samaritan distinctives were crystallized and the schism with Jerusalem Judaism was finalized. The appearance of Samaritanism as a distinct group is not to be seen as the result of a single event—such as the eighth-century BCE fall of the northern kingdom (2 Kgs 17), the sixth-century return of Judah from exile, or the fourth-century building of the temple on Mt Gerizim—which drove an irrevocable wedge between the two movements. Instead the process was gradual, and it continued well into the post-Maccabean period. Cf. R.J. Coggins, *Samaritans and Jews: The Origins of Samaritanism Reconsidered* (Oxford: Blackwell, 1975); J.D. Purvis, *The Samaritan Pentateuch and the Origin of the Samaritan Sect* (Cambridge, MA: Harvard University Press, 1968); J. Macdonald, *The Theology of the Samaritans* (London: SCM Press, 1964), pp. 14-29; and H.H. Rowley, 'The Samaritan Schism in Legend and History', in B.W. Anderson and W. Harrelson (eds.), *Israel's Prophetic Heritage* (New York: Harper and Bros., 1962), pp. 208-22.

conditions which produced within Israel a diversity of sects, parties and movements, held together within a wider unity by means of the religious infrastructure centred on Jerusalem. It could be mentioned in addition that the Roman destruction of Jerusalem in 70 CE led directly to a decrease of diversity and a narrowing of Judaism, both by destroying or seriously weakening a number of sects and parties (Qumran, Zealots, Sadducees), and by eliminating the centripetal unifying force of the Jerusalem infrastructure, which meant that Judaism could not tolerate the same degree of diversity if it was to survive.

With this analysis of the unity and diversity within Israel, we are now in a position to define what we mean by sectarian polemic. Sectarian polemic is characterized by two things: (a) a 'remnant mentality'—the belief that a division is to be made in Israel between the sinners and the righteous, and that the covenant community is to be found not in Israel as a whole but in the smaller sub-group from which sinners had been excluded, and (b) exclusivism—the belief that all outside the sect, especially the Jerusalem establishment, had aligned themselves with the sinners in Israel and were outside the bounds of the true community.

b. *Moses Typology and Sectarian Polemic in Acts 7*
Keeping this definition of sectarian polemic in mind, we can now turn back to Acts 7 and demonstrate that the polemic of Stephen's speech is best understood not as the hostility of Gentile Christians towards Judaism, nor as a radical Jewish-Christian rejection of the religious tradition of Israel, but as sectarian polemic.[47] Since it is not possible here to study the whole speech, our focus will be on the elements of the speech that are tied together by the Moses typology.

The main thrust of much of Acts 7.23-53 is that Jesus is the prophet like Moses promised in Deut. 18.15 in that, like Moses and all the prophets, he was persecuted and rejected by his people. This theme is part of a wider tendency in the speech in which the history of Israel is divided into two streams. On the one hand, there are those like Abraham, Joseph, Moses, the wilderness community in part, and David, who received the promises, obeyed God, and kept the covenant. But there was another tradition within Israel whose history is a litany of sin,

47. Cf. the article by R. Scroggs, in which he attempts, on the basis of a sociological study of sectarianism, to describe the early church as a sect: 'The Earliest Christian Communities as Sectarian Movement', in J. Neusner (ed.), *Christianity, Judaism, and Other Greco-Roman Cults*. II. *Early Christianity* (SJLA, 12; Leiden: Brill, 1975), pp. 1-23.

rebellion, and rejection of God's purposes. Included within this litany is the selling of Joseph into slavery, the rejection of Moses, and the perpetual refusal to keep the law.

For the author of the speech, the two streams continue into the present. Stephen's opponents, those who identify with the 'house made with hands' in Jerusalem, have, by their betrayal and murder of the Righteous One (v. 52), demonstrated that they are sons of those who rejected Moses and persecuted the prophets. Jesus, and presumably those identified with him, are aligned with the stream of the persecuted and abused faithful. The author of the speech understands his opposition to Jerusalem-centred religion not as a rejection of Judaism but as a demonstration of faithfulness to the best in Israel's tradition.

The polemic of the speech vis-à-vis Judaism, therefore, is sectarian, as I have defined that term above: (a) a sharp line of division is made in Israel's history between the sinners and the righteous, the obedient and the disobedient, a division that extends into the present day where it is to be found between the followers of Jesus and Jerusalem-centred religion; (b) the opponents of the speaker are seen, by their very opposition, to have aligned themselves with the stream of the sinners and the disobedient. The polemic is that of a sect which claims to be the legitimate continuation of the authentic stream. Acts 7 falls into the same category as the Qumran recitation of the history of Israel in terms of the sinners and the righteous (1QS 1.21-23), the identification of the Hasmonaeans with the Hellenizers in *Ass. Mos.* 5.1–6.1, or the Samaritan claim that they are Hebrews but not Jews (Josephus, *Ant.* 11.344). This is not to imply that there is necessarily a direct relationship between early Hellenistic Jewish Christianity and Qumran or Samaria, but to say that all three were part of a similar phenomenon within Judaism. Thus, far from being anti-Semitic, the polemic of Acts 7 is part of a phenomenon deeply rooted within the Judaism of the day.

This is particularly demonstrated by the fact that the author of the speech seeks to identify the Christian group with Moses. A feature of first-century Judaism is that each of the sects and groups claimed Mosaic authority for themselves and professed to stand in the true continuation of the Moses tradition. The Samaritans refused to acknowledge any prophet but Moses, 'the great Prophet'. The Pharisees claimed that their oral tradition had been given to Moses at Sinai along with the written law.[48] The Qumran sect saw themselves as the reconstitution of the true

48. *Pirke Aboth* 1.1, and elsewhere, e.g. *Exod. R.* 46.1.

covenant community in the wilderness and looked for the appearance of the eschatological prophet like Moses in their midst.[49] Both Philo and Josephus, attempting to win a hearing for Judaism in the Roman world, pressed the figure of Moses into the service of their apologetic aims.[50] It is likely that the Sadducees also appealed to the authority of Moses in their rejection of oral tradition (*Ant.* 13.297-98). Our sources for the various zealous revolutionary movements are scanty, but in their resistance to foreign domination, emphasis on law observance (*Ant.* 18.23), and penchant for prophet- and wilderness-symbolism (*Ant.* 20.168-72; *War* 6.285-87), similar Mosaic remnant themes may be at work. Early Hellenistic Jewish Christianity was not alone, then, in its appeal to the figure of Moses for support for its own remnant claim.

In addition, the various elements that are woven together into the polemic of Acts 7 by means of the Moses typology are all rooted in the exegetical traditions of first-century Judaism. The interpretation of the prophet like Moses of Deut. 18.15-18 as an eschatological or even messianic figure was widespread in this period. So too was the emphasis on the prophetic role of Moses. These have both been thoroughly documented,[51] and so need not be developed here.

But there are several other elements in this polemic which are not as fully studied but which are also rooted in the common exegetical stock of Second Temple Judaism. One of these is the belief that Israel had persecuted and killed its prophets. This theme is not unknown in the Old Testament (Jer. 2.30; Neh. 9.26; 2 Chron. 36.15-16), but after the time of the Seleucid persecution it was greatly developed and amplified with a variety of exegetical traditions. In the literature of the Second Temple period and later we find straightforward repetitions of biblical accounts of the suffering and death of the prophets,[52] general statements, dating from early in the Maccabean period, to the effect that Israel consistently persecuted and killed its prophets,[53] and apocryphal accounts, often

49. 1QS 9.11, 4QTest.

50. E.g. *Ant.* 2.238–53, 4.327–31; *Apion* 2.279–81; Philo, *De Vita Mosis*.

51. See H.M. Teeple, *The Mosaic Eschatological Prophet* (SBLMS, 10; Philadelphia: SBL, 1957), pp. 31-43; J. Jeremias, 'Μωϋσῆς', *TDNT*, IV, pp. 849-56; and especially W.A. Meeks, *The Prophet-King: Moses Traditions and the Johannine Christology* (NovTSup, 14; Leiden: Brill, 1967), pp. 100-25.

52. E.g. Sir. 49.7; Josephus, *Ant.* 8.330–34; *b. Sanh.* 39b; *Exod. R.* 31.4; *Pes. R.* 2.5; *Cant. R.* 1.6§1.

53. *1 En.* 89.51-53; *Jub.* 1.12; also *Ant.* 9.265–66; *Pes. R.* 26.1-2; *Exod. R.* 31.16; *Lam. R.* Proem 24.

wildly imaginative, of the ill-treatment and death of various prophetic figures.[54] As Fischel has suggested,[55] the intensity of interest in this theme during the Second Temple period is to be explained with reference to the fact that during the period of religious strife initiated by the Hellenizing crisis, the 'faithful' within Israel often met death at the hands of their compatriots and co-religionists. One way of coming to terms with this disturbing situation was the glorification of martyrdom. The other was to see suffering at the hands of the wicked within Israel as the constant fate of the righteous, as the lives (and deaths) of the prophets amply demonstrated. The development of the martyred-prophet motif is therefore closely linked with the development of the remnant mentality within Judaism. Thus the Acts 7 linking of the present suffering of Christ and Christians with that of the prophets, and hence its denunciation of the opponents of the Christian movement as sons of the prophet-slayers, is an exegetical move whose roots go deep into the Judaism of the period.

The second element of the polemic of Acts 7 to be mentioned here is the appeal to the suffering and persecution of the prophet Moses. There is some evidence from this period that there was a tendency within Judaism to link Moses with the theme of the persecution of the prophets. The earliest example of this is found in Josephus. When Josephus recounted that the people wanted to stone Moses after the spies returned from Canaan (*Ant.* 3.307), he was just following the biblical account (cf. Num. 14.10) . But when he said that those who conspired with Korah against the leadership of Moses and Aaron 'attempted to stone Moses' (*Ant.* 4.21–22; cf. Num. 16.1ff.), he was adding an element that was not in the biblical account.

This tendency to generalize from Num. 14.10 and Exod. 17.4, the only other passage which mentions the desire of the people to stone Moses, is also found in rabbinic tradition, where it is tied in with the theme that Israel had killed its prophets. Jeremiah, for example, is made to complain:

54. E.g., for Josephus, the innocent blood shed by Manasseh in Jerusalem (2 Kgs 21.16) was that of the prophets (*Ant.* 10.37–39). The tradition of Isaiah's martyrdom is well known from the *Martyrdom of Isaiah* and from rabbinic literature (*b. Yeb.* 49b, *y. Sanh.* 10.2, *Pes. R.* 4.3). The death of Zechariah (2 Chron. 24.20-22), seen as the death of a prophet (*Ant.* 9.168–69; *b. Giṭ.* 57b), had a great impact on Jewish tradition; see S.H. Blank, 'The Death of Zechariah in Rabbinic Literature', *HUCA* 12–13 (1937–38), pp. 327-46. In the first century *Lives of the Prophets* (ed. and trans. C.C. Torrey; JBLMS, 1; Philadelphia: SBL, 1946), apocryphal accounts of the death at the hands of the Israelites of no less than six of the prophets are recounted.

55. H.A. Fischel, 'Martyr and Prophet', *JQR* 36 (1946–47), pp. 265-80, 363-86.

Master of the Universe, I cannot prophesy to them. What prophet ever came forth to them whom they did not wish to slay? When Moses and Aaron rose to act on their behalf, did they not wish to throw stones at them, as it is said, 'But all the congregation bade stone them with stones?' (Num. 14.10).[56]

In another passage, Moses himself complains about their murderous intent (*Mek.*, Vay. 7.25-28). He should not have been surprised at the attitude of the people, though, for according to *Exod. R.* 7.3 God had already warned Moses and Aaron: 'My children are obstinate, bad tempered and troublesome. In assuming leadership over them you must expect that they will curse you and even stone you.'

In particular, when the rabbis deal with the revolt of Korah and his congregation they speak of it as a revolt against Moses' role as a 'prophet of truth' (*Eccl. R.* 10.1§2), and, in one important passage, link Korah's rebellion against Moses with the persecution of the prophets as recounted in 2 Chron. 36.16:

You will find that Korah and his congregation were smitten only because they stretched out their hands against Moses and Aaron. The citizens of Jerusalem were also smitten because they despised the prophets, for it says: 'But they kept mocking the messengers of God, despising his work, and scoffing at the prophets' (2 Chron. 36.16).[57]

Finally there is the significant reference in *Pes. K.* 13.6 in which the persecution of Moses by his own people is explicitly linked with Deut. 18.18:

R. Judah bar R. Simon [c. 320–350 CE] began his discourse with the verse: 'I will raise up a prophet from among their brethren, like unto thee'... As a matter of fact, you find that much of what is written of the one, Moses, is written of the other, Jeremiah: the one prophesied concerning Judah and Israel, and the other prophesied concerning Judah and Israel; the one—people of his own tribe rose against him, and the other—people of his own tribe rose against him...

None of the five rabbinic references to Deut. 18.15-18[58] gives the passage an eschatological interpretation. Nevertheless, this reference, in which

---

56. *Pes. R.* 26.1-2; cf. *Mek.*, Vay. 3.78-85.

57. *Exod. R.* 31.16.

58. The five references are *b. Yeb.* 90b, *Midr. Ps.* 1.3, *Sifre Deut.* 175–76, *Pes. R.* 13.6, and *Mek.*, Baḥ. 9.62-68. Cf. Jeremias, 'Μωϋσῆς', p. 857, who says that the list of three references in Strack–Billerbeck 'seems to be complete'.

Jeremiah is seen as the prophet like Moses of Deut. 18.15-18 in that (among other things) he was persecuted by his people, offers a striking parallel to the christological exegesis of Deut. 18.15 in Acts 7.

It is true that this rabbinic tradition cannot be dated early with any confidence. But because a similar tendency to depict Moses as a persecuted figure is to be found already in Josephus, and also because it is highly unlikely that rabbinic tradition was influenced by Christian thought at this point, it can be concluded that the tendency to link Moses and the 'prophet like Moses' with the theme of the persecution of the prophets was at least latent in first-century Judaism.

Thus although the combination of elements which are clustered around the citation of Deut. 18.15 in Acts 7 is unique, each of these elements is firmly rooted in the exegetical traditions of Second Temple Judaism and several of the same connections are already to be found in Jewish tradition.

On the basis of our study of the form of the polemic, its appeal to the authority of Moses, and its use of material which was part of the common exegetical stock of the sects and parties of the period, we can conclude that Acts 7 should be classified as sectarian polemic. That is, the anti-Judaism of Acts 7 is best understood when it is seen as an attempt by a Jewish-Christian movement which saw itself as the true remnant of Israel to win a place for Jewish Christianity outside the forms and authority of the Jerusalem-centred mainstream religion. It was therefore polemic from within; it accepted the common tradition of Israel, yet assigned to its Jerusalem opponents the dark side of that tradition: they are the sons of the prophet-slayers.

4. Concluding Remarks

It is easy to see that in Gentile hands these themes could quickly develop the potential for anti-Semitism. As the church gradually separated from Judaism—a process which was the result of the three factors of the narrowing of Judaism after 70 CE, the rapid growth of Gentile Christianity, and the increasing marginalization of Jewish Christianity— the debate with the synagogue was increasingly taken over by Gentile Christianity. In the *adversus Judaeos* tradition of the Gentile church, most of the themes found in Acts 7 were used in the church's attempt to drive a wedge between the Jews and Moses and to deny that they ever were the true people of God, as a glance at Cyprian's *Testimony*

Books will demonstrate.[59] Since we can see the beginning of this process in Acts, where a writer who is in all probability a Gentile uses the polemic of Stephen's speech as part of his presentation of the movement of the gospel from Jerusalem to the Gentile world, we do not completely solve the problem of the New Testament and anti-Semitism by appealing to the sectarian origin of its polemic, though as Jervell has demonstrated,[60] Luke has a more positive attitude to the Jewish roots of the Church and to the place of the Jewish Christian remnant in *Heilsgeschichte* than is to be found in the *Epistle of Barnabas*, Justin, or any of the other second-century Gentile-Christian writers.

But the question of the New Testament and anti-Semitism, with its important ramifications for the understanding of the origins of Christianity and Judaism and for the present relationship between the two, must find its starting point only in the recognition that Christianity emerged in a period which was a time of intense pressure for Israel, a time when Judaism was in a state of flux, with numerous religious movements, all laying claim to the traditions of Israel, competing for the allegiance of the Jewish people. In this period there was a loss of national cohesiveness

---

59. Cyprian's first three articles (*Test.* 1.1-3) deal with the rejection of Moses by the Jews when they chose to worship the golden calf, the subsequent murder of the prophets, and the rejection of Jesus Christ, who is shortly afterwards stated to be the prophet like Moses of Deut. 18.15-18 (*Test.* 1.18). Thus within a short space, most of the elements of the polemic of Acts 7 are to be found. These elements are often encountered in the other literature of the *adversus Judaeos* tradition of the Ante-Nicene church. The church was quick to claim Mosaic authority for its position, seeing Moses as a prophet who prophesied of Christ (Justin, *1 Apol.* 32, 44, 54; *Hort. Addr.* 10, 11, 28; Irenaeus, *Ag. Her.* 2.2.5; Theophilus, *To Autolycus* 18; Clement, *Misc.* 1.24; Lactantius, *Div. Inst.* 4.4; etc.), especially with reference to Deut. 18.15-18 (Tertullian, *Ag. Marc.* 22; Clement, *Instr.* 1.7; Origen, *Commentary on John* 6.4, 8; Novatian, *Trin.* 9; *Constitutions of the Holy Apostles* 20; 'Methodius', *Simon and Anna* 11; Lactantius, *Div. Inst.* 4.17; Archelaus, *Disputation with Manes* 41, 43; cf. *Julian against the Galileans* 253). The killing of the prophets (Justin, *Dial.* 16, 26, 39, 73, 93, 95, 112; *Barn.* 5; Tertullian, *Answer to the Jews* 10; Lactantius, *Div. Inst.* 1.4; *Apology of Aristides* 14) and the rejection of Moses (Justin, *Dial.* 93; *Apology of Aristides* 14; *Constitutions of the Holy Apostles* 6.1-5; Origen, *C. Cels.* 2.75) are presented as proof that the Jews' treatment of Jesus was perfectly in character, and that by rejecting Jesus the present-day Jews had aligned themselves with those who had rejected Moses and killed the prophets. Thus the anti-Judaic polemic of the Gentile church was highly dependent on the polemical material that had been developed in early Hellenistic Jewish Christianity.

60. *Luke and the People of God.*

and an increase of a remnant mentality, as each group claimed the figure of Moses in one way or another to validate its own claims, and defended these claims against competing positions with varying degrees of hostility. The opposition in Acts 7 to Jerusalem-centred religion and the denunciation of those who identified with it is but one manifestation of this wider phenomenon. In its earliest stages, Christian anti-Jewish polemic was a purely Jewish phenomenon, whose origin was prior to and independent of the emergence of Gentile Christianity.

JSNT 32 (1988), pp. 17-26

THE GOD-FEARERS: SOME NEGLECTED FEATURES

J. Andrew Overman

I

The composition of first-century Judaism has received considerable attention over the last fifty years. A significant aspect of this discussion has involved Jewish 'sympathizers' from the Gentile community. This group was in some way involved in the life of the synagogue and the Jewish community.[1]

An important element in this continuing discussion has been the φοβούμενοι/σεβόμενοι τὸν θεόν who appear in the New Testament, but only in the Acts of the Apostles.[2] 'Those who fear God', or 'those who revere God', are such a group of Gentiles interested in and sympathetic to the Jewish religion. While these 'God-fearers' apparently were not full members of the synagogue community through circumcision, they did subscribe to certain aspects of the Jewish religion, and appeared to enjoy a degree of respect and honor from the Jewish community for their piety and faith.

The discussion concerning the so-called God-fearers in Acts took on renewed vitality with the appearance of A.T. Kraabel's article in 1981, 'The Disappearance of the God-Fearers',[3] and a series of articles that

---

1. Some of the more influential discussions have been L.H. Feldman, 'Jewish Sympathizers in Classical Literature and Inscriptions', *TAPA* 81 (1950), pp. 200-208; F. Siegert, 'Die "Gottesfürchtige" und Sympathisanten', *JSJ* 4 (1973), pp. 109-64; B. Lifshitz, 'Du nouveau sur les "Sympathisants"', *JSJ* 1 (1970), pp. 77-84; K. Lake, 'Proselytes and God-Fearers', in F. Foakes Jackson and K. Lake, *The Beginnings of Christianity. I. The Acts of the Apostles*, V (London: Macmillan, 1933), pp. 74-96.

2. The passages in Acts are: 10.1, 22, 35; 13.16, 26, 43, 50; 16.14; 17.4, 17; 18.7.

3. *Numen* 28 (1981), pp. 113-26.

followed Kraabel's essay.[4] Kraabel put forth the thesis that, 'at least for the Roman Diaspora, the evidence presently available is far from convincing proof for the existence of such a class of Gentiles as traditionally defined by the assumptions of the secondary literature'.[5]

Kraabel arrived at his conclusion by using two types of data: archeological and literary evidence from Acts. The archeological evidence largely represents an argument from silence. That is, in the six Roman diaspora synagogues he examines, Kraabel cannot find a single inscription that would indicate the presence of such a group of Gentile adherents known as God-fearers. From a literary-critical viewpoint, God-fearers play an important role in Luke's stylized and creative history of the early church. Kraabel points out the strategic places at which the God-fearers appear and disappear in Acts and concludes that οἱ φοβούμενοι/ σεβόμενοι τὸν θεόν are essentially a literary tool employed by the author. 'The God-fearers are on the stage as needed, and off the stage after they have served their purpose in the plot.'[6]

Accordingly, the 'God-fearers' represent a bridge over which the Christian faith is carried from the Jewish community to the Gentile world,[7] and Acts is the *locus classicus* for the God-fearers. Consequently, Kraabel believes Acts has so informed and defined our picture of the God-fearers that, 'we would not know the term "God-fearer" if it were not for Acts'.[8]

The purpose of this article is to question some of Kraabel's conclusions concerning the God-fearers. Kraabel's view of Luke as primarily a *littérateur* rather than a historian is not at issue here. Nor is the archeological evidence that Kraabel has assembled being disputed, though this is not beyond question.[9] What is being challenged is the conclusion that

---

4.   Ensuing articles are: M. Wilcox, 'The "God-Fearers" in Acts: A Reconsideration', *JSNT* 13 (1981), pp. 102-22; T. Finn, 'The God-Fearers Reconsidered', *CBQ* 47 (1985), pp. 75-84; A.T. Kraabel, 'Greeks, Jews, and Lutherans in the Middle Half of Acts', in G. Nickelsburg and G. MacRae (eds.), *Christians among Jews and Gentiles* (Philadelphia: Fortress Press, 1986); and in the same volume, J. Gager, 'Jews, Gentiles, and Synagogues in the Book of Acts'. And *BARev*, Fall, 1986.

5.   Kraabel, 'Disappearance', p. 121.

6.   'Disappearance', p. 120.

7.   'Disappearance', p. 120.

8.   'Disappearance', p. 118.

9.   The recent discovery in Aphrodisias of a list of names under the heading *Theosebes* bears upon the discussion. This group of names may in fact constitute

we lack sufficient evidence for such a class of Gentiles involved in the life of the Jewish community and synagogue. This will be done by drawing attention to some neglected features of this discussion as it has developed over the last fifty years.

II

The first point concerns the term προσήλυτος. Over fifty years ago Kirsopp Lake raised the question of the proper rendering of the term προσήλυτος in the Septuagint and New Testament.[10] He warned against imposing an anachronistic meaning on the term προσήλυτος in the Septuagint and New Testament.

In the Septuagint, προσήλυτος is consistently used for גר, the Hebrew word for 'foreigner' or 'alien'. The Hebrew Scriptures use two expressions for the 'stranger' or 'foreigner'.[11] One is נכרים, which refers to the strangers who were only in the land temporarily, often for purposes of trade (cf. e.g. Deut. 29.21-23; and 1 Kgs 8.41-43). The other term for 'foreigner' is גר. The גרים are distinguished from the נכרים in that, though often non-Israelites, they have in some way become a part of the life of the Jewish community. The גרים eventually worked their way into the Pentateuchal regulations. Exod. 22.21 and 23.9 reflect legislation involving the גר. The גרים were sufficiently part of the community as to deserve protection, as Exod. 22.21 and 23.9 make clear. Deut. 10.18 and 24.19 group the גרים with the widow and the orphan and further express the legislation and protection afforded them.

Eventually the גרים became a part of Israelite worship and were expected to follow certain religious observances (cf. Exod. 20.10; 23.12; Num. 15.13-16).[12] It is clear that the גרים, while recognized as foreigners,

---

just such a class. See Gager, 'Jews, Gentiles, and Synagogues'; Finn, 'The God-Fearers Reconsidered'; M.J. Mellink, 'Archeology in Asia Minor', *AJA* 81 (1977), pp. 306-16.

A problem relating to Kraabel's archeological evidence is the late date of the synagogues under investigation. All but Delos are no earlier than late second century and probably later. Synagogues so far removed in time from Acts do not constitute evidence about the nature of diaspora Judaism at the end of the first century.

10. 'Proselytes and God-Fearers', p. 83.

11. M. Guttman, 'The Term "Foreigner" Historically Considered', *HUCA* 3 (1926), p. 1.

12. K.G. Kuhn, 'προσήλυτος', *TDNT*, VI, pp. 727-44.

enjoyed a special relationship with Israel. They were incorporated in some way into its communal life and worship.

προσήλυτος renders גר 77 times in the Septuagint. πάροικος renders it 11 times.[13] Yet a consistent distinction exists between these two terms in the Septuagint. When πάροικος renders גר, it refers to an Israelite or Israel itself as the 'alien' or 'sojourner' (cf. Gen. 15.13; 1 Chron. 29.15; Ps. 39.12). When προσήλυτος renders גר, it refers to a non-Israelite as the 'alien' or 'foreigner' (cf. Deut. 10.18; 26.13; Mal. 3.5).[14]

Since in the Septuagint προσήλυτος stands for the resident alien of the Hebrew Scriptures, there is no reason to understand it as a technical term referring to a convert to Judaism. Rather, in the Septuagint it consistently refers to a non-Israelite who is in some way involved in the Jewish community and sympathetic to Jewish religious worship and practice.

Philo confirms this understanding of προσήλυτος in his description of גרים in Exod. 22.20ff.; 23.9.[15] As Feldman pointed out, if the more technical meaning of προσήλυτος was widely in vogue at this time, Philo has used it in an erroneous and confused manner.[16] Wolfson writes that the use of this term by Philo 'reflects the actual existence at his time of a class of Gentiles who, while uncircumcised, had renounced idolatry and otherwise led a virtuous life'.[17] Philo uses προσήλυτος here in the same manner as the Septuagint to translate גרים. These are the resident aliens, friendly or allied with Jews, but in no technical sense are they converts to Judaism.[18]

In late rabbinic literature the term גר takes on the more technical meaning of a full convert to Judaism (cf. e.g. *Mek. Mišpatim* 18; *Sifre*

---

13. Kuhn, 'προσήλυτος', p. 731.

14. The four exceptions to this noted by Allen do not conflict in this respect. προσήλυτος speaking of Israel is technically correct because while in Egypt, Israel was a 'sojourner', not a convert. See W.C. Allen, 'On the Meaning of *Prosēlutos* in the LXX', *The Expositor* 4 (1894), p. 269.

15. Philo, *Virt.* 102–103; *Quaest. in Exod.* 2.2. See R.D. Hecht, 'Scripture and Commentary in Philo', *SBLSP* 20 (1981), pp. 146-47. See also Finn, 'The God-Fearers Reconsidered', p. 82.

16. Feldman, 'Sympathizers', pp. 205-206.

17. H. Wolfson, *Philo* (Cambridge: Cambridge University Press, 1948), II, pp. 372-73.

18. S. Belkin, *Philo and the Oral Law* (Cambridge: Cambridge University Press, 1940), pp. 47-48. Philo uses προσήλυτος in several ways; he does not fix on one single meaning for the term. See also Hecht, 'Scripture and Commentary in Philo'.

Deut. 307; *b. Šab.* 31a).[19] Here גר is usually rendered 'proselyte', which accounts for the confusion of this term in both the Septuagint and Acts. It has been the mistaken assumption of many commentators, despite Lake's warning, to read this rabbinic meaning into the term προσήλυτος in Acts.[20]

With the exception of Mt. 23.15, Acts is the only New Testament document to use the term προσήλυτος. A close examination of these passages in Acts reveals that Luke employs the term with the same general meaning that one finds in Philo and the Septuagint. Acts 2.10 and 13.43 mention προσήλυτος together with Ἰουδαῖοι. Though together, each forms a distinct group. If one were to understand προσήλυτοι here in the technical sense of converts to Judaism, Luke would be speaking nonsense, because, according to this meaning, 'proselytes' are Jews.[21] But Luke does not employ the term in this technical manner in any one of the passages. In Acts προσήλυτοι are Gentiles closely allied with the synagogue and the Jewish people, yet are a group distinct from the Ἰουδαῖοι.

That Luke's usage of προσήλυτος corresponds with that of the Septuagint and Philo is not at all surprising. One would assume Luke to be aware of this meaning of the term, given his extensive use and familiarity with the Septuagint.[22] Further, the προσήλυτοι in Acts emerge as a group strikingly similar to the φοβούμενοι/σεβόμενοι τὸν θεόν as they have been classically understood. In other words, the προσήλυτοι in Acts are distinct from the Ἰουδαῖοι yet closely related to the synagogue and the Jewish community.[23]

19. H.C. Kee, *The Origins of Christianity: Sources and Documents* (London, 1980), pp. 155ff.

20. This is a mistaken assumption made by Kraabel, 'Disappearance', p. 123, and Wilcox, 'A Reconsideration', p. 108.

21. Rather than reevaluating their understanding of the term προσήλυτος, some scholars have accused Luke of misunderstanding this term! Cf. Kuhn, 'προσήλυτος', p. 743; W. Bauer, *A Greek–English Lexicon of the New Testament and Other Early Christian Literature* (Chicago: University of Chicago Press, 1957), p. 722; E. Haenchen, *The Acts of the Apostles* (Philadelphia: Westminster press, 1971), p. 413.

22. For Luke's understanding and use of the Septuagint, see H.J. Cadbury, *The Style and Literary Method of Luke* (Cambridge, MA: Harvard University Press, 1920); C.H. Dodd, 'The Fall of Jerusalem and the "Abomination of Desolation"', *JRS* 37 (1947), pp. 47-54.

23. The parallel between the προσήλυτος and the God-fearers is further highlighted in Acts 13.43, where the προσήλυτοι are described as σεβομένων προσηλύτων.

By contrast, προσήλυτος in Mt. 23.15 seems to carry the more technical meaning as understood in later rabbinic literature: 'Woe to you,
scribes and Pharisees, hypocrites, because you travel about on sea and
land to make one προσήλυτον; and when he becomes one you make
him twice the son of Gehenna as yourselves'. Therefore, it would appear
that there were at least two different understandings of the term
προσήλυτος operative at the time of Luke and Matthew. One meaning,
as reflected in Matthew, resembles the more technical reference to a
convert to Judaism. The other meaning has its roots in the Septuagint
and refers to a non-Israelite who is sympathetic to Jewish beliefs and is
involved in the life of the Jewish community. This meaning is reflected
in Luke's use of the term.

III

A second neglected feature is the use of the phrase οἱ φοβούμενοι in
the Septuagint. There are at least five instances where such a group
appears in the Septuagint (2 Chron. 5.6; Pss. 115.9-11; 118.2-4; 135.19-
20; Mal. 3.16). In the Psalms and Malachi this group is οἱ φοβούμενοι
τὸν κύριον, a title with obvious parallels with the 'God-fearers' of Acts.
In the Psalms they are mentioned together with the house of Israel, the
house of Aaron, the house of Levi, 'and those who fear the Lord'.

In Malachi these 'Lord-fearers' are distinguished from those Israelites
who do not serve God but 'test God'. The term φοβούμενοι τὸν κύριον
refers to a group who remain faithful to God and 'esteem his name'.
These 'Lord-fearers' are 'the righteous' and 'the ones who serve God'
(3.18).

In 2 Chronicles τὸν κύριον is absent. The group is simply οἱ
φοβούμενοι. The passage is significant for two reasons. First, this group
does not appear in the Hebrew text. We find it only in the Septuagint.
Secondly, the group appears to be distinct from the Israelites. The phrase
in 5.6 reads: πᾶσα συναγωγὴ Ἰσραηλ καὶ οἱ φοβούμενοι. The translators were not content with the phrase, 'all the synagogue of Israel' as a
description of those gathered with King Solomon before the Ark. A
second group was added to the assembly, 'the whole synagogue of
Israel', called simply οἱ φοβούμενοι, and even a third, οἱ ἐπισυνηγμένοι
αὐτῶν, 'those gathered about them' (i.e. Solomon and the congregation
of Israel).

Unfortunately, the evidence is too limited to know the precise identity of οἱ φοβούμενοι τὸν κύριον in the Septuagint. However, two observations can be made. First, Kraabel's statement, 'we would not know the term "God-fearers" were it not for Acts',[24] is not entirely correct. The phrase οἱ φοβούμενοι τὸν κύριον is essentially the same as οἱ φοβούμενοι τὸν θεόν in Acts. Since for Luke and his audience, κύριος referred specifically to Jesus, the writer would have needed to select a word that meant 'God' for his audience when borrowing this phrase from the Septuagint. κύριος meant for the Septuagint what θεός meant for Luke.

Secondly, the phrase 'God-fearer' would be familiar to the person, like Luke, steeped in the Septuagint. One cannot say that Luke necessarily understood οἱ φοβούμενοι τὸν κύριον of the Septuagint to refer specifically to a group distinct from, yet allied with, the synagogue. But in light of the passages noted above this conclusion is certainly possible. What is clear is that Luke took over from his tradition a term to describe a group of Gentiles in Acts who were associated with the synagogue and sympathetic to Judaism.

Finally, recent discussions concerning the God-fearers have tended to focus too narrowly on the phrase φοβούμενοι/σεβόμενοι τὸν θεόν. This is particularly true in Kraabel's article where he is concerned simply with the term φοβούμενος or σεβόμενος in his study of more than 100 synagogue inscriptions.[25] The specific name or title of a group of Gentile 'sympathizers' is far less important than the question concerning evidence from this period which might indicate that Jewish communities of the diaspora had included such a group of Gentiles in their life and worship.

Literature from the period in which Acts was written suggests the involvement of non-Jews in the life and worship of the Jewish community. For example, Josephus mentions Greeks who respect and emulate the religion of the Jews.[26] Speaking of the Jews of Antioch, he writes: 'They were constantly attracting to their religious ceremonies multitudes of Greeks, and these they had in some measure incorporated with themselves'.[27] Collins notes correctly that this report accords well

24. 'Disappearance', p. 118.
25. Kraabel, 'Disappearance', p. 116. The same could be said of Wilcox in his focus on these and other terms in light of the question of Lukan redaction ('A Reconsideration', p. 103).
26. Josephus, *Apion* 2.282.39.
27. Josephus, *War* 7.3.3.

with the book of Acts and Paul's encounter in the synagogue with the God-fearers.[28]

Juvenal's *Satire* 14, c. 130, tells of those who have 'Sabbath-fearing' fathers who revere certain Jewish customs. Their sons fully embrace the Jewish religion. They abstain from pork, follow the Law of Moses and 'get themselves circumcised'.[29] Though this is satire, there is no reason to assume this does not reflect a situation familiar to both Juvenal and his audience.

Kraabel's own work on Judaism in western Asia Minor reveals that some Jewish communities of the diaspora were closely related to the predominantly Gentile environment around them. The Jews of Sardis, for example, were part of the economic and social life of that city and seemed to have influenced religious practices there. Sardis, Kraabel suggests, was a logical place for missionary activity, given the age and status of that Jewish community.[30] Acmonea emerges in Kraabel's study as a Jewish community closely related to the Gentile community around it. The patroness of the synagogue was Julia Severa, a Gentile benefactor of whom Kraabel writes: 'She was probably a gentile sympathizer like her contemporary Poppaea, the mistress of Nero; she is proof of the attractiveness of Acmonian Judaism to Gentiles in the first century'.[31] Both Acmonea and Sardis provide evidence for the involvement of sympathetic Gentiles in the life and worship of the Jewish communities of the late first and early second century.

The account from Juvenal, the passages from Josephus and Kraabel's description of the Jewish communities of Sardis and Acmonea concur in one respect. All indicate the presence of Gentile sympathizers or adherents in the synagogues and communities of late first- and early second-century diaspora Judaism.

The aim of this essay has been to question the thesis of Kraabel's paper that we lack convincing proof from the Roman diaspora for the

28. J.J. Collins, *Between Athens and Jerusalem: Jewish Identity in the Hellenistic Diaspora* (New York: Crossroad, 1983), p. 163.

29. Juvenal, *The Sixteen Satires* (ET and introduction by P. Green; London, 1967), p. 266.

30. A.T. Kraabel, 'Judaism in Western Asia Minor under the Roman Empire' (doctoral dissertation, Harvard University, 1968), pp. 201ff., 242.

31. 'Judaism in Western Asia Minor', p. 78. Acmonea is of particular interest in view of the late first-century date Kraabel assigns it.

existence of a class of Gentiles associated with the synagogue and sympathetic to Jewish beliefs.[32]

The term προσήλυτος, properly understood, in both the Septuagint and Acts represents just such a class of people. The προσήλυτος of the Septuagint and Acts was a Gentile related to the synagogue and viewed as sympathetic to the beliefs and practices of the Jewish religion. The rich background of this term in the Hebrew Scripture (גרים), and the numerous references to such a class in the Septuagint, demonstrate that the προσήλυτοι were not a rare breed but rather formed a class of considerable size. Just such a group is represented in Acts.

We have seen that the literature from this period also supports the same phenomenon. Philo, Josephus and Juvenal all report the attraction of the Jewish religion to both Greeks and Romans. These Gentiles were apparently drawn to Judaism in significant numbers and on occasion, according to Juvenal, fully participated in Jewish worship and practice.

Kraabel's account of the Jewish communities in Sardis and Acmonea is consistent with this picture in that these communities attracted Gentiles to their religion. Kraabel identifies the benefactor in Acmonea, Julia Severa, as a 'gentile sympathizer' and as proof of the attraction of Judaism in this area to certain Gentiles.

Since we have found ample evidence for the existence of such a class of Gentiles associated with the synagogues of the diaspora, the absence of the particular phrase οἱ φοβούμενοι/σεβόμενοι τὸν θεόν in synagogue inscriptions poses no real problem. Luke may well have taken this term, or one approximating it, in the Septuagint and used it to describe a class of Gentiles regularly found in and around the synagogue. Indeed, Luke may have understood οἱ φοβούμενοι τὸν κύριον as a group similar in piety and composition to the οἱ φοβούμενοι τὸν θεόν.

The recognition of such a class of Gentile 'God-fearers' or sympathizers is important for the reconstruction of late first-century Judaism and Christianity because this group illustrates the grey area that existed between Jew and Gentile in this period. The presence of such a group of Gentiles in the life of the Jewish synagogue indicates that the boundary between these two groups was vague.[33]

Luke may be writing 'theological history',[34] but there is no reason to assume he has manufactured the picture of the synagogues and their

32. Kraabel, 'Disappearance', p. 121.
33. Collins, *Between Athens and Jerusalem*, p. 245.
34. Kraabel, 'Greeks, Jews and Lutherans in the Middle Half of Acts', p. 149.

surrounding communities in Acts. On the contrary, in light of this evidence there is every reason to assume that the presence of a class of Gentiles associated with the synagogue is an authentic reflection of the diverse composition of diaspora Judaism in the late first century.

JSNT 41 (1991), pp. 97-119

ONESIMUS FUGITIVUS:
A DEFENSE OF THE RUNAWAY SLAVE HYPOTHESIS IN PHILEMON

John G. Nordling

The situation behind Paul's letter to Philemon may be summarized as follows: Onesimus, a slave owned by Philemon, was 'unprofitable' (ἄχρηστον, v. 11) in the past and had fled his master (ἐχωρίσθη, v. 15) after having robbed him (ἠδίκησεν, v. 18). Onesimus either voluntarily or accidentally fell in with the apostle Paul, who converted him to Christianity (v. 10). Paul, who had been the grateful recipient of Onesimus's past services (v. 13), now requests Philemon not only to forgive his formerly disobedient slave, but to accept him as a brother in the Lord (v. 16). Paul softens these radical proposals by offering to pay whatever damages Onesimus owes his master (v. 18). As it is clear that Paul found Onesimus 'useful' to himself (καὶ ἐμοὶ εὔχρηστον, v. 11), there may be contained in this short letter a veiled request for the future services, if not the complete manumission, of Onesimus the slave (v. 13; esp. v. 21).

The preceding paragraph may stand, barring a few minor variations, as the 'traditional' interpretation of Philemon.[1] The traditional interpre-

---

1. Of the many biblical commentaries which adopt the traditional view I have considered the following: R.A. Knox, *A New Testament Commentary* (London: Burns, Oates & Washbourne, 1956), pp. 42-45; E. Lohse, *Die Briefe an die Kolosser und an Philemon* (Göttingen: Vandenhoeck & Ruprecht, 1968), pp. 261-88; J.B. Lightfoot, *St Paul's Epistle to the Colossians and to Philemon* (London: Macmillan, 1904), pp. 304-307; C.F.D. Moule, *The Epistles to the Colossians and to Philemon* (Cambridge: Cambridge University Press, 1957; rev. edn, 1980), pp. 140-49; W. Oesterley, 'Philemon', in *Expositor's Greek Testament* (5 vols.; Grand Rapids: Eerdmans, n.d.), IV, pp. 203-17; W. Roehrs and M. Franzmann, *Concordia Self-Study Commentary* (St Louis: Concordia, 1979), pp. 231-32; M.R. Vincent, *Epistles to the Philippians and to Philemon* (New York: Charles Scribner's Sons, 1897),

tation owes much to the idea that Onesimus ran away from his master. Yet this is not explicitly stated in the text of Philemon. In 1935 John Knox suggested that 'the runaway slave stereotype' had long been responsible for a grave misunderstanding of Paul's little letter.[2] Knox argued that Philemon was not so much a personal letter of reconciliation between Onesimus and his owner (whom Knox believed was Archippus, not Philemon) as a public appeal to the Colossian congregation for the full-time services of Onesimus, whom Paul wished to have henceforth as a missionary companion. Knox's interpretation has been championed, and decidedly amplified, in a pair of recent articles by Sara Winter,[3] in which it is argued *inter alia* that Onesimus did not run away at all. Both Knox[4] and Winter[5] emphasize the fact that the runaway slave interpretation is only hypothetical, since there is nothing in the text of Philemon which explicitly requires it.

In spite of the considerations raised by Knox and Winter, I would like to defend the hypothesis that Onesimus was a runaway slave. Not only

pp. 157-94; *idem, Word Studies in the New Testament* (New York: Charles Scribner's Sons, 1901), pp. 515-26.

Many more articles and pertinent specialized studies either assume, or actively promote, the idea that Onesimus was a runaway slave. Cf. the following representative selection: F.F. Bruce, 'St Paul in Rome. 2. The Epistle to Philemon', *BJRL* 48 (1965), pp. 81-97; P.R. Coleman-Norton, 'The Apostle Paul and the Roman Law of Slaves', in P.R. Coleman-Norton and P. Robinson (eds.), *Studies in Honor of A.C. Johnson* (Princeton, NJ: Princeton University Press, 1951), pp. 155-77; F.O. Francis and J.P. Sampley (eds.), *Pauline Parallels* (Philadelphia: Fortress Press, 2nd edn, 1984), p. xvi; E.R. Goodenough, 'Paul and Onesimus', *HTR* 22 (1929), pp. 181-83; D. Guthrie, *New Testament Introduction* (Downers Grove, IL: InterVarsity Press, 3rd edn, 1970), pp. 635-42; W.A. Meeks, *The First Urban Christians* (New Haven: Yale University Press, 1983), pp. 59-60, 64; C. Osiek, 'Slavery in the New Testament World', *Bible Today* 22 (1984), pp. 151-55; W.J. Richardson, 'Principle and Context in the Ethics of the Epistle to Philemon', *Int* 22 (1968), pp. 301-16.

2.   J. Knox (*Philemon among the Letters of Paul* [Chicago: University of Chicago Press, 1935]) refers to the runaway slave hypothesis as a stereotype on p. 10. Knox's views are aptly summarized by Bruce, 'St Paul in Rome', pp. 91-96; and Richardson, 'Principle and Context', pp. 301-303. Cf. also Knox's article on Philemon in *IB* (New York: Abingdon, 1955), p. 555.

3.   'Methodological Observations on a New Interpretation of Paul's Letter to Philemon', *USQR* 39 (1984), pp. 203-12; and 'Paul's Letter to Philemon', *NTS* 33 (1987), pp. 1-15.

4.   *Philemon*, p. 2.

5.   'Methodological Observations', p. 204; 'Paul's Letter', p. 3.

does that hypothesis suit the evangelical spirit of Philemon, but there is important extra-biblical evidence which ought to be considered before an informed decision can be reached about Onesimus. The evidence suggests a rather uniform pattern of runaway slave behavior which Onesimus may well have adopted before he met Paul and departed from his former manner of life. In his efforts to persuade Philemon to be reconciled to his formerly 'useless' slave, Paul has deliberately mini-mized Onesimus's past crimes against his master and softened the fright-fully harsh language ordinarily associated with the criminal runaway slave. Yet Paul's euphemistic tone cannot quite obscure subtle textual indications that Paul knew precisely the sort of person Onesimus had been and the dubious manner of life in which he had engaged. The pastoral reasons for drafting Philemon on Onesimus's behalf fully account for the undeniable differences between this letter and other documents which describe runaway slaves more explicitly.

I have divided this paper as follows: (1) extra-biblical texts that men-tion runaway slaves; (2) passages in Philemon that support the runaway slave hypothesis; (3) the runaway slave problem in light of Roman law; (4) conclusion.

1. *Extra-Biblical Texts*

Philemon is most often compared to the younger Pliny's letter of intercession to Sabinianus (*Epist.* 9.21) on behalf of a freedman who had somehow offended his patron and sought Pliny's advocacy to effect a reconciliation. Pliny's letter fully describes the penitence of the freed-man: *flevit multum, multum rogavit, multum etiam tacuit; in summa, fecit mihi fidem paenitentiae* (9.21.1). The remainder of the letter con-sists almost entirely of repeated pleas for the master's indulgence and mercy: *Remitte aliquid adulescentiae ipsius, remitte lacrimis, remitte indulgentiae tuae* (9.21.3).[6]

Given the common purposes of the two letters, one might expect to find similar sentiments in Paul's letter. But this is not the case. In fact,

---

6. R.A.B. Mynors (ed.), *C. Plini Caecili Secundi Epistularum Libri Decem* (Oxford: Oxford University Press, 1963). The text is translated in J. Knox, *Philemon*, pp. 2-3; Lightfoot, *St Paul's Epistle*, pp. 318-19; S.K. Stowers, *Letter Writing in Greco-Roman Antiquity* (Philadelphia: Westminster Press, 1986), p. 160; E.M. Blaiklock, *From Prison in Rome* (London: Pickering & Inglis, 1964), pp. 71-72.

due to the apparent lack of common ground between Philemon and Pliny (*Epist.* 9.21), J. Knox argued that the two documents were quite different. Knox maintained that Pliny's letter included two elements absent in Paul's epistle: (1) a reference to the penitence of the runaway; and (2) an explicit plea for the master to forgive. Knox consequently suggested that perhaps Paul had written his letter with some 'deeper purpose' in mind than the one traditionally assumed.

Paul's letter certainly is not as explicit as Pliny's, and in this respect the two letters are quite different.[7] Yet in conceding this point to Knox, one should not automatically assume that the runaway slave hypothesis cannot stand in Philemon. Such a position fails to allow for variations in epistolary style and in the unique circumstances underlying the respective letters. I believe Paul's agenda required him not to remind Onesimus's owner of his slave's past infidelities. And although Paul does not explicitly require Philemon to forgive his slave, the overall tone of the letter seems to presuppose at least a forgiving *attitude* on Philemon's part so that he may the more readily accede to the apostle's radical request: 'Receive him as me' (v. 17b).[8]

The next three documents are not as immediately applicable to Philemon as Pliny, *Epist.* 9.21. However, these texts provide some of the clearest evidence of runaway slaves to have emerged from antiquity and so provide an impartial background against which to evaluate Onesimus and Philemon. I have found it necessary to explicate each text briefly.

The papyrus fragment *UPZ* 121,[9] dated approximately 156 BCE,[10]

---

7. 'Given a common purpose, Pliny is more forthright, direct, and explicit than Paul. Pliny says exactly what we should expect such a note to say. Paul, on the other hand, does not say some things we should certainly expect and says others which seem scarcely relevant' (J. Knox, *Philemon*, p. 3).

8. I shall say more about Paul's request in v. 17b at a later point in this paper. Here it is enough to mention that there are other plausible reasons why Paul did not mention Onesimus's penitence and include an explicit plea for the master to forgive his slave. Richardson ('Principle and Context', pp. 302-303) points out that Onesimus's willingness to return to his master (ὅν ἀνέπεμψα, Phlm 12) is sufficient evidence that Onesimus had already repented of past wrongs; therefore Paul would not have needed to mention separately Onesimus's repentance. Richardson also observes that Paul would never have based forgiveness among Christians upon the *indulgentia* of the person against whom the wrong had been committed—which would have been a Stoic, not a Christian, virtue. Lohse (*Die Briefe*, p. 275) makes the same point.

9. U. Wilcken, *Urkunden der Ptolemäerzeit* (*UPZ*) (Berlin: de Gruyter, 1927),

has been compared to Philemon.[11] The document gives an extremely detailed description of two runaway slaves, who had absconded (ἀνακεχώρηκεν) with as much of their master's property as they could carry. Of the two slaves Hermon, alias Neilos, seems to have been the more important as his description is about twice as detailed as that of Bion, Hermon's 'fellow runaway' (ὁ συναποδεδρακώς, l. 18). Hermon's age (about 18 years), race and origin (τὸ γένος Σύρος ἀπὸ Βαμβύκης, l. 4), stature (medium), and distinguishing physical features at time of flight are painstakingly noted. An inventory of stolen items follows: three *mnaieia* [sic] of coined gold, ten pearls, an iron ring upon which are engraved a flask and scrapers, etc. A complicated reward formula appears next, parts of which are repeated for Bion in the final third of the document.[12] The last item of the document is an appeal for information pertaining to the two runaways' whereabouts (ll. 15-16, 25-26).[13]

In *P. Oxy.* 1643,[14] dated 298 CE, Aurelius[15] Sarapammon, a native of Oxyrhynchus, appoints a friend to go to Alexandria in order to conduct a search there for a runaway slave. Aurelius's actual request provides a rare glimpse of the punishments a master might impose upon a captured runaway slave through his legal representative:

I, no. 121, pp. 566-76. Cf. the extensive literature on this text in R. Taubenschlag, *The Law of Greco-Roman Egypt in the Light of the Papyri* (Warsaw: Panstwowe Wydawnictwo Naukowe, 2nd edn, 1955), p. 84 n. 83.

10. Wilcken believes that the date 'the 25th year, Epeiph 16' represents 13 August 156 BCE, the 25th year of Ptolemy Philometer. Dating is difficult because the exact time and place of discovery are no longer known. Letronne, one of the first to publish the document (*Journal des Savants* [1833]), wrote: 'Il serait curieux de savoir dans quelle ville le papyrus a été trouvé; mais je l'ignore absolument, et je ne sais pas davantage les circonstances de sa découverte'. The alternative date is 145 BCE.

11. E.J. Goodspeed and E.C. Colwell, *Greek Papyrus Reader* (Chicago: University of Chicago Press, 1935), no. 59; and Moule, *Colossians and Philemon*, pp. 34-35.

12. The words τοῦτον ὃς ἂν ἀγαlγάγῃ (ll. 12-13) are applied *verbatim* to Bion in l. 24.

13. For a fuller translation and more detailed attempts to explain some of the rare (and thus semantically unclear) words, cf. Wilcken, *UPZ, passim*; and Moule, *Colossians and Philemon*, pp. 34-37.

14. The text and translation of this document are provided by B.P. Grenfell and A.S. Hunt (eds.), *Oxyrhynchus Papyri* (London: Egypt Exploration Fund, 1920), XIV, pp. 70-72.

15. The left-hand side of the papyrus has suffered substantial damage so this and other names have been restored by the editors.

5   ἀποσ[υ]νίστημί σε κατὰ τόδε τὸ
     [ἐπίσταλμα ὥσ]τε σε ἀποδημοῦντα εἰς τὴν λαμπροτά-
     [την Ἀλεξάνδρια]ν ἀναζητῆσαι δοῦλόν μου ὀνόμα-
     [τι.........]ν ὡς (ἐτῶν) λε, ὃν καὶ σὺ αὐτὸς γνωρίζεις
     [...........], ὅνπερ ἀνευρὼν παραδώσεις

10   [ἐξουσίας σοι] οὔσης ὅσα κἀμοὶ παρόντι ἔξεστιν
     [...........]ασθαι καὶ εἵργιν καὶ μαστιγοῖν καὶ ἐνα-
     [γωγὴν ποιεῖν? ἐ]φ' ὧν δέον ἐστὶν πρὸς τοὺς ὑποδεξα-
     [μένους αὐτὸν] καὶ αἰτεῖσθαι ἐκδικείαν.

I appoint you by this my instruction as my representative to journey to the
most illustrious Alexandria and search for my slave called..., aged about
35 years, with whom you too are acquainted...; and when you find him
you are to deliver him up, (10) having the same powers as I should have
myself, if present, to..., imprison him, chastise him, and to make an
accusation before the proper authorities against those who harbored him,
and demand satisfaction.

Aurelius's representative is given only the name and approximate age
of the slave in question because he knew the runaway personally (l. 8).
There is no inventory of purloined goods, nor is Aurelius's representative
promised a reward upon recovery of the slave, although possibly some
type of reward was assumed by both parties. Especially noteworthy in
this document are the precise instructions which were to be carried
out when the representative apprehended the slave. Not only was the
representative authorized to imprison and flog the slave, he was also
empowered to take legal action against 'those who harbored him'
(ll. 12-13).[16]

    P. Oxy. 1423,[17] a document of the fourth century CE, is an autho-
rization from Flavius Ammonas, the Egyptian prefect's *officialis*, to F.
Dorotheus, a neighboring *officialis*, for the arrest of Magnus (l. 6), a
slave who had run away with his master's property. The request and
descriptive formulas of this papyrus are comparable to those of the two
preceding documents:

    16. The two types of legal action mentioned are: (1) ἐνα[γωγὴν ποιεῖν ἐ]φ' ὧν
δέον ἐστίν (ll. 11-12) and (2) αἰτεῖσθαι ἐκδικείαν (l. 13). The precise legal
significance of both is unclear, although Grenfell and Hunt cite ἐνάγειν in *P. Leipz.*
38.1.14 as a possible parallel to the first formula, and ἐκδικίαν ποιεῖσθαι in
Onasander *Strategikos* as parallel to the second.
    17. I have used the text and translation of *P. Oxy.* 1423.

Φλαού[ιος] Ἀμμωνᾶς ὀφφικιάλιος
τά[ξ]εως ἐπάρχου Αἰγύπτου
Φλαουίῳ Δωροθέῳ ὀφφικιαλίῳ
χαίρειν. ἐντέλλομαί σοι
5 καὶ ἐπιτρέπω δοῦλόν μου
Μάγνον κ[α]λούμενον δράσαν-
τα καὶ ἐν Ἑρμοῦ πόλι διατρίβοντα
καὶ τινά μου εἴδη ἀφελόμενον
δι[α]δήσας δέσμιον ἀγαγεῖν
10 με[τ]ὰ τοῦ ἐπὶ τῆς Σέσφθα.
κυρία ἡ ἐντολὴ καὶ ἐπερωτηθὶς
ὁμολόγησα...

Flavius Ammonas, *officialis* on the staff of the prefect of Egypt, to Flavius Dorotheus, *officialis*, greeting. I order (5) and depute you to arrest my slave called Magnus, who has run away and is staying at Hermopolis and has carried off certain articles belonging to me, and to bring him as a prisoner (10) together with the head-man of Sesphtha. This order is valid, and in answer to the formal question I gave my consent...

After a formula of commissioning (ll. 4-5) the document describes the runaway in a series of participial clauses which informed Dorotheus of Magnus's name (l. 6), status as a runaway (δράσαν|τα, ll. 6-7), location (l. 7), and crime (l. 8). Upon the retrieval of Magnus, Dorotheus was enjoined to imprison the slave (l. 9) and lead him away as a prisoner (δέσμιον, l. 9), 'together with the head-man of Sesphtha' (l. 10). Grenfell and Hunt believe that the title τοῦ ἐπὶ τῆς Σέσφθα designates the office of *comarch*, a position of minor importance in the lower toparchy of the Oxyrhynchite nome. Like the persons designated by the mysterious phrase 'those who harbored him' of the previous document (*P. Oxy.* 1643.12-13), the unnamed *comarch* of Sesphtha had probably coaxed Magnus to rob his master and run away with the stolen property; for this reason Dorotheus was commissioned to arrest the *comarch* and lead him away as a prisoner with the recaptured slave.

The two preceding documents may be interpreted as evidence that outside agents induced slaves to steal from their masters and then abscond.[18] This illegal activity, which existed between dissatisfied slaves and sympathetic outsiders, was first identified by David Daube:

18. There may be further evidence of this type of activity in *P. Oxy.* 1422, a document of c. 128 CE. The papyrus, though quite fragmentary, seems to mention a certain Achilles who was accused of harboring a slave: [ἐνκεκλῆσθαι] ὑπὲρ ὑποδοχῆς (ll. 6-8).

> Your slave would run away to a *fugitivarius* [slave-catcher]. The latter
> would approach you, tell you that with much effort he might perhaps dis-
> cover the fugitive, and declare himself prepared to buy him right now at a
> low figure. You had no choice but to accept, whereupon the slave-catcher
> could resell or even manumit the slave.[19]

If the runaway slave (*fugitivus*) brought the slave-catcher a substantial
peculium (the private savings of the slave), supplemented, perhaps, by
his master's silver or his mistress's jewelry, he might expect immediate
resale to another more congenial master, or even complete manumission
at far below the legitimate price of freedom. There was a tug-of-war
between slave-owning legislators, who wanted to stamp out the illegal
activity, and profit-hungry slave-catchers, who wanted to keep it going.
The struggle between the two interests was fierce and protracted but
eventually the slave-owners prevailed. Legislation requiring that a slave
bought by a slave-catcher might not be freed during the next ten years
without his former owner's consent effectively killed the racket in the
early third century CE according to Daube.[20] However, *P. Oxy.* 1643
and *P. Oxy.* 1423, dated respectively to the late third and early fourth
centuries CE, indicate that slaves and slave-catchers benefitted from each
other long after legislation had supposedly brought the problem under
control. By the same token, indications of slave-catching in *UPZ* 121[21]
suggest that the illegal racket flourished at least 200 years before Paul
wrote Philemon.[22]

There is one final type of evidence to consider before returning to

19. D. Daube, 'Dodges and Rackets in Roman Law', *Proceedings of the
Classical Association* 6 (1964), 61.28; the scheme is more fully described in 'Slave-
Catching', *Juridical Review* 64 (1952), pp. 12-28. Cf. also K.R. Bradley, *Slaves and
Masters in the Roman Empire* (New York and Oxford: Oxford University Press,
1987), p. 32 n. 43; J.A. Crook, *Law and Life of Rome* (Ithaca, NY: Cornell University
Press, 1967), pp. 186-87; A. Watson, *Roman Slave Law* (Baltimore and London:
Johns Hopkins University Press, 1987), pp. 64-66.

20. 'Slave-Catching', pp. 25-27.

21. The elliptical phrase παρ' ἀνδρὶ ἀξιοχρείωι καὶ δωσιδίκωι (ταλ.) γ. (*UPZ*
121.14) probably represents the slave-catcher to whom Hermon and Bion had fled.
Moule (*Colossians and Philemon*, p. 36) translates: '(anybody [bringing the slave
back] by indicating that he is) with a substantial person who is subject to the law
[will receive] 3 talents)'.

22. Though various proposals are given, Philemon can confidently be dated to
within a decade: 53–55 CE (Winter, 'Paul's Letter'); 61 CE or six years earlier
(Bruce, 'St Paul in Rome'); 62 CE (Oesterley, 'Philemon'); 59–61 CE (Roehrs and
Franzmann, *Concordia Self-Study Commentary*).

Philemon. Slaves often wore iron neck-collars on which were inscribed messages intended for the eyes of alert passers-by in case of flight. Although these inscriptions are often misspelled and severely abbreviated, making translation difficult, the general meaning is clear enough:

> *Asellus se|ruus Praeiecti | officialis praefec|ti annon[e]s, foras mu|ru exivi, tene me, | quia fugi, reduc| me ad Flora| ad tosor|es (ILS 8727).*

> I, Asellus, slave of the *officialis* Praeiectus, superintendent of grain, have gone outside the wall. Catch me because I have fled, lead me back to Flora, to the barbers.

That Christian owners also exerted such control over their slaves is suggested by the Chi–Rho symbols displayed in the following inscription:

> ☧*tene me*☧*|et revoca me in| foro Martis ad | Maximianum| antiquarium. tene me qui|a fugi et revo|ca me in Celimon|tio ad domu El/pidii v.c.| Bonoso (ILS 8730).*

> ☧ Catch me ☧ and summon me back to Maximianus the antiquarian in the forum of Mars. Catch me because I have fled and summon me back to the house of Elpidius *v.c. Bonoso* in the Caelimontian [quarter].

Neck-collar inscriptions typically record the name of the runaway, the name and occupation of the master, and some terse formula instructing the reader to return the slave to custody. Rewards may also be listed:

> *Fugi, tene me;| cum revocu|veris me d. m. [domino meo]| Zonino, accipis| solidum (ILS 8731).*

> I have fled, hold me; when you have recovered me you receive a *solidus* [gold coin] from my master Zoninus.

The documents which have now been examined vividly attest to the grave social problem which existed both long before and long after Paul wrote Philemon. In a society which granted absolute powers to owners,[23] it is scarcely surprising that some slaves willingly assumed the frightful risks of flight in order to attain a better life for themselves at their master's expense.

2. *Passages in Philemon*

It may seem that Philemon has little to do with texts documenting runaway slaves. The difference between Philemon and the texts we have

---

23. Bradley's thesis is that masters enjoyed maximum control over their slaves by exploitation of servile fears and desires for self-betterment.

now examined is this: Paul nowhere specifically mentions that Onesimus ran away, whereas the papyri fragments and neck-collar inscriptions explicitly describe the runaway and encourage a reader to recapture, punish, and restore the slave to his former status.

I would like to suggest, however, that Paul's purposes in writing to Philemon prevented him from describing Onesimus in the usual terms. The runaway slave hypothesis seems quite plausible if Paul can be permitted to have described Onesimus's past crimes against his master in an oblique and euphemistic manner. Even if Paul were fully aware of the runaway slave racket and of the financial loss Philemon had suffered as a result of Onesimus's flight, we should not expect him to badger Philemon with painful reminders of details already known too well.[24] Paul's purpose here is primarily conciliatory: to persuade Onesimus's angry owner to welcome back his previously disobedient slave: προσλαβοῦ αὐτὸν ὡς ἐμέ (v. 17b). To accomplish this Paul strives to present Onesimus in the best possible light, recalls Philemon's past services to Paul and other saints (vv. 5, 7), and even engages in a mild form of flattery (v. 21) to induce Philemon to comply with the apostle's radical request.[25]

Certain passages provide solid support for the runaway slave hypothesis in Philemon:

v. 12   ...ὃν ἀνέπεμψά σοι,...

Winter[26] believes that Paul is not sending Onesimus back in any literal sense, but is simply 'referring his case to the proper higher authority'. On this point Winter follows Knox[27] who thought Paul was 'referring

24. Several scholars have noted the extreme delicacy by which Paul addresses his appeal to Onesimus's owner: 'Der Apostel wählt seine Worte mit Bedacht und gestaltet den Aufbau des Hauptteils so, dass der Adressat behutsam an den Inhalt der Bitte herangeführt wird' (Lohse, *Die Briefe*, p. 275); Coleman-Norton, 'Roman Law of Slaves', p. 169.

25. For the suggestion that Paul flattered Philemon, cf. Martin Luther ('Lecture on Philemon', *Luther's Works* 29 [St Louis: Concordia, 1968]): 'We take pleasure in the honor that people trust us. This is good flattery; but it is holy, because it proceeds as in Christ. Whomever I praise, I praise as a Christian; therefore I neither flatter him nor am disappointed in him, because it is impossible to praise Christ enough. If I flatter a Christian man, I do so not for his sake but for the sake of Christ, who dwells in him; and Him a Christian should honor' (pp. 98-99).

26. 'Paul's Letter', p. 7.

27. *Philemon*, p. 6.

Onesimus's case to his legal owner for decision'. The legal significance of ἀναπέμπω is evident in extra-biblical usage.[28] A technical meaning may well be attached to the other occurrences of ἀναπέμπω in the New Testament: the word is used three times in Luke's account of Jesus' trial (Lk. 23.7, 11, 15) and once in connection with Paul's appeal to Rome (Acts 25.21).

The fact that ἀναπέμπω is a technical term, however, need not mean that Paul only referred Onesimus's case to the owner, and not Onesimus himself. The other New Testament passages make it clear that actual people, not just 'cases', were referred from one ruling authority to another: Pilate sent Jesus to Herod for proper sentencing (Lk. 23.7); Herod's soldiers mocked Jesus and sent him back to Pilate (Lk. 23.11, 15). In Acts 25.21 Festus told King Herod Agrippa that he had been holding Paul in custody until he could 'send him up' to Caesar (ἕως οὗ ἀναπέμψω αὐτὸν πρὸς Καίσαρα). Festus meant that Paul would actually be conveyed to Rome for trial (cf. Acts 27.1). In Phlm. 12, therefore, the words ὃν ἀνέπεμψά σοι should be translated literally: 'whom I am sending on to you'.

Several commentators (Vincent, Oesterley, Moule, Lohse) have noted that ἀνέπεμψα is an epistolary aorist, a special nuance of the aorist tense writers would use to put themselves at the same point in time as their readers.[29] We should imagine that the first thing Onesimus did after returning to his angry master was to hand him Paul's little letter. If Onesimus was not only forgiven his past flight, but also manumitted (cf. vv. 13, 21), he may well have treasured this document as his charter of liberty.[30]

v. 15   τάχα γὰρ διὰ τοῦτο ἐχωρίσθη πρὸς ὥραν...

Several scholars (Winter, Vincent, Lohse, Dittberner) have observed that the passive voice of the verb ἐχωρίσθη denotes God's agency: 'he was parted (by God from you) for a while' (cf. Gen. 45.5: 'God did send me before you'). It has also been suggested that ἐχωρίσθη is a euphemism

---

28. Of a decree: ἀναπ. ψήφισμα πρὸς βασιλέα (*OGIS* 329.51); of disputed laws: ἀναπεμφθῆσαι πρὸς ἡμᾶς (*SIG*³ 344.52-53); of important matters and capital cases: τὰ γὰρ μείζω πράγματα καὶ τὰς φονικὰς δίκας ἐφ' ἑαυτὸν ἀναπέμπειν ἐκέλευσεν καὶ τοὺς ἑβδομήκοντα (Josephus, *War* 2.57). For additional references cf. T. Nageli, *Der Wortschatz des Apostels Paulus* (Göttingen: Vandenhoeck & Ruprecht, 1905), and BAGD, p. 59.

29. BDF §334.

30. Bruce, 'St Paul in Rome', p. 97.

for 'he ran away', an interpretation which goes back to Chrysostom: 'He does not say, "*for this cause he fled*", but, "*for this cause he was parted*": for he would appease Philemon by a more euphemistic phrase'.[31] By this oblique expression Paul comes as close as he dares to mentioning Onesimus's illegal flight from his master. Paul may even have intended the deliberate ambiguity of ἐχωρίσθη to protect Onesimus yet also give his master a precise hint of Onesimus's crime.[32]

v. 18   εἰ δέ τι ἠδίκησέν σε ἢ ὀφείλει, τοῦτο ἐμοὶ ἐλλόγα

ἀδικέω denotes general harm or injury, although the term is listed in LSJ (*verb. cit.* II.1) in connection with financial fraud. Many commentators, therefore, believe that Phlm. 18 is a discreet reference to the robbery Onesimus had perpetrated just before he ran away. Robbery and flight commonly occurred together, as we have seen. The typical *fugitivus* loaded himself with as much of his master's goods as possible in order to purchase the sympathies of a resourceful slave-catcher. We should assume that Onesimus similarly plundered Philemon. Unlike the documents examined earlier, however, Paul does not inventory the stolen property, mention the slave-catcher, provide a detailed description of Onesimus, or post a reward for the slave's recapture. Such information would of course thwart Paul's purpose for writing Philemon. The use and mutual proximity of the words ἀδικέω and ὀφείλω, however, are at least suggestive of Onesimus's robbery.[33] Yet Paul states the case hypothetically (εἰ δέ τι...): '*If* he has wronged you somehow or owes you anything...' By shifting Onesimus's gross infidelities to a subordinate clause, Paul focuses Philemon's attention upon his own promise to

---

31. Cited in Lightfoot, *St Paul's Epistle*, p. 340; cf. Oesterley, 'Philemon', p. 215: 'a very delicate way of putting it'; Vincent, *Epistles*, p. 188.

32. By the time of Polybius (c. 200–118 BCE) χωρίζω in the passive voice came to mean 'depart', 'go away' (LSJ); that the stem of χωρίζω could be used in a technical sense meaning 'to run away' appears likely in light of the compound form of the verb (ἀνακεχώρηκεν, *UPZ* 121.3, 21), used to denote the flight of the two runaways, Hermon and Bion. Possibly the verb ἐχωρίσθη possessed a peculiar double sense which would have been useful to Paul in writing Philemon: (1) 'he was parted' (euphemism); (2) 'he ran away' (technical).

33. Cf. the formula ἀδικοῦμαι ὑπό τινος in *P. Mich.* 71.1 and 6, and *P. Mich.* 173.3, used of people who refuse to pay personal debts and thus incur criminal prosecution. ἀδικέω and ὀφείλω occur together in the latter document and also in *P. Mich.* 58.

make amends: '...charge that to my account; I, Paul, write this with my own hand: I will repay' (vv. 18-19).[34]

v. 10   παρακαλῶ σε περὶ τοῦ ἐμοῦ τέκνου...

J. Knox[35] and Winter[36] interpret these words as a legal summons in which the genitive noun following the preposition περί is the object of the request: 'I ask you *for* my child', rather than the more traditional 'I appeal to you *on behalf of* my child' (RSV, TEV). Winter[37] supports the first translation by appealing to four extra-biblical parallels which clearly demonstrate a legal summons.[38] The more traditional translation cannot stand, claims Winter, because there is a substantial difference in the New Testament between the παρακαλῶ...περί construction (which she contends occurs only at Phlm. 10) and παρακαλῶ...ὑπέρ. Winter also claims that the παρακαλῶ ὑπέρ construction occurs three times (2 Cor. 5.20; 12.8; 1 Thess. 3.2) and that these passages demonstrate the differing sense 'request *on behalf of*'.

It is necessary to point out, however, that in the third passage that Winter uses to support her position, περί (*not* ὑπέρ!) occurs: παραπαρακαλέσαι ὑμᾶς περὶ τῆς πίστεως ὑμῶν...(1 Thess. 3.2). This fact alone severely damages Winter's argument that there must be a difference in meaning between the παρακαλῶ περί and παρακαλῶ ὑπέρ constructions. To be sure, New Testament grammarians do make a slight distinction between περί and ὑπέρ with the genitive case.[39] Yet it is widely acknowledged that the two prepositions overlap semantically, at least in epistolary and *Koine* Greek.[40] This accounts for the near

34. On the legal and commercial significance of the verb ἐλλόγα (Phlm. 18) cf. H. Preisker, 'ἐλλογάω', *TDNT*, II, pp. 516-17 and the many papyrus fragments cited in Lohse, *Die Briefe*, p. 284 n. 2. Several scholars (Bruce, Moule, Lightfoot, Vincent, Roehrs, Franzmann, Oesterley) have noted that Phlm. 19 is an example of a χειρόγραφον, an autograph 'IOU'. ἐγὼ ἀποτίσω is probably a stronger form of the more common repayment formula ἐγὼ ἀποδώσω (Oesterley, 'Philemon', p. 216).

35. *Philemon*, p. 5.

36. 'Paul's Letter', p. 6.

37. 'Paul's Letter', n. 45.

38. Aurelius Sakaon 37.15-17; Appianus, *Punic Wars* 136; *P. Tebt.* I, 58.52-55; *P. Oxy.* 1070.7-10.

39. S.G. Green, *Handbook to the Grammar of the Greek New Testament* (New York: F.H. Revell, 1904), pp. 250-52; E. Van Ness Goetchius, *The Language of the New Testament* (New York: Charles Scribner's Sons, 1965), pp. 155-56.

40. C.B. Welles, *Royal Correspondence in the Hellenistic Period* (New Haven: Yale University Press, 1934): 'as used with the genitive, the preposition [ὑπέρ]

interchangeability of περί and ὑπέρ in several New Testament passages.[41] The semantic fluidity between the two prepositions can make it difficult to determine between the meanings 'for', 'on behalf of', or 'about/concerning', as any translator knows when confronted by either preposition in a given passage. To maintain, therefore, that Philemon *must* be a summons because of formal correspondences with extra-biblical parallels seems rather risky; this position is admittedly possible,[42] although it rests upon a semantically uncertain preposition. It is difficult to avoid the suspicion that the whole argument has been ingeniously invented to suit an alien interpretation of the text.

It seems more exegetically sound to determine Paul's use of the verb παρακαλῶ, in Phlm. 10 and elsewhere. Careful consideration of the 52 occurrences of this verb in Paul[43] will reveal that the apostle used the word in two ways: (1) 'to exhort/beseech' (e.g. Rom. 12.1; 1 Thess. 4.1, 10; 1 Tim. 2.1); and (2) 'to comfort/encourage' (e.g. 1 Cor. 4.13; 2 Cor. 1.4; 1 Thess. 4.18; Eph. 6.22). The two meanings are closely intertwined.[44] Even passages which clearly designate a specific exhortation by Paul (Rom. 15.30; 1 Thess. 4.10) should be translated, 'I encourage you to [verb]...', a peculiar request idiom of Paul's which is not duplicated in the extra-biblical examples Winter provides. The idiom should be

encroaches more and more on the field of περί' (p. lxxxi); BDF §§229.1 and 231; C.F.D. Moule, *An Idiom Book of New Testament Greek* (Cambridge: Cambridge University Press, 1953): 'With the genitive [ὑπέρ] means *on behalf of, with a view to, concerning*—though the latter sense, identical with certain uses of περί...is said to be almost confined to Paul in the New Testament' (p. 64); J.H. Moulton and G. Milligan, *The Vocabulary of the Greek Testament* (London: Hodder & Stoughton, 1929): 'The transition to the meaning "on account of", "for", is easy, when περί becomes practically identical with ὑπέρ' (p. 504); A. Buttmann, *A Grammar of the New Testament Greek* (Andover: W.F. Draper, 1895): 'Sometimes [περί] stands in the sense of ὑπέρ *for* (as, on the other hand, ὑπέρ is used for περί...)' (p. 336).

41. Mt. 26.28; Jn 17.9, 20; Acts 26.1; 1 Cor. 1.13; Gal. 1.4; 1 Tim. 2.2; Heb. 5.3; 1 Pet. 3.18. Additional examples of such 'rival prepositions' are presented in M. Zerwick, *Biblical Greek* (ed. J. Smith; Rome: Ponticifal Biblical Institute Press, 1963), p. 31.

42. Further instances of the summons formula can be provided: παρακαλῶ σε γράψαι μοι περὶ τῆς ὑγιείας σου (*P. Sarap.* 92); παρακαλῶ οὖν σε...γράφε περὶ τῆς σωτηρίας (*P. Sarap.* 95); παρακαλῶ οὖν ἀντιγράψαι μοι περί τε τῆς σωτηρίας σου...(*SB* 10.102).

43. W.F. Moulton and A.S. Geden, *A Concordance to the Greek Testament* (Edinburgh: T. & T. Clark, 1957), p. 757.

44. O. Schmitz, 'παρακαλέω, παράκλησις', *TDNT*, IV, p. 797.

translated this way because Paul's requests are really invitations—'encouragements'—for his original readers to offer him service out of hearts which have been freed by the gospel (cf. Rom. 6.20-23; Eph. 6.6; 1 Tim. 1.5).

Paul has the Christian freedom of Philemon in mind as he gently broaches a sensitive issue. The two verses preceding the words παρακαλῶ σε περὶ τοῦ ἐμοῦ τέκνου indicate that Paul is leading up to something far more significant than a mere summons for the future services of Onesimus. There is an odd tension here. On the one hand, Paul parades his apostolic boldness and alludes to his power to 'command that which is necessary' (v. 8) by using vocabulary and hence concepts which occur nowhere else in Paul's letters;[45] on the other hand, Paul makes his appeal out of *agape*-love, as an 'old man' (or 'ambassador', πρεσβύτης, v. 9), and as a prisoner of Christ. These latter words highlight Paul's humanity and weakness, whereas his divinely given authority remains in the background.[46]

Paul plainly prefers gentle persuasion to outright commands, yet he fervently desires Philemon to attend to 'what is required' (τὸ ἀνῆκον, v. 8). Just what Paul intended by this latter expression is unknown,[47] although Paul's original reader would certainly have apprehended correctly the intended meaning. It would not have been out of character for Paul to use the pregnant expression as an allusion to the forgiving attitude which Philemon, as a Christian, ought to assume toward repentant Onesimus. This solution to the problem would correspond well with Paul's climactic request of Philemon in v. 17, toward which the epistle tends all along: 'Receive him as you would receive me' (RSV)—that is, as a forgiven brother in Christ. It would also match other more explicit Pauline references to the necessity of forgiving a former wrongdoer.[48] Paul, the outspoken advocate of Christian freedom (Gal. 2.4; 5.1), does

45. J.H. Schütz, *Paul and the Anatomy of Apostolic Authority* (London: Cambridge University Press, 1975), pp. 221-22.

46. Cf. A. Stoger, *The Epistle to Philemon*, published in the same volume with J. Reuss, *The Epistle to Titus* (New York: Herder & Herder, 1971): 'His [Paul's] authority to command is veiled under the form of a helpless petitioner, his power under his powerlessness, his right to rule under his will to serve' (p. 80).

47. '"*What is required*" of the slave-owner must be a moral obligation; it can scarcely be a legal one' (Schütz, *Anatomy*, pp. 222-23).

48. Col. 3.13b; Gal. 6.1; and 2 Cor. 2.7-10. The requisite forgiving attitude of a believer is also developed elsewhere in the New Testament. For example, see Mt. 6.14-15; 18.21-22; Mk 11.25; Lk. 6.37.

not force Philemon charitably to forgive Onesimus for his former crimes; he *appeals* to Philemon to do this. This is the sense in which the words παρακαλῶ σε περὶ τοῦ ἐμοῦ τέκνου ought to be interpreted.

Mere forgiveness may not seem an imposing request to so loving (v. 5) and generous (v. 7) a man as Paul states that Philemon was: 'Philemon is known as a public benefactor'.[49] But such acclamation ought to be considered in light of the circumstances which undoubtedly surrounded the letter. Paul gently persuades Philemon to accede to an extremely radical request: forgiveness of the latter's runaway slave.[50] Paul must have known that such forgiveness was rare indeed (though cf. Pliny, *Epist.* 9.21), and for Philemon now to think of this former thief and scoundrel as a Christian brother—as an equal before God—must have strained Philemon's Christian charity to breaking point.

3. *Runaway Slaves and Roman Law*

Returned runaways were ordinarily given a far different reception by their masters than the one proposed in this letter by Paul. It is difficult to discover the precise punishments to which recovered runaways were subject during the early Empire.[51] However, 'it is safest to start with the assumption that a slaveowner who was a Roman citizen had by Roman law the legal right to do anything that he desired to any slave'.[52] The important question whether Onesimus's owner was a Roman citizen or peregrine cannot be determined on the basis of Philemon. Yet even if

49. Knox, *New Testament Commentary*, p. 44.

50. The text itself registers Paul's hesitancy to suggest so radical a measure: 'The slight hesitation in mentioning the name of the slave, and the delay in coming to the point of the letter, are noticeable' (Vincent, *Epistles*, p. 184); 'The name is withheld until Paul has favourably disposed Philemon to his request' (Vincent, *Word Studies*, p. 518). The doubled παρακαλῶ...παρακαλῶ (Phlm. 9-10) may indicate a similar hesitancy to impose such extreme advice upon Philemon.

51. Cf. the limited comments of W. Buckland (*The Roman Law of Slavery* [Cambridge: Cambridge University Press, 1908; repr. New York: AMS, 1969], p. 268 n. 11) and P. Garnsey (*Social Status and Legal Privilege in the Roman Empire* [London: Oxford University Press, 1970], p. 130 n. 7) which are generally directed to periods either much earlier or later than the mid-first century CE. Ordinary commentators are content to make severe statements about the punishments to which Onesimus was subject yet rarely ground these upon ancient sources. The best attempt at solving this problem is provided by Coleman-Norton's appendix ('Roman Law of Slaves', pp. 172-77).

52. Coleman-Norton, 'Roman Law of Slaves', p. 175.

Philemon were a provincial (Coleman-Norton believes he was), the fact that Paul interceded at all for Onesimus would make it likely that Philemon wielded powers of life and death over his slave, as was usual.

It was an important point of later Roman law[53] that recovered runaway slaves should be returned to the owner: *Fugitivi...dominis reddendi sunt* (*Dig.* 11.4.2, Callistratus, 193–200 CE); *reddi ergo eos oportet* (*Dig.* 11.4.5, Tryphoninus, 193–217 CE). The dates of these rescripts may seem too late to have much to do with Philemon; however, the attitudes of the owners towards their runaways were probably fairly consistent throughout antiquity, as evidence from both before and after the writing of Philemon would suggest.[54] We have already seen that owners' interests were sorely jeopardized by the mere existence of a runaway; therefore the civil authorities, acting in concert with propertied, slave-owning citizens, generally held a recovered runaway in custody until the owner had personally retrieved the slave.[55]

What treatment did runaways receive after they had been returned to their masters? This is the great mystery. The relative silence of many jurisprudents on this question probably means that owners might yield to capricious, or even sadistic, whims. Masters were permitted to punish

---

53. Although the *Digest* was not compiled until the early sixth century CE, it contains the names and legal pronouncements of many earlier jurisprudents. In the discussion which follows I have used the dates provided in E.C. Clark, *History of Private Law* (Cambridge: Cambridge University Press, 1906; repr. New York: Biblo & Tannen, 1965), I, pp. 156-63. The text and translation are from A. Watson (ed.), *The Digest of Justinian* (4 vols.; Philadelphia: University of Pennsylvania Press, 1985).

54. Thus e.g. a rescript attributed to Ulpian (200–220 CE) in the *Digest* appears quite similar to the much earlier *UPZ* 121, discussed earlier in this paper: 'The magistrates should be told the names and distinguishing features of runaways so that they may the more easily be recognized and caught. (The term "distinguishing features" also includes scars.) The law is the same if this information is posted up in public notices or on a sacred temple' (*Dig.* 11.4.1.8a).

55. 'Harbor masters and police, when they arrest runaways, should keep them in custody' (*Dig.* 11.4.4, Paulus, 193–222 CE); 'A runaway slave cannot escape his owner's power even if he volunteers for the arena and subjects himself to its dangers, which present so great a risk to his life. For a rescript of the deified Pius says that such slaves *should always be returned to their owners* whether before they have fought with wild beasts or after; for sometimes they have embezzled money or committed some more serious crime and have chosen to volunteer for the arena, in order to escape an investigation or the punishment they deserve; so *they ought to be returned*' (*Dig.* 11.4.5, Tryphoninus; emphasis added).

slaves for delicts that had been perpetrated against themselves (*Dig.* 13.7.24.3; 24.3.24.5) and a runaway, regarded as a stealer of himself (*sui furtum facere, Dig.* 47.2.61), was manifestly delictual. It is perhaps unnecessary to review the many gruesome torments masters could potentially inflict upon their slaves, sometimes for trifling offenses. Yet 'crucifixion was the standing form of execution for slaves'.[56] Runaway slaves had been thrown to beasts (*damnatio ad bestias*) since the time of Scipio's victory over the Carthaginians (Livy, *Per.* 51).[57] Coleman-Norton[58] mentions branding as a common lesser punishment (cf. Petronius, *Satyr.* 103.4; Plautus, *Aulular.* 325). Petronius, a contemporary of St Paul, describes a notice affixed to Trimalchio's doorpost which appears to have dictated an extremely severe corporal punishment for runaways: *Quisquis servus sine dominico iussu foras exierit, accipiet plagas centum* (*Satyr.* 28).[59] By Roman law, therefore, Philemon would have been free to impose any one of these penalties, or others of his own choosing, upon *Onesimus fugitivus receptus*.

Much of the legislation pertaining to runaway slaves can be dated close to the time Paul wrote Philemon. Contemporary with Paul's missionary journeys, a number of jurisprudents had tried to define precisely what a runaway slave was. Ofilius's (*flor.* 45 BCE) original definition (*Fugitivus est, qui extra domini domum fugae causa, quo se a domino celaret, mansit, Dig.* 21.1.17) apparently was not specific enough. Later jurists believed that a slave's intent at the time of leaving his master was determinative. Caelius (*flor.* 70 CE) said that a slave who left with the intention of not returning was a *fugitivus* even if he should later change his mind and return, for 'no one purges his offense by remorse' (*Dig.* 21.1.17.1). A more compassionate view is attributed to Vivianus (*flor.* 60 CE) who thought that a slave's flight ought to be viewed against his purpose in fleeing: *ab affectu animi cuiusque aestimandum* (*Dig.* 21.1.17.4).[60]

56. Garnsey, *Social Status*, p. 127; sources, n. 2.

57. Tryphoninus mentions embezzlement (*pecunia interversa*) as the specific crime which motivated captured runaways to prefer the dangers of the arena to certain punishment meted out by owners. Onesimus's crime against Philemon was probably connected to stolen property also.

58. 'Roman Law of Slaves', p. 176.

59. A heavy beating (*verberatio*) was generally imposed on members of lower social classes who could not afford to pay a punitive fine (Garnsey, *Social Status*, p. 138), especially during imperial times.

60. Vivianus cites an earlier jurist (Proculus, *flor.* 40 CE), who mentions as a

It was important to determine the status of such slaves, because a vendor who sold a slave without apprising purchasers of any disease or defect (*morbus vitiumque*) in the wares could be liable to prosecution.[61] An owner who could not warrant was required to sell his slave *pileatus*, that is, with a cap on his head—a recognized sign that no warranty was given (Aulus Gellius, *Noct. Att.* 6.4). Liability might also be avoided by means of certain pacts (*simplariae venditiones*, *Dig.* 21.1.48.8) for which there was no redhibition. Buckland[62] believes that these were cases in which the buyer took the slave, for good or ill, irrespective of quality. In applying these legal considerations to Onesimus, Goodenough may well be correct when he says: 'In a sale of this kind...[a slave] would probably be purchased only for the roughest sort of service, such as the galleys or the mines'.[63]

4. *Conclusion*

Enough of the ancient evidence has now been considered to impress on one the widespread nature of a common, though serious, problem in antiquity: '*Fugitivi* were a great administrative difficulty, and no doubt a public danger'.[64] A runaway slave brought such financial ruin upon his master that ruthless measures were adopted to recover the slave and punish him and other responsible parties, as we have seen. A master could exact a frightful punishment on a recovered runaway by law. Paul must have known that Philemon would be tempted to avenge himself upon Onesimus by the strict letter of the law, as was his right. Paul wrote the letter, therefore, to inform Philemon that the formerly useless

hypothetical case a situation which Goodenough speculated lay behind Philemon: 'but if he [the runaway] concealed himself until his master's wrath abated, he would not be a fugitive any more than one who, having in mind that his master wished physically to chastise him, betook himself to a friend whom he induced to plead on his behalf' (*Dig.* 21.1.17.4). These rescripts aptly demonstrate how contradictory the jurists could be on a single point of Roman law.

61. *Dig.* 21.1.1.1; Buckland, *Roman Law of Slavery*, p. 55. The general rule was that the expression 'defect and disease' applied only to physical defects (*Dig.* 21.1.4.3); however, a venditor was obliged to inform a buyer that a prospective purchase was either 'prone to flee' (*fugax*) or a 'wanderer' (*erro*), although these latter were, technically, mental defects (*Dig.* 21.1.4.3).

62. *Roman Law of Slavery*, p. 53.

63. 'Paul and Onesimus', p. 181.

64. Buckland, *Roman Law of Slavery*, p. 53.

Onesimus was now a fellow believer and, as such, deserving of rein-statement (v. 17), not punishment. He also wrote to remind Philemon that he was a Christian and thus himself beholden to Paul for his former conversion (v. 19) and present submission to apostolic boldness (v. 8). He wanted gently to persuade, not force, Philemon to attend to 'that which is necessary' (v. 8), an expression which, under the circumstances, may well have referred to Philemon's complete pardon and forgiveness of Onesimus, the returned runaway.

These conclusions are consistent with the long-standing *theological* interpretation of Philemon, an interpretation which has been with the church since antiquity:[65] Onesimus wronged his master when he ran away; therefore Paul begs Philemon to accept the former thief and run-away as a brother in the Lord, just as God accepts the repentant sinner for Christ's sake. The radical nature of Christian forgiveness is thus contrasted with the harsh laws of this world. The theologically minded apostle apparently seized an opportunity to apply the gospel to a specific problem, just as the modern priest or pastor is often called upon to reconcile quarrelling parishioners. Such an interpretation cannot prove the runaway slave hypothesis, of course, and the fact remains that the text of Philemon nowhere directly states that Onesimus ran away. Yet Paul's pastoral reasons for not reminding Philemon of the all too obvious fact of Onesimus's past flight quite account for the silence. To base a radical reinterpretation of the letter upon Paul's pastoral discretion in this matter seems to require an undue reliance upon the *argumentum e silentio*.

The ultimate danger of the 'new' interpretation is that it could turn a letter which manifestly 'breathes the great-hearted tenderness of the apostle'[66] into a rather dispassionate, non-theological financial tran-saction between Paul and Onesimus's owner. Yet I doubt that such a routine scrap of business correspondence would ever have become part of the canonical New Testament. Philemon, though given to a rather mundane theme when compared to the apostle's longer epistles, is striking evidence that Paul never ceased to be a theologian. The spirit of Christ (whose name is mentioned eight times in 25 verses) animates this little letter, and Paul never lost sight of the gospel (εὐαγγέλιον, v. 13)

65. Onesimus is explicitly designated as a runaway slave in Jerome, NPNF[2] 6.101; Ambrose, *Fathers of the Church* 26.357; and especially Chrysostom, NPNF[1] 9.109, NPNF[1] 11.133, NPNF[1] 13.545-57.

66. Guthrie, *New Testament Introduction*, p. 638.

to which he had dedicated his life and ministry. The theological dimension of Philemon assured the letter's eventual inclusion in the New Testament, and thus its preservation. However, the real-life circumstances which prompted the letter in the first place prevented Paul from explicitly mentioning *Onesimus fugitivus*.

JSNT 48 (1992), pp. 107-19

THE PRAGMATICS OF POLITENESS AND PAULINE
EPISTOLOGRAPHY: A CASE STUDY OF THE LETTER TO PHILEMON

Andrew Wilson

The substantial corpus of sociological research on Pauline Christianity
has hitherto concentrated almost exclusively on the membership of the
church, community typologies and the sociology of knowledge: little
attention has been paid to the actual relationships between Paul and the
addressees of the letters.[1] These relations, however, are of great importance both for the study of the social setting of Pauline Christianity in its
own right and for the interpretation of the letters, for as I hope to show,
the social setting constitutes a powerful constraint on the linguistic
expression of ideas. I shall argue that the techniques of modern linguistic
pragmatics—in particular those aspects which are normally subsumed
under the heading of 'politeness'—may be of help in elucidating the
writer–reader relationships and kinds of persuasive activity which exist
in the letters and in other ancient literature.[2] I shall use as a case study
example the letter to Philemon. This letter, being the shortest in the
Pauline and deutero-Pauline corpus, provides the opportunity to discuss
at greater length the theoretical underpinnings of the kind of analysis I
am proposing; furthermore, the social situation is more clearly defined
and hence may allow clearer instances to be demonstrated of the
phenomena which I shall discuss.

---

1.   For a survey and bibliography, see P.J. Richter, 'Recent Sociological
Approaches to the Study of the New Testament', *Rel* 14.1 (1984), pp. 77-90.
2.   Note that J.G. du Plessis ('Pragmatic Meaning in Matthew 13:1-23', *Neot* 21
[1987], pp. 33-56) used Leech's principles to aid analysis of the parable of the
sower. However, his analysis did not extend in any detail to the politeness principle.

Pragmatics and Politeness Theory

Pragmatics is that discipline within general linguistics which is concerned with the study of meaning in interaction,[3] that is to say the full meaning of a discourse may only be constructed when it is placed in context with a speaker or writer and a listener or reader. Language has a habit of tricking us. For example, the sentence 'Is that your house?' may indicate surprise or admiration, ridicule, may contain an implicature (e.g. 'May I come in for a coffee?'), or may indeed be simply a request for information: it all depends on the context and the relationships between the participants. This kind of indirectness is very common in linguistic communication, and there may be several reasons for it. One of these is politeness.

The notion of politeness is a social commonplace. However, we need to define more clearly what we understand by 'politeness' when we use the term in the context of pragmatics. One of the most succinct definitions of politeness is that of Hill *et al.* who define it as 'one of the constraints on human interaction, whose purpose is to consider others' feelings, establish levels of mutual comfort, and promote rapport'.[4] This is necessary as any utterance may potentially involve some cost to the speaker or hearer. This cost may be at least partially definable in material terms—for example in a request for money—but more often it will involve some cost to the speaker's or hearer's *face*. Face is an important construct in politeness theory. In their classic study of politeness, Brown and Levinson define it as 'the public self-image that every member [of a society] wants to claim for himself':[5] in other words, it subsumes such concepts as prestige, standing in the community and self-respect. Clearly certain kinds of utterance constitute threats to a person's face (what are termed Face-Threatening Acts—FTAs); these include requests and orders (which involve taking a subordinate role to the speaker), criticisms (which involve a perceived loss of standing within the community), and less obviously certain assertions (which may bring into doubt or refute strongly held beliefs). To use FTAs without giving consideration to ways of mitigating

3. J.A. Thomas, *Meaning in Introduction: An Introduction to Pragmatics* (London: Longman, 1995), pp. 22 and 208.

4. B. Hill *et al.*, 'Universals of Linguistic Politeness', *Journal of Pragmatics* 10 (1986), pp. 347-71 (349).

5. P. Brown and S. Levinson, *Politeness: Some Universals in Language Use* (Cambridge: Cambridge University Press, 1987), p. 61.

the threat to face is considered impoliteness, whereas to construct utterances in such a way as to include forms of words which offset the threat constitutes politeness. Thus, as Leech demonstrates, considerations of politeness form an 'input constraint' on the linguistic encoding of ideas.[6]

Hitherto, most politeness research has concentrated on spoken discourse. However, recent work has begun to extend this to written texts. Roger Cherry's work concentrated on dyadic (i.e. one-to-one) communication between those requesting a professor's tenure case to be reviewed and a university president—a situation analogous to many of those studied in oral communication.[7] Greg Myers has extended research beyond the dyadic writer/reader situation to the more complex situation where there are potentially very many readers.[8] This extension of politeness research is particularly valuable in considering the Pauline letters. Although collation took place most probably in the late first century CE and was not Paul's intention when writing, many letters are addressed to groups rather than individuals. Philemon is no exception, as several commentators have pointed out.[9] Although the primary addressee is Philemon himself, the situation is more complicated as the contents of the letter are also for the attention of the group of Christians which meets at Philemon's house. Hence Philemon's position is particularly vulnerable, for any FTA contained in the letter is made the more so by its public mention before Philemon's immediate community. We might therefore expect Paul to take particular care to mitigate any FTAs with politeness strategies to reduce the apparent cost to Philemon in both face and material terms, in order to avoid damaging his standing within the Christian community at Colossae.

---

6.   G. Leech, *Principles of Pragmatics* (London: Longman, 1983), esp. p. 58.

7.   R. Cherry, 'Politeness in Written Persuasion', *Journal of Pragmatics* 12 (1988), pp. 63-81.

8.   G. Myers, 'The Pragmatics of Politeness in Scientific Articles', *Applied Linguistics* 10 (1989), pp. 1-35.

9.   Cf. J.M.G. Barclay, 'Paul, Philemon and the Dilemma of Christian Slave Ownership', *NTS* 37 (1991), pp. 161-86. S.C. Winter goes further and suggests that this is a completely public letter ('Paul's Letter to Philemon', *NTS* 33 [1987], pp. 1-15 [1-2]). I see no reason to accept this view: on the contrary, the traditional view of a private letter with a wider audience is more strongly supported by the text itself. I do not accept that an argument from vocabulary can supplant the evidence of the text.

Framework for Analysis

The model of politeness which I shall adopt is that of Geoffrey Leech.[10] Although this has been criticized by certain linguists, it is valuable in that it is the only model which seeks to define probabilistic rules ('maxims' and 'principles') for politeness strategies and to incorporate these within a wider process model of language use which gives attention to textual as well as interpersonal considerations.[11]

Leech, following the lead of Michael Halliday, divides language use into two sets of principles or 'rhetorics'. The interpersonal rhetoric, with which we shall be mainly concerned here, deals with the constraints of the social situation upon linguistic expression, while the textual rhetoric deals with the linguistic forms of discourse. Each rhetoric is divided into a number of principles. For the textual rhetoric, Leech employs the set of principles postulated by Dan Slobin in his comparison of child language, pidginization and language change.[12] However, these principles for the communicative properties of language need not detain us here.

The interpersonal rhetoric divides into two major principles: the co-operative principle and the politeness principle. For the co-operative principle, Leech adopts, as others have done, the conversational maxims of the linguistic philosopher Paul Grice, which are briefly:

1. Maxim of Quantity: give the right amount of information.
2. Maxim of Quality: try to make your contribution one which is true.
3. Maxim of Relation: be relevant.
4. Maxim of Manner: be perspicuous, that is, avoid obscurity, ambiguity, disordered discourse and unnecessary verbosity.

The co-operative principle is thus concerned with being considerate about the other party in a conversation or other rhetorical context where there is a speaker/writer and an audience: it is concerned with providing truthful (or what is believed to be truthful) information as quickly and clearly as possible. Obviously, this has some connection with, and trade-off with,

10. Leech, *Pragmatics*, esp. pp. 79-151.

11. Criticism has concentrated on pointing out that Leech's principles are incomplete and can be added to in an *ad hoc* manner. This is equally true of the general principles of Brown and Levinson.

12. D. Slobin, 'Language Change in Childhood and in History', in J. Macnamara (ed.), *Language Learning and Thought* (New York: Academic Press, 1977).

politeness. Verbosity and ambiguity, as we shall see, are sometimes necessary in order to be polite; also, consideration of the audience clearly reflects some of the import of politeness contained in Hill *et al.*'s definition.[13] However, the major politeness strategies are contained in Leech's politeness principle.

The politeness principle divides into the following six maxims:

1. The Tact Maxim: minimize cost to other; maximize benefit to other.
2. The Generosity Maxim: minimize benefit to self; maximize cost to self.
3. The Approbation Maxim: minimize dispraise of other; maximize praise of other.
4. The Modesty Maxim: minimize praise of self; maximize dispraise of self.
5. The Agreement Maxim: minimize disagreement between self and other; maximize agreement between self and other.
6. The Sympathy Maxim: minimize antipathy between self and other; maximize sympathy between self and other.

Obviously, we shall not expect to find all these maxims attested in a given text. The idea of a set of maxims is that they are probabilistic: they present speakers/writers with a set of options which they may or may not choose to use depending on various contextual factors, unlike grammar which is governed by much less flexible rules. However, we should certainly expect to see at least some of them: their complete absence in interactive communication such as letters and conversations would suggest that the speaker or writer was deliberately being impolite.

Setting of the Letter

The letter to Philemon is written by Paul from prison to Philemon (the main addressee) and the Christian community at Colossae. Paul has met up with Onesimus (Philemon's slave) who is also in jail for running away from his master.[14] Onesimus has become a Christian and Paul feels that he will be a valuable member of the community and hence ostensibly

---

13. Hill *et al.*, 'Linguistic Politeness', p. 349.
14. As Barclay ('Paul, Philemon', pp. 163-64) points out, there is no need to adopt the suggestion of Winter ('Philemon', pp. 2-5) that Onesimus is not a runaway, but on an errand to Paul from Philemon.

entreats Philemon to take him back without punishment, possibly also manumitting him.[15] This, of course, would be quite out of keeping with the customs of the time: indeed, the law permitted the death sentence for runaway slaves. If, therefore, Philemon were expected by the society in which he lived to punish severely, and even execute, Onesimus, then a request for him to take him back would be an act particularly costly to him in terms of face as it would be to flout the conventions of his society. In fact this letter is not the sole surviving request of this kind—Pliny also wrote to a friend on a similar matter (Pliny, *Epist.* 9.21)—but it still constitutes a controversion of the norm. It also puts the master in a complex position with regard to the other slaves he possesses (if any), for although his act may be regarded as pious by either Christian or Stoic principles, it may also be construed as weakness both by society and by the other slaves who may perceive the risk in running away to be diminished. The request is thus very costly to Philemon, and we would expect Paul to use various politeness devices to mitigate the cost.

Salutation

We see at the very outset of this letter an instance of Leech's modesty maxim. This maxim, it will be recalled, requires the speaker or writer to minimize praise of himself or herself and maximize dispraise of himself or herself: according to Leech, this may include such strategies as refusing praise from another or minimizing the size or value of a gift which the speaker/writer has given. I take it to have a wider set of manifestations than Leech explicitly allows it. Minimizing self-praise or 'not blowing one's own trumpet' may also involve the on-record reduction of one's own status within a community, especially in comparison to the hearer or reader, and this is what Paul appears to be doing in the salutation to Philemon. In the salutations of nine of the fourteen letters in the Pauline and deutero-Pauline corpus, Paul is referred to as ἀπόστολος. Two letters (1 and 2 Thessalonians) have no epithet, and Hebrews has no salutation at all. Apart from Philemon, only Philippians has an epithetic salutation with no mention of ἀπόστολος. That Paul has omitted this epithet from Philemon may already suggest that he is attempting to minimize his on-record authority as apostle; however, there is more to it than that. In contrast to the δοῦλοι of Phil. 1.1, Paul uses the epithet

---

15. Barclay ('Paul, Philemon', p. 171), however, casts considerable doubt on the clarity of Paul's exact request to Philemon.

δέσμιος Χριστοῦ Ἰησοῦ, the only time this phrase appears in the epistolary salutations. It seems quite clear that by using this epithet Paul is
seeking to emphasize his situation as a prisoner and hence by analogy his
social solidarity with Onesimus. This epithet is echoed in v. 9 immediately before the request to Philemon, a position which seems to support
the hypothesis that it is being used in mitigation of the face-threatening
act. Philemon is no longer seen as the party who has most to lose; rather,
Paul is seeking to boost Philemon's status by diminishing his own. This
is thus the second part of the modesty maxim in operation: maximize
dispraise of self.

Paul's solidarity strategy is, however, bivalent. Emphasizing solidarity
with Onesimus is perhaps a useful persuasive device in that it points out
to Philemon a similarity between Paul and the runaway slave and lessens
Paul's on-record authority. However, Paul also needs to express his
solidarity with Philemon if he is to reduce the size of the imposition he is
about to make on him. In other words, he needs to use Leech's agreement maxim. He does this by the use of pronouns, kinship terms, and
συν- compounds which are heavily distributed throughout the letter.
The choice of pronouns and the expression of solidarity has been
demonstrated many times to be an important aspect in reducing cost to
face.[16] Although Paul's use of first person plural pronouns in this letter
is not unusual in New Testament Greek—for example the genitives in
the phrases θεοῦ πατρὸς ἡμῶν and τῷ συστρατιώτῃ ἡμῶν—we should
also note, for example, the conjunction of first and second person pronouns in v. 11—σοὶ καὶ ἐμοί—emphasizing the unity of Paul's and
Philemon's needs.[17] The use of kinship terms such as ἀδελφός and the
συν- compounds also emphasizes a togetherness and familial bonding
between Paul, Philemon and Onesimus.[18] Paul is seeking a common
base of shared hopes, beliefs and assumptions by which to reduce the
disparity of status among Philemon, Onesimus and himself, and hence

16. Cf. R. Brown and A. Gilman, 'The Pronouns of Power and Solidarity', in
T.A. Sebeok (ed.), *Style in Language* (Cambridge, MA: MIT Press, 1960), pp. 253-
76.

17. F. Blass and A. Debrunner, *A Greek Grammar of the New Testament and
Other Early Christian Literature* (Chicago: University of Chicago Press, 1961),
pp. 146-48. The use of the genitive pronoun in these examples would be unusual and
hence emphatic in classical Greek, but not in the New Testament. This is not Semitic
influence but a colloquial tendency.

18. See Barclay, 'Paul, Philemon', pp. 177-82, for a discussion of what this may
imply for the relationship between Philemon and the Christian Onesimus.

make his request less costly to Philemon. Authority and social distance (for example the relative age or the degree of intimacy between participants in a discourse) are factors in determining how far politeness strategies need to be used in a particular discourse: friends and equals can generally be more forthright in making requests whereas for someone in authority it may be unreasonable to make a request that falls outside his or her direct sphere of responsibility.[19]

Thanksgiving

We have in the next sentence the standard Pauline thanksgiving. A statement of thanksgiving introduced by εὐχαριστῶ or a similar verb occurs at the beginning of nine of the letters in the Pauline and deutero-Pauline corpus. The interesting question, of course, is what function did it serve? Schubert considered that its main function was to provide information to set the scene for the letter.[20] However, I do not believe that this is the best explanation for it. I agree with Schubert that the emphasis in these Pauline thanksgivings is on the indirect statement which the verb of thanking introduces rather than on the act of thanksgiving itself—in Philemon, for example, the thanksgiving extends over four verses. If the emphasis were on the act of thanksgiving itself, it would be reasonable to suggest that Paul had flouted the maxim of quantity ('give the right amount of information') in the amount of information which he supplies in the indirect statement. What I want to suggest is that these thanksgivings may be interpreted as instances of Leech's approbation maxim. By including such detail in his thanksgivings, Paul appears to be expressing his admiration and affection for the people to whom he is writing, perhaps to stand in mitigation to the often quite fierce polemic which follows in the more theological letters. The extended thanksgiving thus appears to function as a sustained politeness device in Paul's writings.

Intercession for Onesimus

The intercession for Onesimus is introduced in a very indirect way. Although Paul has the boldness in Christ to command Philemon to do

19. Leech, *Pragmatics*, p. 126.
20. P. Schubert, *The Form and Function of the Pauline Thanksgiving* (Berlin: Töpelmann, 1939), pp. 166-81.

his bidding (πολλὴν ἐν Χριστῷ παρρησίαν ἔχων), he prefers to beseech him (μᾶλλον παρακαλῶ). It has been commented that Paul is at the same time being polite but making it quite clear that he expects to be obeyed by placing his apostolic authority on record.[21] This may be so, but I do not think that it is the most likely explanation of what is going on here. Such a strategy is little more than blackmail: 'I'm asking you to do this, but if you don't, I'll order you to do it anyway'. This is not what we would expect in the context of a personal letter whose general tone is otherwise non-authoritarian. What Paul in fact appears to be doing is negotiating new pragmatic parameters.[22] Leech and others assume that these are 'givens', not negotiated but an inherent part of the language and social structure. However, this letter seems to support the view that reliance by language users on a fixed set of principles may result in certain cases in 'pragmatic failure' where what the speaker or writer says may be misunderstood by another person who has different expectations of the force of that particular utterance.[23] Ordinarily, a request from Paul would have the *prima facie* force of an apostolic command. If Paul genuinely wants to reduce the force of such a command, and turn it into a friendly request, he needs to formulate a new pragmatic principle, and this he can only do by describing the new 'rules'. What Paul seems to be doing here, therefore, is formulating a new pragmatic parameter where his request is quite clearly seen as that of a friend, not as the command of an apostle of Jesus Christ. It could be argued that this may again be interpreted as an instance of Leech's modesty maxim. Paul's linguistic behaviour certainly fits the requirements of such a maxim. What is different here, however, is the explicitness of what Paul is saying. It is not just a question of the choice of the verb of asking ('beseech' as opposed to 'ask' or even 'order') but the full description of the pragmatic parameters (Paul is *bold enough* to order, but *prefers* to beseech) which suggests that this instance goes beyond the modesty maxim to an extension of it, freshly negotiated for this particular social situation. Indeed, this arrangement is repeated at v. 14, where Paul says again that he prefers to do nothing without Philemon's consent so that Philemon will comply with his request through his free will rather than compulsion (ἵνα μὴ ὡς κατὰ ἀνάγκην

---

21. See, for example, Barclay, 'Paul, Philemon', p. 171.

22. J.A. Thomas, personal communication.

23. J.A. Thomas, 'Cross-Cultural Pragmatic Failure', *Applied Linguistics* 4 (1983), pp. 91-112.

τὸ ἀγαθόν σου ᾖ ἀλλὰ κατὰ ἑκούσιον). The repetition of the negotiated pragmatic parameter appears to signal its importance to Paul for
Philemon's interpretation of the letter.

In the context of the intercessory section of the letter, Barclay comments on the lack of evidence as to what Paul is asking Philemon to do:
'it is extremely unclear what Paul is actually requesting'.[24] This lack of
clarity may also perhaps be explained in terms of politeness. There is a
constant trade-off in language between the requirements of Leech's co-
operative principle and the requirements of the politeness principle. The
co-operative principle is concerned with quick, clear communication while
the politeness principle, as suggested earlier, employs such techniques as
hedging, indirectness and so on. One strategy to reduce the perceived
cost to the hearer or reader is to avoid making the face-threatening act
explicitly 'on record' and leave it to the hearer's or reader's inference to
determine what is being requested.[25] This appears to be what Paul is
doing in Philemon; as Barclay comments, 'I am driven to conclude that
it [the letter] is deliberately open-ended'.[26] The recipient of the letter
needs to draw on his knowledge of the context in order to fill out Paul's
request and determine what exactly he is requesting. This may perhaps
explain why it is so difficult for modern interpreters to come to an agreement about Paul's request: we simply do not know the full circumstances
of composition.

We see also in this section of the letter the use of Leech's generosity
maxim. At v. 18 Paul offers to be responsible for any debts (presumably
not just financial) which Onesimus has incurred. Of course there is no
compulsion for him to do this, but by turning the situation on its head
Paul is able once more to reduce perceptually the cost of his request to
Philemon. He is asking Philemon to perform an act which is costly in
both face and material terms: what better way to redress this cost than
to offer to perform an act which will be beneficial to Philemon but costly
to Paul and thus voluntarily to accept a mirror image of what Paul is
asking Philemon to do? Again, therefore, what I believe is happening
here is that Paul is using the generosity maxim to reduce the cost of his
request to Philemon: he is shifting much of the perceived cost from
Philemon onto himself.

Thus through a careful analysis of the use of language in the inter-

24. Barclay, 'Paul, Philemon', p. 171.
25. Myers, 'Pragmatics of Politeness', p. 22.
26. Barclay, 'Paul, Philemon', p. 175.

cession of this letter, we have found that its request is not expressed directly but is characterized by a heavy use of politeness strategies. What in essence is a simple request is carefully formulated with suitable redresses to cost so that the threat to Philemon's face is minimized. As Barclay rightly comments, there is 'plenty of evidence of Paul's diplomatic skill'.[27]

Domestic Arrangements and Conclusion

The most curious aspect of this letter from a pragmatic point of view is the sudden switch to very direct language use in v. 21. We no longer have the indirectness and politeness strategies used earlier in the letter: the requests are made very simply and clearly. This, I believe, tells us something more about Paul's relationship with Philemon and his fellow church members at Colossae. Both Christian and non-Christian writers in this period comment particularly on the church's προξενία or hospitality. Arguably Paul's self-invitation and request for a room is not a serious imposition in this social setting and thus does not need to be couched in 'polite' language. Some requests are less costly to the hearer/reader than others, and hence the extent to which politeness strategies are required to redress the cost also varies: the more costly a request is, the more likely it is to be expressed with the use of politeness strategies. Cost is often relative to a particular culture. In the former Soviet Union, for example, a request for a cigarette was less costly than a request for a match: in the United Kingdom this position is reversed.[28] It seems possible, therefore, that a request for hospitality which may seem costly in our society was not as costly in Paul's society, and such a suggestion appears to be supported by the literary evidence. However, what are we to make of the phrase 'confident of your obedience' (πεποιθὼς τῇ ὑπακοῇ σου)? It is highly unlikely that this is a slip. The letter is too carefully constructed, and its length is a major obstacle to inconsistency as compared with, say, the Homeric poems. This must surely be interpreted, as Carson has said, as Paul expecting the highest of a fellow church member.[29] Such a situation may be directly paralleled by a letter which a colleague of mine recently received from an old friend and

27. Barclay, 'Paul, Philemon', p. 171.
28. Thomas, 'Cross-Cultural', pp. 104-105.
29. H.M. Carson, *Colossians and Philemon* (Leicester: Inter-Varsity Press, 1960), p. 112.

colleague. After asking a favour of her, he said in the closing of his letter 'I'm sure I can count on you'. There was no power disparity between these two people and hence no suggestion of its being an implicit order: rather it was a friend expecting the best of his friend. Thus there is no real inconsistency in the switch to direct language as has often been implied and used to support a claim of the subtle use of 'hidden' authority in this letter;[30] on the contrary, this fits in perfectly well with a request from a friend to a friend.

Conclusions

This analysis of the letter to Philemon has refuted the claim of Collinge that Ancient Greek is 'timid over indirect illocutions and hostile to presuppositions'.[31] Indeed, the Greek of Paul's letter to Philemon shows a very wide range of politeness strategies with much evidence of indirectness. These strategies have parallels in modern English usage and hence they appear to provide further evidence for the universality of politeness strategies in human communication.[32] We have also seen expressed through these strategies the complex relationship which exists between Paul and Philemon in this social situation. As the apostle of Christ, Paul has the authority to direct the church and its members, but at the same time he shows considerable respect for Philemon's face in front of the church at Colossae. It is clear how far these considerations have affected Paul's linguistic expression. Further work could valuably extend this form of analysis to the theological letters where an analysis of language use from the perspective of politeness might pay important dividends for exegesis.

30. Cf. Barclay, 'Paul, Philemon', p. 171.
31. N.E. Collinge, 'Thoughts on the Pragmatics of Ancient Greek', *Proceedings of the Cambridge Philological Society* NS 34 (1988), pp. 1-13 (12).
32. Myers, 'Pragmatics of Politeness', *passim*.

JSNT 10 (1981), pp. 42-60

CONFLUENCE IN EARLY CHRISTIAN AND GNOSTIC LITERATURE:
THE *DESCENSUS CHRISTI AD INFEROS* (*ACTS OF PILATE* 17–27)

R. Joseph Hoffman

I

Bousset observed as long ago as 1907 that Christian belief in the descent
of Christ into the netherworld (*descensus Christi ad inferos*) represents
the assimilation and spiritualization of a much more primitive myth.[1] The
legend of a redeemer who invades the kingdom of the dead to assert his
power and thwart the demons originally had nothing to do with the
person of Jesus; rather, as Christianity developed a spiritual understanding
of salvation, the mythic figure of a vindictive conqueror was gradually
replaced by the figure of the glorified Christ.

   Two traditions were at work in this Christianizing process: a popular
and archaic one, which retained much of the ancient mythology, and a
theological one which was, in effect, a spiritual elaboration of the first.
The more mythological emphasis survives only in ambiguous allusions
(e.g. Rev. 1.18) and in such apocryphal expansions of the *descensus* as
those that occur in the *Acts of Thomas* and the *Gospel of Nicodemus*. In
these narratives, Jesus' mission is something of a *matière de roman*, his
purpose in hell being not to declare the news of salvation but to wage an
assault on the powers of sin and death. In the Patristic literature of the
second and third centuries, however, the *descensus Christi* was deprived
of many of its mythological features.[2] The Christ of Justin and Irenaeus,

1.   W. Bousset, *Die Hauptprobleme der Gnosis* (Göttingen: Vandenhoeck &
Ruprecht, 1907), esp. pp. 244ff. See also chapter 6, 'Die Gestalt des gnostischen',
regarding Hibel-Ziwa as 'savior'.

2.   The Patristic controversy surrounding the *descensus Christi* cannot be treated
here in any detail. J. Turmel addresses the subject in his *La Descente du Christ aux*

for example, visits hell not to war against the demons but to proclaim the gospel to the captive patriarchs and prophets who have anticipated his coming.[3] The spiritual and intellectual power of Christianity in the late

enfers (Paris: Picard, 1903), tracing the early speculation through the end of the fifth century. A subsequent attempt to provide a history of the motif is J.A. MacCulloch's *The Harrowing of Hell: A Comparative Study of Early Christian Doctrine* (Edinburgh: T. & T. Clark, 1930).

The prevalent understanding of the purpose of Christ's mission to Hades is that he undertook to preach the gospel to those who waited in darkness. Origen wrote in his exegesis of Rom. 5.14: *Christum vero idcirco in infernum descendisse, non solum ut ipse non teneretur a morte, sed ut et eos qui inibi non tam praevaricationis crimine, quam moriendi conditione habebentur abstraeheret.* Both Origen (*Com. Matt.*) and Irenaeus (*Adv. Haer.*) interpreted Mt. 12.29 to refer to the binding of Satan in the underworld ('How can anyone break into a strong man's house and make off with his goods, unless he has first tied the strong man up before ransacking the house?'). Elsewhere (*Adv. Haer.* 4.33) Irenaeus opined that Christ descended to 'deliver and to rescue the dead', while Ignatius of Antioch was inclined to see the mission of Jesus as an evangelical one: 'The prophets were expecting him as their teacher and for this reason he whom they rightly expected, when he came, raised them from the dead' (*Adv. Magn.* 9). And Justin Martyr: 'The Lord God remembered his dead people of Israel and descended to preach for them that lay in their graves' (*Tryph.* 72). Tertullian, on the other hand, held that 'Christ in Hades underwent the law of human death, nor did he ascend until he had descended to the lower parts of the earth, that he might make the patriarchs and prophets sharers in his life' (*De Anima* 55).

Among later writers, Ambrose (*De fid. ad Grat.* 4.1) and Jerome (*Com. in Eccl.* 100.3) followed Origen's lead in arguing for Christ's spiritual presence in hell. Cyril of Jerusalem (*Cat.* 4) classed the *descensus Christi* among the ten necessary dogmas; and Eusebius, citing an apocryphal saying of Thaddeus (*Eccl. Hist.* 1.13) wrote, 'He descended into hell and opened the closure... He descended alone, but he ascended with multitudes to the Father.'

The identity of the beneficiaries of Christ's mission was also a matter of contention among the Fathers. According to Irenaeus, the gnostic Marcion held that the message was intended to convert the wicked. Justin (*Tryph.* 72) and Irenaeus (*Adv. Haer.*) believed that the preachment of Christ was restricted to the righteous of Israel, while Clement held that its benefits would be reaped by Jew and Gentile alike.

3.   Bousset's conclusion may be compared to Hans Jonas's appraisal of the function of the Messenger in the gnostic speculation: 'By the mere fact of his descent, the Messenger prepared the way for the ascending souls. Depending on the degree of spiritualization in the different systems, however, the emphasis may shift from this mythological function to the purely religious one embodied in the call, as such, and the teaching it has to convey, and thereby also to the individual response to the call as the human contribution to salvation' (*The Gnostic Religion* [Boston: Beacon Press, 1958], p. 78).

second century was successful in translating the myth of the harrowing of hell into the doctrine of universal salvation.

Faithful to the principles of the *religionsgeschichtliche Schule* of which he was a pioneer, Bousset wanted to show the prevalence of the *descensus* motif in Western and Oriental literatures prior to its reception by the church. His chief purpose in so doing was to document the cultural diffusion of the ancient mythological *topos* rather than to suggest the ways in which the motif had been tailored to fit the interests of particular religious communities. Thus, while he succeeded in locating instances of the motif in Orphic, Greek philosophical, Assyro-Babylonian, and Latin writings, he failed on the whole to identify the legendary accretions and ideological patterns which distinguish the Christianized *descensus* from other mythologically encumbered adaptations of the legend.

Nevertheless, Bousset's suggestion that the *descensus Christi* was taken over bodily from Oriental mythology[4] raises a number of questions about the relative orthodoxy of the apocryphal expansions of popular belief in Christ's visit to hell: does the *Gospel of Nicodemus*, for example, by far the most elaborate of these expansions, mark a primitive phase in the erosion of the mythological stratum of Christian belief, or the survival of a popular legend that was later to be appropriated and canonized by the church? What historical and religious context serves to explain the expositor's adherence to pre-Christian legend? To what degree has the author of the *Gospel* succeeded in bringing the ancient *topos* into harmony with the yet fluid orthodoxy of his age—and at what expense to Christian doctrine? It is the purpose of the present study to examine these questions with particular reference to the confluence of Gnostic and Christian treatments of the *descensus ad inferos*, and to suggest that while literary parallels certainly exist, they are not decisive for assuming a Gnostic provenance for Christian (credal and theological) adherence to the belief in Christ's visit to the lower regions.

In approaching the text of so full a literary exposition of the *descensus*

4.   In the *Gilgamesh*, Istar (like Christ) descends to the underworld to redeem her lover from the bonds of Death. She is defeated by the consummately evil Erishkigal in spite of her attempts to placate the demons and to disguise herself and her purpose. A bit later in the epic, Nergal invades the nether-regions, and in a venture reminiscent of Christ's harrowing of hell, vanquishes Erishkigal. Finally, however, Nergal requires sixteen accomplices to defeat the demon and capitulates in the end to become her husband and overlord of the dead.

Christi as that supplied in the *Gospel of Nicodemus* (*Acts Pil.* 17–27),[5] it is intriguing to consider not only its most obviously mythic trait—the visit of the hero to the lower regions—but also the literary and theological characteristics that define the work against the background of its time—a time which also saw the rise of Christian Gnosticism.[6] A consideration of the folkloristic and popular appeal of the *descensus* is a precondition of discovering its obscure theology, indeed of determining just how 'Christian' that theology may be. This consideration requires, in turn, that one ask certain form-critical questions of the text and of the myth (or myths) which it supposedly incorporates: What are its typical metaphors, images, and scenic fixtures? To what extent do they vivify the special content of the message they are designed to convey? How does that message contribute to the nascent orthodoxy of the second century? And finally, to what degree has the mythic element been eroded or transfused by the spiritual?

An attempt to respond to some of these questions was made a generation ago by Père Chaine in his article, 'La descente du Christ'. His substantial investigation of the matter led him to conclude the following: (1) Jesus came to hell *because* he died.[7] This is not the case with any pagan or Jewish hero. (2) While in hell, Jesus preached the gospel to the Old Testament faithful who had awaited his coming. The idea of a preaching mission is absent from pagan mythology, and notably from Greek and Babylonian accounts of the *descensus ad inferos*. Even those

---

5. See A. Vaillant (ed.), *L'Evangile de Nicodeme (Texte Latin)* (Paris: Droz, 1968). I have preferred Vaillant's text throughout this study. The *Evangelium Nicodemi* (to which the *descensus Christi* is a late addition) is supplied in Tischendorf, *Evangelia Apocrypha* (Leipzig: Mendelssohn, 1876), in M.R. James *The Apocryphal New Testament* (Oxford: Clarendon Press, 1924), and in E. Hennecke, *et al.*, *New Testament Apocrypha* (ET Philadelphia: Westminster press, 1963), pp. 470-76 (*descensus* portion). The Latin A text has been used as the key in my collation (cf. James's remarks, pp. 94-95; F. Scheidweiler in Hennecke, *New Testament Apocrypha*, pp. 444ff.) and is noted in context as 'A'. The *passus*-numeration is that of Tischendorf in *Evangelia Apocrypha*.

6. See Scheidweiler in Hennecke, *New Testament Apocrypha*, pp. 444-49.

7. Chaine was not alone in finding Jesus' death the distinctive feature of the descent. J.H. Bernard, writing in 1916 ('Descent into Hades', *DACL*, pp. 289-92), observed that Jesus' passage to hell was irrefragable testimony to the fact of his humanity. None, Bernard observed, would have doubted that the souls passed through Sheol after death. Thus to say that 'Jesus descended into hell' was a figurative way of asserting his humanity. Bernard proof-texted his conclusion with reference to Zech. 9.11; Ps. 49.15; Rom. 10.7; and 1 Cor. 15.26.

pagans who possessed a concept of salvation assigned no parallel function
to their redeemer. (3) The notion that Jesus undertook physical combat
in hell is a primitive point. According to Rev. 1.19-20, Jesus triumphs over
sin and death at the moment of his resurrection, whereupon he is given
the keys to the underworld.[8] Chaine concluded: 'The descent of Christ
into the underworld is, more than the other points of Christian doctrine,
compared and brought to the level of myth... The ides of a battle in
Hades is later; it is a literary way of putting into relief the triumph of
Christ.'[9]

But besides degrading the form-critical questions that could be asked
of the apocryphal versions of the *descensus Christi*, Chaine finally
exempted the Christian doctrine of the descent into hell from scrutiny
for apologetic reasons. If the dogmatic idea of salvation of the just is
original to the Christian interpretation of the story, he wondered, how
can one say that the belief represented fragmentarily in the Apostle's
Creed[10] owes anything at all to Oriental mythology?[11] He assumed, presumably in opposition to the conclusions of the *religionsgeschichtliche
Schule*, that the transmission and diffusion of the *descensus* motif as

8.   In fact, however, the passage in Revelation makes no mention of how or
when Jesus obtained the keys to Death's domain.

9.   J. Chaine, 'La descente du Christ aux Enfers', in F. Vigouroux (ed.),
Dictionnaire de le Bible (ed. L. Pirot; Paris: Letouzey et Aue, supp. edn, 1934), II,
pp. 395-430.

10.   On the credal controversy surrounding the inclusion of the *descensus* article,
see T. Zahn, *Das apostolische Symbol* (Erlangen: Deichert, 1893); McGiffert, *The
Apostle's Creed* (New York: Scribners, 1902), and Kelly, *Early Christian Creeds*
(London: Longmans, Green, 1950). The Sirmium formula (389) reads, '(Who) was
crucified, died and descended into hell, and regulated things there, whom the gate-
keepers of hell saw and shuddered'. The doxology of the Syrian *Didascalia* (third
century) contains the sentence, 'Who was crucified under Pontius Pilate and departed
in peace in order to preach to Isaac and Jacob'. Although the Constantinopolitan
formula of 381 omits the article, the Council of 360 had included in its formulation a
rather dramatic interpolation: 'According to the Father's will, he was crucified, died,
and was buried, and descended to the lower regions of the world, at whom Hell itself
quailed'. Kelly has noted (*Early Christian Creeds*, pp. 389ff.) that as the Descent
began more and more to appear in the creeds, the notion of Christ's mission to the
patriarchs was coming to be understood as a symbol of his triumph over Satan and
death, and consequently of the salvation of all humanity.

11.   Chaine's meaning, however, seems not to be that other religions were without a redeemer who preached a message of salvation, but that such a message when
measured against the dogmatic truth of Christianity is not to be regarded as significant.

such was irrelevant to the apprehension of the essential dogmatic message which the Christianized myth had incorporated. The truly distinctive thing about the *descensus Christi*, Chaine argued, is the fact that Jesus is said to have ventured into hell to preach the good news of salvation to those who waited in darkness: not physical combat but illumination by the redeemer distinguishes the Christian belief from all of its supposed sources and analogues.

In the present study I propose to consider Chaine's thesis in the light of evidence which he did not examine, that is, the impressive similarities between Christian (or meta-Christian) and gnostic varieties of the *descensus* motif. It may be shown on the basis of parallels from Mandaen, Valentinian and related literature that the *Gospel of Nicodemus* represents a point of confluence between two ancient and competing systems of thought, without sacrificing to the vestigial mythic elements (e.g., the prominence of physical combat) its fundamentally Christian point of view.

We turn first to consider similarities between the *Gospel* and the Mandaen *Ginza*.

II

The personified power of darkness (Hell) in the *Gospel of Nicodemus*, fashioned after the Gehenna of Rev. 21.8, bears striking resemblance to the netherworld described in the Mandaen *Ginza*.[12] In the more elaborate geography of the gnostic source, the sphere of darkness is shown to be a place of bondage, torpor, and alienation for the pneumatic (spiritual) human being—the 'threshing floor of creation', presided over by the female Archon, Ruha ('Holy Spirit'). The seven archonic circles that move outward from the lower world constitute a formidable hyperbole of the barrier that exists between the captive spirit and the True God who summons it. Inasmuch as this immense space constricts the spirit, it is understood to possess a demonic quality in its own right.[13] Reality and good lie beyond the created order; the lower world into which the pneumatic has been 'thrown' is in itself the gnostic hell, portioned out to

---

12. *Ginza, der Schatz oder das grösse Buch der Mandäer* (ed. and trans. M. Lidzbarski; Göttingen: Vandenhoeck & Ruprecht, 1925), p. 126.

13. Jonas (*Gnostic Religion*, p. 52) writes: 'It is to be understood that the role of these intervening forces is inimical and obstructive: with the spatial extent they symbolize at the same time the anti-divine and imprisoning power of the world. No less demonized is the time-dimension of life's cosmic existence.'

demonic powers that work to prevent the *pneuma*'s escape through the
closure. (Thus Marcion's designation of the world as 'Haec cellula
creationis'—an obvious radicalizing of the Platonic metaphor.[14])

To be sure, the meta-Christian cosmogony presented in the *Gospel of
Nicodemus* differs from the Gnostic description in the *Ginza*, but the
spatial metaphor functions in approximately the same way. Hell signifies
that condition in which the regenerates have been cut asunder from their
divine source: the True God lies beyond the impenetrable closure. Those
who wait in darkness, anticipating the news of their salvation, are in
bondage to powers no less sinister than the archonic lords of this world
(cf. Rom. 5–9).

Since creation is understood by the writer of the *Gospel of Nicodemus*
to be fundamentally and aboriginally good, however, the world (and in
consequence human existence) carries no specifically demonic implications.[15] The gnostic speculation insists on the idea of pneumatic humankind's imprisonment *in factum esse*. The apocryphal *Christian* Gospel
bespeaks the traditional understanding that humankind has either ances-
trally (by the transmission of Original Sin) or wilfully (by virtue of the
concupiscence that clouds the reason) negotiated its own separation from
God. In the *Gospel*, this separation, with its legacy of sin and death, is
assumed to have been revoked. Salvation has been wrought in the death
of Jesus, whereby the impenetrable closure has been breached. Moreover,
the salvation suggested in the *Gospel of Nicodemus* does not appear to
apply only to an elect group of pneumatics, as in the gnostic system, but
rather to all those who heed the words of the divine revealer. The
expositor makes his point in the form of a question: *Quis es tu qui
originali peccato adstricti tenentur absolvis captivos et in libertatem
pristinam revocas?* (A. 22).

By the same token, the *dramatis personae* of the narrative are, on the
whole, quite 'Christian', the chief figures being Old Testament prophets
and patriarchs whose function it is to render forecasts of redemption:

14. Plato, *Phaedrus* 246–47 (Jowett's translation).

15. The medieval development of the motif in dramatic literature challenged
orthodoxy on this point. Middle English versions of the 'harrowing of hell', for
example, commonly grouped the allegorical figures of World, Flesh, and Devil
together as the demonic forces overcome in the *descensus Christi*. On literary developments of the motif, see W.H. Hulme, *The Middle English Harrowing of Hell and
Gospel of Nicodemus* (Early English Text Society Publications Extra Series, 100;
London: Paul, Trench, Trubner, 1907); and J. Monnier, *La descente aux enfers:
Etude de pensée religieuse d'art et de littérature* (Paris, 1905).

Esaias dixit: Nonne cum essem in terris vivis praedixi vobis: Exsurgent
mortui et resurgent qui in monumentis sunt, et exultabunt qui in terris
sunt, quoniam ros qui est a Domino sanitas est illis. Et sicut iterum dixi:
Ubi est, mors, aculeus tuus, ubi est, infere, victoria tua? (Latin A., 12).

Besides its generally high regard for and usage of the Old Testament, something not characteristic of gnostic literature, the *Gospel* provides an at least arguably orthodox interpretation of the doctrine of the Incarnation, the vehicle for the presentation of this theology being a debate between Hell and Satan. The fact that the metaphor of ransom is implied in the subterfuge by which Jesus gains access to the lower world (*in forma hominis*) also argues, however tenuously, for the orthodoxy of the expositor's interpretation of the doctrine of the Atonement.[16]

Whatever its claims to orthodoxy, however, there is a sense in which the *descensus Christi* remains primarily mythical. It shares with its Gnostic analogues not only much of the same epic scenery and the *persona* of a divine illuminator sent by God to wrest humankind from the dark powers of the lower world, but also a suggestion that humankind depends for its salvation on the *gnosis*, or spiritual knowledge, which the illuminator alone can impart. Each system develops this perception in its own fashion, but always in terms consistent with the assimilated and spiritualized myth. Let us look first at the use of the *descensus* in the *Gospel of Nicodemus*.

a. *The Descensus Christi ad Inferos*
(Conflation of Latin A/B and Greek)
The drama opens in hell at a time specified to be just after the crucifixion of Jesus. A blinding light appears in the stygian depths, causing Satan and Hell to tremble. There follows an altercation between the demons over the source of the light. As a precaution, Satan causes the iron gates

16. M.R. James in his introduction to the *Gospel* rejects the early notion that it represents a gnosticizing stance toward Christian doctrine. The narrators of the *Gospel* are given the names Leucius and Charinus, and the association with Leucius Karinos, the gnostic author of the *Acts of John*, was long inferred. James has projected a fifth-century date for the addition of the *descensus Christi* to the *Acts of Pilate*. See also the discussion of the *Gospel*'s supposed provenance in Hennecke, *New Testament Apocrypha*, pp. 444ff. On the dating of the recensions of the *Gospel of Nicodemus*, see G.C. O'Ceallaigh, 'Dating the Commentaries of Nicodemus', *HTR* 56 (1963), pp. 21-58; A. Maury, 'Nouvelle Recherches sur l'epoque...d'Evangile de Nicodeme', in *Mémoires de la Societé des Antiquaries de France*, 20 (Paris: Societé des Antiquaries de France, 1850), pp. 341-92; and R.A. Lipsius, *Die Pilatus-Akten kritisch untersucht* (Kiel: Schwerssche Buchhandlung, 1871).

to be barred. When a cry is heard from without, David and Isaias begin to speak (the bulk of the dramatic narrative consists of additional oracles taken over more or less verbatim from the Old Testament). After a second cry, the Christ appears, *in forma hominis*, having trampled down the iron gates, whereupon Hell demands to know the identity of the invader, and derides Satan for his failure to recognize Jesus as the true God. Jesus then delivers Satan over to Hell in chains, takes Adam by the hand,[17] and leads the whole company of saints into paradise where they are met by Enoch and Elias. (In the Greek version only, the victorious Christ erects his cross in hell prior to his departure.)

b. *The Descensus Motif in the Mandaen Ginza*

On two different occasions in the *Ginza* a divine revealer undertakes a journey to the lower regions of the cosmos, the first coming in Book 3. There the savior Manda d'Hayye ('Knowledge of Life') is sent by his father, the Supreme God, to fight against the powers of darkness, led by Ruha. Once arrived in the netherworld, Manda d'Hayye struggles against the giant, Our ('King of Darkness'; cf. *Gos. Nic.*, Greek, 20). The battle is vigorous, but in the end, Our falls wounded and is enchained by Manda d'Hayye (*Gos. Nic.*, Latin A. 22: Latin B. 24). Our and Ruha lament their defeat (*Gos. Nic.*, Greek 6) while Manda d'Hayye ascends to the Father (*Gos. Nic.*, Greek 24, etc.).

Book 5 of the Ginza contains an allegorical interpretation of the cosmic struggle of the godhead to refund its perfections. Here the Manas (spiritual beings) ascertain the imminent birth of Evil in the world of darkness. Hibel-Ziwa (or Uthra), approximating the role of Manda d'Hayye in Book 3, is sent to confound the demonic powers. He is armed only with an ambiguous magic called 'the great secret', which turns out to be nothing less than the truth of his divine origin and identity (*Gos. Nic.*, Latin A. 20). Hibel gains access to the lower world by seeming to be one of the created order of beings, advancing like Dante from one sphere to the next, 'into the world of darkness where Ruha lives, into the world where the black waters have their source, into the world of

---

17. *Et tenens dexteram Adamae ascendit ab inferis et omnes sancti secuti sunt eum*; in A. 24: *Adam vero genibus Domini advoltus lacrimabili cum obsecratione deprecatus dixit: Exaltabo te Domine* (&c). Cf. *Ginza*, p. 126: 'As (the noise of the) Evil Ones fell upon Adam's ear, he awoke from his slumber and lifted his eyes to the place of light... He spoke to Hibel-Ziwa, the man who had made him hear his voice. As Adam spake thus, a tear gathered in his eye... I came near him, took him by his right hand, and made his heart to rest on my support.'

the dragon-faced Gaf and Gafan'. He arrives after a space of a thousand years—a conventional hyperbole of the barrier between the True God and the imprisoned soul—at the abode of Our, where he uncovers the mystery of his power, enchains the giant, and casts him farther into the infernal world. Vanquished, Our cries out that he had no strength to contend against the Light (*Gos. Nic.*, Latin A. 22).[18]

Like Hibel-Ziwa, the Christ of the *Gospel of Nicodemus* throws the lords of the netherworld into panic and confusion by virtue of the enigmatic reconciliation of corruptible flesh and incorruptible godhead which he embodies. Having gained access to hell by using the 'bait' of his humanity to trick the demons, Jesus reveals almost at once the hook of his divinity.[19] He is the redeemer (ransom-giver), sent from on high to plunder the dominion of evil and to enchain Satan. (The Latin B recension of the *Gospel*, usually more economical in its recitation of the events, is particularly explicit in describing the trampling of the gates and the binding of Satan [24]). Neither in the gnostic *Ginza* nor in the *Gospel* has the mythological element of physical combat been expurgated.[20]

There is, however, a significant difference in the morphology of the myth as it occurs in the apocryphal *Gospel*. Unlike the Mandaen redeemer of the *Ginza*, who behaves typically as a *héros de roman*, the Christ who descends into hell is clearly acting as the mythic enfiguration of the doctrine of universal salvation. The reiteration of the ransom theme, also prominent in the Patristic exegesis of the period, has persuaded the author of the *Gospel* to retain the metaphor of physical combat, but it is a watered-down usage at best. It is not the enchaining of Satan *per se* but the theme of *apocatastasis* (cf. Gen. 3.15; 1 Cor. 15.45-49; Rom. 6.14, etc.) which is programmatic for the exploitation of the myth. The *Gospel* provides an allegorical expansion of a belief already widespread in the

18. Père Lagrange found an analogue to the defeat of Our in Murdok's defeat of Tiamat in the *Gilgamesh*, where the former is finally enthroned as the Lord of Life. *RB* (1927), pp. 321-49, 481-515.

19. 'The Godhead was hidden under the cloak of our nature that it might be within the grasp of the purchaser and that, as in the case of the fish, the hook of divinity might be swallowed under the bait of flesh' (Gregory of Nyssa, *Cat. Or.* 22).

20. And cf. in the *Gilgamesh*, 'If you do not open the gate that I may pass / I shall burst it and smash the lock / I shall destroy the threshhold and break the doorposts / I shall make the dead to rise, and they shall outnumber the living', and *Gos. Nic.*, Greek, 7: 'And then there came a voice saying, "Lift up your heads, ye gates"… And straightaway the gates were broken into pieces, and the bars of iron were ground to powder and the dead that were bound were loosed from their chains.'

Christian East (e.g. Clement of Alexandria, Gregory of Nyssa, Origen) and available to the church at large in the epistles of Paul. The myth has provided a framework and imagery for the allegorical presentation of the doctrine, but there is very little that can be termed 'gnostic' about the account. Indeed, universalism of this kind is a contradiction of the gnostic doctrine of election.

Jesus' presence in hell is meant to be understood from the outset as evidence of an already accomplished redemption. This is far from being the case in the *Ginza*, where the *mise en scène* has no historical context and the contention of good and evil is understood to be acosmic. In the *Gospel*, the action commences directly after the historical action of the crucifixion; the event at issue is the death of Jesus, and it becomes the function of the *Gospel* to explicate and spiritualize the significance of that event. Whereas the Docetic tincture is quite evident in the *Ginza*, it is altogether absent from the *Gospel* where there is a clear-cut distinction between historical and mythological time.[21] Indeed, it is possible to say that the *Gospel of Nicodemus* represents one of the earliest attempts outside Lukan literature to construct a comprehensive *Heilsgeschichte*.

Moreover, the christic illuminator does not call the faithful in hell to arcane knowledge; the prisoners await only the coming to pass of an event spoken of in history—thus the emphasis on the prophetic oracles. *Gnosis*, accordingly, does not refer in the *Gospel* to a complicated system of divestiture imparted only to the pneumatic, but rather to the revelation of God in Jesus. The Christ, as it were, bears only himself as a message, and his message is that salvation has been achieved *pars pro toto* on the cross. Doubtless it was the universalism of the *descensus Christi* that recommended its use as a literary as well as a doctrinal *topos* throughout the Middle Ages.[22]

While both the gnostic and the apocryphal Christian developments concern a salvation perfectly embodied in the person of the redeemer and the abrogation of evil, the terms 'salvation' and 'evil' appear to differ radically in the two accounts. Both symbolize the opposition between truth and ignorance by the powerful antithesis of light and darkness. But what is imaged by that contradiction (or more precisely, what knowledge consists in) depends in either case upon the theological or theogonic system that overlays the myth of the *descensus*. This matter can be profitably explored by referring to gnostic literature outside the *Ginza*.

21. See Jonas's discussion, *Gnostic Religion*, pp. 264ff.
22. See Monnier, *La descente aux enfers*.

III

In the apocryphal *descensus Christi* of the *Gospel of Nicodemus* the antithesis of light and darkness is pervasive from the beginning:

> *Nos autem essemus cum omnibus nostris positi in profundo (inferni) in caligine tenebrarum, subito factus est aureus solis color purpureaque regalis lux illustrans super nos. (Omnibus) exultaverunt dicentes, Lux ista autor luminis sempiterni est, quae nomis promisit transmittere lumen coaeternum suum* (Latin A. 18: cf. A. 2, 7).

The light is more than a revelation of glory; it works as the primary symbol of a salvation already brought to completion in the death of Jesus on the cross. This dual revelation is the cause of elation among the patriarchs and prophets, and the source of consternation for the dark powers that war against the truth but have failed to comprehend the light (cf. 'And the light shines in the darkness, and the darkness does not comprehend it', Jn 1.5). Upon seeing the faintest glimmer in the dim recesses of hell, the saints rejoice that victory is theirs.

A similar theme is developed in the gnostic *Pistis Sophia*:

> Deliver me, O Light, from evil. I looked upwards to the place of light that it might rescue me. I was in that place mourning and weeping, seeing the light I had seen on high. And the Watchman at the gate of the Aeons saw me (*Pist. Soph.*, 32).[23]

Here, however, the dominant theme is not salvation but alienation, the utter hopelessness of the human condition *in factum esse*. To see the light in the distance is not a source of hope for the pneumatic; indeed, the distance serves only as a reminder of the enormous space between the True God and the incarcerated spirit. Whereas the prophets and patriarchs are able to rejoice in the promise that the light declares to have been fulfilled, the gnostic sees the light and awakens to the darkness of the world, for it illuminates the primordial error of human existence.

As already noted, the testimonies of prophets and patriarchs occupy considerable space in the *Gospel*, and they are construed in a consistently spiritual fashion as adumbrations of the New Man, the Deliverer. Hope grows out of the continuity of assurance, with Adam, Abraham, Isaias, and John the Baptist acting, each in turn, as a spokesman for the truth of salvation and a clarion for the new day that has come to repel

---

23. Hennecke, *New Testament Apocrypha*, I, pp. 250-62.

the darkness. The oracles are thus transformed into the documentation of universal redemption, just as the arrival of Jesus in the netherworld is its guarantee:

> *Glorificate dominum Jesum Christum filium Dei, quia...nunc viderunt oculi mei salutare tuum, quod praeparisti ante faciem omnium populorum lumen ad revelationem gentium et gloriam populi tui Israel. Haec audiens omnis multitudo plus exultaverunt* (A. 18).

This emphatic reassurance, grounded in the witness of the Old Testament, possesses none of the pathos that characterizes gnostic hopes for redemption:

> Lead me out of the embracement of Death![24]

> A vine am I, a lonely one that stands in the world. I have no sublime planter, no keeper to instruct me.[25]

> Having strayed into this labyrinth of evil
> the wretched soul finds no way out...
> She seeks to escape from bitter chaos,
> and knows not how she shall get through.[26]

> Save us out of the darkness into which we are thrown![27]

> Sheol saw me and was made miserable;
> Death cast me up, and many along with me.
> I made a congregation of the living among these dead men,
> And I spoke with them, my lips saying, Son of God,
> bring us out of the bonds of darkness.[28]

In both the gnostic and meta-Christian developments of the *descensus*, the coming of the divine revealer is a source of bewilderment and confusion for the evil powers (cf. Jn 1.5). In the *Gospel of Nicodemus* this

24. Turfan Fragment M.27. Given in Jonas, *Gnostic Religion*, p. 58.
25. *Ginza*, p. 346.
26. *Naasene Psalm*, Hippolytus 5.10.2 (Hennecke, *New Testament Apocrypha*, II, pp. 807ff.).
27. *Ginza*, p. 254; cf. pp. 457, 323.
28. *Odes of Solomon* 42 (Hennecke, *New Testament Apocrypha*, II, pp. 808ff.). There is nothing 'unorthodox' about the *Odes*, as such; the *Pistis Sophia* incorporates five. *Ode* 31 is an analogue of the *descensus Christi*: 'The abysses were dissolved before the Lord / Before his appearance: Error went astray / Perishing in his hand, and folly found no path to walk upon...'

confusion is configured in the debate between Satan and Hell (*passus* 20), the former holding fast to his prerogative as overlord of the dead and repudiating Hell's quite accurate suggestion that the stranger *omnipotens est in divinitate*. There is no hint of Docetism here. The main point of the debate is to argue the humanity of Jesus (*ita potens est in humanitate*) in concert with his divinity. *Passus* 20 represents in effect the literary development of the doctrine of the Incarnation. Christ is *tam magnus et parvus, humilis et excelsus imperator, in forma servi admirabilis praeliator et rex gloriae*.

The use of *collusio oppositorum* and rhetorical paradox to image the godhead is also a feature of Gnosticism. In *The Thunder*, for example, one discovers a litany of contradictory predicates intended to suggest the divine plenitude of the *Pleroma*:

> I am the whore and the holy one.
> I am the wife and the virgin.
> I am the mother and daughter.
> I am the members of my mother.
> I am the barren one.
> And many are her sons.
> I am she whose wedding is great.
> And I have never taken a husband.
> I am the bride and the bridegroom.
> And it is my husband who begat me.[29]

But it will be noticed that many of these androgynous self-predications are only tautonyms designed to contradict sense. Their purpose is to enfigure the all-in-all, the inclusiveness, of the True God. The paradox of the Incarnation to which the antitheses in the *Gospel* refer, on the other hand, signifies the interpenetration of the human and the divine rather than the singular plenitude of the godhead and its diffusion in the created order.

The hiddenness of the godhead plays a crucial part in the Mandaen theogony as well, but there, as we have noted, the savior's humanity is illusory. The gnostic redeemer's 'suffering', as the Suffering Son of Man, is only an emblem of the human condition. His purpose is not to redeem the whole person, nor especially humankind for its own sake, but to gather himself out of all things.

---

29. *The Thunder; Perfect Mind*, Nag Hammadi Codex 6.13.20-21. Trans. G.W. MacRae in J. Robinson (ed.), *The Nag Hammadi Library in English* (New York: Harper & Row, 1977), pp. 271-72.

> Draw the elect out of the world... Instruct the souls that they may not
> perish and die, not be kept back in the dense darkness; whenst thou comest
> to earth, the Evil Ones shall know thee not.[30]

The reaction of the evil powers when the secret of the messenger's
identity is revealed and their destruction appears imminent is predictably
similar in both developments of the motif; both have accepted the
mythological *mise en scène*:

> *Ego enim tunc quando audivi imperium verbi eius contremuni perterritis*
> *parvore, et omnia officia mea impia simul mecum conturbata sunt* (A. 20).

The gnostic Archons (or Worlds), having quite as much to fear from the
refunding of the created order to the *Pleroma*, behave in a comparably
frenzied manner:

> When Jesus went up into the heaven, all the powers were troubled, and
> they all trembled together, and all their orders and the whole earth was
> moved, and all that dwell upon it...and all the powers of heaven ceased
> not from their agitation... They were afraid because of the great earth-
> quake that took place, and wept with one another.[31]

And in the *Gospel of Truth*:

> When the Word appeared, a great confusion reigned among the vessels...
> All the spaces were shaken and confused. Error was agitated, not knowing
> what it should do. It was afflicted and lamented and worried because it
> knew nothing. (When) the Powers that are the perdition of Error and all
> its emanations approached it, Error became empty, there being nothing
> more in it.[32]

Like the personified Hell of the *Gospel of Nicodemus*, what Error fears
most from Truth (the Word) is the voiding of its power and the dissipa-
tion of its content. The two accounts differ, however, with respect to the
nature of that content. In the gnostic system, the abrogation of Error
entails the end of the world. In the *Gospel of Nicodemus*, it means
reclaiming the world for God, the created order being fundamentally
good.

Let us attempt to summarize and restate those features of the apocryphal *descensus Christi* which appear to mark it off from gnostic
developments of the *descensus* motif. In the *Gospel of Nicodemus*, the

---

30. *Ginza*, p. 295.

31. *Pistis Sophia* in Hennecke, *New Testament Apocrypha*, I, p. 254.

32. *Gos. Truth* 26.4-27 (Hennecke, *New Testament Apocrypha*, I, pp. 523-24;
and see discussion, pp. 233ff.).

call of Jesus to the imprisoned faithful is inclusive rather than selective;[33] nor is it a call to arcane *gnosis*. The *Gospel* possesses no doctrine of eternal damnation (*Et ipso de coelo in terram prospexit ut gemitum compeditorum et solveret filios interemptorum.*) The Christ does not call to humankind from the recesses of the world, like the gnostic Savior, but confronts the imprisoned multitudes directly, thereby claiming the divine as a category of human existence: *Venite ad me, sancti mei, omnes qui habetis imaginem et simultudinem meam* (A. 24). In contrast to the strong antinomian emphasis in Gnosticism, the Jesus of the *Gospel* appears in hell not symbolically to acquit human beings of responsibility to the lords of this world, but to liberate humanity from the bonds of sin, understood as that which defiles and enslaves the world and those who rule it.

In all that concerns mythological origins, epic architecture, imagery, and dramatic irony, the *descensus Christi* bears a striking resemblance to gnostic developments of the *descensus* motif. In both cases, a redeemer lays aside his heavenly glory, descends from the heights *in forma hominis*, breaches the impenetrable closure, and frees the captives who have awaited his coming in darkness. In sometimes subtle and sometimes obtrusive ways, the gnostic edges toward the Christian, the Christian toward the gnostic. Nonetheless, the common mythological element is overlaid by two significantly different conceptual systems: one that employs the myth in order to argue the hopelessness of the human condition and the error of life itself, and another that interprets humankind as fallen and destitute of God, but ultimately destined to triumph over the demonic powers that surround it.

33. Cf. Greek 21 and especially Greek 23: 'Turn and see that not one dead man is left in me, but all whomsoever thou didst gain by the tree of knowledge, thou hast lost forever by the tree of the cross'.

INDEXES

INDEX OF REFERENCES

OLD TESTAMENT

CLASSICAL

PAPYRI

This item is to be returned on or before
the last date stamped below.
Items can be renewed 3 times unseen. If a
fourth renewal is required the item must
be brought to the Library.

- 9 DEC 2003